CITIES ON THE MOVE

A WORLD BANK
URBAN TRANSPORT
STRATEGY REVIEW

THE WORLD BANK
Washington, D.C.

Library of Congress Cataloging-in-Publication Data

World Bank.
    Cities on the move : a World Bank urban transport strategy review.
          p. cm.
    "The author of the report is Ken Gwilliam"—Ackn.
    Includes bibliographical references.
    ISBN 0-8213-5148-6
     1. Urban transportation. 2. Urbanization. I. Gwilliam, K. M. II. Title.
    HE305. W67 2002
    388.4—dc21

2002025882

CONTENTS

ACKNOWLEDGMENTS   vii

ABBREVIATIONS AND ACRONYMS, CITIES AND COUNTRIES   ix

EXECUTIVE SUMMARY   xi

1   CONTEXT FOR THE REVIEW   **1**

2   URBAN TRANSPORT AND CITY DEVELOPMENT   **5**
Urban Transport and City Efficiency   5
Sources of Declining Urban Transport Performance   8
Urban Transport in City Development Strategies   11
Development Strategies for Making Urban Transport More Efficient   12
Coordinating Sector Policies in City Development Strategies   21
Conclusions: A Strategy for Urban Transport in City Development   22
Notes   23

3   URBAN TRANSPORT AND POVERTY REDUCTION   **25**
Urban Poverty and Social Exclusion   25
Transport Patterns of the Urban Poor   25
Pro-Poor Economic Growth and Poverty Reduction   28
Focusing Infrastructure Policies   29
Public Transport Service Planning for the Urban Poor   32
Fare Policies, Subsidies, and Budget Constraints   34
Conclusions: A Strategy for Poverty-Focused Urban Transport   36
Notes   37

4   TRANSPORT AND THE URBAN ENVIRONMENT   **39**
The Scale of the Issue   39
Global Warming   40
Noise and Other Disturbances   42
Urban Air Pollution   42
Conclusions: A Strategy for Urban Transport and Environment   60
Notes   61

5   URBAN TRANSPORT SAFETY AND SECURITY   **65**
The Scale of the Issue   65
Safety   66
Security   72
Conclusions: A Strategy for Urban Transport Safety and Security   75
Notes   76

6	**THE URBAN ROAD SYSTEM**	**77**
	Elements of Road Strategy	77
	Road Maintenance	77
	Traffic Management	79
	Demand Management	83
	Infrastructure Provision	84
	Poverty Focus	88
	Conclusions: A Strategy for Roads	90
	Notes	91
7	**PUBLIC ROAD PASSENGER TRANSPORT**	**93**
	The Urban Bus Sector	93
	Conclusions: Toward a Strategy for Public Transport	106
	Notes	107
8	**MASS RAPID TRANSIT**	**109**
	The Scale of the Issue	109
	Objectives and Role of Mass Rapid Transit within the City Development Strategy	110
	Relationship to Urban Structure and Land Use	111
	Mass Rapid Transit and the Urban Environment	111
	Choice of Mass Rapid Transit Technology	112
	Ownership and Financing	117
	Public Transport Integration	121
	Pricing	121
	Conclusions: Toward a Strategy for Mass Rapid Transit	122
	Notes	123
9	**THE ROLE OF NONMOTORIZED TRANSPORT**	**125**
	The Importance of Nonmotorized Transport	125
	Walking Is Transport	126
	Walking on Wheels	126
	The Policy Package	128
	Municipal Institutions and Organization	132
	Conclusions: A Strategy for Nonmotorized Transport	134
	Notes	134
10	**URBAN TRANSPORT PRICING AND FINANCE**	**135**
	The Role of Prices in Urban Transport	135
	Charging for the Use of Infrastructure	135
	Public Transport Pricing and Finance	141
	Urban Transport Financing	146
	Conclusions: A Strategy for Urban Transport Pricing and Financing	150
	Notes	151
11	**STRENGTHENING URBAN TRANSPORT INSTITUTIONS**	**153**
	The Importance of Institutions	153
	Major Institutional Weaknesses	154

Organizational Options 156
Capacity Building 165
Conclusions: A Strategy for Institutional Reform in Urban Transport 167
Notes 168

**12 MEETING THE DEVELOPMENT CHALLENGES:
    HOW CAN THE BANK CONTRIBUTE?** **169**
Development Challenges 169
Strengthening the Focus on Poverty 170
Facilitating Decentralization 171
Mobilizing Private Participation 173
Increasing Transport Safety and Security 175
Protecting the Environment 176
Conclusions 179
Notes 182

APPENDIX: URBAN TRANSPORT PORTFOLIO IN THE WORLD BANK 183
A.1   Urban Transport Projects under Preparation and Implementation as of
      February 26, 2002 183
A.2   Special Project Features 187
A.3   Urban Portfolio: Project Cost and World Bank Group Loan and
      Grant Amount Allocation 190

BIBLIOGRAPHY 193

INDEX 201

TABLES

2.1   A Categorization of City Circumstances 7
2.2   Estimates of External Costs of Road Transport 9
3.1   Poverty-Focused Urban Transport Interventions: Road Infrastructure 30
3.2   Income of Users of Rail Systems in Brazil 31
3.3   Poverty Impacts of Interventions: Rail Infrastructure and Management 32
3.4   Average Income of Users by Transport Mode 33
3.5   A Poverty-Focused Agenda: Public Transport Service Planning 35
3.6   Poverty-Focused Urban Transport Interventions: Finance Strategies 37
6.1   Functions and Responsibilities of a Typical Traffic Management Agency 82
6.2   Typical Functional Classification of Road and Path Networks 86
7.1   Efficiency of Bus Operations in Delhi, 1995 94
7.2   A Classification of Informal (Noncorporate) Urban Transport Operations ... 102
8.1   Performance and Cost of Some Typical Mass Rapid Transit Systems 113
8.2   Variation of Cost in Recent Metro Contracts 117
8.3   Financial Performance of Some Metro Systems 118
11.1 Allocation of Strategic Functions 154
11.2 Professional Organization for Municipal Transport Functions 158

FIGURES

2.1   Motorization and Incomes: Growth of Cars versus Growth of per Capita Incomes in France, Japan, Spain, and the United Kingdom, 1950s to 1995; and the Relative Positions of Selected Other Countries, 1995   10

4.1   Overview of Ambient Air Quality in Selected Cities: Subjective Assessment of Monitoring Data, Various Years in the 1990s   44

7.1   Urban Public Transport Competition: Regimes and Transitions   97

7.2   Effects of Competition on Bus Transport in London   99

11.1   Effect of Transport Integration in Madrid   157

11.2   A Typical Metropolitan Planning Process   161

BOXES

2.1   City Development Strategies   12

2.2   Matching Locational Characteristics and User Demands   17

2.3   Internal Consistency in Planning   18

2.4   The Market and Land Use and Transport Integration: The Tama Garden City Development   20

4.1   Fuel Adulteration in Thailand   46

4.2   Electric Three-Wheelers in Kathmandu   49

4.3   The Benefits of Information: Lubricating Two-Strokes   53

4.4   Private Sector Vehicle Inspection and Maintenance in Mexico City   54

5.1   Road Accidents and the Poor in Sri Lanka   66

5.2   Saving Lives in Brasília   72

5.3   Crime, Violence, and Diminishing Mobility   73

6.1   Financing Urban Road Maintenance in the Kyrgyz Republic   78

6.2   Paving Roads in Low-Income Areas in Brazilian Cities   90

7.1   Introducing Competitively Tendered Franchises in Uzbekistan   100

8.1   Leveraging Urban Transport Coordination in Brazil   116

8.2   TransMilenio: Bogotá's Bus Rapid Transit System   119

8.3   The Hopewell Project in Bangkok   120

9.1   Some Recent Experience with Facilities for Cycling in China   128

9.2   The Bogotá Bicycle Master Plan   129

9.3   Shova Lula (Ride Easy): A National Bicycle Transport Partnership   130

9.4   Stakeholder Participation in Nonmotorized Transport Development in Tanzania   133

10.1   The Namsan Tunnels in Seoul: Simple Road Pricing Reduces Congestion and Finances Traffic Management   137

10.2   Electronics Improves Road-Pricing Efficiency in Singapore   138

10.3   Recovering Fixed Costs: The Ramsey Pricing Rules   143

11.1   Engaging Civil Society in Planning Resettlement of the Poor in Mumbai   165

ACKNOWLEDGMENTS

This strategy review was undertaken on the initiative of John Flora, Director of the Transport and Urban Development Department of the World Bank. The author of the report is Ken Gwilliam, Economic Advisor to the Transport Department of the World Bank. The report has been discussed and approved by the Transport and Urban Sector Boards of the World Bank.

The work was undertaken in collaboration with the Urban Transport thematic group, which discussed and agreed on the report in detail. Important contributors to this review process included the coordinators of the group, Ed Dotson and Richard Podolske, together with Patrick Bultynck, Sally Burningham, Robin Carruthers, Jean-Charles Crochet, Ben Eijbergen, Pierre Graftieaux, Paul Guitink, Jeff Gutman, Ajay Kumar, Zhi Liu, Gerhard Menckhoff, Slobodan Mitric, Hubert Nove-Josserand, Jorge Rebelo, Binyam Reja, Richard Scurfield, Graham Smith, Antti Talvitie, and Lou Thompson.

Colleagues from the Urban Development, Environment, and Energy sectors who made important contributions, particularly to chapters 2 and 4, include Samir El Daher, Fitz Ford, Vincent Gouarne, Sonia Hammam, Christine Kessides, Masami Kojima, Magda Lovei, and Margret Thalwitz.

In support of the review, several background reports were commissioned, funded by trust funds or direct government commissioning. These reports, listed in the bibliography, are all separately available on the World Bank Web site. The assistance of the governments of France, Germany, Japan, the Netherlands, Spain, and the United Kingdom is gratefully acknowledged.

A consultation draft of this report was discussed with major stakeholders in client countries, including governments, transport operators, and nongovernmental organizations, as well as with representatives of other international institutions in consultation meetings held at Accra, Ghana; Santiago, Chile; Budapest, Hungary; and Yokohama, Japan. Gerhard Menckhoff, Ben Eijbergen, Patrick Bultynck, and James Edezhath organized those meetings, with particular assistance from Ian Thompson of the Economic Commission for Latin America and the Caribbean (Santiago), staff of the Japanese Ministries of Transport and Communications (Yokohama), the Közlekedéstudományi Intézet Rt. Institute for Transport Sciences (Budapest), and the Sub-Saharan Africa Transport Program (Accra). We are also grateful to the approximately 250 people from all over the world who were involved in those consultations.

ABBREVIATIONS AND ACRONYMS, CITIES AND COUNTRIES

ABBREVIATIONS AND ACRONYMS

ALS	Area licensing scheme
CBD	Central business district
CDS	City development strategy
CNG	Compressed natural gas
CO	Carbon monoxide
CO_2	Carbon dioxide
ERP	Electronic road pricing
GDP	Gross domestic product
GEF	Global Environment Facility
GHG	Greenhouse gas
GNP	Gross national product
I/M	Inspection and maintenance
IBRD	International Bank for Reconstruction and Development
IFC	International Finance Corporation
ITS	Intelligent Transport System
IU	In-vehicle unit (Singapore)
km/h	Kilometers per hour
LIL	Learning and Innovation Loan
LPG	Liquefied petroleum gas
LRT	Light rapid transit
mg/dl	Micrograms per deciliter
MMS	Monthly minimum salary
MRT	Mass rapid transit
NDoT	National department of transportation (South Africa)
NMT	Nonmotorized transport
NO	Nitric oxide
N_2O	Nitrous oxide
NO_2	Nitrogen dioxide
NO_x	Oxides of nitrogen
OECD	Organisation for Economic Co-operation and Development
PM	Particulate matter
pphpd	Passengers per hour in the peak direction
PRSP	Poverty Reduction Strategy Paper
RON	Research octane number
SO_2	Sulfur dioxide
SO_x	Sulfur oxides
SRT	Thailand State Railway
SSATP	Sub-Saharan Africa Transport Program
USAID	U.S. Agency for International Development
WBI	World Bank Institute
wt ppm	Parts per million by weight

CITIES AND COUNTRIES

Abidjan, Côte d'Ivoire
Accra, Ghana
Addis Ababa, Ethiopia
Ahmedabad, India
Almaty, Kazakhstan
Bangalore, India
Bangkok, Thailand
Beijing, China
Beirut, Lebanon
Berlin, Germany
Bilbao, Spain
Bishkek, Kyrgyz Republic
Bogotá, Colombia

Brasília, Brazil
Bremen, Germany
Bucharest, Romania
Budapest, Hungary
Cairo, Arab Republic of Egypt
Cali, Colombia
Cape Town, South Africa
Caracas, República Bolivariana de Venezuela
Casablanca, Morocco
Colombo, Sri Lanka
Copenhagen, Denmark
Cotonou, Benin

Curitiba, Brazil
Dakar, Senegal
Damascus, Syrian Arab Republic
Dar es Salaam, Tanzania
Dhaka, Bangladesh
Douala, Cameroon
Gothenburg, Sweden
Guangzhou, China
Hanoi, Vietman
Hamburg, Germany
Harare, Zimbabwe
Hong Kong, China
Ibadan, Nigeria
Jakarta, Indonesia
Johannesburg, South Africa
Karachi, Pakistan
Karlsruhe, Germany
Kathmandu, Nepal
Kinshasa, Democratic Republic of Congo
Kolkata (formerly Calcutta), India
Kraków, Poland
Kuala Lumpur, Malaysia
Kunming, China
La Paz, Bolivia
Lagos, Nigeria
León, Mexico
León, Nicaragua
Liaoning, China
Lima, Peru
Lomé, Togo
London, United Kingdom
Madras (now Chennai), India
Manila, Philippines
Maputo, Mozambique
Maracaibo, República Bolivariana de
    Venezuela

Medellín, Colombia
Mexico City, Mexico
Montevideo, Uruguay
Morogoro, Tanzania
Mumbai (formerly Bombay), India
Nairobi, Kenya
New Delhi, India
Ouagadougou, Burkina Faso
Porto Alegre, Brazil
Phnom Penh, Cambodia
Pusan, Republic of Korea
Quito, Ecuador
Recife, Brazil
Rio de Janeiro, Brazil
Rostov, Russian Federation
Rotterdam, Netherlands
Samarkand, Uzbekistan
Santiago, Chile
São Paolo, Brazil
Seoul, Republic of Korea
Shanghai, China
Singapore
Stockholm, Sweden
Stuttgart, Germany
Sydney, Australia
Tehran, Islamic Republic of Iran
Tunis, Tunisia
Urumqi, China
Vienna, Austria
Vientiane, Lao People's Democratic
    Republic
Warsaw, Poland
Wuhan, China
Yokohama, Japan
Zurich, Switzerland

EXECUTIVE SUMMARY

A previous World Bank urban transport strategy paper concentrated on economic and financial viability. "Urban Transport" (World Bank 1986) emphasized efficient management of existing transport capacity, good traffic management, and efficient pricing. It discouraged subsidies, recommended competition and minimal regulation, and questioned the value to the urban poor of capital-intensive projects that might not be cost effective in countries with limited resources.

Subsequent sector strategy papers have taken a broader view. The transport sector strategy paper "Sustainable Transport" (World Bank 1996) emphasized the integrity of economic, social, and environmental dimensions of a sustainable transport policy. The urban development strategy paper "Cities in Transition" (World Bank 2000a) stressed that the livability of cities depends on their being economically competitive, financially sustainable, well governed, and well managed.

This volume links the urban development and transport sector strategies with a strong poverty focus. Its objectives are (a) to develop a better understanding of urban transport problems in developing and transitional economies, (b) to articulate an urban transport strategy framework for national and city governments, and (c) to identify the role of the World Bank in supporting governments. It concentrates on the problems of people who are very poor, not only in terms of income but also in terms of the broader dimensions of social exclusion associated with inaccessibility: inaccessibility to jobs, schools, health facilities, and social activities.

Some well-established urban trends continue. Urban population continues to expand at more than 6 percent per year in many developing countries. The number of megacities—cities with over 10 million inhabitants—is expected to double within a generation. More than one-half of the developing world's population, and between one-third and one-half of its poor, will then live in cities. Per capita motor vehicle ownership and use continue to grow by up to 15 to 20 percent per year in some countries. Traffic congestion and air pollution continue to increase. Pedestrian and other nonmotorized transport (NMT) continue to be poorly served. Increased use of private vehicles has resulted in falling demand for public transport and a consequent decline in service levels. Sprawling cities are making the journey to work excessively long and costly for some of the very poor.

The context has changed in some significant respects since 1986. Cities are increasingly involved in trading patterns on a global scale, which makes the efficiency of their transport systems more critical. At the same time, responsibility for urban transport is being decentralized to the cities, which are often strapped for cash and are institutionally ill prepared for the new challenges. Under these conditions the financial state of public transport has deteriorated drastically in many countries. The safety and security of urban travelers are emerging problems, particularly in Latin America.

THE FUNDAMENTAL PARADOX OF URBAN TRANSPORT STRATEGY

Urban transport can contribute to poverty reduction both indirectly, through its impact on the city economy and hence on economic growth, and directly, through its impact on the daily needs of poor people. However, urban transport exhibits a fundamental paradox. How can a sector with such an obvious excess of demand over supply and with such a heavy involvement of private suppliers of service fail so completely to meet the aspirations of both politicians and citizens? Why has it not been possible to mobilize commercial initiative to yield the kind of revolution in service quality and cost that has been achieved in the telecommunications, water, and energy sectors? Finally, why does increasing affluence seem to have the effect of reducing the quality of travel, at least for poor people?

Urban growth increases transport costs. From the viewpoint of efficiency and growth, it is not too difficult to characterize the central problem. Economies of agglomeration generate the growth of cities. As cities grow and become richer, vehicle ownership and use grow more rapidly than the available road space, resulting in increased congestion and traffic-generated air pollution.

Urban growth often has perverse distributional effects. As cities expand, the price of more accessible land increases. Poor people are forced to live on less-expensive land, either in inner-city slums or on city peripheries. As average incomes grow and car ownership increases, the patronage, financial viability, and eventually quality and quantity of public transport diminishes. Motorization, which is permitted by the growth process, may thus also make some poor people even poorer. In particular, in the absence of efficient congestion pricing for road use, piecemeal investment to eliminate bottlenecks will almost certainly benefit the relatively wealthy at the expense of the poor.

An eclectic strategy is proposed. The strategy includes four main ways to address these problems: (a) structural change, (b) improved operational efficiency of the transport modes, (c) better focusing of interventions to assist the poor, and (d) policy and institutional reform.

STRUCTURAL CHANGE

Deconcentration has a limited role to play. The most fundamental structural response is to try to shift activity away from megacities, concentrating new development in medium-size cities. Unfortunately, it is not clear at what city size the economies of agglomeration run out or how a policy of deconcentration can be effectively implemented. Nevertheless, central governments can encourage the development of smaller regional hubs by eliminating fiscal and public expenditure distortions, including elimination of price distortions in land and transport markets, such as the underpricing of congested road space and the absence of full-cost connection charges and impact fees for land development. They can also lead by the location of their own activities.

Improved structure within cities can contribute greatly. A less-radical approach emphasizes coordination of land use and transport infrastructure and service planning, to ensure provision of adequate and well-structured road space as the city grows. This requires improved development control skills and practices at the city level. Critics of this approach argue that such an emphasis on road capacity fosters a level of motorization that will create dependence on the automobile, and will eventually overtake space availability. In any case, it is unlikely to be socially or environmentally acceptable to balance supply and demand solely by increasing road capacity in larger cities.

Good road infrastructure does not necessarily mean total auto dependence. Indeed, it is the combination of land-use and transport planning that has made it possible for some cities to reconcile high mobility with high quality of urban life. In order to achieve that reconciliation, traffic has been restrained (as in Singapore, by road pricing) and has been managed to maintain safe, efficient, and environmentally acceptable movement of people, not just of vehicles. This implies prioritization of infrastructure to protect movements of public transport and NMT against unrestricted expansion of private motorized trips (as in Bogotá, Colombia, and Curitiba, Brazil, through busway systems). In these more-constrained circumstances, rigorous appraisal of investments in road capacity needs to take into account (a) the effects of induced traffic on benefits; (b) the benefits to, and disbenefits of, NMT; and (c) the environmental impacts.

IMPROVING THE OPERATIONAL EFFICIENCY OF TRANSPORT

To improve the efficiency of transport, the needs of each mode must be addressed—the road system, NMT, public passenger transport, and mass transit. In addition, the role of the private sector as a means of promoting efficiency deserves special attention.

THE ROAD SYSTEM
Even in highly congested cities, urban road transport efficiency can be improved through better system management. Although rapid development of technology has reduced the cost—as well as the maintenance and operational skill requirements—of modern traffic management techniques, many cities are still too poorly organized and inadequately staffed to make effective use of this development. Both technical assistance and investment are capable of yielding high returns in this field, as long as fundamental institutional and human resource problems are addressed.

Urban road decay is a serious problem in many countries. Road decay contributes to conges-

tion and increasing operating costs. It often arises from jurisdictional conflicts—such as conflicts over which authority is responsible for which roads, lack of clear ownership of neighborhood roads, or inadequate allocation for urban roads from the national road funds through which road funding is channeled.

NONMOTORIZED TRANSPORT
NMT is systematically underrecognized. Walking still accounts for the largest proportion of trips taken, although not of distance traveled, in most low- and middle-income countries. All income groups are involved. Despite this fact the welfare of pedestrians, and particularly the welfare of mobility-impaired pedestrians, is frequently sacrificed in planning to increase the speed of the flow of vehicles. Cycling is similarly disadvantaged. Without a continuous network of secure infrastructure, people will not risk bicycle travel. Without users, investment in infrastructure for cycling may appear wasteful.

A comprehensive vision and action plan for NMT is required. In the planning and management of infrastructure, the excessive emphasis on motorized transport may be redressed by (a) clear provision for the rights as well as responsibilities of pedestrians and bicyclists in traffic law; (b) formulation of a national strategy for NMT as a facilitating framework for local plans; (c) explicit formulation of a local plan for NMT as part of the planning procedures of municipal authorities; (d) provision of separate infrastructure where appropriate (such as for safe movement and secure parking of vehicles); and (e) incorporation of standards of provision for bicyclists and pedestrians in new road infrastructure design. Incorporation of responsibilities for provision for NMT should also be included in road fund statutes and procedures.

Traffic management should be focused on improving the movement of people rather than on improving the movement of motorized vehicles. In order to achieve that goal, police need to be trained to enforce the rights of NMT in traffic priorities as well as in recording and preventing accidents. Furthermore, the development in poor countries of small-scale credit mechanisms to finance bicycles, credit mechanisms that are increasingly successful in rural areas, might also be developed in urban areas.

PUBLIC PASSENGER TRANSPORT

Public transport is for all. Concentrating on the transport modes of poor people in middle-income countries essentially means the provision of affordable forms of public transport, both formal and informal. But it should not be viewed as only for the poor, as the importance of public transport to all income groups in many rich European cities demonstrates. Improving efficiency in public transport must be concerned not only with keeping costs down but also with providing a flexible framework within which the less poor as well as the very poor can use public transport with confidence and comfort.

Most urban public transport is road based. Bus lanes and automatic priority at intersections can improve public transport performance significantly, but these solutions tend to suffer from inadequate enforcement by police, who are untrained in traffic planning and management. In contrast, exclusive busways in developing countries have proved to be capable, except in very high traffic volume corridors, of performance nearly equivalent to rail-based systems but at much lower cost.

Pricing and financing issues are at the heart of public transport problems. Formal bus operations face financial collapse in many countries, partly as an unintended consequence of good-hearted but wrong-headed fare and service controls. Some prescriptions can easily be made to forestall this. General fare controls should be determined as part of a comprehensive city transport financing plan, and their effect on the expected quality and quantity of service carefully considered. Fare reductions or exemptions should be financed on the budget of the relevant line agency responsible for the categories (health, social sector, education, interior, and so on) of the affected person. Modally integrated fare schemes should be assessed for their impacts on poor people. It is in the interests of poor people for sustainable financing and efficient targeting of public transport subsidies to be paramount.

There is a rich agenda of urban public transport policies that is both pro-growth and pro-poor. The recent decline in both the quality and quantity of public transport has resulted partly from the absence or disappearance of a secure fiscal basis for support. Public transport, however, can be improved in many ways that are consistent with the fiscal capabilities of even the poorest countries. Giving priority to public transport in the use of road space makes public transport faster and more financially viable.

Competition is pro-poor. Supply costs can be reduced through competition between private sector suppliers. In Buenos Aires the urban rail system has been revolutionized through concessioning. Regulated competition in the bus market has also worked well in cities such as Buenos Aires and Santiago—but care is needed in system design. Total deregulation in Lima, although it has increased supply, has worsened road congestion, the urban environment, and user safety and security. The lesson is that it is not privatization or deregulation per se that improves public transport, but rather the introduction of carefully managed competition, in which the role of the public sector as regulator complements that of the private sector as service supplier.

Cities should strive to mobilize the potential of the informal sector. Informally supplied small vehicle paratransit (publicly available passenger transport service that is outside the traditional public transport regulatory system) is often dominant in providing for dispersed trip patterns and in flexibly addressing the demands of poor people, particularly in low-income countries, but it is typically viewed as part of the problem of public transport and not part of the solution. Certainly, anticompetitive or antisocial behavior should be controlled through quality controls and enforcement, but its potential can be better mobilized through legalizing associations and through structuring franchising arrangements to give the small operator an opportunity to participate in competitive processes.

MASS TRANSIT

Rail-based mass transit systems have a role to play in very large cities. Rail-based mass transit systems are less congesting than are road-based systems and can be very important for those who are peripherally located and have long journeys to access employment in the cities. In Latin America, in particular, rail-based systems carry significant numbers of very poor people. The Bank has financed several major urban rail developments in the past decade, typically in metros and existing suburban railway refurbishment but occasionally in new construction. Often the restructuring of bus services, which eliminates direct competition and can harm the interests of poor bus-users unless skillfully planned, supports the rail-based systems. The position that has been adopted is that such developments must be integrated into a comprehensive urban transport strategy and that arrangements should include physical and fare integration between modes, to ensure that the poor are not excluded from or disadvantaged by the Bank's investments.

Urban rail-based systems should be cautiously appraised. Urban rail-based systems are costly to build and operate, are more expensive for the passenger to use than road-based modes, and can impose a large burden on the city budget. It remains appropriate, therefore, to advise cautious examination of the fiscal sustainability of rail investments and their impact on poor people before making expensive commitments. The most critical lesson the Bank has learned is that mass transit investment decisions should be driven by a thorough examination of strategic objectives of technological alternatives, and financial implications, and not by short-term political or commercial opportunism.

THE ROLE OF THE PRIVATE SECTOR

Private financing of urban transport infrastructure is possible. Recognizing the burden of investments in major roads and metros on municipal budgets, cities such as Bangkok, Buenos Aires, and Kuala Lumpur have already managed to secure private capital finance for them. Experience so far has shown that this requires very high demand for faster movement in the affected corridor and a realistic stance by government on the relationship between price controls and commercial profitability. Experience has also shown opportunistic development on an ad hoc basis to be damaging, and usually costly to the public purse. Mass transit systems, in particular, appear to yield greatest benefit when they are incorporated into a citywide price-level and structure plan in which the full cost of new mass transit investments on the municipal budgets, on fares, and on poor people has been estimated in advance.

Planning and regulatory arrangements for private participation in urban transport are fundamental. The interaction of transport with land use requires its careful integration into the planning of metropolitan structure and finance within a comprehensive long-term plan for the city. The public sector must set a strategy; identify infrastructure projects and describe them in some detail; and confirm the acceptability of environmental consequences, tariffs, and any contingent changes to the existing transport system. It must acquire the necessary land and rights-of-way, ensure development permissions, commit funding, and provide some necessary guarantees. Physical coordination (to achieve convenient modal interchange) and fares coordination (to keep public transport attractive and to protect poor people) need to be embodied in a comprehensive transport strategy plan that recognizes the relationships between modes of transport.

BETTER FOCUSING OF INTERVENTIONS TO ASSIST THE POOR

There are two possible approaches when designing poverty-targeted transport interventions—directly serving the locations where poor people live and work, and targeting disadvantaged groups. In addition, institutions must address two issues that have a particular impact on the poor—the polluted urban environment, and safety and security.

SERVING THE LOCATIONS WHERE POOR PEOPLE LIVE AND WORK

Transport improvements can be focused on where poor people live and work. These improvements may involve concentrated efforts to improve access to slum areas or to improve public transport to peripheral locations. The Bank-supported Pavement Program in Low-Income Areas (Programa de Pavimentação de Baixo Custo em Areas de Baixa Renda—PROPAV) in Brazil proved highly successful, and was extended throughout the country, as well as to other Latin American countries.

Leakage through land rent changes must be taken into account. Transport investments or service improvements change the structure of land values. If there is strong competition for the use of land and highly concentrated ownership of land, rents increase in improved areas and the benefits of transport improvements accrue to rich landowners rather than to poor land occupants. Some investments— such as improvements in bus or NMT systems—are less likely to drive poor people out to more distant, less-expensive locations than are others—such as primary roads or more highly priced, mass transit systems. This find-

ing further emphasizes the need for transport to be part of a comprehensive urban development strategy.

TARGETING DISADVANTAGED GROUPS

Transport provision can be part of a social safety net. A complementary approach is to focus on the specific categories of disadvantaged people. Given the overwhelming importance of the ability to access employment, the work journeys of poor people may be a prime target for support. The cost of ensuring that these trips are affordable may be shifted to the employer (as with the "vale-transporte" in Brazil) or the state (as with the commuter subsidy system of South Africa). Although they may be less-than-perfectly targeted (for example, the vale-transporte misses very poor informal workers), may distort residential location incentives, and are inferior to direct income transfers, targeted transport subsidy arrangements may be the best practicable safety net for poor workers.

Low income is not the only form of deprivation. Gender confers some particular disadvantages in terms of diffused trip patterns and timings, as well as particular vulnerability to safety and security problems. Age and infirmity pose rather different problems, calling for sensitive "inclusive" design of physical facilities. Both locational resettlement and occupational redeployment impinge in a particularly harsh way on poor people, requiring adequate safety nets.

Fare controls can do more harm than good. Experience teaches two important lessons about what not to do with respect to fare controls. First, controlling fares in the absence of realistic analysis of, and provision for, the resource needs of that social strategy actually destroys public transport service and may cause serious harm to some poor people. Second, cross-subsidy within public sector monopolies does not eliminate the fundamental resource problem, and instead adds some extra burden of inefficiencies in supply.

POVERTY OF "LIFE QUALITY": TRANSPORT AND THE URBAN ENVIRONMENT

Poor people tend also to be the most vulnerable to environmental pollution. The most damaging pollutants are lead, small suspended particulate matter, and in some cities, ozone. Local air pollution from transport in developing countries contributes to the premature deaths of over 500,000 people per year, and imposes an economic cost of up to 2 percent of gross domestic project (GDP) in many countries. A strategy for improvement of the effects that urban transport has on the environment is thus not a luxury to be afforded at the expense of poor people, but an important element of an urban transport strategy. The Intergovernmental Panel on Climate Change (IPCC) also forecast that developing countries will suffer disproportionate costs of from 5 to 9 percent of their GDP should the global level of carbon dioxide double (IPCC 1996).

Understanding of the environmental impacts of urban transport remains deficient. There are some clear technological priorities. While it is generally preferable to concentrate on performance standards, rather than on specific technology preference, there are also some relatively clear technological priorities for the sector. These include the elimination of lead from gasoline, the replacement of two-stroke motorcycles with four-stroke motorcycles, and the elimination or cleaning up of high-mileage, heavily polluting vehicles. The Bank can help with technical assistance in these fields and, in some cases, with the financing of infrastructure and incentive mechanisms to stimulate change.

There is no quick technological fix for developing countries. Local air quality can be improved in the long run by new fuel and vehicle technologies. In the short run, however, the vehicle stock is dominated by an older generation of technology, which is often badly maintained. In some countries the emphasis on identifying and acting to improve the worst, highest-mileage polluters—often buses, taxis,

and some trucks—has helped. Inspection and maintenance programs, if undertaken by technologically efficient instruments in a corruption-free context, can have great impacts. At the extreme there are assisted, or forced, scrappage schemes.

Some robust "win-win" environmental strategies exist for the urban transport sector. Good traffic management can reduce environmental impact as well as congestion. Tax structure reform can encourage the use of cleaner fuels and stimulate better vehicle maintenance. This reform, however, requires the design of fiscal measures to handle problems associated with the use of fuels (for example, kerosene, which is used in several sectors), and to handle the associated conflicting policy objectives, such as those associated with the taxation of diesel fuel (see the more detailed discussion in the main text of the report). The integration of transport interventions in general municipal development packages may offer better leverage in this respect than the integration of transport-specific projects.

SAFETY AND SECURITY

Road accidents are a global pandemic. Nearly 0.5 million people die and up to 15 million people are injured in urban road accidents in developing countries each year, at a direct economic cost of between 1 and 2 percent of GDP in many countries. Accidents occur widely on roads between intersections rather than being concentrated at intersections, as is the case in industrialized countries, and the majority of victims are poor pedestrians and bicyclists.

Adequate data are the basis for policy formulation and implementation. The first steps to improve traffic safety are the development of national road accident data collection and analysis capability, and the formation of institutional arrangements to ensure that the data are transmitted to those who need them for policy purposes. Accident frequency and severity can be reduced by improved road design and traffic-management policies. While some infrastructure investment is specifically safety oriented (such as infrastructure for NMT in Lima, or grade-separated railway crossings in Buenos Aires), there is a strong case for mandatory safety audits in the design process for all transport infrastructure. Improved medical response can be achieved by some relatively inexpensive and simple institutional innovations. Increasing safety awareness to change traffic patterns and pedestrian behavior requires development and training of staff for specific road-safety coordinating agencies or councils, at both the national and municipal levels.

Personal security is a growing social problem in many countries. While this problem encompasses much more than the transport sector, it is important to analyze the nature and significance of insecurity in the urban transport sector and to devise policy instruments to counter it. That might include collection and analysis of data on personal security in the transport sector to enhance official awareness of the problem, and might include commitment of police authorities to arrest and the courts to appropriately penalize offenders. Strengthening public participation in projects, particularly at the neighborhood level, is important. Some transport policy initiatives can contribute directly to better personal security. For example, street lighting—designed to improve pedestrian security—can be included in street improvement, and particularly in slum-upgrading, projects. Franchise conditions for public transport can give incentives for improved attention to security by public transport operators.

POLICY AND INSTITUTIONAL REFORMS

Technical measures alone are unlikely to resolve the fundamental paradox of a sector's combining excess demand with inadequately financed supply. Improvements in the efficiency of roads, vehicles, public transport operations, and traffic management can undoubtedly improve the efficiency of urban transport. This will not be enough, however, because of three structural characteristics that distinguish urban transport from most other urban service sectors. These characteristics are (a) the separation of infrastructure from operations, (b) the separation of interacting modes of transport, and (c) the separation of infrastructure finance from infrastructure pricing. What is required, therefore, is an integrated package of strategies for infrastructure pricing, service pricing, and urban transport system financing, founded in well-designed institutions within an appropriate political framework.

SEPARATION OF INFRASTRUCTURE FROM OPERATIONS

Charging for road infrastructure is the core of a strategy for both efficient allocation of resources and sustainable finance. Congestion increases private transport costs and contributes to the decline of public transport service. While these two phenomena are logically connected, in most cities they are institutionally and financially separated. In principle, vehicular users of congested urban road space should be charged a price at least equal to the short-run marginal cost of use, including congestion, road wear and tear, and environmental impacts.

In the absence of direct charging, fuel taxation should be structured concurrent with vehicle license duties to give a proxy charge for road use and its external impacts. In practice, a range of direct and indirect mechanisms is used to charge for road use. The most common of these mechanisms—the fuel tax—reflects global warming impacts well, but is a poor surrogate for either congestion or road-maintenance impact pricing. Nevertheless, if it is the best proxy there is, the fuel tax should be structured to reflect its relative contributions to urban air pollution, again in conjunction with the structuring of vehicle license duties.

Parking charges should be related to an overall infrastructure pricing strategy. Although they are also a poor proxy for congestion charges, parking charges should, in any case, always cover the full opportunity-cost of land used for parking. Where parking policy is the only available proxy for congestion, pricing controls need to cover all forms of parking space (including that provided privately by employers for their employees).

Direct charging for roads requires careful political and administrative preparation. Although cordon pricing and tolling of specific roads is a step in the right direction, the long-term solution lies in more systematic congestion charges. Of course, it is not easy to raise prices or taxes, particularly for goods that have traditionally been viewed as free. For instance, resistance to increased fuel prices in the República Bolivariana de Venezuela in the late-1980s was very violent. Riots following an increase in public transport fares in Guatemala in 2000 cost five lives. This suggests that such increases in charges must be linked with a perceptible improvement in provision of services. There would remain a large education requirement to explain the link between the increased cost and the improvement of services, and to offer realistic choices of alternatives. The second part of the integrated solution thus refers to service provision and pricing.

SERVICE PROVISION AND PRICING

Pricing principles for public transport modes should be determined within an integrated urban strategy. This means that they should reflect the extent to which road infrastructure is adequately charged. Given the high level of interaction among modes, and the prevalent undercharging of road use, financial transfers between roads and public transport services—and between modes of public transport—are potentially consistent with optimal pricing strategy.

Subsidies or compensation payments do not mean that there should be a monopoly supplier of transport services. In the interests of effi-

cient service supply, transport operators should operate competitively, with purely commercial objectives, and with financial transfers achieved through contracts between municipal authorities and operators for the supply of services. Any noncommercial objectives imposed on operators should be compensated directly and transparently, where appropriate, by the nontransport line agencies in whose interests they are imposed. Above all, in the absence of appropriate contracting or other support mechanisms, the sustainability of public transport service should be paramount, and should generally have precedence over traditional price regulation arrangements. The completion of an integrated policy thus requires an integrated urban transport financing system.

URBAN TRANSPORT SYSTEM FINANCING

Urban transport financing should be fungible. Given the interaction among modes, there is a strong case for treating the urban transport system as an integrated whole. Because neither congestion nor environmental impacts are currently subject to direct charges in many countries, optimizing the performance of the sector as a whole might justify using revenues raised from private automobile users to fund improvements in public transport. Private sector financing for transport infrastructure, raised through competitive tendering of concessions, may be supported by public contributions as long as these have been subject to proper cost-benefit analysis.

There are different ways of securing fungibility of funding. In a well-managed unitary authority, such as in Singapore, this occurs through the normal budgetary process. In more complex, multitiered administrative systems, achieving this flexibility may require the pooling of urban transport financial resources within an urban transport fund administered by a strategic transport authority at the municipal or metropolitan level. Under such an organization, all local transport-user charges, including congestion charges and any allocations of local taxes or intergovernmental transfers for transport, should normally be made to the fund.

Urban transport funds do not imply earmarking of taxes. Earmarked taxes, such as the payroll tax on employers, that supports the public transport agency Régie Autonome des Transports Parisiens (RATP) in Paris, have the advantage of a secure legal and budgetary foundation, and are often the basis on which sound long-term service planning can be undertaken. However, the value of having an integrated urban transport fund does not depend on any specific tax source being earmarked for transport. Moreover, in order to develop the credibility of the fund, and particularly to gain political and popular support for the payment of congestion charges, it is essential that the objectives and scope of an urban transport fund be clearly defined, that allocations be subject to rigorous appraisal, and that the operations of the fund be transparent.

INSTITUTIONS

Policy integration has significant institutional implications. In the interests of urban transport integration and sustainability, developing countries could therefore profitably move toward prices reflecting full social costs for all modes, to a targeted approach to subsidization reflecting strategic objectives, and to an integration of urban transport funding, while still retaining supply arrangements for individual modes that give an important incentive to operational efficiency and cost-effectiveness. The implementation of such a policy package has significant institutional implications, requiring close coordination both between jurisdictions and between functions, as well as between private and public sector planning and operating agencies.

The basis for institutional coordination is often very weak. Few cities have a strategic agency for land-use and transportation planning, or a competent traffic management unit. Traffic police are therefore often involved with traffic

management planning, for which they are ill equipped and untrained. Public transport planning and regulation is also often tied to operations. The few institutions that do exist tend to be understaffed and their staff poorly trained.

Urban transport institutions need both restructuring and strengthening. Action is required on two levels. First, authorities need to recognize what kind of technical organization is necessary to address urban transport issues. Second, the organizations need adequate human, as well as physical, resources to perform their functions. While no single institutional blueprint for public transport is appropriate for all countries, there is enough experience to establish some general principles for the reduction of institutional impediments to effective policy integration.

Jurisdictional coordination may be facilitated through the clear establishment in law of the allocation of responsibility between levels of government. Formal institutional arrangements can be made for collaboration where multiple municipalities exist within a continuous conurbation. The process of decentralization in developing countries may offer an excellent opportunity to address the problems. In particular, intergovernmental transfers need to be carefully planned to be consistent with the allocation of responsibility, but structured to avoid distorting local priority setting. Central governments might also encourage coordination at the metropolitan level; in France, for example, the central government made both local taxation powers and intergovernmental transfers conditional on appropriate jurisdictional and functional collaboration.

Functional coordination should be based on a strategic land-use and transport plan. Detailed planning, both of transport and land use, should be aligned with a municipal or metropolitan structure plan. Coordinated operation is further enhanced by the clear allocation of functions among agencies, with the more strategic functions being retained at the metropolitan level.

Obligations statutorily imposed on local authorities should be linked to specific channels of finance (such as direct line agency funding of reduced public transport fares). Responsibility for traffic safety should also be explicitly allocated, with an institutional responsibility at the highest level of the local administration. Traffic police should be trained in traffic management and safety administration, and involved in transport and safety policy planning.

Responsibility for planning and operating public transport should be institutionally separated. For effective involvement of the private sector, technical regulation should be separated from procurement and economic regulation. A clear legal framework should be established for competition in public transport supply, either in the market or for the market. Operations should be fully commercialized or privatized, and the development of new competitive private suppliers of service encouraged through legal recognition of associations, and so on. The public sector should develop strong service procurement and contract enforcement skills.

POLITICS, PARTICIPATION, AND PERFORMANCE

Decentralized democratic process must be complemented by high technical competence. Ultimately, transport policy formulation involves an element of tradeoff between conflicting interests. It is therefore bound to be a political process. Too often (not least in Latin America) bad investments have been made, and serious urban transport issues trivialized, by the political process. Cities that have exhibited good transport planning and management, such as Curitiba and Singapore, have often developed under strong leadership and have been founded on a high level of technical and professional competence in the planning function. The question is how to reconcile coherent technical vision with more decentralized and fragmented democratic processes.

Public participation and technically strong planning can be complementary. The development of public participation and consultation, in parallel to the local democratic process, is an important means of improving local policy design. This may occur through advance exposure of plans to a free press and other media, as well as through more formal processes of public consultation or public inquiry. For small-scale, very localized, infrastructure projects it may be possible to incorporate local preferences in the design process itself. Public transport users may also be involved in service franchising arrangements by complaints and consultation processes and by linking bonus payments for franchised operators to public or media appraisal. At a more strategic level, and for larger, more complex projects, consultation often functions more as a means of trying to reconcile inherently competing or conflicting interests; it is nevertheless central to the development of consensus-based city development strategies.

Public participation must be timely and well structured. Developing strategic involvement requires action at two levels. First, the public processes must be organized to facilitate timely but well-informed consultation. Second, particularly where formal local political processes are weak, the existence of effective local community groups is extremely important. In developing countries, such groups are often well developed in rural areas but much less so in cities. As both policy and financial responsibility for urban development is decentralized to the cities, it is thus possible to create institutional and financial arrangements that better reflect the complex interactions both within the urban transport sector and between urban transport and the rest of urban development strategy. It is only on such a carefully considered institutional and financial basis that the fundamental paradox of urban transport can be resolved.

1 CONTEXT FOR THE REVIEW

Cities in the developing world are growing rapidly; with this growth comes increased congestion. At the same time, public transport is declining in many cities to the detriment of the city economy, its environment, and the welfare of its poorer inhabitants. The purposes of this review are (a) to refocus urban transport strategy on the issues of urban poverty, and (b) to offer a vehicle for enhancing collaboration between the World Bank and other agencies involved in urban development lending or aid.

The primary focus of all World Bank activity is the reduction of poverty. The essence of its approach, embodied in the comprehensive development framework and in the poverty reduction strategies being developed with the highly indebted poor countries, is a holistic view of the development process, recognizing the interdependence among sectors, concentrating on the weak links in any particular country, and aiming to better coordinate the activities of the many agencies involved.

Economically, transport is the lifeblood of cities; in most countries, including developing countries, cities are the major sources of the national economic growth. Cities, and the growth of cities, make poverty reduction possible. Poor transport inhibits the growth of cities. Socially, transport is the means of (and the lack of transport is the impediment to) accessibility to the jobs, health, education, and social services that are essential to the welfare of the poor; inaccessibility emerges as a major cause of social exclusion in studies of the poor in urban areas. Urban transport strategy can thus contribute to poverty reduction both through its impact on the city economy, and hence on economic growth, and through its direct impact on the daily needs of the very poor.

Urban transport is already an important part of the Bank portfolio. At the end of 2000 there were 48 active projects with urban transport components and an additional 12 projects at a sufficiently advanced stage of preparation for World Bank investment to be estimated. One-half of the 48 active projects were registered as urban transport projects. The total sum of Bank lending in these projects is estimated at $4.4 billion.[1] Of that amount 35.3 percent was accounted for by metro and suburban rail investments (most of these in Latin America), and 13.7 percent by investments in buses, busways, and other high-occupancy vehicle facilities. An additional 19.2 percent of the investment was on new road construction (most of this investment in China), and 15.4 percent on road and bridge rehabilitation and maintenance. In addition, the International Finance Corporation has, since 1995, invested in seven urban transport projects, including toll roads, buses, and a metro project, as well as a number of major airport and seaport developments in capital cities.

The context for this review is the progressive decentralization of political and financial responsibility for urban development, either by deliberate institutional shifts of decentralization policy—for example, in Brazil—or by political and economic reality—for example, in many countries of the former Soviet Union. As a recent World Bank urban development strategy paper argues

(World Bank 2000a), decentralization will inevitably force city governments to confront the issues of fiscal balance and creditworthiness ("bankability") and of good governance of their assets, as a necessary condition for improving the competitive position of the city's economy and the social and environmental conditions ("livability") for its inhabitants. Fostering the development of these institutional characteristics is the primary thrust of the urban development strategy paper (World Bank 2000a). That strategy paper did not, however, attempt to translate the philosophy into specific service supply strategies for different sectors. That is what this volume attempts to do: to view urban transport in the wider context of city development and within a comprehensive development framework that puts increased emphasis on poverty and on enhanced collaboration between the World Bank and other multilateral and bilateral agencies involved in development lending or aid.

The last World Bank urban transport policy paper (World Bank 1986) emphasized the importance of planning and managing infrastructure and traffic to secure economically efficient urban movement. Since then, a broader perspective on transport sector policy has been developing. In late 1996 the Bank published its general transport policy paper, which emphasized the essential integrity of economic, social, and environmental dimensions of a sustainable transport policy (World Bank 1996).

The objectives of this urban transport review volume are therefore (a) to develop a better common understanding of the nature and magnitude of urban transport problems, particularly with respect to the poor, in developing and transitional economies, and (b) to articulate a strategy to assist national and city governments to address urban transport problems within which the role of the World Bank (and other agencies) can be identified.

This is not a narrow technical matter. There is some tension among the objectives of growth (of which motorization is, to some extent, an enabling element), poverty, and the environment. Moreover, transport is mainly an intermediate good, facilitating the production of final goods and services that satisfy human needs. As such it is an essential element of a city development strategy, but not a freestanding one. It is only in the integration of urban transport strategy with other sector strategies in responding to the problems and opportunities of development that transport strategy adds its value.

The critical point is that such integrated, strategic thinking should be realistic and should be convertible into action plans and programs within the capability of the cities. Urban transport is a sector more than normally subject to such disconnect between vision and reality. New road construction in the absence of a balanced urban development program that includes demand management, public transport provision, and supporting land-use policies may not improve traffic or environmental conditions. Low-fare policies for public transport, in the absence of a realistic understanding of implied resource needs for implementing this social strategy, may actually cause deterioration in service. For that reason the review tries to balance a concern for the way transport fits into the strategic vision of the city development strategy with a concern for better ways to deliver transport, a matter that is far from trivial.

The first part of this volume considers how urban transport can be used as an instrument of urban development and poverty reduction. The strategy has two main thrusts. First, as discussed in chapter 2, "Urban Transport and City Development," poverty may be reduced through the contribution that transport makes to the efficiency of the urban economy and hence to the overall growth of incomes. Second, as discussed in chapter 3, "Urban Transport and Poverty Reduction," urban transport policies can be focused more specifically on meeting the needs of the poor. The inability to afford good transport service is not the only transport-related aspect of the quality of life of poor people, however. Chapter 4, "Transport and the Urban Environment," considers the urban environment and shows that the poor are particularly vulnerable to transport-related air pollution, while chapter 5, "Urban Transport Safety and Security," considers problems of personal safety and security in transport.

The second part of this volume considers how the objectives (to develop a better common understanding of urban transport problems, with particular reference to the poor, and to articulate a strategy to address them) can be pursued using a range of instruments. Chapter 6, "The Urban Road System," considers the provision and management of road infrastructure. Chapter 7, "Public Road Passenger Transport," discusses road-based public transport, including the role of the informal sector. Chapter 8, "Mass Rapid Transit," considers the role and limitations of mass transit. Chapter 9, "The Role of Nonmotorized Transport," pays special attention to nonmotorized transport, which plays a very important, but often neglected, part in meeting the needs of the poor (and increasingly the less poor). Chapters 10, "Urban Transport Pricing and Finance," and 11, "Strengthening Urban Transport Institutions," address two common areas of weakness identified in the preceding chapters: the issues of pricing and financing of urban transport, and the institutional arrangements for the sector. Finally, in chapter 12, "Meeting the Development Challenges: How Can the Bank Contribute?" we consider implications for the instruments and lending strategies of the Bank.

NOTE

1. All dollar amounts are current U.S. dollars, unless identified otherwise.

2 URBAN TRANSPORT AND CITY DEVELOPMENT

Deteriorating transport conditions associated with urban sprawl and increased motorization are damaging the economy of large cities. Structural policies such as well-planned transport infrastructure expansion, planned deconcentration, comprehensive management of land-use structure, or liberalization of land markets can help, but they require careful coordination of transport policies within a broader city development strategy.

URBAN TRANSPORT AND CITY EFFICIENCY

In this chapter we consider the impact of urban transport on the development of the city economy. In most developing countries the urban sector accounts for at least 50 percent of the gross national product (GNP); in some countries that number is over 70 percent. Cities in developing countries often devote 15 to 25 percent, and sometimes much more, of their annual expenditures to their transport systems. Between 8 and 16 percent of urban household income is typically spent on transport, although this can also rise to more than 25 percent for the poorest households in very large cities. About one-third of all city infrastructure investment need is for the transport sector. Despite recent developments in private sector involvement in transport infrastructure finance, most of this investment will have to come through the city budget.

Urban population is expanding at more than 6 percent annually in most developing countries. In many formerly rural economies, such as China, because of the need to decrease the number of persons dependent on agriculture and to improve productivity in rural areas, urbanization is viewed as a prerequisite of growth. Within a generation more than one-half of the developing world's population will live in cities. This implies an increase of 2 billion—equal to the present-day total urban population of developing countries.[1] The number of megacities—cities with over 10 million inhabitants—is expected to double, with three-quarters in developing countries. Some growth will be in high-density peri-urban settlements outside the range of the existing urban facilities and authorities. Much growth is likely to consist of urban sprawl, which militates against adequate public transport service supply, encourages auto dependence, and hence reduces accessibility to employment and to urban facilities for the poor and very poor. It is therefore important to explore possibilities of improving the economic performance of cities by better integrating transport with other aspects of city development strategy (CDS).

Cities exist because of economies of agglomeration associated with industrial and trade activities. The "advanced" sectors are located there, and labor productivity is typically higher in cities than in rural areas. The dominance of large and dense capital cities in many developing countries suggests that these advantages continue up to megacity size.

Within these cities motorized road transport is the main mode of movement. While longer-distance movements of goods and passengers may make significant use of other modes, and nonmotorized transport (NMT) may perform an important role in short-distance movements of passengers (and in some cities, of freight), most large cities in the world that are not dependent on mechanized road transport for the majority of internal freight and passenger movement are poor, relatively unproductive, and wish to change their situations. Of all cities, megacities have the highest travel times, the greatest congestion, and the most polluted environments. The strategic quandary, particularly in countries where the capital city dominates, is how to retain the economic benefits of city scale while limiting the deterioration of transport performance that may be associated with size and density.

Particularly in Asia, this deterioration of transport performance appears to be generating a rapid growth of motorized two-wheelers that are faster than either bicycles (because of their power) or buses (because of their personal nature, thus their maneuverability). The new two-wheelers are so inexpensive that even the relatively poor can afford them. For example, a recent study of Delhi, India, showed that with an average per capita income of less than $2,000 per year, over 80 percent of households have motorized vehicles, mostly two-wheelers. They offer personal motorized mobility, albeit presently at a high environmental and accident cost (see chapter 5), although technology exists to clean them up very substantially at little extra cost. Moreover, there is also evidence that they make more effective use of road space per person than either bicycles or private cars. In the short term, therefore, there does appear to be a rather different development path available for the developing countries involving greater personalized mobility than was available in the industrialized countries at equivalent income levels in their development. The long-term strategic question is whether motorcycles are simply going to be viewed as a transition step to an unsustainable level of private automobile ownership and use, or whether by good traffic management and segregation they can be sustained as the core of a more mobile, but safe and sustainable, urban transport system.

In addressing that quandary, it must be recognized that cities differ greatly in economic, social,

and spatial characteristics. Moreover, any individual city will change its characteristics over time. We cannot hope to produce a simple blueprint for the development of urban transport systems that is appropriate for all cities at all times. Nevertheless, although each city has its own peculiarities, four characteristics stand out as explanations of transport differences:

a. *Income.* Vehicle ownership is primarily dependent on income, in developing as in industrialized countries. Though rich countries tend to have more road infrastructure than do poor countries[2]—and at the national level, paved roads tend to be undersupplied in countries with low and middle per capita incomes[3]—the growth of urban road space with income is likely to be slower than that of traffic volume with income. Hence, unless vehicle use is dramatically restricted, as it has been in Singapore, traffic levels and congestion are likely to increase with income.

b. *Size and size distribution.* As city size, and particularly spatial extent, increases, so typically do the average length of commute, the level of traffic congestion, and the environmental impact of road traffic. Megacities have some of the worst problems of urban poverty, as well as the worst problems of urban transport.[4] This is accentuated in countries that are dominated by their capital cities.[5]

c. *Political history.* The form of modern cities inevitably reflects their historical transition between economic and social systems. The most notable are those differences between former socialist planned cities, many of which had widely dispersed pockets of high-density residences served by mass transit, and those cities where market forces played a greater role in shaping land use.[6] In particular, the transition economies combine rapidly increasing motorization with a rapidly declining fiscal capability to support their traditionally extensive public transport systems.

d.   *Population growth rates.* Rapidly growing cities are distinct for two reasons: they appear to have above-average car ownership rates in relation to income for the national average income levels, and they tend to have below-average proportions of land space devoted to circulation. Together these militate for high congestion.

These influences clearly overlap and interact. Abstracting from the issue of city size, they give us a taxonomy of city types into which major cities can be divided (table 2.1), but which to some extent explains the type of public transport systems that they have acquired. For example, high-income countries are highly motorized and congested, but also tend to be more able to afford rail-based mass transit systems. Where growth has been very rapid, the development of mass transit is less likely to have kept pace. Where population growth has been slower, and particularly for the cities in formerly centrally planned economies that have suffered stagnating incomes, the probability of there being mass transit systems is greater than income alone would suggest. These differences between types of cities, and the influences which cause the differences, should be borne in mind when interpreting the more generic discussions that follow.

THE ECONOMIC IMPACT OF POOR URBAN TRANSPORT

The pressures on urban transport systems are increasing in most developing countries as part of the process of growth. Motor vehicle ownership and use are growing even faster than population, with vehicle ownership growth rates of 15 to 20 percent per year common in some developing countries. The average distance traveled per vehicle is also increasing in all but the largest, most-congested cities. This growth exceeds the ability to increase road space, and the major impediment to the efficient working of the urban economies in large-size cities, and particularly in megacities, is the level of road traffic congestion. Travel speeds are decreasing and the travel environment for pedestrians and people-powered vehicles is deteriorating. Downtown weekday traffic speeds are reported to average 10 kilometers per hour (km/h) or less in Bangkok (Thailand), Manila (Philippines), Mexico City (Mexico), and Shanghai (China); 15 km/h or less in Kuala Lumpur (Malaysia) and São Paulo (Brazil). It is estimated that congestion increases public transport operating costs by 10 percent in Rio de Janeiro (Brazil) and 16 percent in São Paulo. Of the 16 developing-country cities with populations of more than 4 million, 5 of them (Bucharest, Romania; Jakarta, Indonesia; Kinshasa, Republic of Congo; Lagos, Nigeria; and Manila) cited aver-

TABLE 2.1 A CATEGORIZATION OF CITY CIRCUMSTANCES			
	Income/motorization rates		
	Low	**High**	
Population growth — **High**		Singapore	**Formerly centrally planned**
	Dhaka, Bangladesh	Bangkok; Manila; Hong Kong, China	**Market**
Population growth — **Low**	Samarkand, Uzbekistan; Almaty, Kazakhstan; Bishkek, Kyrgyz Republic	Moscow, Russian Federation; Warsaw, Poland; Budapest, Hungary	**Formerly centrally planned**
	Dakar, Senegal; Nairobi, Kenya	Prague, Czech Republic; Buenos Aires, Argentina	**Market**

Source: Authors.

age one-way commute times of one and one-quarter hours or more (UNCHS 1998). Growth of measured gross domestic product (GDP) is also reduced by freight congestion, delays and unpredictability, difficulties of conducting business, and increasing signs of disarticulation of the labor market in some large cities such as São Paulo, Mexico City, and Manila. All this is occurring despite the fact that motorization is still at a relatively early stage in most developing and transitional economies; most developing countries have fewer than 100 cars per 1,000 people, compared with 400 or more per 1,000 people in the richer industrialized countries.

Furthermore, most transport-originated air pollution, as well as nonbusiness time lost to congestion, is efficiency reducing but is not directly reflected in GDP statistics. The safety and security of travelers is also diminishing in many large cities. Some of these impacts can be, and have been, valued in monetary terms. Table 2.2 presents a summary of some estimates of external costs of road transport at national and regional levels. Recent World Bank estimates suggest that the total economic damage of air pollution represents up to 10 percent of GDP in polluted cities such as Bangkok, Kuala Lumpur, and Jakarta.[7] For six developing-country cities with a total population of over 50 million (Mumbai, India; Shanghai; Manila; Bangkok; Kraków, Poland; and Santiago, Chile), World Bank estimates show the costs of particulates and other vehicle emissions (excluding lead) as equivalent to 60 percent of the import cost of gasoline and over 200 percent of the import cost of diesel.[8]

SOURCES OF DECLINING URBAN TRANSPORT PERFORMANCE

It is sometimes presumed that the deteriorating state of urban transport in many developing countries has been caused by relatively higher levels of motorization with respect to income levels than are experienced in the industrialized countries. The evidence does not support that proposition.

In terms of the relationship between income and car ownership, the developing countries are following a pattern very similar to that followed by the industrialized countries, as figure 2.1 shows. Most developing countries fall in the development track shown for France, Japan, Spain, and the United Kingdom. Only Argentina, Brazil, Mexico, and some of the transition countries of Eastern Europe have higher car-ownership-to-income ratios than the industrialized countries experienced. Chile, the Republic of Korea, the Philippines, and Thailand all have lower national rates, but all have highly congested capital cities that have much higher incomes and (contrary to experience in most Western industrialized countries) much higher car ownership rates than the national average.

The problems of the developing countries thus do not generally seem to result from motorization occurring at lower per capita income levels or at higher rates of income growth than that experienced in the earlier growth of the industrialized countries. Nevertheless, there are some respects in which the present situation does appear to differ from that of the industrialized nations at a similar stage in their income growth:

- High concentration of national population, economic activity, and motorization itself in one or a very few major cities that are expanding rapidly in size and population
- Inadequate quantity and structure of road infrastructure, often associated with rapid population growth
- Poorly developed institutional, fiscal, and regulatory arrangements at the municipal level.

LONG-TERM DYNAMICS OF URBAN ECONOMIC STRUCTURE

There is also a long-term dynamic interaction between transport and the nature of the city economy. Cities have economic cores explained by various forms of agglomeration economies, which are often based on a traditional industrial or trading base. Those employed in the city center choose their places of residence by trad-

TABLE 2.2 ESTIMATES OF EXTERNAL COSTS OF ROAD TRANSPORT (AS PERCENTAGE OF NATIONAL AND REGIONAL GDP)

Country or city	Year	Source	Road costs	Land and parking	Con-gestion	Accidents, net of insurance	Pollution				Sub total	Revenue from road users	Net sub-total	Others	Total
							Noise	Local air	GHGs	Other					
United States 1	1989	WRI	1.64[a]	1.56	—	1.00	0.16	0.18	0.50	—	5.04	[a]	5.04	0.46	5.5
United States 2[b]	1990	NRDC	1.25[a]	0.43–1.74	0.19	1.71	0.05	2.09–3.83	—	0.07	5.69–8.84	[a]	5.69–8.84	0.78–2.61	6.47–11.45
United States 3	1991	Lee	1.76	2.41	—	0.24	0.19	0.73	—	0.26	5.59	0.88	4.71	0.87	5.58
EU1	Early 1990s	ECMT	1.75	—	0.74	2.40	0.30	0.60	0.50	—	6.30	1.67	4.63	—	4.63
EU2	Early 2000s	ECMT	1.49	—	0.75	1.20	0.30	0.15	0.47	—	4.36	1.67	2.69	—	2.69
United Kingdom	1993	CSERGE	0.24	—	3.03	0.46–1.49	0.41–0.49	3.12	0.02	—	7.28–8.39	2.60	4.68–5.79	—	4.68–5.79
Mexico City	1993	Ochoa	—	0.08	2.56	2.32[c]	—	0.64	—	—	5.60	—	5.60	—	5.60
Poland	1995	ISD	1.14	—	0.30	1.60	0.10	0.30	—	—	3.44	2.81	0.63	—	0.63
São Paolo	1900	IRBD	—	—	2.43	1.11	—	1.55–3.18	—	—	—	—	5.09–6.72	—	5.09–6.72
Buenos Aires	1995	FIEL	0.73	—	3.42	0.5–2.00[d]	—	0.97	—	—	5.62–7.12	1.01	4.61–6.11	—	4.61–6.11
Bangkok	1995	Misc.	—	—	1.00–6.00	2.33	—	2.56	—	—	5.89–10.89	—	5.89–10.89	—	5.89–10.89
Santiago	1994	Zegras	1.37	1.92	1.38	0.94	0.15	2.58	—	—	8.35	1.64	6.71	—	6.71
Dakar	1996	Tractebel	—	—	3.37	0.16–4.12	—	5.12	—	—	8.65–12.61	—	—	—	8.65–12.61

— Not available.

Note: GHGs = greenhouse gases; EU = European Union. In most cases, congestion costs are calculated in comparison with either a free-flow speed or an "acceptable" traffic performance, and not with a calculated "optimum" level of congestion. The calculated values may thus overestimate what it would be economic to eliminate.

a. Road costs given net of revenues from road users.

b. Cars only.

c. Gross of insurance compensation.

d. Calculated on nationwide basis and gross of insurance compensation.

Source: Willoughby 2000a.

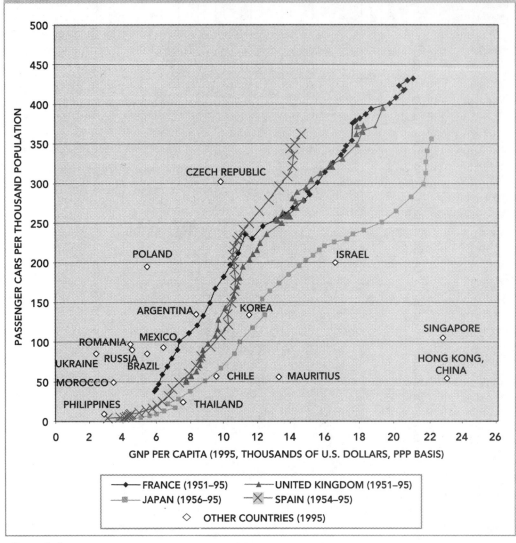

FIGURE 2.1 MOTORIZATION AND INCOMES: GROWTH OF CARS VERSUS GROWTH OF PER CAPITA INCOMES IN FRANCE, JAPAN, SPAIN, AND THE UNITED KINGDOM, 1950s TO 1995; AND THE RELATIVE POSITIONS OF SELECTED OTHER COUNTRIES, 1995

Source: Authors.

ing off increased travel costs against the lower land costs (and greater availability of space and amenities) as the distance between places of residence and employment increases. As both city-center congestion and incomes increase, people are willing to pay more for space and amenities, so they travel farther to live where land is less expensive and home-based movement easier. Thus the area of the city increases. Paradoxically, to avoid road congestion, people move to loca-

tions in which they become increasingly dependent on the car. This trend is accentuated by investments in radial trunk route capacity and by technology improvements that increase speed and reduce cost.

Similar considerations motivate firms. As the city grows and its economic base diversifies, those which need more space—often the larger export-oriented companies engaged in modern assembly-line production technology—may flee from the old, high-rent, congested city center to locations with less expensive land cost and better external access to ports or intercity trunk road systems, while firms in trades and services may stay in the center to maintain access to customers.[9] In many industrialized countries, this has already led to a relocation of freight movement–intensive activities to peripheral locations. The existence of a limited number of major radial transport routes may lead to star-shaped patterns. There may be several subcenters along any radial; where radials intersect with external rings, new nodes of high commercial density emerge. Despite this the old city center survives, retaining the highest-value commercial activities.

In richer industrialized countries, urban sprawl is characterized by unbounded outward spread of development from the urban core, at low density, often "leapfrogging" areas of undeveloped land to enter new jurisdictions competing for development.[10] When employment follows residential development, it creates the phenomenon of the "edge city."[11] It is generally agreed that sprawl increases the public and private costs of infrastructure per residence, while draining the fiscal capability of the traditional core causing decay of the core's infrastructure and decline of its services. In transport terms it is generally agreed that this increases trip lengths (even when employment is also decentralized) and auto dependence, although it does not necessarily increase household travel expenditure, trip times, or overall congestion. Sprawl fosters a spatial mismatch between the places of work and residence of the poor. Despite these disadvantages, suburbanization appears inexorable in higher-income cities.[12]

Not all of these features of sprawl are replicated in the municipal development process of transitional and developing economies. In many of the former socialist cities, leapfrogging was part of the planned structure, with high-density enclaves in peripheral areas surrounded by undeveloped land and linked to centralized employment by high-capacity public transport links. The new sprawl in these economies tends to take residences even farther out, however, and away from the traditional high-capacity public transport axes. In many of the rapidly growing developing cities, it is the poor rural-to-urban migrant who is located in the peri-urban settlements; land-use policies may even counter inner-city densification. The peri-urban settlements are too low income to be served by private automobiles, so that their development is associated with increases in household travel time and household budgets.

From the individual or company point of view, this outward shift of activity is an economically rational adjustment to increase accessibility, either to the amenity of space in the case of households or to markets and suppliers in the case of firms. In making decisions to change locations, however, neither individuals nor firms need to take into account the indirect effects that their decisions are having on others. If transport prices are less than real costs (because they do not take into account congestion or environmental effects) or if infrastructure is provided below cost in new peripheral locations (because connection charges and impact fees are too low), then the city will sprawl farther and faster than is economically optimal. Some administrative action will then be necessary to curb this distortion. Planning intervention may also be necessary at the micro or local level, where new industrial developments may have adverse effects on the amenity of existing residential activities for which they are not charged, with the consequence that the mix of activities (or environmental protection in mixed activities) is suboptimal.

URBAN TRANSPORT IN CITY DEVELOPMENT STRATEGIES

The process of strategy development will vary from city to city. It is likely to require collective vision for the city shared by city government and the major stakeholders in civic society; an agreed-on strategic framework for realizing that vision;

a technical capacity to convert the strategy into practical actions; and a fiscal and financial system able to mobilize and allocate the necessary resources efficiently (box 2.1).

Our starting point is the common observation that transport is not usually demanded for its own sake, but that the demand for transport is derived from the demand for final consumption goods and services and for the raw materials and intermediate products that go into the production of final goods and services. The implication is that transport problems have two quite different generic types of solution. The first type, discussed below, involves instruments internal to the transport sector to make the sector more efficient. This may involve large infrastructure investments but may also involve improvements in the management of infrastructure to make it more productive.

The second type of solution is to operate on the sectors that generate the demand for transport. Most attention is usually given to the location of activities, discussed below. There is a range of other structural impacts that result from the role of transport in servicing developments in other social sectors, such as health, education, and so on. Hence urban transport policy needs to be integrated with other sector developments, not only at the activity planning level but also in municipal budgetary arrangements, as discussed below.

DEVELOPMENT STRATEGIES FOR MAKING URBAN TRANSPORT MORE EFFICIENT

When preparing development strategies, a number of issues must be examined, including expansion of the road infrastructure, urban freight policies, and the roles of the private sector.

ROAD INFRASTRUCTURE EXPANSION
High levels of traffic congestion certainly give an impression of inadequacy of urban road infrastructure in many developing countries. It is well

---

BOX 2.1 CITY DEVELOPMENT STRATEGIES

A CDS is an action plan for equitable growth in cities, developed and sustained through participation, to improve the quality of life for all citizens.

The goals of a CDS include a collective city vision and action plan aimed at improving urban governance and management, increasing investment to expand employment and services, and systematic and sustained reductions in urban poverty.

It is not intended to substitute for integrated master plans, general land-use plans, or even investment plans. Rather, it forms the basis for planning of land use, transport, and other sectoral needs, and for setting policy, resource allocation, and investment priorities.

Cities such as Bilbao (Spain), Rio de Janeiro, Sydney (Australia), Bangalore (India), and Yokohama (Japan) have successfully guided their growth with CDSs through a wide variety of approaches, with the lead being taken by the city itself, and with the urban poor and local business leaders actively engaged within a wider participatory process. In this way each of the cities secured a better alignment and more efficient mix of public and private resource commitments. The Bank and its partners, through the Cities Alliance partnership, is engaged in more than 50 cities that are currently preparing CDSs.

Source: Tim Campbell and Peter Palesch, World Bank.

---

known that the 10 to 12 percent of land space devoted to all forms of road rights-of-way in the major cities in Asia[13] falls far short of the 20 to 30 percent common in U.S. cities. It is clearly necessary to provide an adequate basic road network and to extend it as the city expands in space. Primary rights-of-way or easements for these roads should be acquired at the outset of any development for future extensions of main arteries. This will give clarity for all parties about the broad future shape of the city and allow the land market to operate more effectively to support rational land-use patterns. Moreover, the character and capacity of this infrastructure provision needs to be tailored to the nature and density of the planned or anticipated developments. It is particularly important for secondary cities to use transport infrastructure to structure urban growth.[14]

Nevertheless, simple statistical comparisons should be viewed very cautiously. In fact, only about 13 percent of land space is devoted to roads in London (out of about 18 percent devoted to total transport); the figures for Paris and Moscow are not much higher. There are several reasons for these relatively low figures. Much rail movement space is underground in the European cities. Land-occupation density also has an important influence on the performance of the transport infrastructure network. The structuring of the road network is also very important. It is necessary to provide for local distribution of traffic as well as for longer-distance trunk movements within and between towns. These functions do not mix well, and a given amount of road space will always give better performance if it is organized hierarchically to try to separate functions. Some cities, such as Bangkok and Manila, suffer particularly badly from the absence of an appropriate structure of local distribution capacity. Thus it is the management and use of the space devoted to transport, rather than the simple proportion of land devoted to roads, that is critical to system performance.

Furthermore, even if the proportion of space devoted to movement in an already highly congested city or in a megacity is low, that does not mean that it can escape its problems simply by building more roads. First, once the city fabric is established, it becomes increasingly expensive and both socially and environmentally disturbing to superimpose substantial additional road infrastructure. Second, where congestion is already suppressing demand, increasing capacity may simply generate such a large amount of extra traffic that the congestion-reduction effects are much lower than anticipated.

These considerations have some technical implications for the appraisal of investments in extra road infrastructure. Taking the economic and environmental impact of new traffic generation into account will reduce the benefits attributed to the reduction of congestion for existing traffic, offset to some extent by the marginal benefit of the newly generated trips. Similarly, the alternative possibilities—improving the efficiency of existing infrastructure by traffic management, restraining traffic by demand management, and shifting traffic from private to public transport—should always be considered as the basis for assessing the need for additional capacity.

URBAN FREIGHT TRANSPORT POLICIES

Freight transport attracts relatively little attention in the methodology of conventional Western urban transport planning, mainly because it does not contribute much to the peak-hour flows, which are the predominant generators of congestion and which drive both physical investment and traffic management responses to congestion. However, it does tend to attract specific attention where freight vehicles impinge on the amenities of residential areas. In the short term this is often addressed by restraining the movement of freight vehicles. In the longer term these problems tend to be addressed through zoning and land-use controls. Consequently, both light industry and warehousing tends to move to the peripheries of the cities. Given the increased importance of reliable delivery time in integrated logistic systems, and the more footloose nature of much modern light industry that makes it easier to move to alternative locations, this focused strategic treatment of freight movement tends to channel freight movements in ways that are mutually acceptable to those concerned with local congestion and the environment, and those concerned with efficient freight movement. Even in the great port cities of the world, the shift of port facilities downstream has usually shifted concentrated freight traffic flows out of the cities rather than into them.

Very different considerations apply in many developing-country cities.[15] Ports, industry, and commodity markets often remain in their historic city-center locations. Roads in these areas are often narrow and encumbered, requiring the use of more, and smaller, vehicles for freight flows, including very small nonmotorized vehicles—such as handcarts, bicycles, and rickshaws—in many places. Peripheral infrastructure, which attracts much freight-intensive activity out of the center of developed-country cities, is less well developed. Freight vehicles therefore account for a larger proportion of urban road traffic flows, freight transport performance tends to be inferior, and the perceived congestion and environmental impact of freight transport greater.

Many of the most successful developing countries have achieved rapid growth through export-led industrial development. This development is often based, initially, on the exploitation of inexpensive domestic labor. As incomes rise, however, it depends more on the labor force's quality and its ability to participate efficiently and flexibly in global manufacturing and distribution systems. Reliable transport, both within cities and in connections to international networks, is critical to this development.

For the most part, logistic networks are entirely private sector, and often led by multinational companies. However, there are some important external requirements for these networks' development. An open domestic transport market, with freedom for modal integration and good

seaport and airport facilities, is central to these requirements. This transport market must be supported by good telecommunication facilities. These elements are to be found in the rapidly industrializing economies, and are notably absent in the stagnating ones. City growth thus depends not only on actions that can be taken at the city level but also on the support of a national government committed to liberalizing freight movement.

That still leaves some important supporting policy requirements for economic growth at the municipal level. Development planning, supported by land-use control, can foster well-located industrial development both in relation to external transport links and in relation to domestic labor markets, thus avoiding both local traffic congestion and divisive environmental impacts. A good planned example of this approach is Curitiba, Brazil. The effective protection of the city environment from the impacts of industrial and port-related traffic through the combination of road infrastructure and industrial location policies is also one of the most notable features of the Dutch planning system.

Many large cities draw their wealth from commercial as much as from industrial activities. Here again the combination of a liberal commercial environment with good internal transportation and telecommunication links is critical to the attraction of the city to international business.

THE ROLE OF THE PRIVATE SECTOR

Responsibility for urban transport is being decentralized to the cities in many countries. In this decentralization process, the expenditure responsibilities of municipalities tend to expand much more than the intergovernmental transfer of financial resources. Only a small fraction of the necessary resources can come from the multilateral and bilateral agencies.[16] Cities will therefore have to broaden their financial bases in order to be able to finance the infrastructure that they want, as well as to support any social objectives they are pursuing in controlling transport operations.

As a result cities increasingly look to the private sector to provide facilities and services.

As far as transport services are concerned, it is estimated that at least 80 percent of all urban bus services provided around the world are now privately owned and operated, including those operated privately for public sector clients. The onus for financing both rolling stock and, to a lesser extent, the supporting infrastructure is thus transferred to the private sector to be financed through fares. There is increasing concern, however, about the quality of service available in many unregulated regimes. As discussed in chapter 7, some of these concerns can be addressed effectively with competitively tendered franchising of services. That requires a clear legal and regulatory framework, as well as a strong public planning and public procurement capability. While the legal framework is typically provided through national legislation, the planning and procurement is essentially a local responsibility that depends heavily for its success on how well these arrangements relate to the rest of the city development strategy (CDS).

Many municipalities harbor parallel expectations that transport infrastructure capacity can also be privately financed. In many cases they have seen successful privatization or concessioning of power, water, and telecommunication utilities, and believe that roads and mass transit systems can be similarly financed. Although some existing urban expressways and urban railways have been successfully concessioned in a number of countries (see chapter 7), new infrastructure is more difficult to finance privately. In the road sector, the scope for private financing through tolls is limited by the need to be able to limit access. In any case, the proportion of the network that can be financed in that way is relatively limited. Shadow toll systems have been developed to extend the scope of private participation, but experience is so far limited, and in any case the charges of such systems remain on budget.

As far as urban rail systems are concerned, pure private finance has not yet been successful in a developing country (though the Bangkok Transit System [BTS] could change this conclusion). The financial difficulties arise partly due to undercharging of the competing, congested road space. Significant operational difficulties have also been experienced in cities such as Kuala Lumpur, Manila, and Bangkok because of their failure to integrate the private systems effectively within a comprehensive urban transport and development strategy. These issues are discussed further in chapters 8 and 10.

It is not the intention here to discourage increasing private sector participation in urban transport infrastructure finance, but there are some general observations that can be made on the requirements for success in utilizing private finance effectively. First, purely opportunistic finance is to be avoided. Unless the private developments conform to a general structure plan, they may impose unforeseen, and sometimes very significant, contingent costs on the public budget. Second, careful attention is required to individual contract design to ensure that the objectives of the CDS and the financial requirements of the private financiers are effectively reconciled. Third, cities may need to consider carefully their priorities for private finance in order to strengthen their creditworthiness to be able to access domestic and international capital markets. These considerations all highlight the need for any attempt to secure private financing of transport infrastructure to be integrated within a CDS, both with respect to physical and to financial planning.

STRATEGIES FOR STRUCTURAL CHANGE: LAND-USE AND TRANSPORT PLANNING

In most countries local transport performance is better, and costs lower, in smaller rather than in larger cities. In a number of developing countries, of which Thailand is the extreme example, the dominance of the capital city is such that these differences are very large. Structural strategies to improve transport may therefore focus on the distribution of activities among cities—particularly through planned deconcentration—or the distribution within cities through land-use planning and development controls.

DECONCENTRATION

Limiting the further expansion of the major cities by consciously promoting the development of lower-order urban developments is a beguiling strategy. France and the United Kingdom have both adopted policies of controlling the capital, encouraging the provinces, and developing peripheral new towns. China has similarly been seeking effective policies to discourage all rural migrants from going to the booming coastal cities. The case for limiting further capital-city growth because of intolerable transport conditions has been argued even for a city of only 2 million inhabitants, such as Nairobi.[17] Given the transport problems of many large cities, it is tempting to see decentralized urban growth as a solution.

There are two major problems with that strategy for attenuating the transport problems, and other problems, of the megacities. First, neither the magnitude of agglomeration economies nor the significance of environmental externalities are understood clearly enough to be able to make any universal judgment about how far or how fast to push deconcentration. Second, attempts to control concentration, either by land-use and development constraints in the megacities or by inducements to locate outside the megacities, have had limited impact and dubious benefit.[18] Many capital-city authorities prove to be lukewarm in their support for such policies and tend to resist even the dispersion of some central government activities.

Given these doubts, it is likely to be better to concentrate on using macroeconomic policies to allow markets to work more effectively in locating activity, rather than to engage in strong administrative redirection of economic activity. Protectionism and autarky appear to reinforce the dominance of capital cities. Open markets are likely to create a more-level playing field between core and peripheral manufacturing and between urban and rural activities. The quality of intercity transport and communications can also contribute to that level playing field. For example, it has been estimated that a 1 percent increase in the share of GDP spent on government transport and communications investments is associated with a 10 percent reduction in primacy; barriers to internal trade reinforce primacy.[19] Similarly, the removal of subsidies to the megacity—including transport subsidies—might reduce megacity size without adverse social consequences.

PLANNING AND MANAGEMENT OF URBAN LAND USE

Two extreme approaches to improving the structure of activities within cities may be characterized.[20] Urban planners tend to define a preferred urban form, albeit based on extensive consultation and consideration of transport demand, incorporated in a structure plan. This provides the required physical framework for market forces, private sector investment, and public sector programs for urban change and growth. The plan can be indicative and passive, or it can be actively pursued through public sector transport and urban regeneration investment. Economists, in contrast, tend to concentrate on applying an efficiency criterion to each policy decision, without prejudging the structural outcome.

Neither approach is sufficient in itself. Full internalization of externalities, precluding the need for any planning intervention, has not been achieved even in the most sophisticated of market economies, such as the United States. Moreover, the longevity of major infrastructure is such that conventional financial decisionmaking discounts the effects over much of its life. On the other hand, planning undoubtedly works better if supported by, rather than working against, economic incentives. Thus it is advisable to look at the effectiveness of both administrative and market-based instruments in the search for a strategy on land use and transport.

The possibility of manipulating urban land use for transport policy purposes has been recently incorporated into an environmental argument for densification, based on the undisputed fact that gasoline consumption per capita in cities is highly correlated with the overall density of the city.[21] Proponents of this view argue that reducing density increases trip lengths, makes public transport less viable, encourages greater use of, and dependence on, the private automobile (auto dependence), and hence generates more environmental impact per capita. They also point to the adverse effects of increasing auto dependence on those without access to a private car, who find themselves progressively excluded from access to economic and social activities.

In their simplest form, policies designed to promote land-use concentration so as to save energy have been challenged on the grounds that energy consumption is but one input, and that it is inappropriate to concentrate only on minimizing energy consumption irrespective of its effects on other aspects of the quality of life (particularly the amount of residential space per person).[22] This has also proved to be a very difficult area for policy implementation, even in sophisticated governance systems. There is much evidence to show that where individuals have been free to choose the location of their residence, suburbanization has continued as incomes increase, irrespective of land-use planning policies. This has shifted the focus of research in the direction of obtaining better understanding of the determinants of this behavior and transferred the policy emphasis to other instruments, such as land-use mix, public transport structure and quality, which operate on travel choices in ways that more obviously respect individual preferences.

Effective administrative control of land use requires, above all, the willingness and foresight to plan. One of the defining features of cities that are widely believed to have been most success-

---

BOX 2.2 MATCHING LOCATIONAL CHARACTERISTICS AND USER DEMANDS

In the Netherlands a system called the "ABC" system is used to match the characteristics of land uses to characteristics of the transport network. Types of location and types of activity are both classified at a central government level according to their traffic-generating characteristics and according to their need for accessibility by public transport or by private road transport. The distinction between the locations should then be reflected in public transport planning and in parking restrictions on "A" and "B" locations implemented at the provincial or municipal level.

The approach requires a hierarchical control to avoid competition between adjacent jurisdictions from undermining the functional allocations, as well as parallel financing actions on public transport development to prevent new residential developments from becoming auto dependent. It has had a significant effect in areas directly controlled by the national government. From dispersed sites throughout the country, the Ministry of Housing, Physical Planning, and the Environment relocated to a new office building directly adjacent to the central railway station in The Hague. This resulted in a dramatic drop in commuting by auto from 41 percent to only 4 percent, while commuting by rail increased from 25 percent to 57 percent. Bus and tram use went from 9 percent to 20 percent. Lower-level authorities appear to have implemented the system with varying degrees of commitment. Nevertheless, it has undoubtedly contributed to sustaining the public transport share of trips to major administrative, office, and educational locations, while ensuring good road transport access for industrial and commercial plants.

Source: NEA Transport Research and Training 2000.

ful in managing the relationship between transport and land use (such as Curitiba, Brazil; Zurich, Switzerland; and Singapore) is the early existence of an integrated land-use and transport structure plan in support of which a wide range of sectoral policies were employed. In many countries this is hampered by the lack of appropriate institutions and consistent political leadership at the metropolitan level. The hitherto successful attempt to transfer experience on strategic planning and urban development from Zurich to Kunming (China) through a twinning arrangement enjoys the active support of both Swiss and Chinese central governments.[23] Structure planning also needs to be supported at the implementation level by guidelines relating the nature of the activities being developed in any location with the transport facilities available to it. In the Netherlands national guidelines have been established to foster such consistency in land-use and transport planning (box 2.2).

A second essential requirement is the existence of the necessary technical skills to develop a plan that is comprehensive and internally consistent. In the absence of an internally consistent and fully integrated spatial policy, infrastructure invest-ments and regulations often work at cross-purposes. For example, in some Indian cities attention is given to the avoidance of congestion in existing built-up areas and to the need to provide more city-center parking space, while at the same time developing "suburban" greenfield sites (box 2.3). A more consistent policy might be to let parking space provision be entirely a private, market-driven, activity. This would change relative costs of public and private transport, and might actually improve the split between public and private transport.

A third requirement for effective planning of the land-use and transport interaction is the ability to implement land-use, public transport, and development controls in a coherent manner that consistently supports the planning objectives. For example, many Indian cities adopt an unrealistically low permitted floor area ratio in central areas, which not only restricts the ability of developers to build office and retail buildings where there is most demand (in the central business district [CBD] and around transport nodes), but also pushes new residential construction to the periphery. Similarly, imposition of inappropriate setback and coverage requirements tends to keep the

---

BOX 2.3 INTERNAL CONSISTENCY IN PLANNING

In Bangalore, India, land-use regulations prevent the densification and the creation of new office space in the city center. However, the city is planning a major investment in a light rail transit system whose economic feasibility depends on the creation of new jobs in the current central business district (CBD), and therefore in the building of new office space. Simultaneously, new technological parks are built in distant suburban areas (out of range of the light rail lines) to try to create enclaves of adequate infrastructure and services, while the city-center infrastructure is left to deteriorate. The Bangalore Revised Comprehensive Development Plan for 2011 plans for three concentric ring roads (beltways), which would further contribute to the dispersion of jobs. The main issue is the inconsistency between different projects. This implies that the appraisal of either is dependent on the strategic priority that is given to the other.

Similar problems exist in Ahmedabad, where the imposition of low floor space ratios in the CBD prevents the renovation of buildings in the prime location, and hence contributes to the flight of activities to the suburbs.

Source: Bertaud 1999.

wrong space underoccupied compared with a policy of having a strong position on public open space. Even if effectively enforced, as in Seoul, Republic of Korea, greenbelt policies tend to exert strong upward pressure on the price of housing.[24]

THE ROLE OF MARKETS IN LAND-USE DISTRIBUTION

Even in an administrative planning context, market tendencies and values need to be recognized in implementation. Redevelopment can only happen when regulations allow it, when real estate transaction costs are low, and when the municipality is willing and able to redesign and finance improved infrastructure to accommodate new types of land use and land densities.

Any reduction in unit transport costs will tend to have the effect of reducing density, expanding the spatial scale of the city, separating different land uses, and, possibly, increasing total transport expenditure and transport resource use (including fuel). Any undercharging of transport costs—whether it is for road use, parking, or public transport—will similarly accentuate the sprawl. Urban boundaries and greenbelts may constrain that outward pressure for a time, but they tend to be jumped over without necessarily leading to the establishment of new self-contained cities with a balance of employment and residence. An "efficient pricing" approach to urban structure attempts to reflect costs—both of transport and of land occupation—in prices, and to allow individual preferences on land use to reconcile the variety of tastes with regard to space and other forms of consumption.

There are important limitations to this approach. Given that the major distortions arise from underpricing of environmental and congestion impacts, a quantification of those effects is required, at a highly disaggregate level, accompanied by a charging mechanism to implement the price regime. The same applies to properly internalizing the "costs of sprawl" in land development charges. Finally, it is necessary to handle the redistribution implications of the charging mechanism.

Even if these difficulties exclude the possibility of sole reliance on market forces, it is still prudent to attempt improvement of land-market operation.[25] In developing countries there is a long agenda of actions necessary to facilitate demand-driven land-use change, including:

- Clarification and recording of property rights to generate security of tenure, provide a base for investments and borrowing, and enable efficient transfers of property between owners
- Establishment of procedures for speedy adjudication of land invasions and informal acquisitions, and for assignment of property rights, especially in cities where much of the housing is provided and developed by the informal sector
- Replacement of existing types of title, which often provide only restricted rights, with a full ownership title that is recorded in a single, open, registry containing full information about liens, mortgages, easements, and so on
- Incorporation of the full costs of ancillary infrastructure development in connection charges for on-site public utilities and fees for trunk infrastructure
- Conversion of existing land-use controls into a transparent zoning and building control system, sensitive to demand signals
- Elimination of obstacles to recycling of publicly owned lands, particularly in formerly Communist countries, in which enterprise managers and local government officials often combine to prevent reassignment of industrial land in prime locations
- Broadening and deepening of financial markets' support for housing, with emphasis put on groups who would otherwise be unable to obtain appropriate accommodation.

Regulations should also be revised to avoid distortion of land use. Legally required standards for building and site development (including minimum plot sizes, setbacks, and parking provisions) should reflect the availability and affordability of land. Regulations should be firmly enforced. Market distortions resulting from excessive interjurisdictional competition should be minimized through national standards in order to limit local government ability to grant special favors (such as tax remissions or exceptional relaxation of regulations) that would attract investors away from other jurisdictions.

Public sector pricing and taxing practices are often themselves the source of distortions. Sales and leases of lands owned or developed by public authorities should always be at full market value, and public utilities should set connection charges reflecting actual costs rather than systemwide averages, with any exemptions specifically targeted and funded. Infrastructure cost should be included in land price through transparent impact fees or in-kind obligations. Developers should be required to cover the costs of neighborhood infrastructure and whatever expansions of public facilities are needed to maintain service levels for services such as fire and police stations, stormwater infrastructure, schools, roads, and bus stops.[26] Usually this involves a substantial public sector planning effort. However, where government provides an enabling framework, the private sector can be stimulated to undertake a fully coordinated development of the land-use and transport infrastructure (box 2.4).

BOX 2.4 THE MARKET AND LAND USE AND TRANSPORT INTEGRATION: THE TAMA GARDEN CITY DEVELOPMENT

The Tama Garden City Development Project is widely viewed as a model of integrated land-use and transport development. The project, promoted by the Tokyu Railway Company, was planned to transform a vast, hilly, and sparsely inhabited area into a community of some 5,000 hectares with 0.5 million residents, as well as to construct a railway of 22 kilometers (the Den-en Toshi Line) passing through the newly developed area and linking it to central Tokyo. The first phase of the railway construction (14.2 kilometers) was completed in 1966, followed by a second phase (5.9 kilometers), which started in 1967 and was completed in 1984. The total construction cost was 22 billion yen ($200 million), 50 percent of which was financed by commercial loans and the rest from the Japan Development Bank. No direct government subsidy was provided. On completion of the railway, bus routes, largely operated by Tokyu, were rearranged to provide feeder services for rail users. Between 1959 and 1989, nearly 3,000 hectares were developed for a population of 440,000, and the Den-en Toshi Line carried about 729,000 riders per day in 1994.

Among the key features of this project was the use of "land readjustment" to assemble the land needed to accommodate the railway and to develop real estate. Rather than acquiring all of the land, Tokyu organized landowners to form a cooperative that consolidates properties, redevelops them without transferring ownership, and returns smaller but fully serviced parcels to landowners. A unique aspect of this project was that Tokyu undertook the whole construction without charging the cooperatives for the redevelopment works; in return, Tokyu acquired the reserved housing sites after completion of the redevelopment. The success of the first readjustment phase accelerated the formation of cooperatives, thereby leading to large-scale area development within a relatively short time. Tokyu and its affiliated companies actively promoted the area's development in a variety of ways in order to increase population and rail ridership, including selling land, constructing housing, developing and attracting shopping centers, and inviting schools to locate themselves within the development.

Source: PADECO 2000.

While a free land market can thus improve the efficiency with which land use is allocated and adjusted to changing economic conditions, there is a potential tension between the operations of the land market and the desire to focus transport policies to benefit the poor. Transport investments change the structure of land values. If there is strong competition for the use of land and highly concentrated ownership of land, rents increase and the benefits of transport improvements accrue to rich landowners rather than to poor land occupants. Focused transport investments may, through this process, simply drive poorer people out to other, less-expensive, locations. This potential of perverse redistribution, further discussed in the next chapter, emphasizes the need for transport to be part of a comprehensive urban development strategy in order to prevent the benefits of transport improvements being appropriated exclusively by the better-off inhabitants. Some mechanism to capture, for the public good, the land value increases resulting from public infrastructure investments is critical.

COORDINATING SECTOR POLICIES IN CITY DEVELOPMENT STRATEGIES

The implications of transport's being a derived demand are not confined to the level of general spatial structure. There are also important implications for the formulation of a range of social sector policies and for institutional and financial planning arrangements.

SOCIAL SECTOR POLICIES
In the provision of *health services,* the public sector dominates in most countries. Whether health service provision is formally a national or local responsibility, the local health authority typically has a high degree of independence from the municipal authorities. This can have a number of adverse effects. First, decisions on the size and location of hospitals and clinics tend to be taken in the interest of minimizing health sector costs or improving health sector service quality. Considerations of

accessibility of facilities, both for patients and visitors, tend to be given lower weight. Second, even in countries such as Bangladesh, where the burden of road accidents on health facilities is very large, little weight seems to be given to designing medical strategies to improve on-site availability of medical services, or to combining sector interests to give road safety a higher priority.

In the *education sector,* there is an even wider range of issues. Location of facilities is usually less of a problem, although in some cities, such as Santiago, Chile, the combination of liberal school choice policies with the location of the more attractive schools in higher-income areas puts very heavy demands on the public transport system. That problem is often accentuated by the planned coincidence of the journey to school and journey to work peaks, especially in higher-income countries where some parents take children to work by car. From a public transport operational point of view, that problem tends to be accentuated by the traditional (and sometimes mandatory) provision of reduced fares for students. As long as the financial burden of these fares falls on the transport budget, and there is no institutional channel through which the potential tradeoffs can be examined and negotiated, the outcome is likely to be suboptimal.

A similar set of problems relate to *social security.* In some countries there is a statutory or constitutional basis for free or reduced-fare travel for pensioners or the unemployed, without reference either to any limitations on that right (off-peak only) or to the financing of it. Where that applies only to public sector transport providers, it tends to obscure the issues in deciding how best to organize public transport services. Particularly in some of the republics of the former Soviet Union, the proliferation of ostensibly socially motivated concessions has played a significant part in the decline of public transport service capability.

Public sector administrative activities can be used as a leading sector, particularly in capital cities, where government employment is concentrated. For example, moving activities from the former central district of Mumbai to new locations farther up the peninsula may make a very important contribution to improving the transport situation in the old city center.

INSTITUTIONAL AND FINANCIAL PLANNING IMPLICATIONS

Most of these problems of intersector strategy coordination have both an institutional and a financial dimension. Institutionally they call for channels of coordination, both between functions and between jurisdictions. It is not possible to propose a blueprint institutional structure applicable to all countries and all political systems. The most critical point, however, is that there should be some effective integrating mechanism or process through which the issues become explicit and receive attention. Some relevant principles and models are discussed in detail in chapter 11.

In parallel with the need for an appropriate coordination of institutional responsibilities is the need for coordinated financial planning. Chapter 10 presents the argument for a flexible financial system for urban transport, allowing resources to be efficiently allocated between modes. In some cases this may justify the establishment of a multimodal urban transport fund. The relationship between that arrangement, justified in terms of intrasector efficiency of resource allocation, and the municipal budgetary allocation process needs careful structuring.

CONCLUSIONS: A STRATEGY FOR URBAN TRANSPORT IN CITY DEVELOPMENT

It has been argued that cities are the engines of economic growth in most developing countries, and that urban transport is the oil that prevents the engine from seizing up. Unfortunately, deteriorating transport conditions are already damaging the economy of many large cities,

particularly the megacities, worldwide. Because demand for transport is essentially a derived demand, urban transport must be viewed strategically as an integral component of the city economy and hence of its development strategy.

The economic performance of the sector can be improved by more careful attention to the requirements of freight transport and logistics, as well as by improvements to infrastructure, including privately financed infrastructure, where appropriate. While expanding cities require adequate infrastructure, it is physically and economically impossible to escape from congestion by building roads in the densest cities. Broader structural approaches are also required. Deconcentration of activities can be encouraged, but is difficult to achieve. Planning and management of land-use structure is essential, but has practical limitations. Liberalization of land markets can help, but the direct impact is weakened by the inability to internalize the external costs of development. Integration and coordination of sector policies are also central to the more integrated development approach.

Although no single, simple, structural policy offers a complete solution to the transport-related problems of urban growth, it is possible to identify some elements of each policy that can be advocated as robust components of a strategy for transport within an urban development strategy. These elements include:

- Elimination of policies favoring the capital city together with properly appraised investment in intercity transport outside the capital region
- Development of a structure-planning capability as the basis for positive CDSs.
- Provision within structure plans of space for transport infrastructure that would be adequate for immediate demand but also capable of adaptation as the city grows
- Coordination of the planning and development of land use with that of transport infrastructure and services

- Encouragement of development-control skills and practices at the city level
- Elimination of obvious price distortions in both land and transport markets, including the introduction of congestion prices for road use and full-cost connection charges and impact fees for land development
- Improved road investment appraisal to take account of the economic and environmental effects of induced traffic in assessing the need for capacity expansion
- Strategic consideration of the benefits that could be achieved through traffic management, and demand restraint in the base-case for road investment appraisal
- Coordination of transport sector policies with the policies of the sectors that transport serves.

NOTES

1. *World Urbanization Prospects* (United Nations 1996), projects urban population of 1.9 in 2000 and 3.7 billion in 2025. By that date it is projected that there will be 500 cities of over 1 million inhabitants and 35 megacities of over 10 million inhabitants.

2. Ingram and Liu 1999.

3. Canning and Bennathan 2000.

4. There is less agreement, however, concerning the size of city at which these problems begin to dominate the advantages of agglomeration, or why some cities, particularly in developing countries, continue to grow despite having reached this situation.

5. City size distribution is very skewed in many Asian and African developing countries, but not in most Latin American or Eastern European countries. In Thailand the capital city is over 40 times as large as the second city, and this ratio (the "primacy index") is above three for other highly populated countries such as the Philippines, Malaysia, and Indonesia (Karan 1994).

6. Dutt and others 1994.

7. Hughes and Lovei 1999.

8. Lvovsky and others 2000.

9. This pattern, well documented in industrialized countries, has been shown to be equally forceful in developing cities such as Bogotá, Cali (Colombia), and Seoul. See K.S. Lee 1989.

10. Burchell and others 1998.

11. Garreau 1991.

12. Fouchier 1997.

13. It is 11 percent, for example, in Bangkok and Kolkata (India).

14. Koster and de Langen 1998.

15. For a comparison of the cities of Rotterdam (the Netherlands), Dhaka, and Nairobi, see Arcadis Bouw/Infra 2000.

16. In the case of the World Bank, the requirement of a sovereign guarantee is a particular impediment for cities in countries whose governments are unwilling to give such guarantees.

17. Howe and Bryceson 2000.

18. For example, the Korean greenbelt policy for Seoul appears to have produced perverse density gradients, high housing costs and travel distances, and arguably has militated particularly against the interests of the poor.

19. Krugman 1991.

20. D. B. Lee 1999.

21. Newman and Kenworthy 1989.

22. World Bank 1996.

23. Joos 2000.

24. Dowall 1995.

25. Elaborations of these points are to be found in Dowall 1995.

26. Pendall 1999.

3 URBAN TRANSPORT AND POVERTY REDUCTION

Poor people's inability to access jobs and services is an important element of the social exclusion that defines urban poverty. Urban transport policy can attenuate this poverty, both by contributing to economic growth and by introducing a conscious poverty reduction focus to infrastructure investment, to public transport service planning, and to fare-subsidy and financing strategies. There is a rich agenda of urban transport policies that are both pro-growth and pro-poor, yet which are consistent with the fiscal capabilities of even the poorest countries.

URBAN POVERTY AND SOCIAL EXCLUSION

Poor households derive their standard of living from a variety of activities, not all of which are marketed or assigned a monetary value. That standard of living, and its security, depends not only on current income but also on the stock of assets, including the social and human capital, as well as the money and physical assets, at the disposal of the household. Poverty is thus a multidimensional concept involving the lack of the social and cultural, as well as economic, means necessary to procure a minimum level of nutrition, to participate in the everyday life of society, and to ensure economic and social reproduction.[1] In this general notion of poverty as "exclusion," accessibility is important, not only for its role in facilitating regular and stable income-earning employment but also for its role as part of the social capital that maintains the social relations forming the safety net of poor people in many societies.

Deteriorating urban transport conditions have a particularly severe impact on poor people.[2] Growing reliance on private vehicles has resulted in a substantial fall in the share of, and in some cases an absolute decline in the number of, trips made by urban public transport in many cities. Consequently there has been a decline in urban public transport service levels. Sprawling land-consuming urban structures are making the journey to work excessively long and costly, particularly for some of the very poor. Surveys of commuters in Mexico City have shown that 20 percent of workers spend more than three hours traveling to and from work each day, and that 10 percent spend more than five hours.[3] Poor people also suffer disproportionately from deterioration of the environment, safety, and security because they are locationally and vocationally most exposed, and less able to afford preventative or remedial action.

TRANSPORT PATTERNS OF THE URBAN POOR

Poor people make fewer trips per capita than do the nonpoor. The difference in total number of trips per day per person is not usually extreme, falling in the range of 20 to 30 percent, though some earlier studies have suggested much greater disparities.[4] Consistent with the difference between trip rates of the poor and the nonpoor, average trip rates have also tended to increase over time as income increases.[5] In contrast, the composition of the trip making of the poor and the nonpoor differs very substantially. The nonpoor typically make two or three times as many motorized trips per capita as do poor people, even when total trip rates are fairly similar. In most poor countries, private motorized vehicle trips are restricted to the wealthiest 20 percent of the population, with the motorcycle extending this down to those with average incomes in middle-income countries.[6] As might be expected, poor people's journey purposes are more restricted, with journeys to work, education, and shopping dominating.

The burden of transport on household budgets often cannot be determined precisely. Incomes may be difficult to establish, especially where there is some payment in kind or where there are incentives not to disclose the total income. Household expenditure is therefore probably a better base than is income, although it is believed that household consumption surveys tend to understate transport expenditures, while transport surveys tend to overstate them.[7] Subject to those caveats, it has been estimated that transport accounts for between 8 and 16 percent of household expenditures in a range of developing countries in Africa.[8] Estimates for major cities in some other countries also fall in this range, with 15 percent for an industrialized country such as France.

In the context of poverty assessment, the proportion of income spent on transport by different income groups is of more interest. Typically there are two steps in transport expenditures corresponding to the progression from nonmotorized to motorized public transport, and from public transport to motorized private transport, respectively. Where those steps take place in any country depends on income level and distribution, as well as on the quality, availability, and cost of public transport. Studies in Ouagadougou (Burkina Faso) and Dakar show that the highest quintile spends 20 times as much on transport as the lowest quintile, but this only amounts to double the proportion of income (Godard and Olvera 2000). In virtually all countries, richer groups spend a higher proportion of their incomes on transport than do most of those with lower incomes.

However, the proportion of income spent on transport varies greatly for the very poorest groups.

Some of the very poor may be forced to accept precarious living conditions in order to be able to access work. For example, a survey of pavement dwellers in Madras, India, showed that 59 percent walked to work at no cost.[9] In other circumstances, however, the burden of transport expenditure on poor people may be very high. A study of low-income households in Temeke, Tanzania, 8 kilometers from the center of Dar es Salaam estimated that households spent between 10 and 30 percent of their incomes on transport, with an average of 25 percent (Howe and Bryceson 2000). The upper limit was very income constrained, while many low-income earners in the formal sector claimed that they could only afford public transport in the period immediately after being paid. Later, after their pay was exhausted, they walked.

Given the high cost of transport, the time taken by the poor who are working to travel to work varies greatly. The Madras pavement dwellers, walking less than one-half an hour to work, are a polar case of the tradeoff between transport cost and residential quality. More generally, land-price differentials reflect local environmental quality, and are likely to do so more as the middle classes grow and environmental expectations rise. Even in the largest cities, there may be areas of barely habitable or accessible land, such as those of the "favellas" (squatter developments) in Brazilian cities, which are relatively close to areas of potential employment but which are unserved by formal transport providers.

The other polar case in the tradeoff concerns those who live remotely in order to inhabit affordable space, and who thus incur both high travel costs and long travel times. As a result of apartheid policies, the average distance of the black townships from the central business districts (CBDs) of the seven largest South African cities is 28 kilometers.[10] Some poor people in Latin American cities—such as Lima (Peru) and Rio de Janeiro—are also driven out to inexpensive dwelling space in remote locations, some 30 or 40 kilometers out of the employment center (the average commuting time per day for the poorest group in Rio de Janeiro exceeds three hours). Such peripheral locations typically involve exclusion from a whole range of urban facilities, a deprivation only partly overcome by family or neighborhood solidarity.[11]

The transport patterns of poor people thus exhibit a complex tradeoff among residential location, travel distance, and travel mode, in an attempt to minimize the social exclusion associated with low earning potential. Differences in land prices in developing countries generally reflect variations in accessibility to the CBD or other centers of employment. Since good transport contributes to accessibility, it tends to drive up land rents and drive out poorer residents, who can only afford to live closer in as pavement dwellers or in slums which are often inaccessible to motorized transport and are very difficult to inhabit.

The role of transport in this complex concept of exclusion may be characterized as follows. The "income poor" make fewer trips, and more of their trips are undertaken on foot. For most purposes they are restricted to whatever services (usually poor services) that can be accessed within walking distance, making them "accessibility poor." The journey to work may be relatively long. Even if it is not, it will use slow modes and may be very time-consuming, so they are also "time poor." For poor people, and particularly for women, children, and the elderly, trip making is often deterred because of their vulnerability as pedestrians, both to traffic accidents and to personal violence, making them "safety poor." Finally, there is evidence that long walking distances and times also creates tiredness and boredom that reduces their productivity by adding an "energy-poverty" dimension to their deprivation. In assessing transport provisions for poor people, it is therefore necessary to look at the total package that defines "exclusion," and not simply to look at the proportion of income, or even of time, spent on transport.

Where public transport is not available, access to a private mode of mechanized transport may play a critical role in the extent of exclusion. In the United Kingdom, experiments with inexpensive car loans for rural workers who can only access jobs by private transport are improving the lot of some relatively poor people. The equivalent in poorer countries may be the development of mechanisms for inexpensive finance of private bicycles—together with public investment in infrastructure for the safe movement of those bicycles. This is discussed further in chapter 9.

In addition to household characteristics, there are also some specific personal characteristics that accentuate deprivation. In most countries, over 10 percent of the population has some form of physical disability imposing serious disadvantage both in terms of mobility and safety (Merilainen and Helaakoski 2001). For the physically impaired, as well as for the elderly, public transport accessibility is often very poor and pedestrian facilities are often nonexistent or are blocked by parked cars. Increasing attention is now being paid to these groups in industrialized countries, and guides to good design practice are available.[12] While some aids to mobility are expensive, and raise issues of expenditure priorities in circumstances where affordability of basic transport itself is an issue, many are not. Provision of pavement ramps to make road crossing easier for wheelchairs, tactile strips on station platforms to assist the blind, large brightly colored signage to help the partially sighted, and well-designed grab bars and handles to assist the less mobile are all matters of a more inclusive focus in design rather than of expense.[13] Good practice can be found in developing as well as in industrialized countries.[14]

Gender-related disadvantage is also endemic. Many activities typically undertaken by women (childcare, household management, informal sector employment, and so on) require them to make more frequent and shorter trips than are required of men. They make more trips at off-peak hours and more trips that are off the main routes, and engage in more complicated multileg trips, all of which tend to make their movements relatively expensive for public transport to provide, and hence more highly priced or more poorly supplied.[15] Women are very vulnerable to these cost characteristics because they frequently have less capacity to pay than do male household members, who, in many cultures, also control any bicycles or other vehicles available to the household. Cultural factors may constrain women's abilities to use public transport or bicycles. In many countries there is also a problem of the "social safety or security" of public transport for women, especially after dark.[16] This may force them to depend on more expensive alternatives. Peripheral location may be particularly damaging to women's employment potential.[17] To confirm this, a heavy agenda of necessary gender-related research is required. This includes a need for more activity-based, as opposed to trip-based, research; better estimates of the economic value of women's time; and direct evaluation of the impacts of some gender-related projects.

Reforms aimed at improving economic efficiency may sometimes have the immediate effect of reducing employment of the poor or the relatively poor. Constraints on the development or behavior of the informal transport sector, discussed in chapter 7, may take away the only source of livelihood for some of the very poor. Rail reform has also often been associated with substantial severance of redundant staff, as has occurred in Buenos Aires. In World Bank projects this adverse side effect is mitigated by the imposition of resettlement provisions based on a policy of no detriment. But there is a wider issue. Not all impacts are so directly apparent. Identification of distributional effects of infrastructure works and of reform policies, and the fuller involvement of project-affected persons in decisions, is thus a sine qua non for the avoidance of incidental damage to the interests of poor people.

Some general conclusions may be derived immediately from the analysis of the travel patterns of poor people.

a. "Exclusion" is multidimensional, so low travel costs may be achieved through the acceptance of other heavy transport quantity, time, or quality penalties, or through the acceptance of very bad housing conditions.

b. The transport capability of a household is critically dependent on its stock of private vehicles (bicycles, motorbikes, cars, and so on), as well as on its income and locational characteristics.

c. The structure of provision of formal public transport services tends to reflect and accentuate the distribution of poverty rather than to compensate for it.

d. Some specific categories of people—defined in terms of age, gender, or infirmity—may suffer particular disadvantage in transport terms.

PRO-POOR ECONOMIC GROWTH AND POVERTY REDUCTION

At the individual level, the urban poor are very conscious that access to employment is critical to their fight against poverty, and that the availability of good transport infrastructure and services is a basis on which this access can be achieved. "The lack of basic road, transportation, and water infrastructure is seen as a defining characteristic of poverty,"[18] but the relationship between urban transport infrastructure and poverty reduction is complex. The "income poor" may in fact have chosen to live in poorly served peripheral locations precisely because they are the places where their overall welfare (in terms of availability of shelter, access to activities, and so on) is best served. High transport cost is then a *symptom* of their poverty rather than its fundamental cause. Hence transport policies that improve the general economic viability of the city are very important to poor people. For example, the lot of poor people in Cairo, Egypt, has been improved more through relocation of their residences in order to improve their access to transport links, which are not primarily designed for poverty alleviation, than through poverty-targeted transport investments.[19]

This finding has a parallel at the macroeconomic level. World Bank research indicates that income of the poorest quintile of the population varies in direct proportion to national income (Dollar and Kraay 2001). Moreover, there is no evidence of a lag between increases of overall incomes and the incomes of poor people to suggest that benefits accrue to poor people only in a prolonged process of "trickle down."[20] That being so, urban transport interventions that are particularly effective in generating growth may also be particularly effective in raising the incomes of poor people. Moreover, aggregate-level analysis of poverty and growth indicates that much previous public social sector expenditure has been poorly targeted, having little demonstrable effect on either growth or distribution, while, in contrast, policies to improve market functioning has yielded proportionate benefits to poor people. Policies that most benefit the poor appear to be those associated with reducing government expenditures and stabilizing inflation.

While these general analyses do not refer specifically to urban transport, they highlight some critical questions about poverty-oriented urban transport interventions. Many governments view urban public transport policy as an instrument of their social policy. It is thus important both to establish how effectively urban transport infrastructure, service planning, and investment targets the needs of poor people, and to establish the indirect effect of urban transport pricing and financing policies on the poor through those policies' impact on government expenditures and macroeconomic stabilization.

FOCUSING INFRASTRUCTURE POLICIES

The selection and design of infrastructure investments, whether in facilities for motorized or nonmotorized road traffic or for rail traffic, must consider their impacts on the poor.

ROAD INVESTMENTS

Most urban transport is road based. The availability of an adequate road infrastructure is there-fore a prerequisite for efficient urban movement. Some of the most intransigent urban transport problems arise where the space devoted to movement is both inadequate and poorly structured; an example of this is Bangkok. Rapidly expanding towns need adequate road capacity, which may involve investment in limited-access primary roads as a structuring element. Some of the developing-country cities that appear to have the best public transport facilities are also notable for well-designed and managed road infrastructure; an example of this is Curitiba.

But, there is a fine balance to be struck. Unless road space is already very abundant, there is a danger that more roads will simply encourage people to make extra trips to an extent that nullifies the intended reduction of congestion, increases auto dependence, and contributes to urban sprawl. In the absence of a strategic vision of the desired transport system, which addresses the management of available space as well as the planning of additions to it, and particularly in the absence of efficient congestion pricing, piecemeal adjustment to emerging bottlenecks will almost certainly benefit the wealthy at the expense of the poor (see chapter 6).

This finding has some consequences for the economic appraisal of urban road projects. As we argued in chapter 2, allowance should be made for the effects of generated traffic in limiting the extent to which congestion can be reduced and time and operating cost savings achieved. This has long been accepted in the context of more sophisticated, model-based appraisals in industrialized countries, but it tends to be forgotten in simpler, more abbreviated appraisals. The problems associated with differences in the ways the rich and poor value time can also be handled by assigning a common value to all nonworking time for evaluation purposes.

Some more difficult issues remain unresolved. Because conventional transport planning is driven by the willingness to pay (either demonstrated, in the case of commercial services, or synthesized from behavioral studies, in the case of public infrastructure), relatively low value tends to be assigned to investments that cater to more dispersed and off-peak transport needs. These needs often include those of the very poor, and of women. Moreover, much of the travel of poor people is on foot and typically receives low priority in conventional transport planning, which is often oriented to vehicle movement rather than to person movement. If conventional evaluation cannot recognize such categories of movement, it should not be relied upon. Even participatory planning methods may fail to accommodate this if they underrepresent both women and the very poor.

To some extent investments in road infrastructure can be focused to specifically benefit poor people. Several such types of investment have been commonly favored in Bank projects (see table 3.1).

a. Road investment and rehabilitation expenditures can be concentrated on major public transportation routes so that public transport can benefit, as is the case in the current Kyrgyz Urban Transport Project.

b. Investments can be made in the provision or segregation of routes for nonmotorized transport (NMT), including walking, to make NMT quicker and safer; this has been the case in recent projects in Lima, Accra (Ghana), and others.

c. Road and sidewalk design can be more sensitive to the needs of disabled persons.

d. Road expenditures more generally may be directed specifically to improve access to poor areas, or informally settled areas (for example, the "pueblos jovenes" of Lima).

e. Particularly in informally settled areas (such as in the Hanna Nassif project in Dar es Salaam),[21] the use of employment-intensive methods may be an important source of income for the very poor and may also create a local sense of ownership conducive to good maintenance.

NONMOTORIZED TRANSPORT

The most obvious policy mismatch is that between the significance of NMT (walking and cycling) to poor people and the attention given to these modes, both in infrastructure design and in management. In the poorer countries more than one-half of all trips are undertaken on foot, yet are typically treated as a peripheral issue rather than as a core element. Cycling offers a relatively inexpensive means of improving the accessibility of poor people, but is often vulnerable both to accidents and crime; planning and providing for cycling is often poor. Because this is such an important issue, we devote a separate chapter (chapter 9) to NMT.

TABLE 3.1 POVERTY-FOCUSED URBAN TRANSPORT INTERVENTIONS: ROAD INFRASTRUCTURE

Specific intervention	Nature of impact	Cost and fiscal impacts	Implementation ease	Bank examples
Maintaining public transport routes	Faster and less-expensive public transport	Moderate	Easy	Kyrgyz
Paving poor areas	Access for public transport	Moderate	Easy	Lima
Bicycle and pedestrian tracks	Safer trips; encouraging NMT	Moderate	Moderate	Lima, Accra
Separation of NMT on existing roads	Safety; speed for all modes	Low	Difficult	Dhaka; Guangzhou, China

Source: Authors.

RAIL INVESTMENTS

The poverty impact of investment in mass rapid transit (MRT) has been very controversial. It may improve quality of the transport that poor people receive and give them a wider choice of household location, employment, and lifestyle. It can increase their incomes indirectly through its effect on the efficiency of the urban system. But it may concurrently increase the fares that they must pay. Prescriptions to subsidize MRT to offset the effect of higher fares may actually militate against the interests of poor people unless it is clear that the subsidies are well targeted to them, do not precipitate declines in service quality (which are more harmful than higher fares would be), do not leak away through inefficient operation, and do not impose a burden on city finances by preempting other socially desirable expenditures.

The most basic consideration is what modes of public transport poor people actually use. In some cities in East Asia, buses are the transport of poor people and rail transport the mode of the relatively affluent. The same is not true in many Latin American cities, where the average income of rail users is much below the average income, and very similar to that of bus users (table 3.2). The pattern disclosed is one of great variety, defying simple norms and emphasizing the importance of relating policies sensibly to objectives on a case-by-case basis.

Metros may incidentally serve low-income areas, as in Cairo, but have rarely been designed specifically for that purpose. Even where they are designed to serve low-income areas, the operations of the land market mechanism may result in the benefits passing on to others. Insofar as a metro reduces travel time to central areas of the city, it will tend to increase city-center land values and hence land rents at the newly advantaged locations. Poor people only capture those benefits if they own the land themselves, and hence acquire the windfall capital gain, or are protected against charges for the increased value of the land in property rents. That can be done if public housing programs and mass transit developments are undertaken jointly by a development authority with a specific responsibility for the welfare of poor people, as has been done systematically in Singapore and more sporadically in a number of other cities, such as Fortaleza, Brazil.

The link between efficiency and equity is sometimes very subtle. For example, restructuring of bus services to feed into higher-capacity trunk links (either rail or bus) is commonly advocated as a central part of integrated urban transport developments, as in Singapore and Curitiba. However, this restructuring will tend to increase the number of multileg trips involving separate payment, which, given the typical flat or very shallowly tapered fare structure, can increase total

Rail system	City/region average income (MMS)	Users' average income (MMS)	Percentage of users below city average income
Recife suburban rail (1997)	4.1	2.7	55.7
São Paulo Metro (1997)	13.6	13.8	57.4
São Paulo train (1997)	13.6	8.8	80.4
Rio de Janeiro suburban rail (1996)	10.0	3.2	85.5
Belo Horizonte (1995)	8.1	4.6	55.6

TABLE 3.2 INCOME OF USERS OF RAIL SYSTEMS IN BRAZIL

Note: MMS = monthly minimum salary.
Source: World Bank, project files.

fare costs, particularly for those (often poor people) living in locations most remote from the MRT line.

That impact may be reduced by the introduction of multimodal through-ticketing systems, which have been shown to yield high benefits to users in a number of countries (table 3.3). These multimodal systems may be difficult to establish where there are a number of independently operated modes. Certainly it will tend to be easier to achieve when the bus industry is relatively highly concentrated (as in many Brazilian cities). Even where it is achieved, however, adverse distribution effects on the very poor may occur if the effect of incorporating a high cost–high fare metro in a revenue pool is to raise fares, even for those who do not benefit from the new investment. The lesson is that wherever integration is introduced, it is necessary to analyze and design fare structures and cross-modal revenue support very carefully.[22]

Poor people may lose their jobs because of a reform; both severance compensation and retraining finance is necessary to counteract this consequence. The poor may also suffer involuntary displacement in the process of urban rail (or road) infrastructure development, especially where they occupy land illegally, or where they do not hold title (that is, squatters). The expansion

of capacity of the suburban rail system in Mumbai is estimated to involve the resettlement of 60,000 persons. In that case full consultation with local slumdwellers' associations at the project preparation stage, as well as adequate financing for their resettlement, has been essential for avoiding harm to some of the very poor people.

PUBLIC TRANSPORT SERVICE PLANNING FOR THE URBAN POOR

Even in some of the most highly motorized cities in Latin America, the average income of those who use cars is more than double the income of those who do not use cars (table 3.4). For the very poor, transport service is synonymous either with NMT (mostly walking) or public transport, often very inexpensively provided by the informal sector. Hence a poverty-oriented urban transport strategy needs to concentrate on the movement of people rather than of vehicles.

That does not mean that municipal authorities should be disinterested in the phenomenon of road congestion, which affects the movement of freight as well as people and which reduces the efficiency of the city. Congestion also tends to disadvantage those in crowded public transport vehicles even more than those in private cars. But

TABLE 3.3 POVERTY IMPACTS OF INTERVENTIONS: RAIL INFRASTRUCTURE AND MANAGEMENT

Specific intervention	Nature of impact	Cost/fiscal impacts	Implementation ease	Bank examples
Concessioning	Improved service to users: fare effects uncertain	Cost saving	Moderate	Rio de Janeiro, Buenos Aires
Severance payments	Protects (poorer) workers	Small	Moderate	Buenos Aires
Resettlement arrangements	Protects disturbed residents from consequences of development	Small/medium	Difficult	Mumbai
Converting suburban railways	Improves speed and frequency	Moderate	Moderate	Fortaleza, Brazil

Source: Authors.

TABLE 3.4 AVERAGE INCOME OF USERS BY TRANSPORT MODE

City	Average income car users	Average income noncar users	Average income car users/ noncar users	Percentage of all motorized trips done by car
Bogotá[a]	462.4	196.8	2.3	19.2%
Buenos Aires[b]	607.2	299.1	2.0	40.0%
Lima[c]	1,157.0	312.0	3.7	20.0%

a. Monthly income in dollars of 1995 for 1995 (Exchange rate is $1 = 1,000 pesos). Figure assumes 160 hours worked per month. Source: JICA-Chodai 1996.
b. Monthly income in dollars of 1994. Figure is for 1997. Source: Centro de Estudios del Transporte del Area Metropolitana 1999.
c. Monthly income in dollars of 1999 for 1999 (Peruvian currency seems overvalued). Source: APOYO 1999.
Source: Authors.

it should be recognized that, even in relatively poor cities, scarce but freely provided urban road space is increasingly appropriated by private cars carrying a small proportion of total "person-movements" made by the wealthy. This inequity implies that priority should be given in the use of scarce road space to facilitating the movement of NMT and the more space-efficient public transport modes, rather than to private cars.

THE GENERAL SAFETY NET APPROACH

From the conventional public transport supply side, the challenge of meeting the transport needs of poor people can be approached in two quite different ways. In most socialist economies, public transport was traditionally viewed as a basic social service. Even in some mixed economies, such as France and francophone Africa, concentration on the concept of exclusion of identifiable spatial groups has led to an emphasis on mobility as a "merit good," a minimum supply of which is viewed as a social imperative. This approach leads to a "network completeness and integrity" approach to transport supply, with extensive fare reductions or exemptions for disadvantaged groups. It depends on broad political acceptance of high levels of subsidy of public transport operations, as well as on state contributions, particularly to finance capital. The employment of a single private operator, either under a management contract or under some form of system concession, tends to gener-

ate a continued willingness to supply unprofitable locations, both on the part of the operators, who do not wish to abandon any part of their monopoly domain, and on the part of the public authorities, who wish to sustain urban integration. But this is probably not the least expensive or most efficient way of providing a basic network of services, as we will show in chapter 7.

Maintaining the basic social network is not always easy. Even in France, as car ownership increased and public transport patronage declined, there have been pressures to reduce the fiscal burden through tariff increases. In most francophone developing countries, the attempt to maintain the social obligations in the absence of a fiscal basis for support resulted, initially, in the retreat of the traditional supply agencies to be suppliers only of those with fare concessions (who may not be the very poor, but who may fall into categories such as middle-class scholars) and ultimately in the bankruptcy and disappearance of the traditional supply.[23]

The safety net approach thus needs a secure financial basis that is often lacking, given general budget weaknesses of many developing-country cities. There are, however, two possibilities, discussed in more detail later, that may avoid the need for any charge on the general budget. The first possibility is that, within a system of competitively tendered franchises, the profits from the more profitable routes may be used to support unprofitable services (chapter 7). The second possibility is that road pricing may be used as a revenue source for a multimodal urban transport fund (chapter 10).

THE TARGETED SUBSIDY APPROACH

The alternative approach is to treat transport supply more as a commercial business and to target subsidies explicitly at disadvantaged groups on a personal basis. In the United Kingdom, where supply of bus services is entirely by the private sector in competitive markets, scholars and pensioners often benefit from fare reductions or exemptions directly funded by the relevant line agencies; this funding hence appears as commercial revenues to the operators. Transfer of responsibility for "social" subsidies from the accounts of the transport operators to those of the relevant line agencies is also being widely advocated as a means of addressing the decline of public transport service in many countries of the former Soviet Union.

The obvious advantage of this approach is that the fiscal burden on the community is lower. It also has the merit of giving clear signals and incentives to the operators to adjust their services and fares in such a way as to maintain their equipment in operation. The disadvantage is that there is no clear institutional channel through which the more strategic and structural considerations concerning the role of public transport .in urban development strategy, and the response to the various externalities that impinge on urban public transport, can be addressed.

COMPETITION, PRIVATIZATION, AND POOR PEOPLE

Introduction of competitive tendering of franchises in major cities in Western Europe reduced costs per vehicle kilometer by up to 40 percent in real terms, and allowed higher service frequencies to be maintained within constrained budgets than under traditional monopoly supply mechanisms. These advantages, which were first exploited in Organisation for Economic Co-operation and Development (OECD) countries, are now being seen to be effective in developing economies (urban rail services in Buenos Aires, Argentina) and transitional economies (bus services in secondary cities in Uzbekistan).

There are, nevertheless, some concerns about competitive private sector supply. These include the loss of internal cross-subsidy, the abandonment of socially desirable services, and the increase in fares associated with commercialization. As discussed in more detail in chapter 6, all of these perceived problems can be overcome by good design and administration of the competitive regime. The capability to combine some central service coordination with competitive supply varies from country to country according to administrative capability and integrity, so that there is no single pattern that fits all economies. The lesson is that attention to the potential for competitive process can be a powerful contributor to improvement of the services on which poor people depend. Some examples are provided in table 3.5.

FARE POLICIES, SUBSIDIES, AND BUDGET CONSTRAINTS

Controlling public transport fares, ostensibly to help the poor, may adversely affect service quality unless supported by subsidy. This raises questions both about the concept of an affordable fare and about the financing and targeting of subsidies.

THE CONCEPT OF THE AFFORDABLE FARE

The price and quality of service provided is obviously important in assessing the impact of urban transport on poor people. The concept of "affordability" of public transport is popular and seductive, and governments frequently control public transport fares because fares above some threshold level would be unacceptably burdensome to poor people. Although it was not originally intended as a pricing policy prescription, the "Armstrong-Wright maxim" (that situations in

TABLE 3.5 A POVERTY-FOCUSED AGENDA: PUBLIC TRANSPORT SERVICE PLANNING

Specific intervention	Nature of impact	Possible cost/ fiscal impact	Implementation ease	Bank examples
Introduce competition in public transport	Cost-reduction service growth	Cost saving	Moderate	Uzbekistan and Kazakhstan
Public transport interchange	Faster, safer trips	Medium	Moderate	Pusan, Republic of Korea; Manila
Bus priorities	Faster, less expensive trips	Low	Politically difficult	Bangkok
Develop informal sector	Lower-cost service	None	Moderate	Uzbekistan, secondary cities

Source: Authors.

which more than 10 percent of households spend more than 15 percent of household incomes on work journeys can be regarded as discriminatory) has often been interpreted as a reasonable rule for determining the level of a politically administered price.[24]

Caution should be advised over this maxim. First, the impact of any particular level of transport costs on the aggregate welfare level of the household does not depend only on household income and the price of transport. If shelter and heating are provided very inexpensively through tax-financed public subsidies, then the proportion of disposable income for transport might be correspondingly higher. More important, though, price is not the only thing that matters. There is evidence from social surveys of public transport users in Uzbekistan, the Kyrgyz Republic, and various Brazilian cities that even relatively poor people may be willing to pay more for the better service offered by the informal sector, with their small vehicles, compared with the inexpensive but slow and unreliable service offered by the public sector, with their traditional buses. Similarly, where metro fares are higher than those of buses, poor people may choose to use the metro because of the better quality of service that it provides; this is the case, for instance, in Cairo.[25]

The most serious problem, however, is that many governments control general fare levels without making any accompanying fiscal provision for subsidies. The rationale for this, often explicitly stated, is that it will force operators to cross-subsidize unprofitable services from profitable services, leading to cross-subsidy of poor people by the rich. In practice, in many countries there is no such basis for cross-subsidy (the rich do not use public transport and there are no profitable services from which to squeeze cross-subsidy finance). In these circumstances the main effect is to reduce the quality, and eventually the quantity, of public transport service.

Sometimes the adverse effect of the failure of the traditional formal sector is attenuated by the development of informal sector services, usually provided with smaller and less expensive vehicles, frequently at fares above the controlled formal sector fares. Insofar as this informal sector service involves the provision of a quality of service that could be improved by the traditional larger vehicle if allowed to operate at the fare adopted by the informal sector, it represents a distortion with unintentionally adverse effects on poor people. The lesson is that tinkering with the symptoms of poverty may actually make things worse for the poor. The policy prescription arising from this is that the likely supply outcomes of different levels of fare intervention and subsidy should always be estimated. Fares should be set at levels consistent with the outcome preferred by poor people as shown by surveys, and not on the basis of some "normative" concept of what an affordable fare might be.

FINANCING TARGETED SUBSIDIES

Many countries have extensive lists of categories of passengers qualifying for free or reduced-fare travel. Rarely is there any specific mechanism for remunerating suppliers for these fare exemptions or reductions. This has two effects. First, it means that some passengers are paying more, or receiving poorer service, than would otherwise be the case in attempts to secure cross-subsidy. Because the rich often do not use public transport, this means, at best, subsidy of the poor by the poor. Second, it creates a vested interest of benefiting nontransport agencies (health, education, police, and so on) in maintaining a subsidy for their particular user group, that they might not favor if it had to be financed from their own budgets. The lesson is that, in the interests of poor people, any public transport fare reductions or exemptions should be carefully considered in the light of other uses that might be made of the resources involved. That consideration is probably best ensured by putting the responsibility for finance of fare exemptions or reductions directly on the benefiting line agencies, with the obligations on the transport operators contingent on the receipt of the appropriate compensation.

Even where a fiscal basis for corrective action to reduce poverty exists, the question arises as to whether intervention in the transport sector is the most appropriate use of such funds. The answer to that question turns partly on the relative efficiency with which funding can be targeted in different sectors, and partly on the political feasibility of taking poverty-reducing actions in various sectors. The relationship between the average income of the users of specific modes and the overall average incomes is usually known, or can be established, and the distribution of general fare subsidies can thus be assessed. There are two main impediments to the use of general subsidy, however. First, there may be wide variations of income among users of a specific mode, so that targeting is very imprecise.

Second, there is substantial evidence that a large proportion of subsidy to public transport through deficit financing of public sector monopoly operators "leaks" away, either through inefficiency of operations or through the capture of the subsidy by organized labor in the supply industry. While there remain some problems in achieving adequate targeting, it is clear that public transport users include the poorest, and usually exclude the richest, groups, so that in the absence of any means of transfer through taxation structures, it may be a reasonably good discriminator in many developing countries. As further discussed in chapter 6, competition is the best protection against leakage of the benefit to suppliers or their employees.

CONCLUSIONS: A STRATEGY FOR POVERTY-FOCUSED URBAN TRANSPORT

Inadequate and congested urban transport is damaging to the city economy and harms both rich and poor. But the simplistic solution of increasing road capacity in an attempt to speed up the movement of vehicles, accompanied by public provision of fare-controlled public transport, is likely to be inequitable (because it leads to a progressive decline of public transport services) and ineffective (because it will tend to generate more congesting car traffic). Rather, there is need for a more poverty-focused policy (see table 3.6) reflecting the following general conclusions concerning the impacts of urban transport policies:

- Costs should be properly charged for all vehicle movements, both to secure efficient use of infrastructure, and to generate a secure financial basis for urban transport provision.
- The importance of walking and other NMT activities, and the special needs of the mobility-impaired should be recognized both in infrastructure design and in traffic management.

TABLE 3.6 POVERTY-FOCUSED URBAN TRANSPORT INTERVENTIONS: FINANCE STRATEGIES

Specific intervention	Nature of impact	Cost/ fiscal impact	Implementation ease	Bank examples
Subsidy finance reform	Line agencies to finance exemptions; better focus of support	Uncertain	Moderate	Russian Federation
Public transport fare integration	Enables use of faster modes	Low	Moderate	São Paulo and Fortaleza, Brazil
Congestion pricing	Direct impact small. Provides basis for public transport improvement	Generates revenue	Difficult	Kuala Lumpur, Bangkok

Source: Authors.

- Ill-judged policies on general public transport fare controls in the absence of secure subsidy mechanisms can actually harm poor people.
- Constraints on the informal transport sector often harm poor people. The message here is that policies for the informal transport sector need to be framed with their impacts on poor people carefully taken into account.
- Absence of competition in public transport is likely to both increase costs and reduce supply to poor people. A preference for stable, disciplined supply should not be interpreted as a case for uncontested monopoly.
- Efforts to secure multimodal integration need to be carefully managed to ensure that these efforts do not increase the number of times poor people must pay per trip, and that fares on the services on which they are particularly dependent do not increase.
- Attention needs to be given to financing of support mechanisms, avoiding deficit financing of monopolist suppliers, and, wherever possible, targeting very specific groups.
- Because of the effect of transport infrastructure investment and transport pricing policies on land values, it is important that ostensibly poverty-oriented urban transport interventions be integrated in a broader strategy incorporating housing, health, education, and other social service policies.

Based on these principles, there is a rich agenda of urban transport policies that are both pro-growth and pro-poor, yet that are consistent with the fiscal capabilities of even the relatively poorest countries.

NOTES

1. World Bank 2000c.

2. In this volume, poor countries are defined as those falling below the threshold that qualifies for International Development Association borrowing terms, currently an average annual gross national product per capita of $885. Much of the distributional analysis referring to the conditions of poor people uses data on the bottom quintile of income per capita within a country (and hence are not strictly comparable across countries). Little transport-related data are linked to the commonly quoted absolute poverty standard of $1 per day per capita.

3. Schwela and Zali 1999.

4. An early study in Salvador, Brazil, showed that the lowest income groups on average made one trip per person per day, compared with three trips per day for the highest income groups, with a constant distance per trip of 6 kilometers across all income groups. See Thompson 1993.

5. The recently observed exceptions to this in some of the major cities of Latin America may reflect the increasing insecurity of travel, which is now affecting the nonpoor as well as the poor.

6. A curious exception to this, which is worth further investigation, is the city of Ouagadougou, where public transport is almost nonexistent and 57 percent of households falling in the bottom income quintile possessed a motorized two-wheeler.

7. Godard and Diaz Olvera 2000.

8. Godard and Diaz Olvera 2000.

9. Madras Metropolitan Development Authority 1990.

10. De St. Laurent 1998.

11. Cusset 1998.

12. European Conference of Ministers of Transport 1999b.

13. Merilainen and Helaakoski 2001.

14. Wright 2001.

15. Diaz Olvera, Plat, and Pochet 1998.

16. Gomez 2000.

17. In a study of squatter resettlement in Delhi in the late 1970s, it was found that male employment among the colony decreased by 5 percent, but female employment decreased by 27 percent after resettlement (Moser and Peake 1987).

18. Narayan 2000a.

19. CATRAM 2000.

20. Dollar and Kraay 2001.

21. Howe and Bryceson 2000.

22. Recent MRT development packages in some Brazilian cities have been subject to detailed analysis of the effects of changes in bus service structures and integrated ticketing arrangement on the money, and generalized costs of transit for zones with populations at different income levels.

23. Teurnier and Mandon-Adolehoume 1994.

24. Armstrong-Wright 1986.

25. See White 1999.

4 TRANSPORT AND THE URBAN ENVIRONMENT

Road transport contributes significantly to urban air pollution in many countries. The World Health Organization estimates that suspended particulate matter leads to the premature death of over 0.5 million people per year. The economic costs of air pollution have been estimated to be equivalent to about 2 percent of gross domestic product in many countries. Incorporation of environmental issues within an urban transport strategy requires the identification of the main transport-generated pollutants (usually suspended particulate matter, lead, and ozone) and the mobilization of technical, fiscal, and system management controls on fuel and vehicle technology to reduce these pollutants. Frequently these will also contribute to a desirable reduction of greenhouse gas emissions.

THE SCALE OF THE ISSUE

For many poor people in developing countries, the inability to access jobs, education, and health facilities is viewed as the most serious constraint on their quality of life (Narayan 2000a). Motorized transport is often crucial to poor people, but because they frequently live and work in the shadow of motorized transport, they are also the most vulnerable to its adverse environmental impacts. Environmental protection must therefore be seen as an essential part of the task of improving the quality of life of the poor, and not as a luxury to be purchased at the expense of the poor's mobility.

A comprehensive strategy for transport and the urban environment should cover the built environment, including land take, urban form, visual intrusion of infrastructure and traffic, and cultural heritage; the social effects of transport in causing occupational or locational resettlement and community severance; personal safety and security; and the more commonly recognized problems of noise and air pollution (local, regional, and global). All of these concerns must be formally addressed in a typical project's environmental assessment.

In this review we deal with matters concerning the built environment in chapters 2 and 6, with the social effects in chapter 3, and with safety and security in chapter 5. In this chapter we deal only with various forms of pollution, especially air pollution.

In developing countries an estimated 0.5 million to 1 million people die prematurely each year as a result of respiratory and other illnesses caused by exposure to urban air pollution. This is a larger number than those dying as a consequence of urban traffic accidents, although because of the age distribution of those afflicted, traffic accidents probably reduce life-years more. Exposure to lead contributes to behavioral problems and learning disabilities in urban children. It also reduces the quality of life.

GLOBAL WARMING

It is now generally agreed that a global climate change is occurring. It also appears that the poorer countries stand to suffer most as a consequence of this change, with estimated costs in the range of 5 to 9 percent of gross domestic product (GDP) for some of the poorer countries—several times greater than the relative effect in industrialized countries.[1] It is estimated that the transport sector is responsible for about 25 percent of emissions of the gases contributing to global warming in industrialized countries, but only about one-half this amount in developing-country cities.[2] While the proportion appears to have been stabilized in the Organisation for Economic Co-operation and Development (OECD) countries, it is still growing in the developing countries as motorized transport increases. This increase in motorized transport is concentrated in urban areas. Although controversy continues over the optimal greenhouse gas (GHG) reduction strategy, and the distribution of action between industrialized and developing countries, it is accepted that some mitigating strategy is called for in all countries.

Despite this, GHG mitigation has a negative connotation in many developing countries, where exhortations to limit GHG emissions are perceived as a denial of the right to develop the services and lifestyle being enjoyed by industrialized countries. The apparent unwillingness of some industrialized-country governments to take strong action also does not help, while the inherent long-term and nonlocal nature of the negative impacts of GHGs feeds this attitude.

A "business-as-usual" scenario for the transport sector offers little prospect of relief. The principal components determining the level of GHG emissions in transport are the level of activity (in ton or passenger kilometers), the modes of transport used, the energy intensity of each mode, and the mix of fuels used. In the industrialized countries, transport activity has increased pari passu with economic growth, the shift to the pri-

vate car and air transport has worsened the modal balance effect, and changes in the balance of fuels has had little impact. It is only the dramatic increase in fuel efficiency that has acted as a brake on GHG emissions. Even so, transport GHG emissions continue to grow in the industrialized countries even though overall emissions have been stabilized. Economic growth in the developing countries similarly threatens to dominate any attenuating effect of technology improvement.

To avert this outcome requires a combination of transportation policy reforms in the short term and technological changes in the longer term. The question is how to get such policies adopted. The suggested key to changing this situation is to link GHG-mitigation policy initiatives to goals that are perceived to be of immediate relevance (such as local air pollution and balance-of-payments considerations) and to try to uncouple, or at least "flex," the link between economic growth and GHG emissions from the transport sector.[3]

We start from the observed synergy between GHG reduction and local environmental and economic interests. The GHGs that most contribute to global warming in the transport sector include carbon dioxide (CO_2), methane, and nitrous oxide (N_2O). Emissions of CO_2 are directly proportional to the quantity of carboniferous fuel consumed; other things being equal, reduced fuel consumption will reduce economic costs and global pollution simultaneously. Better traffic flow conditions typically reduce fuel consumption per kilometer. In chapter 6 we advocate both road-based traffic management and traffic restraint measures to that end, while the measures that are suggested to improve public transport in chapter 7 and to improve nonmotorized transport (NMT) in chapter 8 should have similar effects. More generally, local air quality improvement programs for urban transport in middle-income countries such as Mexico and Chile have also shown some collateral benefits for reducing GHG emissions.[4] While the rest of this chapter focuses primarily on local air pollution reduction, much of it also relates, by implication, to the global warming issue. Because these types of interventions can be shown to be in the immediate self-interest of city residents themselves, it is believed that concentrating on exploiting the synergy between GHG reductions and local economic and environmental interests is likely to be the most productive strategic stance.

This must be supported by economic incentives. Fossil fuel consumption is influenced directly by fuel choice, vehicle size, and fuel efficiency, and indirectly by individual and corporate decisions on activity location and style, and transport mode. Emissions of methane come largely from leakages of gasoline, diesel, and unburned natural gas and are thus susceptible to influence by fueling infrastructure improvement. The strongest incentive to fuel economy in actions in all these dimensions is the monetary cost of fuel. It has been shown that pollution controls supported by appropriate prices or taxes are much more effective than is the use of regulations alone.[5] In chapter 10 we discuss this in detail, arguing for fuel prices that at least cover the full social costs of fuel consumption.

Unfortunately there is not always a synergy between local air pollution and GHG emission–mitigation measures. The current generation of diesel vehicles appears to be more damaging to public health than are gasoline or gas-powered vehicles. Thus, while diesel is a particularly efficient fuel from the point of view of reducing GHG emissions, only the new generation of clean diesels should have a role in GHG strategy. Furthermore, mitigation measures for local pollution focus on emissions of vehicles in use, whereas the entire life cycle (from well to tailpipe) is relevant for analysis of GHG emissions. Worldwide policies to reformulate transport fuels to mitigate local pollution by means of severe hydrotreating (particularly recent moves in North America and the European Union [EU] to limit sulfur in gasoline and diesel to 10–50 parts per million by weight [wt ppm] or lower) make refinery processes increasingly energy intensive, increasing GHG emissions. N_2O can increase significantly when catalysts used to convert nitric oxide (NO) or nitrogen dioxide (NO_2) begin to be deactivated.

A strategic response is therefore required to address situations where the synergy is weak or negative and where a tradeoff between local and global effects appears. In this context, the Global Environment Fund (GEF), a multidonor fund administered by the World Bank, has promoted the concept of the "global overlay." This is a procedure in which measures developed to target other objectives are subject to a scrutiny exploring the possibility and cost of modifying them to yield GHG reductions. In this way an attempt is made to identify and concentrate on those areas where GHG reductions have the least "opportunity cost." Through GEF's Operational Program 11, on transport, GEF funding is available both for the development of new globally friendly technologies and, on an incremental cost basis, for other interventions that pilot promising current GHG reduction policies. An early grant under this scheme is supporting the development of infrastructure for bicycle movement in an outer area of Manila. The Bank has also established a "Prototype Carbon Fund" to foster the international transfer of certified emission reductions under the Clean Development Mechanism, as defined in Article 12 of the Kyoto Protocol.

Technological measures to secure GHG reduction perform primarily through the replacement of the vehicle stock. This may take up to 20 years to complete for cars and up to 30 years for freight vehicles. In developing countries, however, most of the change of vehicle stock is through growth, so that strategies affecting new vehicles may have a more rapid effect on emissions per unit of activity. Hence, with GDP rising, the best way to achieve a decline in GHG emissions by transport vehicles is a combination of policy reforms in the short term and technological changes in the longer term. Because most vehicle users are driven by economic motives, this implies a need for strong support from taxation and pricing instruments. "Closing the loop," so that revenues from increased taxation or charges for vehicles or fuels are seen to contribute to improvement in the transport sector, is likely to be a necessary condition to secure acceptance of the policies at the political level. This is further discussed in chapter 10.

NOISE AND OTHER DISTURBANCES

Noise from transport appears to be considered much less seriously in developing countries than in high-income countries. While there have been studies of the physical damage resulting from exposure to occupational noise, these have been mostly in manufacturing establishments. The levels experienced in developing-country streets, while not pleasant, approach but do not exceed the lower limits above which noise is considered an occupational hazard. Attitude surveys do not show urban transport noise to be perceived as a serious hazard.

Other disturbances exist. Heavy road traffic volumes can make roads dangerous and difficult to cross, causing *community severance.* It is reported that in Jakarta, businesspersons routinely take taxis just to get safely to the other side of the busiest thoroughfares. Barriers, footbridges, and tunnels may reduce the danger but increase the severance, particularly in countries where these facilities appear to be constructed and located to improve motor vehicle flow rather than to assist pedestrians (see chapter 5).

Severance can in some circumstances be reduced by the grade separation of motorized traffic and mass transport from pedestrian movements. In established cities, tunneling is often too expensive (and technically difficult for major flows of road traffic for ventilation reasons) so that elevation is the only viable possibility. This can cause significant *visual intrusion* as well as restrict the dispersion of fumes from traffic remaining at ground level. The elevated rail transport system so dominates Silom and Sukhumvit roads in

Bangkok that the government has decided to avoid any further elevated mass transit in the central area. The problems of community severance and visual intrusion can, to some extent, be reduced by good engineering design. The main lesson from experience is that community severance and visual intrusion have often developed because of inadequate coordination among strategic planning, transport infrastructure investment planning and design, and management of private participation in infrastructure. That emphasizes some institutional requirements, to which we will return in chapter 11.

URBAN AIR POLLUTION

By far the greatest environmental concern about urban transport in most cities relates to local air pollution. Designing an appropriate strategy, with limited resources, to address this concern requires careful identification of priorities, both in selecting targets and in selecting instruments.[6] This section first identifies the major local air pollutants produced by urban transport, and assesses the significance of their contribution to the total urban environmental burden. On this basis, we then discuss four main types of instrument for consideration as components of a strategy for reducing the impact of transport on the urban environment. The first two types—actions on transport vehicles and transport fuels—are primarily technological. The other two types of instrument—traffic management and fiscal instruments—while requiring technological support for effective implementation, are "softer" policy instruments. In some countries, such as Mexico, public transport improvements are sought primarily for environmental reasons.

MAJOR TRANSPORT-GENERATED AIR POLLUTANTS AND THEIR SIGNIFICANCE

Vehicular emissions are very damaging to health.

a. High *lead* concentration in the bloodstream may increase incidence of miscarriages in women, impair renal function, and increase blood pressure. Most significantly, it retards the intellectual development of children and adversely affects their behavior. More lead is absorbed when dietary calcium intake is low, in cases of iron deficiency, when the stomach is empty, and by the young, so poor malnourished children are particularly susceptible to lead poisoning. Suspended particulate matter, particularly particles from vehicle emissions and tire wear that fall predominantly in the submicron range, are able to penetrate deep into the respiratory tract, cause respiratory problems, exacerbate asthma, and damage lung function. There is also a growing consensus that diesel exhaust poses a serious cancer risk.[7]

b. *Carbon monoxide (CO)* inhibits the capacity of blood to carry oxygen to organs and tissues. People with chronic heart disease may experience chest pains when CO levels are high; at very high levels, CO impairs vision, manual dexterity, and learning ability, and can cause death.

c. *Sulfur oxides (SO$_x$)* which are emitted in direct proportion to the amount of sulfur present in fuel, cause changes in lung function in asthmatics and exacerbate respiratory symptoms in sensitive individuals; they contribute to acid rain and to the formation of secondary particulate matter.

d. *Oxides of nitrogen (NO$_x$)* cause changes in lung function in asthmatics, contribute to acid rain and secondary particulate formation, and are a precursor of ground-level ozone. Both diesel- and gasoline-fueled vehicles contribute to NO$_x$ emissions.

e. *Ozone* is responsible for photochemical smog and decreases pulmonary function in individuals taking light to heavy exercise. NO$_x$ (which is emitted in significant quantities by gasoline- and diesel-fueled vehicles) and photochemically reactive volatile organic compounds (to which emissions by gasoline-fueled vehicles contribute) are the two main precursors of ozone.

While all of these emissions are potentially damaging, their incidence and their health impacts differ substantially, both between pollutants and between regions. World Health Organization (WHO) studies of megacities, although now somewhat dated, show that, although health norms of all major pollutants are widely exceeded, the significance of the problem varies considerably (WHO 1992). Lead excesses over norm are very serious where leaded gasoline is used, but not usually elsewhere. Excess of CO is typically not nearly as great as that of fine particulate matter, particularly in countries where the consumption of gasoline is relatively low compared with that of diesel. Significantly elevated levels of ambient SO$_2$ tend to come from the combustion of coal much more than from the transport sector. Ambient NO$_2$ concentrations are often below the WHO guidelines, but are on the increase, as are those of ozone (figure 4.1).

When risk assessment of susceptibility to physical excesses are combined with evidence of health impacts from dose and response analysis, studies in a number of cities (for example, Bangkok; Cairo; Mexico City; Quito, Ecuador; and Santiago) have indicated that the greatest damage to human health comes from exposure to fine particulate matter (particles smaller than 2.5 microns in aerodynamic diameter, or PM$_{2.5}$) and to lead. Depending on topographical and meteorological conditions, ozone can also be a serious health problem in large metropolitan regions, as it is in Mexico City and Santiago.[8]

Transport is not the only source of urban air pollution. In particular, industrial and domestic use of fossil fuels—especially heavy fuel oil, biomass, and brown coal—is a significant source of ambient particulate matter and sulfur dioxide (SO$_2$), especially in temperate regions such as China and Eastern Europe.

FIGURE 4.1 OVERVIEW OF AMBIENT AIR QUALITY IN SELECTED CITIES: SUBJECTIVE ASSESSMENT OF MONITORING DATA, VARIOUS YEARS IN THE 1990s

CITIES	POLLUTANTS					
	CO	NOₓ	Lead	SPM	SO₂	O₃
OECD						
London	Moderate to heavy	No data	No data	Low	Low	No data
Los Angeles	Moderate to heavy	Moderate to heavy	No data	Low	No data	Serious
New York	Moderate to heavy	No data	No data	Low	No data	Low
Tokyo	No data	No data	No data	No data	No data	Serious
East Asia						
Seoul	Low	No data	Low	Serious	Serious	No data
Beijing	No data	No data	No data	Serious	Serious	Low
Jakarta	Low	Low	Low	Serious	No data	Low
Bangkok	Low	No data	Low	Low	No data	No data
Manila	No data	No data	Low	Low	No data	Low
South Asia						
Karachi	Low	No data	Serious	Serious	Low	No data
Mumbai	Low	No data	Low	Serious	Low	No data
Delhi	Low	No data	Low	Serious	Low	No data
Latin America						
Lima	No data	Low	Low	Low	Low	No data
Mexico City	Low	Low	Low	Serious	Low	Serious
São Paulo	Low	Low	No data	Low	Low	Serious
Buenos Aires	Low	No data	No data	Low	No data	No data
Rio de Janeiro	Low	Low	No data	Low	Low	Low
Central Asia, Africa, and Europe						
Tehran	Serious	Low	Serious	Low	Low	Low
Cairo	Low	Low	Low	Serious	Serious	No data
Lagos	Serious	No data	Low	Low	Low	No data
Moscow	Low	Low	No data	Low	No data	No data

Legend:

- Low pollution — Relevant WHO/national guidelines are normally met (short-term guidelines may be exceeded occasionally).
- Moderate to heavy pollution — Relevant WHO/national guidelines exceeded by up to a factor of two (short-term guidelines exceeded on a regular basis at certain locations).
- Serious problem — Relevant WHO/national guidelines exceeded by more than a factor of two.
- No data available — Information on ambient polluted concentration not available.

CO = Carbon monoxide   SPM = Suspended particulate matter   O₃ = Ozone
NOₓ = Oxides of nitrogen   SO₂ = Sulphur dioxide

Source: The data for figure 4.1 have been assembled by Asif Faiz and Surhid Gautam, World Bank, from various sources. These include: World Bank project reports; Urban Air Quality Management Strategy reports, World Resources Institute; a study of seven cities undertaken for the Latin America and the Caribbean Clean Air Initiative; Indian Central Pollution Board reports; and unpublished data obtained by direct inquiry from various cities (São Paulo, Santiago, Bangkok).

Any strategy to reduce pollution from the transport sector needs to be seen in this broader context.[9] However, urban transport is generally identified as a high-priority action area for several reasons.

- Urban traffic is a large contributor to the most harmful fine particulate emissions, and it is responsible for up to 80 to 90 percent of atmospheric lead in cities where leaded gasoline is still used, for the greatest part of

CO emissions, and for significant contribution to the formation of ground-level ozone.

- Large stationary sources of air pollution, which are often located at a distance from densely populated city centers, disperse into the higher layers of the atmosphere while vehicles emit near ground level in highly populated areas. Consequently, vehicles contribute more to human exposure than their share in total emissions loads would indicate. In a study of six megacities, vehicles accounted for only 6 percent of emissions in tons emitted but 32 percent of average exposure for the population.
- The urban transport sector is one of very rapid growth and change, which makes it very susceptible to positive and to protective actions. An understanding of the environmental significance of alternative transport policies and actions may enable growing cities to avoid the environmental impacts already endured in the megacities.

FUEL POLICY

Fuel policy measures may affect the polluting characteristics of existing fuels, the selection among available fuels, and the total amount of fuel consumed.

Improving fuel quality

For the World Bank's client countries, the first step in improving the quality of transport fuels is to phase out lead in gasoline. Lead has historically been added to gasoline as an octane enhancer. Because of its toxicity, there is now a worldwide move to ban its use in gasoline. More than three-quarters of the gasoline sold worldwide today is unleaded. Virtually all OECD countries and many large developing and transition countries, including Bangladesh, Brazil, Honduras, Hungary, Malaysia, and Thailand, have already eliminated lead in gasoline.[10] Some very large countries, including Indonesia, Venezuela, and most countries in Sub-Saharan Africa, remain to be converted.

In the absence of other significant sources of lead, eliminating lead additive in gasoline can reduce

ambient concentrations of lead to less than 0.2 micrograms per cubic meter ($\mu g/m^3$) and the level of lead in blood to lower than 5 micrograms per deciliter ($\mu g/dl$), below the 10 $\mu g/dl$ level now considered by many health organizations to be the appropriate norm. The necessary strategy should attend both to the introduction of unleaded fuel and the elimination of leaded fuel.

Eliminating lead additive from gasoline can also trigger wider environmental improvement. The availability of unleaded gasoline throughout a country is a prerequisite for the introduction of catalytic converters to reduce the emissions of NO_x, CO, and hydrocarbons. The level of CO emissions can also be reduced by incorporating oxygenates into gasoline. It is important, however, to stress that lead elimination should not be carried out in isolation because many of the gasoline-blending components used to increase octane after elimination of lead have their own adverse health effects. Excessive presence of benzene and total aromatics in unleaded gasoline would be of particular concern. However, controlling gasoline volatility and adjusting refinery operations and processing units can manage these blending components at a reasonable cost during the lead phase-out process.

Sulfur in diesel and gasoline generates emissions of SO_2, causes acid rain, and contributes to particulate emissions. It can be reduced by hydrotreating the base fuels. However, in countries where the carbon component of vehicular particulate matter remains high, it may not make economic sense to attempt to match North American and EU sulfur standards immediately in order to mitigate particulate emissions from diesel engines.[11] Rather, tightening of standards should be carefully phased in the light of country-specific circumstances. In some extreme cases, proposed emissions standards are incompatible with the transport fuels available on the market. For example, insistence on Euro 2–compliant buses when the sulfur level in the diesel available in the country may be as high as 5,000 wt ppm is not technically coherent. Some regional effort may also be necessary to harmonize refining and import standards to avoid local black markets in high-sulfur diesel. Transport, environment, and energy policies must always be carefully aligned.

It is not enough to regulate fuel quality. In many developing countries, old, poorly maintained vehicles dominate vehicle fleets. This reduces the cost effectiveness of imposing stringent fuel specifications.[12] Moreover, in some countries transport fuels are routinely adulterated. For example, the addition of (lower-cost) kerosene to gasoline in Asia (box 4.1), cross-contamination of diesel with crude oil, and addition of lead additives to gasoline downstream of refineries or terminals in Central Asia and the Caucasus all increase vehicle emissions. Regular fuel-quality monitoring, together with costly penalties for noncompliance, could help enforce fuel standards more effectively, although preventing local adulteration is likely to remain very difficult as long as there is any financial incentive to engage in the practice.

Fuel-quality requirements are location specific, depending on climatic conditions, ambient concentrations, vehicle fleet characteristics, and so on. For example, Chile and Mexico have more stringent standards than do other Latin American countries because of the particular pollution char-

acteristics of their capital cities. Countries that have domestic refineries merit special attention in this context because refinery processes are integrated, and changing the specifications of one fuel can affect the quality of other fuels and overall refinery economics. While many countries have fuel standards, most of these standards are stipulated in the form of fuel composition. In the United States, the combination of allowing the option of fuel certification on the basis of vehicle emissions, in lieu of fuel composition, and regional differentiation of specifications has allowed the refining sector the freedom to seek flexible least-cost solutions for meeting specific vehicle emissions standards.

The governments own many refineries in developing countries. Some are not operated economically at present. Revamping refineries to improve fuel mix and quality is likely to render them even less commercially viable. Under these circumstances the government may resist requiring changes in fuel quality, or will embrace them only while maintaining import protection through restrictions or high tariffs. In some developing countries, the net cost to society of improving fuel quality by importing superior fuels would be lower than the costs resulting from the use of domestically manufactured fuels with less-stringent spec-

---

BOX 4.1 FUEL ADULTERATION IN THAILAND

Adulteration of heavily taxed gasoline by highly subsidized kerosene was a serious problem in Thailand in the early 1980s. The government introduced a number of measures, including:

- Dyeing the kerosene blue
- Requiring kerosene to be sold in 20-liter containers only
- Extensive enforcement efforts by the police.

Although these measures had some effect, sales of kerosene remained high until oil taxes were restructured in 1986 and the tax on kerosene increased between 1986 and 1991 to remove the incentive to adulterate. However, the incentive to adulterate gasoline with untaxed industrial solvents remains, and such adulteration is a continuing problem.

Source: Jitendra Shah, private correspondence.

ifications. Downstream petroleum–sector reform through transfer of ownership from the government to the private sector, coupled with liberalization of petroleum product trade and the introduction of competition, can therefore result in improved fuel and, ultimately, urban air quality.

Substituting cleaner fuels

A range of alternative fuels considered to be cleaner than conventional hydrocarbons continue to be under investigation or development in industrialized countries. For substitutes to be attractive in the developing world, they must be seen not only as addressing locally perceived environmental problems but also as economically viable at the individual and national levels. It is in that context that the potential of new fuels for urban transport in the developing world must be appraised.

Compressed natural gas (CNG) is a relatively clean fuel.[13] Natural gas is available in abundance in many developing countries that do not have other indigenous fuel resources—such as Argentina, Bangladesh, and Thailand—and hence is potentially of great balance-of-payments significance. As transport use of CNG alone is not enough to justify the development of gas fields and the construction of gas transport and distribution infrastructure, the availability of CNG for transport is closely linked to its availability through city gas distribution networks. These exist in many large cities in Bangladesh, Brazil, Colombia, Indonesia, Pakistan, Eastern Europe, and the former Soviet Union. Some governments have already specifically mandated the use of natural gas as the transport fuel in highly polluted areas (for example, for taxis in Buenos Aires and, more recently, for buses and all pre-1990 auto-rickshaws and taxis in New Delhi, India).

The environmental benefit of CNG is not disputed. Although recent tests by the New York City Transit Authority have shown that natural gas buses have better local pollutant emission characteristics than do ordinary diesel buses, their emission advantages are significantly lowered or even eliminated when compared with diesel-powered buses running on ultra low sulfur diesel and equipped with a continuously regenerating particulate trap. Similarly, although the overall global warming impact of cars fueled by CNG is lower than that with gasoline (especially where the natural gas would otherwise be flared), gasoline vehicles that are converted to natural gas suffer from potentially high leakage of the GHG methane. Although some good retrofitted kits (for example, those used in Argentina) work efficiently, many do not. For example, the conversion of a fleet of Mercedes buses in Rio de Janeiro is reported to have increased most emissions except those of particulates.

A second disadvantage concerns the economic and technical sustainability of the technology in developing countries. The New York City Transit Authority reported that CNG vehicles pay a 30 to 35 percent energy premium over diesel vehicles. Technically, of a fleet of 40 CNG buses in Jakarta, 20 were out of operation in mid-2001 due to maintenance problems. Dual-fuel vehicles also carry some extra cost penalties and reliability problems. Again in Jakarta, a fleet of Nissan dual-fuel vehicles is now being run as single-fuel (diesel) vehicles for technical reasons.

The economics of CNG are complex. Because the choice of fuel generally rests with the business or individual, the critical factor is ultimately the cost and convenience of CNG compared with that of other fuels. As far as the fuel is concerned, the Intergovernmental Panel on Climate Change (IPCC) estimated the wellhead gasoline equivalent production cost of CNG to lie between 70 and 90 percent that of gasoline or diesel, so that given differences in distribution and storage costs, the cost at the pump (excluding taxes) could be very similar. The actual real resource cost thus depends critically on the local availability of fuel and density of the distribution network.[14] As far as vehicles are concerned, there is extra cost associated with the CNG engine (or its conversion), the fuel control system, and the fuel tanks. Together these increase the cost of a basic vehicle, whether a bus or a car, by up to 30 percent.[15] The convenience factor is also important because CNG vehicles lose significant amounts of luggage and passenger space to fuel tanks; at low penetration levels, refueling can involve some dead-running and can be time-consuming; vehicle range may be reduced by over 50 percent, doubling the refueling frequency. Considering all these factors, international evidence suggests that, except for some very heavy mileage vehicles, the pump price difference would need to be about 50 percent of the production cost of liquid fuels for natural gas to be attractive to users. Hence natural gas would seem to require strong fiscal encouragement if it is to be more than a niche fuel.

Liquefied petroleum gas (LPG) is a mixture of light hydrocarbons, mainly propane and butanes. It is easier to distribute and store than CNG,[16] and although the octane number of LPG is not as high as that of natural gas, it has excellent anti-knock characteristics allowing dedicated propane vehicles to take advantage of engines with slightly higher compression ratios than can be used with gasoline. The limited amount of highly reactive hydrocarbons and the low sulfur content of LPG in comparison with gasoline or diesel are some of LPG's good environmental features; it does, however, contain olefins, which are photochemically reactive. LPG-powered three-wheelers are commercially available in Bangkok, and have already effectively replaced the old two-stroke gasoline-powered "tuk-tuks."

The main problems in introducing LPG to the transport sector are the supply sources and distribution system. Several countries already import significant amounts of LPG. India, Pakistan, and Sri Lanka, for example, import about 30 to 40 percent of their LPG demand. On the distribution side, LPG is stored under pressure both inside the vehicle and in the refueling tanks. Special refueling equipment is needed to transfer the pressurized liquid from storage tanks to the vehicle and to ensure that no LPG escapes during refueling. As with CNG, the required investments

in LPG distribution and refueling stations have not been made in most developing countries, and the need for such stations remains a constraint on widespread LPG use.

Ethanol and methanol. True biofuels (that is, those without substantial fossil fuel use hidden in harvesting and processing) would give a real reduction in GHG emissions, but these are still elusive at costs competitive with those of gasoline or diesel. The only long-term effort to promote biofuels for transport in developing countries, the sugar-ethanol program of Brazil, appeared attractive as a means of saving foreign exchange when oil prices were at their peak, but has lost most of its attractiveness; the new car market in Brazil is now almost exclusively for gasoline vehicles. In any case, many experts argue that only alcohol produced from cellulose can truly claim a GHG benefit.

Electric vehicles. Electric road vehicles are quiet and nonpolluting at their point of use and have obvious attractions as urban vehicles, whether powered directly, as in the case of electric trains or trolleybuses, or indirectly, as in the case of some buses, small vans, and cars. A program for electric three-wheelers is being undertaken in Kathmandu, Nepal (box 4.2). While these have the lowest environmental impacts at point of use, their overall environmental impact depends on the way in which electricity is generated and stored, and the disposal problems associated with expired batteries, which can be substantial. Whatever that environmental balance, the market attractiveness of electric-powered transport depends, as is the case for other fuels, on its economic attractiveness in terms of overall cost and convenience. At present the economics of electric vehicles are far from favorable.[17]

Battery technology is central to the economic success of battery electric vehicles. Lead-acid batteries, currently used in electric vehicles, take 6 to 10 hours to slow-charge, emit hydrogen when recharging (requiring indoor recharging facilities to be well ventilated) and still have very limited range. Other battery types are still in the development

In 1993, faced with growing air pollution in Kathmandu, the government of Nepal banned the sale of new diesel three-wheelers imported from India. In the same year, the Kathmandu municipality invited the United States–based Global Resources Institute to design an electric three-wheeler for the city. The pilot vehicle, known as "safa tempo," was put on the road in September 1993, and U.S. Agency for International Development (USAID) support expanded to buy eight vehicles, promote the program, and train mechanics. When USAID funding ended in 1996, two local business groups started assembling, servicing, and operating electric vehicles, which sell for about $6,000. In September 1999 the government finally banned all existing diesel three-wheelers. There are now six suppliers of electric vehicles, and as of May 2000, the city has over 500 battery-powered three-wheelers, each capable of carrying up to 12 passengers. This is the world's largest fleet of electric passenger transport vehicles for use on public roads. The future is not secure, however. In May 2000 the government approved the import of 300 15-seat vans with the same preferential import duties accorded to the electric vehicles. In May 2001 it decided to ban new or transferred registration of all three-wheelers, including safa tempos, although that decision was later rescinded under pressure from donors.

Source: *The Wall Street Journal Europe*, May 30, 2000.

stage, and significant efforts are being directed to electric–internal combustion engine hybrids rather than pure electric engine vehicles. The economics of electric vehicles also depends on the price of electricity. The power sector in many developing countries is currently undergoing reform and restructuring. The long-term viability of electric vehicles should be evaluated from the standpoint of market-based power pricing. Given the current state of technology, electric vehicles would not be expected to have widespread applications; with carefully considered government intervention, however, they could play a useful, though limited, role in extremely polluted traffic corridors. Moreover, the greenhouse characteristics of electric vehicles depend critically on a full fuel cycle analysis; if the electricity is produced from present mixes (coal, oil, or gas), there may be no greenhouse benefit at all compared with a small internal combustion engine.

Hybrid diesel-electric vehicles are now being developed with some success and tested in industrialized countries under a GEF grant. Their cost is similar to that of a heavy CNG vehicle. Onboard diesel engines operated at constant load to maintain battery power for peak demands and in sensitive areas can give a 30 percent energy savings compared with a conventional diesel vehicle.

Hydrogen fuel cell. This is a widely advocated "sunrise" technology, at least for heavy-duty urban vehicles. Fuel-cell buses are already being used in trial projects, including a program funded by the United Nations Development Programme. The environmental performance of these vehicles—depending on the source of the hydrogen—can far exceed that of CNG or improved diesel engines, and their life-cycle operating costs are projected to be lower than that of CNG or diesel. It is possible that we will see such vehicles deployed in active service in urban fleets (buses and urban freight delivery applications) in the industrialized countries in about a decade. It is unlikely, however, that they will have early application in the developing countries.

Influencing fuel consumption

In industrialized countries technological improvements in engine efficiency tended to decrease both local and global pollution in the 1970s and the first half of the 1980s, although effective reductions in fuel consumption have subsequently been lost in the United States by increases in vehicle size. Possibilities for further improvement in new-vehicle fuel economy arise from reduction of vehicle size or weight; direct fuel injection, lean-burn technology; measures to increase the share of diesel (which may, however, adversely affect local pollution); and optimized engine transmission systems and hybrid vehicles. Fuel-consumption standards, such as the corporate average fuel efficiency (CAFE) standards imposed by the U.S. government and those more recently agreed on between Association des Constructeurs Européens d'Automobiles (ACEA—the organization of the European motor industry) and the European Commission, have attempted to force the pace of technological progress in this respect.[18]

In developing countries, fuel economy is affected by what is occurring in the industrialized countries through the availability and cost of imported second-hand vehicles, but they also have special problems of their own. Fuel economy is often low because of poor vehicle maintenance, fuel adulteration, and a number of other factors. Using gasoline with an octane number that is lower than that recommended by vehicle manufacturers—either because lower-octane gasoline (for example, 80 research octane number [RON]) is available and is less expensive or because gasoline is adulterated with kerosene—can decrease fuel economy, lead to knocking and ultimately to engine damage, and to higher emissions. Hence a rather different focus may be appropriate for policy on fuel economy in developing countries.

The scope for improving fuel economy is greatest in countries where a large fraction of vehicles have low engine compression ratios. In the new independent states of the former Soviet Union, many vehicles run on gasoline with a motor octane number as low as 72. Increasing the octane and the engine compression ratio will result in fuel savings—and reductions in GHG emissions—in the long run.

A staged strategy for fuels

The timing of the development of fuel-cell technology may have a significant part to play in strategic thinking about the alternatives. CNG requires significant investment in gas production, distribution infrastructure, and vehicles, which would only be recouped over a substantial period. The incremental cost of cleaning up the performance of diesel is significantly lower. Except in a few cities where the CNG infrastructure is already in place, it may make more sense, as an interim strategy, to concentrate on getting the diesel vehicles currently on the road performing well and cleanly, to gradually reduce sulfur content in diesel fuel, and to bring in cleaner diesel-vehicle technology in new vehicles on the road, while waiting for the cost of fuel cells to become viable.[19]

VEHICLE POLICY

Environmental issues for vehicles can be divided into those relating to improving new-vehicle technology, those relating to replacing the existing stock by more environmentally friendly technology, particularly with respect to motorcycles, and those relating to the use of the existing vehicle stock. Although we discuss vehicles and fuels separately here, in practice they must be considered simultaneously.

Improving vehicle technology

Largely in response to stricter vehicle emissions requirements, considerable progress has already been made in developing vehicle hardware to reduce emissions. Efficiently operated three-way catalytic converters can reduce exhaust CO and hydrocarbon emissions of gasoline vehicles by as much as 95 percent and NO_x by over 75 percent. Similarly, state-of-the-art diesel vehicles that use ultra low sulfur diesel fuel and continuously regenerating traps can be almost as clean as vehicles that use CNG. Such advanced technologies are unlikely to offer cost-effective solutions in very low income countries in the near future, but their existence makes the point—an important one to keep in mind in formulating incentive policies—that not all diesel vehicles are alike.

The EU, Japan, and the United States lead the world in setting stringent vehicle emissions standards and fuel specifications. These countries are pursuing the best available technology for further reducing emissions from new vehicles. The control measures include a combination of the following: dramatic reduction of sulfur in gasoline and diesel, to extend the useful life of the catalyst and to enable new catalyst technologies for reducing NO_x[20] and particulate emissions; new measures for control of tailpipe emissions (for example, particulate traps with regeneration for diesel engines); emerging vehicle technologies such as common-rail direct-injection diesel engines; and the use of alternative fuels for very low emission or zero emission vehicles (as are mandated in California). Although the rest of the world will probably adopt these standards and technologies some day, the issue for developing countries is how to phase in these measures cost-effectively.

In encouraging the use of catalytic converters in developing countries, a number of conditions need to be satisfied to ensure that they function effectively. These conditions are (a) wide availability of unleaded gasoline and, preferably, complete phase-out of leaded gasoline, to eliminate the chances of misfueling; (b) differentiated taxation during the transition period to prevent misfueling;[21] (c) a reasonably low level of sulfur in gasoline, preferably lower than 500 wt ppm; (d) specification of the emissions performance levels and the length of time during which the catalyst system must meet those levels; and (e) effective inspection and maintenance (I/M) to ensure that converters are operating properly. If these conditions cannot be fully satisfied, the additional cost associated with the installation of converters may not be justified by the benefits.[22] Even where effective use of catalytic converters is considered feasible, governments should consider specifying emissions levels for new vehicles rather than mandating catalytic converters per se. Retrofitting in-use vehicles with catalytic converters is not usually considered cost effective.

Options for motorcycles

Motorcycles account for about one-half of the vehicle fleet in many Asian cities (and up to 75 percent in some). In many cities motorcycles offer substantially greater speed and flexibility of movement than do inadequate and congestion-bound bus services, while being broadly comparable to them in cost. In Taiwan, China, the ownership is already 0.55 per capita. The majority of motorized two- and three-wheelers in Asia are powered by two-stroke engines, which are preferred because they have a (now only slightly) lower capital cost than do four-stroke engines, have more power (higher power-to-weight ratio, higher specific output, higher torque, and low revolutions per minute response) for a given displacement, and are simpler to self-maintain.

Unfortunately, conventional two-stroke engines are environmentally very damaging because of their inherent combustion technology; their poor maintenance and misfiring, particularly at cold start; and their frequent and excessive use of lubricants not manufactured for use in two-stroke-engine vehicles.[23] In Delhi, India, for example, 45 percent of particulate emissions and two-thirds of unburned hydrocarbon emissions in the transport sector are estimated to come from two- and three-wheelers powered by two-stroke engines. Despite this, no country has issued standards for PM (particulate matter) emissions for two- and three-wheelers, largely because there is no proven methodology for measuring oil droplets (although smoke standards might be used as a proxy standard for two-stroke engines).

The balance of advantage between two-stroke and four-stroke technologies is changing. The difference in capital cost is rapidly being eroded.[24] Taking into account differences in fuel economy and the lower cost of crankcase oil than two-stroke oil, the total annual operating cost of owning and operating a four-stroke can already be lower than that of owning and operating a two-stroke. Furthermore, the decision of one of the major market economies, Taiwan, China, to impose stringent environmental standards on two-stroke motorcycles starting in 2004 is likely to shift the economies of scale in production in favor of the four-stroke, and to concentrate future technical development on the four-stroke technology. Already, Japanese manufacturers appear to be concentrating their sales efforts on four-strokes, even where two-strokes are still legal.

Basic two-stroke technology can be improved at source by emissions-reduction technologies including electronic control for fuel metering and improved scavenging characteristics, or by after-treatment.[25] Two-stroke engines manufactured in India, meeting year 2000 emissions standards, emit very little PM. Unfortunately, the durability of catalyst and secondary air systems is limited because of the high concentration of hydrocarbons in the exhaust gas.[26] Retrofitting of improved technology is relatively expensive and ineffective for this category of small vehicle. It is therefore advisable that governments specify emissions levels for new vehicles and adopt policies to secure premature replacement for high polluters, rather than mandate catalytic converters per se. The key is to switch to four-stroke engines.

New technology does not deal with the problem of the high average age and low replacement rate of vehicles currently in use. For these vehicles, emissions on the road are usually much higher than are emissions levels found during tests, due to bad operational and maintenance practice. They are estimated to emit more than 10 times the amount of fine particulate matter per vehicle kilometer than is a modern car, and only a little less than a light diesel truck.[27] In some countries, such as Bangladesh, low-octane gasoline is used (80 RON, compared with a recommended minimum of 87 RON), and gasoline is often adulterated with inexpensive kerosene, causing engine malfunction. It is also common for the proportion of lubricant in the fuel mix to be two to three times the recommended level, even though this both increases cost and reduces performance. Nevertheless, given the strong current preference for the use of two-stroke engines, mandatory scrappage of existing fleets is likely to be politically difficult. Phasing out more gradually might be achieved by the imposition of differential license fees, according to technology and location, to encourage more-polluting vehicles to move into rural areas where pollutant concentration is less. The same effect might be achieved by refusing to license high emitters in the cities or limiting the maximum permissible age of vehicles. Subsidy of environmentally advantageous scrap-and-replace programs might also help. For two-stroke vehicles remaining in use, the first step might be to mandate an appropriate lubricant standard. Maintaining the recommended mixtures (2 percent oil for two-wheelers and 3 percent for three-wheelers) might be facilitated by the sale of premixed fuel. Driver education is an important source of improvement in this respect (box 4.3). Improved I/M are also powerful instruments.[28]

The evidence thus suggests a number of strands in a strategy for addressing the motorcycle problem.

- The information basis for policy needs to be improved through more systematic measurement of ambient air quality, the introduction of PM standards for new two-strokes, public information campaigns on fuel mix and vehicle maintenance, identification of locally cost-efficient retrofit technologies, and the establishment of secure common institutional commitment (police, inspection agencies, and so on).
- Standards on new motorcycles should be regularly reviewed and progressively tightened in the light of technological possibilities. This process would be enhanced if government announced long-term objectives with respect to fuel quality and vehicle emissions standards.
- Existing two-stroke performance should be improved by introducing minimum gasoline octane requirements (87 RON), mandating appropriate oil standards, introducing premixed fuel, introducing systematic I/M, and offering incentives for conversion to clean fuels for three-wheelers.

It is a commonly believed fallacy in some countries that if a little oil is a good thing, more must be better. In Dhaka, Bangladesh, many operators of two-stroke three-wheelers use less-expensive straight mineral oil rather than the recommended two-stroke oil. Because this gives less lubrication, they also tend to use as much as 8 or even 12 percent mix compared with the recommended 3 percent for two-stroke oil. Since two-stroke oil cost twice that of mineral oil in June 2000, following the recommended procedures would actually give a savings of 25 to 40 percent in oil costs as well as reduce engine damage and emissions. But bad habits are inbred in a generation of operators and mechanics. To counter such misinformation, training sessions for mechanics and "auto clinics" for three-wheeler taxi drivers were therefore held in 2000 under the Energy Sector Management Assistance Program. Similarly, in Pakistan, pamphlets containing basic information on fuel and lubricants have been distributed by the Hydrocarbon Development Institute.

Source: Masami Kojima, World Bank.

- High polluters should be eliminated through a program including the statistical identification of high-polluting ages and categories, testing followed by improvement to standard or buy-in of nonconforming vehicles, the introduction of tax- or license fee–incentives for low polluters in cities, and the reduction of import duties on environmentally benign vehicles and parts.

Using the existing stock of vehicles

The share of emissions is not uniformly distributed over the vehicle fleet. A fraction of all vehicles—ill maintained, often old—is typically responsible for a disproportionately high amount of pollution from the transport sector. If these "high emitters" (typically, commercial vehicles and public transport vehicles, including, in some places, two- and three-wheeler taxis with two-stroke engines) can be repaired or eliminated permanently, a considerable reduction in pollution can be achieved at relatively small cost.

The implementation of such a scheme is far from simple. To be cost effective, any scheme targeting high emitters should identify polluting vehicles with high annual vehicle kilometers traveled operating in densely populated areas. Old vehicles in very poor condition may be candidates for retirement. Those that are highly polluting but are better maintained may be considered for repair or for retrofitting with more recent vehicle technology. Complicating the issue is the fact that in some cities, such as Cairo, the proportion of old, gross polluters may be very high, with the result that targeting does not leave very many vehicles out of the scope.

APPLYING ENVIRONMENTAL STANDARDS

To apply environmental standards, it will be necessary to design appropriate vehicle inspection and maintenance programs, scrappage programs, as well as ensure that related policies are appropriate, and provide the correct incentives, including those related to domestic taxation, trade liberalization, and public expenditures.

Inspection and maintenance programs

Vehicle emissions standards and technologies are not effective without proper maintenance. Poorly maintained vehicles are high emitters and are responsible for a disproportionate share of total vehicle emissions. Data collected in India in November to December 1999 during a series of I/M "clinics" for two-wheelers indicated that minor vehicle repairs improved fuel economy by an average of 17 percent and reduced CO emissions by 44 percent. A well-run, uncorrupt I/M program should be able to strengthen the enforcement of emissions standards significantly.

Introducing effective I/M programs has proved difficult. For example, recent experience in Wuhan, China, showed that in roadside testing, 93 percent of vehicles fell short of the standard even though 97 percent of those tested in the same period at the I/M station met it.[29] Thus, wider use of spot-checking equipment capable of identifying major problems from any relevant vehicle type, and of fixed I/M stations for more thorough examination and follow-up of vehicles so identified, holds promise of significant impact on the pollution problem. An appropriate system of fines, and controls thereof, could also make such system self-financing. As far as off-road testing is concerned, experience from various parts of the world suggests that an I/M system based on centralized, high-volume, inspection-only centers with computerized emissions measurement to minimize tampering and corruption, such as the I/M system in Mexico City, is likely to be more effective than is a decentralized system with a large number of private garages participating in the I/M. If the proper controls are in place, the private sector can be an important partner in operating effective I/M programs (box 4.4).

The usual reason for not properly maintaining vehicles is to avoid out-of-pocket expenses. There are, however, certain maintenance practices that would actually yield cost savings. An example is

---

BOX 4.4 PRIVATE SECTOR VEHICLE INSPECTION AND MAINTENANCE IN MEXICO CITY

Mandatory testing for vehicle emissions in Mexico City was introduced in 1988. Initially testing was done in government test-only centers as well as in private garages that were permitted to both test and repair. Although the private sector in Mexico undertook testing more economically, initially as many as 50 percent of vehicles were estimated to obtain passes falsely. A more limited number of private test centers were therefore subsequently licensed for testing only. The Mexican experience shows that an effective testing system must evaluate emissions levels accurately, and issue and enforce certificates without corruption. To achieve this it is necessary that:

- The legal framework provides sanctions to be applied for failure to carry out the testing protocols correctly
- The testing stations must be subject to monitoring by independent bodies, and sanctions must be properly applied
- Repair work should be separate from testing
- The pass certificate must be easy to monitor
- There should be sufficient monitors (for example, traffic police) to ensure a low probability of evasion by vehicle owners
- The fine for not displaying a legal emissions test certificate should be sufficient to discourage evasion
- The technology of testing should exclude the possibility of temporary "tuning" to pass the test
- The number of licensed centers should not be too large, to avoid garages being "soft" to increase market share
- All testing centers should be subject to rigorous implementation of protocols and inspection of their procedures.

Source: World Bank 2001.

---

use of the correct kind and amount of lubricant in the two-stroke engines that are common in South Asia (box 4.3 above). At a minimum, wide public education campaigns should be undertaken to promote cost-effective practices.

Scrappage programs

When emissions standards are enforced effectively, the cost of owning old vehicles actually increases, making vehicle renewal more attractive.[30] Vehicle retirement and scrappage programs can further encourage this phenomenon as long as it is possible to identify gross emitters that are operating at a high annual rate of vehicle kilometers and that still have reasonable remaining economic lives. Considerable care is needed in designing such schemes, however. Using age as a proxy for high emissions does not always identify the worst cases. If the program is directed at urban pollution, it must also prevent the import of old vehicles from outside the city to take advantage of the retirement bonus. Evidence in Europe that may be relevant for some of the higher-income developing countries suggests that—because gross emitters are typically owned by low-income households that are often in no position to purchase much newer vehicles— cash-for-scrappage schemes may be more effective than cash-for-replacement schemes.[31] In the most polluted areas, it may even be possible to use cash-for-scrappage schemes to influence modal split.[31]

In many developing countries, particularly those in which particulate emissions are the most serious pollution concern, commercial vehicles (buses, trucks, and taxis) are the greatest contributors to urban air pollution. Some countries have been quite successful in stimulating early replacement of these vehicles. For example, Hungary offered large cash incentives for replacement of old buses and trucks with new vehicles complying with most recent emissions standards ($3,600 in 1997 dollars for a bus replacement). In the early 1990s Chile combined tax incentives with preferential treatment of environmentally benign vehicles in competitively tendered franchising arrangements to remove the most-polluting diesel buses from the urban transport fleet.

Domestic taxation policies

The importance of taxing fuels at a level that reflects the externalities, as well as the border costs and any proxy charges for road maintenance costs, was emphasized in a recent World Bank sector policy paper.[33] Although the cost of mitigating impacts is logically a better foundation for defining appropriate levels of environmental taxation valuation of damage, the evidence on marginal damage costs of the six megacities, quoted above, suggests taxes around 60 percent of the import cost of gasoline and 200 percent of that of diesel fuel.

These estimates emphasize not only the importance of the absolute levels of fuel taxes and prices but also their relative levels. Around the world the retail price of diesel is typically lower than that of gasoline, because of differential taxation. The trend is particularly pronounced in South Asia. In Bangladesh, for example, the retail price of gasoline was almost double the price of diesel in 1999. The price differential, together with the low profit margin fixed by the government for the sale of gasoline, has led to the adulteration of gasoline with kerosene and, as an unintended consequence, higher particulate emissions from vehicles. In Pakistan, where the price difference is even higher, the diesel-gasoline ratio consumed in the transport reached 5.3 to 1 in fiscal 1999/2000, which is very high by international standards. Relative tax rates may thus be encouraging the highest-mileage urban vehicles (taxis, mini-buses, and so on) to switch from gasoline—not to CNG or other clean fuels but to diesel, the fuel with the most damaging urban environmental impacts. A large price differential between kerosene and gasoline, based on the use of kerosene by the poor as a domestic heating fuel, leads to illegal addition of kerosene to gasoline, resulting in higher pollutant emissions.

The usual reason for low tax rates on diesel is its use for heavy interurban freight movement and agricultural purposes. Given that the health impact of particulate emissions is likely to be lower in low-density interurban and rural areas than in cities, the emphasis on the economic rather than the environmental impact of diesel fueling outside urban areas may not be unreasonable. Hence it is necessary to develop tax structures that protect the urban environment but that do not discourage use of the most economical fuel by agriculture or intercity freight vehicles. One possible way of doing that is to identify the most damaging vehicle types (cars, urban mini-buses, and vans) and use high duties on those types of diesel vehicle, rather than fuel taxation, as the means of changing the balance of economic advantage. That is already being done in some countries by exempting clean vehicles from import duties or vehicle license duties. Another option is to increase the tax on diesel to make the price of automotive diesel comparable to that of gasoline, but to rebate industrial and agricultural users of diesel. This approach has been adopted successfully in Chile. Another is to tax automotive diesel more and use a dye to distinguish automotive diesel from diesel for other uses.

Setting *relative* tax levels is a complex issue. In principle, one should identify the emissions values of different pollutants and structure vehicle and fuel taxes to reflect differences in the summed value of emissions for different vehicle types. In practice, however, emissions levels depend not only on the fuel type and composition but also on where and how it is burned. Moreover, the evidence on the health costs of different pollutants remains sketchy. At best, then, the use of fiscal incentives would be somewhat rough and ready. Nevertheless, on the basis of successful application of fiscal incentives in industrialized countries, it is possible to confidently recommend differentiation of excise taxes between leaded and unleaded gasoline, and between diesel and CNG.

Tax structures that discourage the purchase of new vehicles—for example, registration fees or excise taxes based on the market value of the

vehicle—may have adverse environmental impacts that should be weighed against their perceived distribution effects. Possible measures include replacing import tariffs on new vehicles by ownership taxes reflecting the environmental quality of the vehicle, eliminating the system under which vehicle registration fees are proportional to the book value of the vehicle (which makes it more expensive to own new vehicles than old ones), and minimizing the tax on the purchase of new vehicles. The fiscal impact of these changes might need to be offset by an increase in direct charges for road use. In some middle-income countries, it may be necessary to consider a safety net to offset the immediate impact of making it more costly for the poor to operate old vehicles, particularly in the taxi trade.

Trade liberalization

It is common for developing countries to use tariffs or trade barriers to protect domestic industry and to prevent the expenditure of scarce foreign exchange on luxury goods that are not essential to economic growth. Where either of these arguments is applied to the import of vehicles, the effect is likely to be the protection of outdated technology. Liberalization of vehicle trade is hence an important step, particularly in countries that have automobile-manufacturing facilities. The removal of barriers that hinder access to the technology available in the rest of the world would enable consumers in these countries to meet tighter emissions standards at least cost. Rules such as local content requirements (for example, requiring that 70 percent of the vehicle weight or content must be produced domestically) often result in inefficiency and in heavier vehicles if the percentage is based on weight. High import tariffs on new vehicles, rigid licensing schemes for imports, and quotas are all likely to slow the rate of vehicle renewal, with potentially adverse impacts on air quality (pollution); their distributional impact must therefore be weighed against their environmental effects.

Free trade in used cars raises the question of "environmental dumping." Among the largest recipient markets for used cars are Cyprus, Jamaica, Peru, Sri Lanka, and the Russian Federation, while Japan remains the largest identifiable single source of used-car exports. The forces driving the export of used cars by industrialized countries will become stronger as emissions standards become more stringent and regulations concerning the end-of-life vehicle are implemented, as in the EU.

In the interest of environmental protection, the government may limit the age of the vehicles that may be imported. For example, Hungary set the age limit to 10 years old in 1991 and progressively reduced it to 8, 6, and finally in 1997, 4 years old. Chile bans imports of used vehicles altogether. However, the purchasing pattern of vehicle owners should be carefully balanced against the hypothetical environmental advantage of restricting the import of old vehicles. If commercial operators (and, in some of the transition economies, low-income households) are in no position to buy relatively new vehicles, such an import restriction constrains the supply, and increases the price of replacement vehicles, postponing the replacement of high emitters. However, a combination of higher general taxation on motoring and environmental standards on vehicles is always likely to reconcile restraint on car use with environmental protection better than discriminatory import taxation.

Transport fuel is also an internationally traded commodity. Having an open border and being able to take advantage of superior fuels manufactured in other countries makes it much easier to phase lead out of gasoline and to implement other fuel-quality improvement measures. In some parts of the world, there is a move toward harmonizing fuel specifications to ensure minimal environmental standards, foster intraregional trade, and enhance the efficiency of supply. Fuel specifications in North America, the EU, and the countries of the former Soviet Union are already harmonized, for the most part. Similar measures have been proposed in Latin America.[34]

Public expenditure policies

The traditional role of public sector expenditure in addressing environmental externalities centers on the provision of classic public goods. These public goods include (a) maintenance of an emissions inventory and (b) setting and enforcement of standards, including establishing I/M arrangements (even if these arrangements are implemented by the private sector).

Environmental benefits are often attributed to public transport subsidies because of modal transfers from car to bus, or from bus to rail. Generally, these arguments should be treated cautiously for two reasons. First, the "preferred" modes only yield benefits if they are well patronized. Poorly loaded buses are more environmentally damaging than are well-loaded cars. Second, the environmental benefit only accrues if the subsidized modes draw their patronage from an environmentally inferior mode, rather than from new trip generation. In the case of car–public transport transfers, the evidence is that the cross-elasticity of demand between car driving and public transport is low. In the case of rail-bus transfers, which are the most common, the problems concern the financial and economic cost of securing the transfers. It is therefore wise to draw a cautious conclusion: not that it is impossible to secure environmental benefit from public transport subsidies, but that subsidy alone might be an inefficient means of securing that environmental benefit. Public transport subsidy is best addressed in the much wider context of improving congestion and distribution, as well as in the context of environmental benefits. Other forms of environmentally focused subsidy can represent better value for money. As argued above, well-targeted support of premature retirement of environmentally damaging vehicles or fuel conversions is much more likely to yield high benefits-per-dollar committed.

There is, of course, much more to public expenditure decisions. Giving priority to infrastructure for public transport and NMT may be more effective in changing modal choice than may subsidies,

SYSTEM MANAGEMENT POLICIES

System management policies to reduce the environmental impact of urban traffic can be divided into three categories. These categories are (a) those giving priority to less-polluting modes, (b) those relieving the impact by allowing traffic to perform in a more environmentally friendly way, and (c) those relieving the impact by reducing traffic volumes.

Public transport priorities

In developing countries, buses are often the transport mode of choice for the poor, but they are frequently highly polluting because of the many stops and starts and idle running of engines in heavy traffic. Giving priority to buses not only reduces their direct environmental impact but also improves their attractiveness with respect to the private car. It also improves their finances. The construction of separated busways, as has been done in several Brazilian cities, or even a highly integrated priority bus network, as in Curitiba, appears capable of affecting car ownership and, more significantly, car use. It is still doubtful how far good bus services by themselves can defer or deter motorization. The case for bus priorities will thus be a combination of economic, distributional, and environmental considerations.

In this context it is appropriate to consider the concern that economic liberalization of transport operations will have adverse environmental consequences. In road haulage, where liberalization is best established, it has usually increased both average vehicle size and load factor. As long as this is accompanied by adequate enforcement of emissions standards, the effect should be beneficial rather than harmful. In the bus industry the opposite appears to have happened, with both average vehicle size and load per vehicle falling, often in the context of poor environmental enforcement. In the absence of a well-functioning regulatory system, complete liberalization of

bus services, such as has occurred in Mexico City and Lima, has clearly increased environmental pollution. That outcome is not inevitable, however. For example, faced with this effect in Santiago, the Chilean government successfully introduced competition "for the market," in the form of a competitively tendered franchising system using environmental quality of the vehicle as one of the selection criteria. This highlights the importance of concentrating on regulatory reform, rather than simple deregulation; this is discussed further in chapter 7.

Traffic management

Traffic congestion reduces average speed and increases most emissions (except for NO_x). Traffic congestion worsens the emissions of both local and global pollutants. Increasing the average speed in city traffic from 10 kilometers per hour (km/h) to 20 km/h could cut CO_2 emissions by nearly 40 percent. Increasing vehicle speed from 12 to 15 km/h to 30 km/h in Bangkok and Kuala Lumpur was estimated to be equivalent to installing three-way catalytic converters in 50 percent of the cars in these cities. Experience suggests, however, that though it is possible to reduce congestion in the short run, this favorable result invites greater car use in the long run, thus ultimately resulting in further congestion. Studies have shown that measures to decrease traffic congestion by providing more road space eventually increase the volume of traffic.[35]

More subtle forms of traffic management may be able to reduce unit emissions rates without generating extra traffic to negate the benefit. Coordination of traffic lights is generally beneficial. Traffic-calming devices, which slow traffic down but do not stop it, may also result in cleaner, as well as safer, traffic. Good signage can prevent excessive "hunting" movements for scarce parking space.

Traffic restraint

In the industrial economies, demand for more space in lower-density settlement, and the vehicle ownership and use associated with it, have all proved income elastic, while at high incomes and low motoring costs, the price elasticity of demand for car travel has been low. Increased vehicle fleet and mileage may therefore appear inevitable as economies develop. The political feasibility of denying those economic characteristics has also been widely doubted.

In some of the world's most congested and polluted cities, politicians are reassessing that conservative judgment; some quite direct attacks on vehicle use have been recently made for environmental reasons. Exclusion of some vehicles, selected by registration numbers from all roads on particular days, as in the "hoy no circula" ("do not drive today") scheme, first imposed in Mexico City in 1989 and subsequently copied in other cities, such as São Paulo, can result in dramatic reductions in traffic volume during the first months of implementation. In the longer term, however, the schemes may be counterproductive because some households purchase an additional vehicle or retain an old and polluting vehicle that would have otherwise been replaced, in order to avoid the effect of the restrictions. The most recent variant of this strategy, the "pico y placa" ("peak-hour restrictions by license plate number") scheme in Bogotá, applies only to peak hours, but increases to two the number of days per week on which each vehicle is kept off the road.

Further focusing restraint to exclude all vehicles from particularly sensitive areas (such as pedestrian-only city shopping centers or residential areas) is now adopted in many countries, and is increasingly being provided for in initial planning of new development. When first introduced it was believed that this type of measure would reduce trade in the controlled areas and hence be resisted by traders. In actuality, however, it appears not to have had that effect and, when associated with good planning of preferential public transport access, can reduce private road traffic over a broader area.

For the broadest impacts, economic instruments still look the most promising. The World Bank energy sector strategy argues that it should be the objective for all countries to integrate local environmental and social externality costs into energy pricing and investment decisions.[36] The extreme case is that of Singapore, where very strong political action to limit the stock of cars to that deemed sustainable has been implemented through the auctioning of a controlled stock of certificates to purchase vehicles as well as by congestion pricing in the CBD and some of its major freeway accesses.[37] The existence of a single jurisdiction with the ability to use the revenues from vehicle taxation to finance other supporting elements of a comprehensive policy seems important to that case. Perhaps equally significant, in the United Kingdom the legal provision of revenues from congestion pricing to accrue to the local authority introducing it has been the basis for the development of new enthusiasm for the pricing device from business as well as environmental interests.

In some industrialized countries, studies also indicate that, in the long run, own-price elasticity for gasoline consumption is significant enough to make fuel taxation a potential policy instrument for reducing vehicle usage and kilometers traveled. A World Bank study concluded that a judicious use of gasoline tax could save the citizens of Mexico City $110 million a year more than would an otherwise well-designed control program with no gasoline tax.[38] This might be accentuated by converting some of the other costs of ownership (such as insurance, parking, and vehicle taxation) into costs of use, although in many developing countries these charges are low and often evaded.

NMT modes are the least polluting of all modes, as well as often being the less expensive for short-distance movements. The elimination of impediments to NMT thus has environmental benefits, in addition to the poverty focus advantages discussed in chapter 9.

CONCLUSIONS: A STRATEGY FOR URBAN TRANSPORT AND ENVIRONMENT

A number of strong conclusions arise from the above discussion of strategic priorities.

On basic knowledge
Better basic understanding both improves policy identification and helps to persuade decision-makers to implement the policies:

- Local data collection and analysis on vehicle registrations and on levels and sources of ambient air pollution
- Development of better understanding of the health impacts of different small particulate emissions from transport (although this development may be better left to the industrialized countries)
- Dissemination of basic knowledge on environmental impacts of transport modes (for example, optimal oil/fuel mix for two-stroke gasoline engines)
- Education campaigns on efficient vehicle operation, maintenance, and so on.

On technological priorities
While it is generally preferable to concentrate on performance standards, rather than on specific technology preference, there are some relatively clear-cut technological priorities:

- Elimination of lead from gasoline
- Replacement of two-stroke by four-stroke motorcycles
- Elimination or cleaning up of high-mileage, heavily polluting vehicles; the Bank can help both with technical assistance in these fields and, in some cases, with the financing of public infrastructure and incentive mechanisms to stimulate change
- Introduction of computerized I/M regimes administered by centralized, private sector contractors, subject to scrutiny to prevent corruption, and targeted initially at old and high-polluting vehicle categories.

On managing transport demand
Technological and fiscal measures must be complemented by a coherent transport management strategy lest increasing traffic volumes swamp the beneficial effects of other measures. This would include:

- Public transport investment programs, including improved conditions for walking and cycling
- Traffic management, including rigorously enforced priorities for public transport in congested and environmentally sensitive areas
- Traffic-calming and other measures of demand management.

On incentive systems
Because most critical decisions about travel behavior are made by individuals, and are largely driven by economic self-interest, tax levels and structures are often decisive in determining the amount of transport undertaken, choice of mode, technology, and fuel. This emphasizes:

- Tax reform both to restrain demand for transport to an efficient and environmentally acceptable level and to generate efficient incentives in the choice of vehicle and fuel type, size of vehicle, and location and timing of vehicle use
- Exploration of ways to overcome limitations of fiscal measures associated with multiple sectors and multiple objectives.

On institutions
Because there are multiple pollutants and multiple types of ambient conditions, comprehensive, multi-instrument packages need to be tailored to specific local circumstances. This requires:

- Assessment of environmental impacts as an integral part of transport and land-use structure planning
- Development of technical competence and probity in administration as an essential prerequisite for effective action, because of the complexity of these packages

- Development of concerted action between jurisdictions and tiers of government.

The Bank can help to identify and focus on major polluters, and can help in the international exchange of experience in designing integrated urban environmental strategies. Moreover, integration of transport interventions in general municipal development packages may offer better leverage than transport-specific projects, as cities seek to reduce pollution.

NOTES

1. IPCC 1996.
2. Lvovsky and others 2000.
3. Schipper and Marie-Lilliu 1999.
4. Eskeland and Xie 1998.
5. Eskeland and Devarajan 1996.
6. For technological detail of the issues involved, see Kojima and Lovei 2001.
7. The advisory board to the U.S. National Toxicology Program has recommended that diesel exhaust particles be listed as "reasonably anticipated to be a human carcinogen."
8. Recent studies have found a significant independent effect on premature mortality for ozone if the important nonlinear effects of temperature (and humidity) are taken into account (Holgate and others 1999).
9. Ideally, a comprehensive urban air strategy policy should involve the systematic collection of air quality data and identification of major sources contributing to the pollutants of concern. Source apportionment analysis, emissions inventorization coupled with dispersion modeling, can be carried out to identify which sources should be targeted for control. These steps will then enable comparison of costs and benefits of different identified measures for improving air quality, and to identify priority actions (Kojima and Lovei 2001).
10. Lovei 1996.
11. Sulfur in diesel was lowered to 0.05 weight percent (500 parts per million by weight, wt ppm) in 1993 in the United States and in 1996 in Europe to meet new standards for particulate emissions. This move came after a number of vehicle technology measures had substantially lowered the carbonaceous contribution to particulate emissions.
12. In the United States the Air Quality Improvement Research Program of 1989–95 found that high-emitting, poorly maintained vehicles contributed about 80 percent of total vehicle emissions but represented only about 20 percent of the population. Improving fuel quality decreased emissions somewhat but not nearly as much as changing vehicle technology (for example, by identifying and repairing old vehicles). Similarly, the European Programme on Emissions, Fuels and Engine Technologies found that the spread in emissions levels related to vehicle technologies was wider than the variations attributable to fuels.
13. In comparison with a modern, catalyzed gasoline car, a CNG-fueled car of equivalent size has been estimated to emit approximately 10 to 20 percent less CO_2 and particulates per vehicle kilometer, up to 25 percent less NO_x, and 80 percent less CO, nonmethane hydrocarbons, and other smog-forming emissions. For buses, compared with diesel 80S Euro 2 bus, a lean-burn CNG bus has an advantage in all the major pollutants, including a 20 percent advantage in global warming gases and an 85 percent advantage in particulates, despite the fact that the modern clean diesel bus emits only one-quarter of the NOx and one-eighth the particulates of the diesel bus of 1990. The stoichiometric CNG bus has a smaller advantage over diesel in CO and CO_2 (only 10 percent) than the lean-burn version, but an even greater advantage in NO_x. For a fuller discussion and sources of statistics quoted here, see Gwilliam 2000a.
14. For example, transportation and distribution double the wellhead price for a refueling station on the Atlantic coast of Colombia, but give a station cost five times the wellhead price for the central zone, where the distribution network is only 20 percent utilized. The real economic cost is thus lowest in urban areas close to the gas fields.

15. For example, for the barest 12-meter low-floor bus, the extra cost of a CNG vehicle might be $30,000 on a price of $120,000. For the more sophisticated vehicles used in urban transport in the U.S. and Western Europe, the basic cost might be twice that, while the incremental cost of CNG would not increase proportionately. That might be reduced by international unification of regulations for homologation and safety, and eventually through scale economies in OEM. In developing countries retrofitting is the norm, as the conversion of existing vehicles may be less expensive, even in the long run, than premature replacement by dedicated new vehicles.

16. LPG requires pressures ranging from 4 to 13 bar, compared with 200 bar for CNG.

17. At present the weight of available lead/acid batteries is likely to account for nearly 40 percent of the vehicle mass, limiting speed to about 40 km/h and range to about 55 kilometers. The cost of eight batteries and additional modifications required for a three-wheeler is about $1,000, which doubles the price of electric compared with two-stroke gasoline three-wheelers. While battery technologies under development (Ni MH or Lithium Ion) may raise achievable speeds to over 50 km/h and range to over 100 kilometers, these performance levels are still much inferior to those of existing technologies.

18. ACEA (the organization of the European motor industry) and the European Commission have agreed that average CO_2 emissions from new cars will be reduced by one-quarter compared with current levels, to 140 grams per kilometer by 2008.

19. For further guidance on selection of technology, see TRB 1998a.

20. Nitrogen oxides (NO_x) are formed during combustion as nitrogen in the air reacts with oxygen at high temperatures. The amount of NO_x formed can be reduced by controlling the peak combustion temperature (for example, by recirculating exhaust gas in vehicles), by reducing the amount of oxygen available during combustion, or by converting NO_x to nitrogen and oxygen-containing inorganic compounds after its for-mation (for example, by installing three-way catalytic converters for gasoline engines).

21. Many countries have made effective use of differentiated taxation—taxing leaded gasoline more than unleaded gasoline—to encourage the use of unleaded gasoline and prevent the use of leaded gasoline in cars equipped with catalytic converters. In the absence of such a fiscal policy, control programs need to be in place to prevent permanent deactivation of catalytic converters on a large scale as a result of misfueling. The effectiveness of differentiated taxation depends on the extent to which fuel quality—in this case, leaded versus unleaded gasoline—is enforced.

22. Unfortunately, there are many examples of uncoordinated policies. In one country the government is proposing mandatory installation of catalytic converters in heavy-duty diesel vehicles without taking measures to lower the sulfur level in diesel (currently 0.7 weight percent, or 7,000 parts per million by weight [wt ppm]). At such a high sulfur level, the life of the catalyst will be shortened, and the oxidation catalyst will merely oxidize sulfur completely to SO_3 (and sulfate particulate matter will form), thereby significantly *increasing* particulate emissions. In another country the government mandated catalytic converters in passenger cars without specifying the emissions levels to be met—an omission that could defeat the purpose of the new requirement. In other cases, catalytic converters have been mandated without a reliable system of providing unleaded gasoline.

23. Kojima, Brandon, and Shah 2000.

24. For example, in June 2000 the current prices of three-wheelers from an ex-showroom in Delhi, inclusive of all state and local taxes, are Rs. 66,500 (US$1,359) for a two-stroke vehicle and Rs. 70,500 (US$1,440) for the four-stroke equivalent. In July 2001 no difference was discernible in the average price of equivalent two-stroke and four-stroke machines.

25. Typically consisting of a catalyst to oxidize HC (hydrocarbon) and CO, and secondary air to assist conversion.

26. The durability standard for catalytic converters in Taiwan, China, is still only 15,000 kilometers, although in 2000 the Society of Indian Automobile Manufactures offered to give a warranty of 30,000 kilometers for all two- and three-wheeler vehicles fitted with catalytic converters. Even this is only one year's life for a typical three-wheeler in commercial use.

27. Weaver and Chan 1996.

28. In a recent U.S. Agency for International Development (USAID)–financed program, the Society of Indian Automotive Manufactures undertook free emissions tests for 65,000 participants in 12 locations over a three-week period. Vehicles failing the test were given a free mechanical check involving carburetor adjustment, spark plug cleaning and adjustment, and air filter cleaning. As a result of this minor maintenance, emissions of HC (hydrocarbons) were reduced by 30.9 percent and those of CO by 59.7 percent.

29. Roth 1996.

30. Empirical evidence from Spain suggests that changes in the I/M program may have had considerable effects on trends in first-time vehicle registration (European Conference of Ministers of Transport 1999a).

31. European Conference of Ministers of Transport 1999a.

32. In a pilot program implemented in 1996 in British Columbia, Canada, owners were offered the choice of cash or a one-year free transit pass (worth about 1,000 Canadian dollars) on the local public transport network, to replace vehicles of model year 1983 or older. Fifty-two percent of the owners participating in the program chose the second option.

33. World Bank 1996.

34. There is a tradeoff between harmonizing fuel specifications and setting site-specific fuel standards. Ideally, provided that the distribution system can handle segregation of different fuels, cleaner (and costlier to produce) transport fuels should be used in large cities, and fuels with less-stringent specifications should only be used in areas outside urban centers. Leakages and other enforcement problems, as well as the logistics of delivering fuels of different qualities to different depots, make it difficult to implement regional differentiation cost effectively. Countries that import the bulk of their transport fuels typically find it easier to harmonize with neighboring countries than with countries that have domestic refineries. Trade considerations (between Canada and the United States, within Central America, and within the European Union [EU]) are a strong driving force for harmonizing fuel specifications. In the case of developing countries, harmonizing fuel specifications with North America or the EU is most unlikely to be cost effective.

35. The U.S. Environmental Protection Agency suggests that up to one-half of the annual U.S. traffic growth of 2.7 percent could be a result of construction of added road capacity, while a report of the British Standing Committee on Trunk Road Assessment in 1994 concluded that increasing the capacity of the road network eased congestion only temporarily because of additional generated traffic (Sactra 1994).

36. World Bank 1998.

37. Willoughby 2000b.

38. Eskeland and Devarajan 1996.

5 URBAN TRANSPORT SAFETY AND SECURITY

Nearly 0.5 million people die and up to 15 million people are injured in urban road accidents in developing countries each year, at a direct economic cost of between 1 and 2 percent of worldwide gross domestic product. A majority of victims are poor pedestrians and bicyclists. Fears for personal safety and security significantly deter the use of nonmotorized transport. This burden of physical harm that is borne by the poor can be reduced by improved road design, traffic management, medical service, and by policy improvement. This solution requires comprehensive action by a well-trained, committed, adequately financed, and organizationally integrated public sector.

THE SCALE OF THE ISSUE

This chapter distinguishes between the problems of transport *safety*, which are defined as vulnerability to accidental injury (usually involving at least one vehicle as the instrument causing the injury), and the problems of transport *security*, which are defined as vulnerability to intentional criminal or antisocial acts suffered by those engaged in trip making.

Recent conservative estimates suggest that, in 1999, between 750,00 and 880,000 people died as a direct result of road accidents.[1] The World Health Organization (WHO) puts the number even higher—at 1.171 million people.[2] About 85 percent of these deaths occurred in the developing and transitional economies; about one-half were in urban areas. In addition, between 25 and 35 million people were injured in road accidents worldwide, of which up to 75 percent were in urban areas. The economic cost of the accidents in the developing world has been estimated at $65 billion, which is approximately equal to the total annual aid and lending of the international institutions to these countries. For the developing countries, the economic cost of

accidents is estimated to be between 1 and 2 percent of their gross domestic product (GDP). Road accidents currently rank ninth as a cause of deaths worldwide, and are expected to rise to sixth by the year 2020. Even more significant, because many of the people killed are relatively young, road accidents already rank second in terms of reductions in life expectancy. In Bangladesh, it is reported that nearly 50 percent of hospital beds are occupied by road-accident victims.[3]

The security problem is less well quantified or recognized. It particularly affects pedestrians and cyclists, but also affects people in cars and public transport vehicles. In extreme cases, such as the injuries or deaths of passengers in the South African minibus "wars," there is some record of the occurrence of events. More usually the acts of personal violence or harassment—particularly sexual harassment in public transport vehicles—do not get recorded. Social surveys in Latin America have demonstrated their prevalence (Gomez 2000).

The significance of poor safety and security is twofold. First, there is the direct injury and trauma suffered by victims. According to a recent public transport survey carried out in Lima, 10 percent of those interviewed had been involved in a traffic accident on public transport during the previous six months.[4] Second, there is the effect of the perception of vulnerability on the travel patterns of a much wider spectrum of people. The major constraint on the use of non-motorized transport (NMT) is the fear of accident or attack, or of a bicycle's being stolen while it is parked. The diminishing trip rates now being experienced in some of the larger South American cities have been partly attributed to the sense of insecurity experienced by potential passengers. While this affects all social groups, the most vulnerable people appear to be those who have no alternative to an insecure mode of travel, and whose protection takes the form of withdrawal from a socially important activity (for example, evening education of women). When a wage earner in a poor family is badly injured, the whole family economy may collapse, because there is usually neither insurance compensation nor a social security safety net to protect them (box 5.1).

SAFETY

The World Bank's concern with transport safety is not new. Periodic reviews during the past two decades have shown an increasing proportion of projects with an explicitly stated safety objective and safety components, with nearly one-half of transport projects having safety elements in the latest cohort examined.[5] However, most of these efforts arose as part of the design of infrastructure improvements or traffic management systems, with safety audits becoming a common part of new transport infrastructure projects. Improvement of the accident databases has been included in many projects. The total cost of these activities was estimated as only about 1 percent of total project costs.

Relatively few projects have had transport safety as their primary objective. The Mexico Highway Rehabilitation and Traffic Safety Project included institutional strengthening, research, and training, and a $14 million expenditure on black-spot improvements. The Buenos Aires Urban Transport Project included an even larger sum to eliminate

---

BOX 5.1 ROAD ACCIDENTS AND THE POOR IN SRI LANKA

A study of pedestrian road accidents in Sri Lanka showed that only 5 percent of accidents reported to the police resulted in any form of compensation. Even where compensation was paid, the average amount was 500 rupees (about US$5).

A thousand pedestrians and cyclists are killed in the country each year. The maximum compensation payable is only 100,000 rupees (about US$1,040), compared with the unlimited sum payable for damage to property, which may run to millions of rupees. The victims' loss of earnings is often not covered by motor insurance. Moreover, the legal procedure in making such a claim is too lengthy for the poor to even attempt.

The Motor Traffic Act should clearly stipulate a reasonable and fair compensation for pedestrians and cyclists. There is also need for provision of free (or affordable) legal aid to assist the poor and uneducated in making such claims, and for counseling and rehabilitation in the case of the severely injured.

Source: Kumarage 1998.

---

at-grade road crossings of the urban and suburban rail network, to speed up rail travel, and to reduce accidents. The most comprehensive effort, however, was the collaborative effort with the PHARE program of the European Union (EU) to improve traffic safety in six countries of Eastern and Central Europe from 1992 to 1994.

The outcomes of these interventions, and others of the same type, have been variable. A review of 25 projects in the early 1990s found them to be equally divided between the categories of successful, partly successful, and unsuccessful interventions.[6] Physical measures were usually implemented, but their effects seldom measured; enforcement efforts were often initially successful, but rarely sustained; and road-user education and legislative reform efforts were most successful when carried out by a well-established coordinating body, such as a national safety council. Above all, few projects were judged to have improved institutional capacity to undertake traffic safety activities beyond the project itself. Of growing concern, also, has been the protection of vulnerable road users, with measures to protect NMT being an important part of recent urban transport projects, in China in particular. The core weaknesses have been the poor level of awareness and commitment of governments and an unwillingness to create a strong enough institutional focus for a concerted, sustained effort.

Despite the horrifying statistical evidence, it remains difficult to persuade governments to give priority to road safety either as a transport problem or as a health problem. For example, a study of road safety in Ethiopia estimated that the annual cost of road accidents was the equivalent of 40 million Ethiopian birr ($4.8 million) per year. However, a suggestion that 2 percent of a newly established road fund (equivalent to 400,000 birr, or $47,450) be spent on a comprehensive crash-reduction program each year was rejected by the government.[7] This reflects a certain sense of fatalism and apathy about the problem, nurtured by the belief that, because of the strong human element in accident causation, there can be no well-

established, cost-effective intervention packages for accident prevention, as there are to address other scourges of morbidity and mortality.

To redress that apathy, the magnitude and nature of road accidents must be properly understood. Governments must be convinced that effective action is possible and that institutional arrangements can be put in place so that necessary actions can be effectively implemented. For that reason the Global Road Safety Partnership, established as the result of a World Bank initiative, has concentrated its early efforts on mobilizing the private sector and civil society to assume their responsibilities in road safety, increasing awareness of the nature of the problem, and identifying a limited number of pilot initiatives which can show that something can really be done about it. This section concentrates on the main elements of understanding the phenomenon, policy formulation, infrastructure design, traffic management, medical policies, and institutions.

UNDERSTANDING THE PHENOMENON

A primary source of policy neglect has been the absence of reliable evidence on the magnitude and nature of the problem of transport safety. Road accident fatalities and serious injuries have long been known to be substantially underreported in official police statistics in developing countries, and should be adjusted up by 10 percent, at the very least.[8] The situation is worse with respect to injury-only accidents.[9] Even within the injury-only accidents recorded in hospital statistics, there is likely to be some bias. For example, females represented only one out of every seven casualties in urban Zimbabwe, probably due to the reduced ability of low-wage earners (often including women) to afford hospital treatment.

The impact of road accidents is concentrated on some classes of vulnerable road users. Pedestrians account for more than twice the proportion of those injured in developing, as compared with industrialized, countries. Drivers and passengers of motorcycles and three-wheel motor vehicles account for fewer than 10 percent of those injured in developing countries, but up to two-thirds of those injured in some East Asian cities, such as Kuala Lumpur. Public transport passengers, particularly those traveling in the back of a commercial truck or pickup truck, are very vulnerable. In many countries drivers of trucks and buses have particularly bad accident records.

While males between the ages of 16 and 54 account for the majority of injury from accidents in all countries, about 15 percent of those killed in developing countries are children, which is a much higher proportion than that in industrialized countries. Although the police rarely collect income data, recent interviews of pedestrians involved in road accidents in a number of countries show that the poor were disproportionately affected. The damage is even higher where the injured are the main income earners in a household. Studies in Bangladesh and Zimbabwe have shown that 80 percent of those injured have family members who are entirely dependent upon them.

The location of accidents also varies significantly between countries. The majority of urban accidents in industrialized countries occur at intersections, while most urban accidents in developing countries are reported to occur between intersections. Relatively few accidents occur where there are any traffic controls, including traffic police. This is partly because in the absence of effective development control, unrestricted access to main roads increases the risk of a collision. It is also partly attributable to the different mix of vehicle types that are using the roads; this is particularly seen in the juxtaposition of motorized and NMT users, who are more vulnerable between intersections, where speed differences are greatest.

The absence of adequate accident statistics is important, not only because it diverts attention from the seriousness of the problem but also because it hinders the search for, and selection of, appropriate remedies. Identifying the most vulnerable locations, types of accident, and types of person involved is the basis for road-safety policy

design. Introduction of an effective system of accident recording and analysis is thus a very high priority for international assistance. Because accident analysis would be useful to a range of agencies (including the police, the judiciary, insurance companies, car manufacturers, and traffic management agencies), the case can be made for the analysis to be done as independently as possible, perhaps by a road research institute. Alternatively, it should be a function of the traffic management agency. Computer programs developed for analysis in Denmark, the United Kingdom, and elsewhere are already in use in many countries. But that analysis is only as good as the attention to recording of accident detail in the police records. A critical part of the development of an accident analysis capability is to persuade police chiefs to collect, process, and transfer to the responsible agency the data needed for traffic safety analysis—rather than only those needed for legal purposes—and to train their staff accordingly.

POLICY FORMULATION

In most industrialized countries, increases in road accidents have been associated with the increase in car ownership and usage. A large proportion of deaths and injuries occur to vehicle occupants. Many countries, but most notably Australia, Japan, and the United Kingdom, have developed comprehensive programs to reduce the incidence and severity of road accidents; these programs are based on a combination of engineering, enforcement, and education. Urban traffic safety is also a current priority of the EU.[10] Measures include improvements in infrastructure design (which are often informed by black-spot analysis), vehicle characteristics (particularly compulsory installation and use of safety belts [seatbelts]), and driving behavior (such as blanket speed limits in urban areas and campaigns to discourage "drinking and driving"). High-level goals (such as Sweden's Vision Zero goal of no deaths from road crashes) are typically adopted and advertised at the national level, but are made operational at local levels by municipal and other highway authorities. These programs have been supported by a high level of agreement and coordination between different authorities under different ministries and with different budgets.

Similar comprehensive road-safety programs can be successful in developing countries. For example, in the early 1990s the Asian Development Bank assisted the government of Fiji to develop a broad national road-safety action plan that reduced road deaths by 20 percent. However, because of the differences in traffic composition and consequently in the characteristics of accidents and of the most vulnerable groups, different policy instruments are likely to be of high priority in developing countries.

INFRASTRUCTURE DESIGN

There is no doubt that good design of road infrastructure can help substantially. Improvements in road surface and horizontal and vertical alignment at black spots has proved very effective in a number of cases.[11] Clear definitions of, and implementation of, a road hierarchy can help to match the use and operating speed of roads to their immediate environment. Much is already well known about measures to protect the pedestrians and cyclists, who are the most vulnerable road users. Proper provision of footways, controlled signals for at-grade pedestrian crossings, grade-separated crossings, pedestrian-only areas, and segregated bicycle lanes and tracks are all effective and, in comparison with most infrastructure, relatively inexpensive.[12] For example, on the basis of pilot projects in East Africa, undertaken as part of the Sub-Saharan Africa Transport Program, it was argued that serious urban pedestrian and bicycle traffic crashes can be reduced significantly by a suitable program of road (and intersection) redesign and traffic calming.[13]

That type of experience needs to be generalized and disseminated. Considerable effort has already been put into the preparation of design manuals for safe road infrastructure. In 1991 the British Overseas Development Agency (now the Department for International Development)

funded the preparation of a manual entitled "Towards Safer Roads in Developing Countries," which has been widely disseminated, both in the English and Spanish versions. The Asian Development Bank has funded road-safety guidelines for the Asia and Pacific region, and country-specific road-safety engineering manuals have been developed in a number of countries, including Bangladesh, Indonesia, Kenya, and Malaysia. The Inter-American Development Bank has undertaken similar work in Latin America.[14] Incorporation of a safety audit of road (and traffic management system) designs by an independent consultant is likely to be a cost-effective way of avoiding the need for black-spot improvement programs later.

Safety is a necessity rather than a luxury, but conventional methods of cost-benefit analysis may make it look like a luxury unless the benefits of improved safety are appropriately valued. There is, of course, an understandable reluctance to attribute a money value to the saving of life or to the reduction of pain and grief. Certainly international comparisons of the value of life are invidious. For allocations of committed funds in explicitly safety-oriented projects, the issue can be evaded by use of cost-effectiveness analysis to compare alternative project designs. But where it is a matter of safety-related design components of investments, for which the bulk of impacts are time- or vehicle operating–cost savings, the omission of safety valuation will make safe design appear as an uneconomic luxury. It is therefore suggested that all governments insist that safety benefits be attributed a value that appears reasonable in terms of local conditions. More-detailed advice on how they might approach evaluation is available.[15]

Road-safety plans and action programs have been prepared in many countries, usually by external consultants piggybacked onto other projects. While these programs have been very broad, they were often led by road-safety professionals, with only limited support from the local enforcement and legal authorities.

TRAFFIC MANAGEMENT

Where there is no independent traffic-safety analysis unit, the safety functions of a "traffic management agency" generally commence with retrieval of accident data from the traffic police. There is often no systematic, periodic transfer of data from traffic police to the traffic management agency, with data retrieved on an ad hoc basis to resolve particular accident problems. A methodical approach requires that the traffic management agency obtain data on a regular basis and that procedures be established within the traffic management agency to allow the accident data to be analyzed to determine problematic sites, periods, groups, trends, and so on. Various proprietary accident-analysis software programs are available, but any simple database software package can be used.

Although a traffic management agency may have a separate road-safety group with the responsibility to analyze accident data, promote safety programs, and review schemes, safety should be regarded as an integral part of any traffic management scheme design and should be an important evaluation criterion governing the acceptance of any scheme or measure. In some countries, such as the United Kingdom, all but the simplest of schemes are subject to an "Independent Safety Audit." This involves scrutiny by traffic management designers who were not involved in the original scheme planning and design. In some developing cities, it is acknowledged that there may be few experienced traffic management staff and there may be a lack of resources for hiring consultants. Nevertheless, the savings in social costs from the introduction of "safe" schemes should more than offset costs; the independent safety audit is worth consideration as part of the normal design process.

It is generally accepted that in industrialized countries, the three most common causes of fatalities and injuries are (a) excess driving speed, (b) driving under the influence of alcohol, and (c) inadequate protection of vulnerable persons in accidents. At the national level there should be enforced systematic policies for dealing with each, while at the local level those policies should be rigorously enforced.

Speed limits and controls are powerful instruments to reduce the severity of accidents. On local roads in European cities, a wide range of physical traffic-calming measures for speed control has been used effectively. Typical measures include:

- Pedestrian refuges that narrow the effective road width
- The control of vehicle overtaking (passing) and prevention of vehicles from reaching high speeds
- Road humps, to reduce vehicle speed
- Road narrowing, to prevent heavy vehicles from using a road or to restrict movement of vehicles to one direction at a time
- Chicanes, to force vehicles to follow a tortuous route and thus reduce speed
- Raised intersections, comprising a plateau or flat-topped road hump built across an entire intersection
- Plantings, to change the perceived width of a road in order to encourage vehicles to reduce speed.

On main roads, speed limits must be enforced by the traffic police by various means—direct measurement by radar guns, static or mobile camera enforcement, following vehicles, and so on. Traffic calming can also reduce traffic speeds, especially if carefully related to the hierarchy of roads. On main roads, effective devices include positive signs and road markings emphasizing speed limits, rumble devices, bar markings, road texture and color on the approaches to critical locations (intersections, pedestrian crossings, and so on), and adjustment of intersection traffic-signal timings to control and maintain a desired safe speed of traffic progression. However, some of the more extreme physical traffic-calming measures used on local roads might add to accident hazards if introduced on main roads.

The strict enforcement of stringent national standards on drinking and driving is the basis for reducing the second serious cause of accidents. The right to perform random tests assists enforcement, but may be a platform for corruption in some countries. Holding employers of professional drivers, as well as the drivers themselves, responsible is also a powerful inducement to effective control, especially in public transport companies. Above all, it is important that it is the outcome (reduction of drunken driving) and not any particular procedure (for example, daily medical inspection of drivers as routinely required in many countries of the former Soviet Union) that is subject to control.

In industrialized countries, efforts to protect persons in accidents have concentrated on seat belt and airbag installation and use. In some middle-income developing countries, the emphasis has been on the use of crash helmets by bicyclists and motorcyclists. In many poorer countries, however, the real issue is the protection of pedestrians from motorized vehicles; the provision of adequate sidewalks, barriers, and road-crossing facilities is most important. While the provision of pedestrian bridges or tunnels may offer the greatest potential protection, it may not be the most effective measure, especially where the crossings involve arduous detours or are designed as a potential operating ground for thieves.

MEDICAL POLICIES

There is considerable evidence that the lack of adequate medical facilities contributes to the high level of fatalities in developing-country cities.[16] Many lives could be saved if medical attention were provided within the hour immediately following an accident (the "golden hour"). This requires the improvement of emergency service response time, which can often be improved at modest cost by the following:

- Strategic positioning of emergency service centers (perhaps first aid stations at fuel stations)

- Provision of an emergency telephone number
- Establishment of a control center
- Use of ITS (Intelligent Transport Systems) applications for efficient service control
- Setting up an emergency medical services committee
- Provision of first aid training
- Creation of a mechanism, possibly funded by insurance companies, to cover costs of minor expenses in bringing injured persons to the hospital
- Upgrading hospital emergency rooms and departments.

INSTITUTIONS

In many countries too many different agencies and institutions have some responsibility for road safety for it to be viewed as the primary responsibility—and hence institutional priority—for any of them. Moreover, some of those institutions, notably the police departments, often have such a bad image in developing countries that both citizens and international institutions may be loathe to support them.[17] It is therefore important that emphasis should be placed on the development of an institutional focus for transport (particularly road) safety. Emphasis thus needs to be given to developing an institutional responsibility for coordination of safety efforts at a very high level, while at the same time enhancing the commitment of the interested line agencies (police, traffic management, health, and education), at both the national and local levels. Direct responsibility of the national road-safety agency to the prime minister's office is a device used to focus attention on, and obtain satisfactory commitment to, road safety in countries such as India and Vietnam. Parallel institutional arrangements at the municipal level, with direct responsibility to the head of the city government, have been successful in prosecuting urban road-safety campaigns (box 5.2).

Funding arrangements for road safety need particular attention. Most cities finance safety measures out of limited departmental construction

As a planned new city, Brasília has an extensive road network, which in 1995 sustained an average traffic speed of 40 kilometers an hour (km/h), twice the national urban average, but which also experienced 11 deaths per 1,000 vehicles. On the recommendations of a joint working group of the secretariats of public safety and transport, in July 1995 the governor established by decree a traffic safety program, entitled "Peace within Traffic." The aims of the program included:

• Control of excess speeding
• Control of driving under the influence of alcohol
• Tighter traffic rules enforcement
• Improved medical assistance to accident victims
• Improved road infrastructure safety features
• Vehicle safety inspection and control
• Pedestrian, cyclist, and public transport priority.

Several secretariats were involved in implementing this high-level activity, which was supported by an energetic press campaign, as well as by intensive efforts to involve civil society. Between 1995 and 1997 the number of deaths per 1,000 vehicles fell from 11 to 6.6, and the emphasis and benefit has been subsequently maintained.

Source: Affonso, Rezende, and Vitor 1998.

and management budgets. In Vietnam some dedicated road-safety funding is obtained at a local level from traffic fines. Of the new generation of road funds that have been developed in recent years in Africa and elsewhere, only those funds in Ethiopia are known to specify safety measures, along with road-maintenance activities, as the responsibility of the fund.[18]

Other sources of funding are clearly required. One source of increasing interest in a number of industrialized countries is through contributions from insurance company premiums. However, since a large proportion of road vehicles are operated without insurance in many developing countries, this is only likely to offer a viable source of funds in the wealthier and better-governed countries. In a very few cases private sector support has been mobilized. In Delhi, Indian vehicle manufacturers Maruti Udyog Ltd. have sponsored interceptor patrol vehicles. These patrol vehicles have played a prominent role in traffic law

enforcement and resulted in a considerable increase in revenue from fines—however, it is not possible for the police to reinvest the revenue for road-safety activities. This sponsorship came about following the brokering of a partnership between a nongovernmental organization, the traffic police, the Delhi state government, and Maruti Udyog (Aeron-Thomas and others 2002).

SECURITY

Personal security while engaged in transport activity is an increasing problem throughout the world. In a sense, this is not a transport problem but a symptom of a much wider social malaise. But the inescapable need to undertake travel to pursue essential activities of life—such as work, education, health care, and so on—may force people into situations where they are most vulnerable to attack, with only a limited ability to adjust activities to avoid or ease their vulnerability (box 5.3).

BOX 5.3 CRIME, VIOLENCE, AND DIMINISHING MOBILITY

In a number of major cities in Latin America, such as São Paulo, the number of trips undertaken per day have been declining in recent years, and it has been suggested that this is at least partly a consequence of declining security, particularly in the evening hours when trip rates have declined most. This interpretation is supported by evidence from a survey of poor households in Ecuador. In a six-month period in 1992, one in five women in Cisne Dos was robbed on a bus, and one in two women had witnessed such an attack. There was a drop in the use of public transport at night, and an increase in the relatively safer small trucks operated by the informal sector. For those who could not afford the alternative, travel was curtailed. The lack of safe transport during off-peak hours has caused girls, generally from the poorest families, to drop out of night schools.

Sources: Henry 2000; and Moser 1996.

Threats to security of person and property may be classified into four main types.

a. Theft by stealth, which is largely a function of crowding on public transport vehicles, but which may also involve the unattended parking of bicycles and other vehicles.

b. Theft by force, which can occur in crowded places but is more likely to occur in situations where the victim is relatively isolated. Theft by force includes vandalism and violent physical attack.

c. Sexual harassment, which with different degrees of violence can occur in either crowded or isolated situations.

d. Political and social violence, which may have some transport significance (such as the attacks on South African commuters traveling by rail, bus, or minibus) or for which the transport vehicle may simply be an opportune location.

In each case, while the origin of the problem may not lie primarily in transport conditions, questions arise about the planning and management of transport facilities and services.

Theft by stealth is the most common manifestation of this problem, and is the most difficult to act against, but usually, fortunately, is the least traumatic of the phenomena. Passengers in vehicles can be frequently reminded of the need for caution, and of the best ways to secure themselves against theft. Automatic prosecution and exemplary sentencing of those caught can also be a deterrent. Provision for secure parking of bicycles has been an important element of policies that support bicycle ownership, in some countries. Electronic surveillance may be effective in stations but less so (and more expensive) on crowded vehicles.

Theft by force, because it is more likely to occur in less-crowded locations, is more susceptible to electronic surveillance, which, however, is only likely to be effective if accompanied by adequate arrest-and-arraignment arrangements. The existence of a specialist transport policing force has helped in rail and metro systems in industrialized countries, but is less likely to be affordable for the fragmented bus sector.

Vandalism, which is a form of property theft, and unruly behavior toward passengers are common in poorly managed public transport operations in both developed and developing countries. Management changes or institutional reform can rapidly reduce vandalism. For example, graffiti almost disappeared from the New York subway once public transport management took determined action. In Buenos Aires, service on the government-run suburban railways had become very irregular and unreliable in the 1980s and early 1990s, and windows were broken, seats slashed, and passengers harassed by roving bands of vandals. When railway services were privatized in 1994, the first action of the new concessionaires was to introduce controllers (supported by government security guards) on each train—in part to control fare evasion and in part to establish a safer environment. Within four years the number of passengers had doubled, to a large degree because of the improved safety associated with train travel.

Perhaps even more than the public transport passenger, the pedestrian is increasingly likely to suffer violent attack. This may occur after dark as part of a robbery or, in the case of women, sexual assault. It can occur in business or residential districts, but is most common in low-income settlements controlled by gangs in the absence of a viable police presence. Again, the poor suffer most, because they are vulnerable to physical attack when walking from bus stops to home. Travel by taxi is expensive—and often not even an option when drivers refuse to drive into dangerous neighborhoods. For example, in Caracas (República Bolivariana de Venezuela) it was reported that people missing the last safe opportunity to return home in the evening are obliged to stay overnight at their places of work. In some countries, such as Ghana and South Africa, theft by violence from cars or of cars when stationary or slow moving has been a problem, against which drivers tend to protect themselves by the equally dangerous procedure of ignoring traffic signals, particularly after dark. Civilian neighborhood patrols, common in some industrialized countries, may also play a role in improving safety from violent physical attack in the developing world. Police bicycle patrols, which have become popular in the United States, have also shown promise in Venezuela.

Sexual harassment can be reduced by the provision of women-only vehicles in situations where the density of movement makes this feasible without loss of service availability. Examples of this include buses in Bangladesh, India, and Sri Lanka; and coaches on some trains in the Mexico metros. In Karachi, Pakistan, women-only compartments in buses are physically separated from the larger conductor-controlled compartment of the vehicle. Given increasing personal awareness of the problem, a commercial response is beginning to emerge in some Latin American minibus and taxi markets that specifically protect vulnerable travelers. This response might be stimulated at very little cost by government encouragement and some externally supported experiments. Harassment by male transport staff unwilling to make allowance for the difficulties of women in entering or leaving moving vehicles might be addressed by use of mixed-gender crews on public transport vehicles.[19] Female police officers have become effective, and have a reputation for being tough and incorruptible, in the enforcement of traffic rules in La Paz, Bolivia, and Lima. Women also might have a wider role in responding to issues of sexual harassment.

Political and social violence often finds a focus in burning buses or destroying traffic signals, even where there is no transport-related stimulus. There are also some transport-specific origins of violence. Bus and rail passengers in South Africa were allegedly targeted in order to coerce them to ride the black-operated minibuses. Minibus passengers were also frequently caught up in murderous struggles between competing operators. These types of insecurity are particularly susceptible to actions designed to regularize and give legally defensible property rights to operators of franchised services. Economically motivated policy reform in urban transport operations may thus have a very significant security payoff. The benefit accrued depends on the regulations being enforceable, and on being actually enforced, by legitimate authorities, and not by mafias. For example, in Medellin, Colombia, gangs controlling a low-income area extorted protection money from bus operators serving the area; funds were recovered from the fares of the poor passengers.

Some general points may be made in conclusion. Increasing criminality in many developing cities is a symptom of a much wider social malaise. While it affects the transport behavior of everybody, it is primarily the poor who suffer when essential trips for work or education are curtailed. Lack of security also frustrates environmentally motivated attempts to reduce the need for car travel when children can no longer safely walk or take the bus to school, and many people are obliged to go by car or taxi when even a short walk may have become too dangerous. To some degree, security in public transport might be improved by establishing minimum regulations on service quality. There are some technical fixes to improve personal security for pedestrians, such as better street lighting and use of video or CCTV (closed circuit television) monitoring of public spaces,[20] but ultimately this is a function of much broader and more complex issues, such as social cohesiveness and the tradeoff between police power and human rights concerns.

CONCLUSIONS: A STRATEGY FOR URBAN TRANSPORT SAFETY AND SECURITY

The development of a strategy for urban transport safety should include:

- Development of national road-accident statistics data collection and analysis capability
- Incorporation of safety elements in all transport infrastructure projects by the incorporation of a mandatory safety audit in the design process
- Incorporation of estimation and evaluation safety benefits of improved designs in all infrastructure projects, using values determined by government in collaboration with local safety agencies
- Development and associated training of staff for specific road-safety coordinating agencies or councils, both at the national and the municipal levels

- Specification, clear signing, and enforcement of maximum speed limits for different road categories in urban areas
- National-level specifications, advertising, and enforcement of limits for blood-alcohol levels for vehicle drivers
- Financing of specific safety-related infrastructure investment (such as the financing of infrastructure for NMT, or the railway crossing investments in Buenos Aires) based on the identification of vulnerable groups and locations
- Involvement of police in road safety, such as the collaboration between police and traffic management departments in black-spot analysis in Seoul
- Involvement of medical authorities in joint planning for improved accessibility to medical facilities for victims of accident trauma
- Inclusion of compensation provisions and liabilities in motor traffic and associated insurance legislation
- Creation of high-level committees with responsibility for road safety in all major city administrations
- Development of plans for financing safety activities as part of transport strategy plans in all major municipalities.

With respect to security, serious effort remains necessary both to analyze the nature and significance of insecurity in the urban transport sector, and to devise policy instruments to counter it. That might include:

- Collection and analysis of data on personal security in the transport sector
- Development of an awareness of the problem, together with the commitment of police authorities to arrest, and the courts to appropriately penalize, delinquents
- Development of franchise conditions giving incentives for improved attention to security by public transport operators
- Including street lighting—designed to improve pedestrian security—in street improvement, and particularly in slum-upgrading projects

- Strengthening public participation in projects—particularly those dealing with improvements at the neighborhood level.

NOTES

1. Jacobs and Aeron-Thomas 2000.
2. WHO 1999.
3. TRL and Silcock 2000.
4. Gomez 2000.
5. Amundsen 1996.
6. Ross 1993.
7. TRL and Silcock 2000.
8. A TRL study in Colombo, Sri Lanka, in 1984 showed that fewer than one-quarter of hospital-reported road traffic accident casualties were recorded in police statistics. The problem remains. In Karachi, 1999 police statistics showed only 56 percent of the fatalities and only 4 percent of the serious injuries attributed to road accidents in hospital statistics. Even hospital records can be a poor source for accident research. In Buenos Aires most deaths are attributed solely to a medical condition (broken skull, for instance) and not to the cause of that condition.
9. The number of urban injuries reported for every fatality in official statistics in 1999 was 160 in Great Britain, 22 in Zimbabwe, but only 3 in Dhaka.
10. The DUMAS (Developing Urban Management and Safety) project involves collaboration of research teams in nine countries to produce a framework for the design and evaluation of urban safety initiatives (European Commission 2000).
11. For example, the Amman Transport and Municipal Development Project, funded by the World Bank, planned improvements at 15 intersections. Crash reductions of 98 percent were achieved between 1984 and 1990 at the first two intersections treated. However, these were the only two implemented, and only 18 percent of the planned expenditure on traffic management was achieved.
12. Cracknell 2000.
13. Koster and de Langen 1998.
14. Gold 1999.
15. TRL 1995.
16. TRL and Silcock 2000.
17. For example, there is widespread concern about the provision of equipment—such as cars, cameras, and other enforcement devices—which might also be used for less legitimate, non–traffic-related purposes.
18. Even in this case, the only safety measure finance so far has been the upgrading of traffic signs in Addis Ababa. Since 91 percent of traffic accidents in Addis Ababa involve pedestrians, the provision of new traffic signs is unlikely to be a significant safety benefit.
19. Gomez 2000.
20. Some cameras used for traffic control have also been used for other purposes, but this raises broader questions of personal privacy and possible misuse of government power.

6 THE URBAN ROAD SYSTEM

Most urban transport is based on the use of roads. Congested road infrastructure damages the city economy, increases environmental pollution, and harms the poor by slowing road-based public transport. Particularly in larger cities, however, it may be neither socially nor economically acceptable to balance supply and demand solely by increasing road capacity. A strategy for roads must therefore concentrate on the movement of people, rather than the movement of vehicles, through traffic and demand management, as well as on the provision and maintenance of road infrastructure.

ELEMENTS OF ROAD STRATEGY

Most urban transport, be it public or private, passenger or freight, motorized or nonmotorized, in rich countries or in poor, uses the road system. Roads also provide rights-of-way for utilities, communications infrastructure, and the everyday interaction of the population. The competitiveness of cities, on which the wealth and welfare of their poor as well as their rich increasingly depends in a global economy, requires efficient road transportation.

Despite its economic significance, the road system is usually managed in a fragmented and uneconomic way. Decisions on the management, maintenance, and expansion of road infrastructure rest with separate public sector agencies, while those concerning operations on that infrastructure fall predominantly to the private sector. Increased private demand for infrastructure is not reflected in the price charged for it and does not yield any increase of revenue or fiscal commitment to satisfy it. The juxtaposition of extremely buoyant private demand (demonstrated by high levels of congestion) and a cash-starved infrastructure-supply agency is commonplace. Inadequate road maintenance is pandemic. The most important requirement of a strategy for roads in developing countries is to link those private and public sector decisions in an economically rational way.

A strategy for roads in urban areas to make this linkage must address a number of major issues, including:

- Road maintenance organization and finance
- Traffic management to improve traffic system capacity, quality, or safety, or a combination of all three
- Demand management to secure maximum social value from network use
- Infrastructure expansion planning and appraisal.

While these aspects are primarily concerned with the growth-creating effects of roads, the direct poverty impacts should also be addressed.

ROAD MAINTENANCE

Cities usually have a massive investment in their road systems, which are often very poorly maintained. World Bank–funded projects typically show very high returns on maintenance expenditures, yet there is a persistent tendency to underfund maintenance. In the interurban highway context, this has been confronted by the development of user-managed "second-generation road funds" financed through fuel duty surcharges and other direct charges for use.[1] Such funds do not exist in all countries, however, and even where they do, they do not necessarily solve the problems of urban road maintenance (box 6.1).

The creation of a systematic and secure basis for the maintenance of economically and socially viable roads should be a high priority of urban transport strategy. Where, as is commonly the

---

BOX 6.1 FINANCING URBAN ROAD MAINTENANCE IN THE KYRGYZ REPUBLIC

The Kyrgyz Republic—a small nation in central Asia with a population of approximately 5 million—is facing a serious urban road maintenance problem. Bishkek, the capital, with an estimated population of 1 million, has a road network of 730 kilometers, of which nearly 90 percent is paved. Lack of routine maintenance and deteriorating drainage conditions have resulted in street surfaces that are uneven, heavily cracked, and extensively potholed. Much of the road network needs rehabilitation or complete reconstruction. Other, smaller Kyrgyz cities have similar problems.

A road department of the city corporation is wholly responsible for road maintenance within the city. Work can, in principle, be carried out either by force account or by private sector contractors. In practice, private sector capability remains limited. Asphalt and concrete plants are still operated by the city. Moreover, the embryonic local private sector road construction industry is plagued by the lack of a stable level of contracts and the reluctance of the cities to contract out services.

Providing adequate financing of road maintenance and rehabilitation is critical. The recently established Kyrgyz Republic National Road Fund is permitted by law to allocate up to 10 percent of its resources to urban areas, but has so far allocated much less than this because the needs of the national road network are considered more pressing. Cities are in no better position to fund road maintenance from their own sources. Transfers from central government make up 60 to 75 percent of city budgets, but are mostly earmarked to pay for school and health-care worker salaries. Less than 2 percent of total city expenditures go to roads—about $0.12 per capita per year. As it has such limited authority to raise revenues, Bishkek has resorted to ad hoc lotteries, bazaars, and festivals to finance road maintenance.

In connection with a $22 million International Development Agency credit to help cities catch up on the backlog of maintenance and road rehabilitation of arterial roads carrying the bulk of motor vehicle and public transport traffic, the Kyrgyz government has set up a working group of city- and central-government officials to find ways to make funding of road repairs more sustainable. Agreement has already been reached that National Road Fund revenues could be increased, with a higher percentage coming from user fees (such as gas and vehicle taxes). The ultimate challenge will be to empower cities to generate and retain adequate revenues to fulfill their statutory responsibility for road maintenance and rehabilitation. Urban road finance in the Kyrgyz Republic is thus essentially part of wider national road finance and municipal finance issues.

Source: R. Podolske, from World Bank project files.

---

case, maintenance is financed from general municipal revenues, some general allocation standard should be established as a benchmark. In countries with national road funds, there should be adequate criteria and process to ensure that an appropriate part of the fund is devoted to urban roads. That has not been the case in some of the early road funds.

In terms of funding sources, the second-generation road fund philosophy is that road infrastructure should be maintained with funds collected from users. Ideally, direct or indirect charges to users should be sufficient to cover the full costs of traffic, including environmental impact and road maintenance. Distance- and weight-related licensing fees might be the most accurate instruments for allocating maintenance costs between categories of road user, although allocations of fuel duties or congestion charges might be proxies for those fees.

In practice, many countries do not have such road funds, and road maintenance responsibilities are allocated between levels of government according to whether the traffics using specific roads are considered national, regional, or local. Where such arrangements are in place, it is essential that the delineation of responsibility between authorities is clear, and that the funding arrangements are steady and sustainable, with substantial discretion for municipalities to raise funds locally, if necessary.

Implementation also needs improvement in many countries. A maintenance culture must be established and nurtured in the municipal institutions. Maintenance management systems should be employed to plan and budget for required maintenance on a systematic basis related to surveys of road condition, distinguishing routine, periodic maintenance, and rehabilitation or reconstruction.[2] This establishes the foundations for the development of a private maintenance contracting capability and even possibly for the development of urban road maintenance concessions, as have recently been concluded in Montevideo (Uruguay) and Bogotá.

TRAFFIC MANAGEMENT

The objective of urban traffic management is to make the safest and most productive use of existing (road-based) transport system resources. It seeks to adjust, adapt, manage, and improve the existing transport system to meet specified objectives. By maximizing the efficiency of existing facilities and systems, capital expenditure can be avoided or deferred to gain time in which to develop longer-term policy measures. At the same time, traffic safety can be improved and the adverse impact of road traffic on the city environment reduced.

Many traffic management instruments, such as efficient traffic signal systems, increase the efficiency of movement with negligible adverse side effects. But traffic management policy also involves choices. Priority given to pedestrians may reduce capacity for vehicles or may adversely affect bus operations. An integrated traffic management scheme will require compromises between the competing interests of various users of the road and traffic systems. It is hence not just a technical issue, but must be clearly directed in harmony with the overall urban transport strategy. In practice, in most cities both traffic engineers and traffic police tend to concentrate on keeping the traffic moving. As a result, roads are widened, motorcars (automobiles) receive priority, and pedestrians and bicycles get crowded out. In that process the street system gets rearranged to benefit the generally richer car users at the cost of the generally poorer bus users, bicyclists, and walkers. If it is a policy objective to focus on the needs of the poor, this objective should also motivate traffic and demand management.

TRAFFIC CONTROL

There are numerous traffic management tools, including on-street parking management and control, traffic circulation design, traffic signal systems, public transport (bus) priority, and the enforcement of traffic regulations. These tools can be applied not only to speed the movement of cars but also, if desired, to give priority to pedestrians, bicycles, and other nonmotorized (NMT) or commercial vehicles.[3]

The combination of a coherent circulation system design and an efficient traffic signal system is central. Good signal control technologies are readily available. Moreover, the rapid pace of development of intelligent traffic system technologies offers relatively poor countries the chance to leapfrog to the latest technology, just as some have in telecommunications. Such systems are increasingly robust and need little maintenance, but they do require planning, some minimum maintenance, and a willingness to use them. Unfortunately, many large cities lack even the basic skills to develop and maintain these systems, with the result that, as in Bangkok, traffic control reverts to what the police can achieve at a single intersection.

Traffic management can be applied at a specific site; for example, improvements may be necessary at a key intersection to ensure consistent traffic capacity along a route, or improvements may be made at an intersection to resolve a capacity or severe accident problem. However, traffic management is most effective if applied over an area (for example, a corridor, local area, or town center) in order to develop a consistent traffic management regime. Hence measures are best combined in comprehensive packages to ensure that traffic problems are not simply transferred to new conflict points, that there is synergy between the various interventions, and that users are consistently presented with the same "messages," thereby improving the likelihood of observance of traffic regulations.

PUBLIC TRANSPORT PRIORITY

In most cities in the developing world, buses are the backbone of the motorized transport system and will remain so for the foreseeable future. In poorer cities the bus share of the market may be exceeded by paratransit (publicly available passenger transport service that is outside the traditional public transport regulatory system).

Regular travel by taxi or motorized rickshaw-taxi (as in some cities in India) tends to be by the better-off; the car is not a mode available to most poor people. Even in cities where suburban rail is predominant, such as in Mumbai, or where metros exist, most mechanized journeys are usually still by public road passenger transport.

At peak loading, a bus may carry 30 (or more) times as many passengers as a car, in only three times the road space. The primary objective of traffic management should therefore be to improve travel for **people** and not necessarily for **vehicles.** Not only will this lead to the most efficient use of scarce road space but the policy will have a positive impact on poverty. Such an approach will tend to emphasize:

- Measures to assist public transport generally and bus priority measures in particular
- Pedestrian facilities
- Bicycle facilities.

In many Latin American cities, traffic management already seeks to improve on-street bus operations through busways or bus lanes. Extensive bus lanes and busways exist in many cities, with the most notable being Curitiba, Porto Alegre (Brazil), São Paulo, Bogotá, Lima, Quito, Santiago, Mexico City, and León (Mexico). Many Latin American cities also have pedestrianized areas or streets, particularly in the city centers. Road paving has been undertaken in some poor areas to provide bus access, and most roads are provided with pedestrian footways. Elsewhere, the situation is less encouraging. In Asia few developing cities—including, as far as is known, only Bangkok, Manila, Madras, and Kuala Lumpur—have allocated extensive road space to bus priority and busways. In the latter three cities, enforcement of with-flow bus lanes (as opposed to the contra-flow bus lanes that constitute most of the Bangkok lanes) remains problematic.

The lack of bus priority outside Latin America is partly associated with the absence of a conventional bus system. The prevalence of paratransit makes bus priority difficult to implement due to the high volume of relatively small vehicles, such as the jeepneys in Manila. In some cities, such as Hanoi, Vietnam, bus services are embryonic; even where bus services exist, they may be regarded by users as the transport of last resort, as in some cities in China. In other cases, such as Moscow, bus transport is regarded as a subsidiary mode to the metro and hence given little preferential treatment on trunk routes. For these reasons there is a lack of understanding of the objectives of bus priority, and politicians are unwilling to commit to measures that adversely affect the (rich) private car users. Because of its low status, there is a lack of trained and experienced professional staff with sufficient vision to appreciate the benefits of road-space reallocation to buses. The problems of enforcement of "complex" bus priority schemes that require vehicle selectivity (that is, buses versus others) are viewed as too great to overcome.

The trend in industrialized cities is the reverse of that in developing cities (outside Latin America). Road-space reallocation to buses from cars on a highly preferential basis is increasingly accepted in many richer industrialized cities, particularly in Western Europe. As in Latin America, acceptance for bus priority has been brought about by better planning, better information to decisionmakers, better enforcement or legislation, creation of a better image for buses, and better dissemination of information on the benefits of bus priority. Busways in such cities as Curitiba and Quito are highly valued by the population (most of whom have low incomes), and mayors spearheading busway schemes have subsequently won election to even higher offices.

IMPLEMENTATION

In many cities the high rates of traffic growth may quickly catch up with the initial congestion relief of traffic management measures. Traffic management must not be seen, therefore, as a panacea for urban transport congestion, but rather as a component of a broader strategy

also involving public transport and demand management. Traffic management must not be seen as a "one-shot" intervention, either—rather, it should be seen as a continuous process, adapted and adjusted to meet the changing traffic situation. Hence, the emphasis should be on creating a favorable institutional environment for the effective operation and adaptation of traffic management measures, and on fostering the technical skills to implement them, rather than merely on the financing of specific schemes.

The main traffic management activities to be performed at a city or city-region level are shown in table 6.1. The major institutional problems relating to road provision and management concern the functional separation of responsibility for activities between municipal and district levels in hierarchical systems, and the coordination between local traffic management and overall transport strategy.

Achieving a balance between competing transport modes and interests relies on competent transport institutions working within a clearly defined framework of responsibilities. While there is no single ideal or model institutional framework for traffic and transport administration, a city must have an organizational framework that deals with the basic functions of strategic transport planning; infrastructure planning, design, and construction; road maintenance; public transport planning and procurement; and traffic and demand management, including enforcement. Alternative ways of organizing these functions are discussed in chapter 11.

Some traffic management functions can be contracted out to the private sector. The contracting may be conventional (such as for the maintenance of traffic signals) or include a broader range of functions. Consultants may be contracted to conduct a large part of the traffic management process—for example, to develop and implement a comprehensive corridor plan—although the executive must ulti-

TABLE 6.1 FUNCTIONS AND RESPONSIBILITIES OF A TYPICAL TRAFFIC MANAGEMENT AGENCY

Area	Functions and responsibilities
Traffic management policy	Formulate and implement citywide traffic management policies to comply with objectives defined by the city council to include, at least, such areas as determination of (a) a functional road hierarchy, (b) the appropriate balance between transport system users (private transport–public transport—NMT vehicles–pedestrians), (c) priority programs for action, and (d) "five-year" investment plans.
Traffic research	Survey, monitor, and evaluate all traffic and accident data to enable trends to be identified, problems quantified, and traffic management plans and improvements prepared.
Traffic management plans and improvements	Plan, design, implement, monitor, evaluate, fine-tune, and continuously update traffic schemes and policies to realize the agreed-on traffic management policy. The program would cover all motorized road-based modes (cars, public transport, trucks, and so on) and all NMT modes (pedestrians and cycles). Plans and improvements would range from simple intersection improvements, or marking and signing programs, through to far-reaching citywide strategies such as extensive bus priority or pricing. Accident programs and countermeasures would be included.
Traffic control devices	Plan, design, install, operate, and maintain all traffic control devices including (a) traffic signal systems, including computer-controlled systems; (b) road markings; (c) road signs; and (d) enforcement devices (cameras, and so on).
Traffic regulations	Formulate traffic regulations to realize the proposed traffic management plans and improvements, for enactment by city government and for enforcement by the traffic police.
Parking management	Prepare off- and on-street parking policies and programs, including approval for the location of, and access to, parking areas proposed by others. Parking enforcement and administration, where paid parking applies, would be carried out by a separate "parking authority," or the equivalent.
Approvals and coordination	Evaluate and advise city government on all schemes (such as new roads) and developments (developed both by public and private sector agencies, and including major new land or building developments) that have a significant traffic impact, to ensure that they are consistent with agreed-on traffic policy.
Consultation	Consultation with the public and stakeholders on traffic policy and on the impacts of specific schemes and measures.
Budget	Preparation of an annual budget for submission to city government for (a) implementation of traffic management plans and improvement schemes, (b) traffic operations and maintenance of control devices, and (c) the continuous work of the traffic management agency itself.

Notes: Not all functions would be carried out by the traffic management agency itself. For example, functions such as maintenance of traffic control devices and signals would most commonly be contracted out. In this case, the agency would assume the functional responsibility of supervision. The potential for contracting out significant elements of the functions to consultants is discussed below.
Source: Authors.

mately remain responsible and accountable for those functions. While this may reduce the need for implementation staff at the city level, it does not alleviate the need for a trained core of staff to determine traffic management policy and to manage the consultants. Issues arise over the extent of the consultants' or contractors' responsibility for letting (that is, awarding) implementation contracts and thus responsibility for public funds. However, such an arrangement may assist cities in developing countries, since it may be easier for a city to obtain finance for short-term consultants than for the staff levels required in-house.

DEMAND MANAGEMENT

The economic rationale for demand management is that if the price directly incurred by travelers in making journeys is lower than the full cost of the journey, then some trips will impose a net cost on the community. The full costs of a journey include both the personal costs incurred by the traveler (vehicle-running costs, fuel, parking, and so on), and the social costs imposed by the traveler on the community through the journey's contribution to congestion, the increase in accident potential, and the polluting effects on the environment. As the costs imposed by a traveler on others vary by location, time, and traffic conditions, so, ideally, should the charges incurred by vehicle users also vary. The objective of demand management should be to secure the total level of traffic, and its distribution between modes, locations, and times of day that would exist if traffic by each travel mode were to be charged prices equal to its full marginal social cost.

In order to achieve that objective, all demand-management tools aim to increase the costs of travel, either explicitly through charges (parking or congestion charges or fuel prices) or implicitly by limiting movement through traffic restraint measures. Demand management and restraint in traffic volumes may be realized by a range of pricing measures, many of them touching on national policy (including, for instance, fuel pricing).

Parking controls for demand management

Parking control and pricing are the most commonly applied demand management measures in both industrialized and developing-country cities. At its most basic, parking policy in many developing cities is limited to the control of on-street parking (usually simple parking prohibitions on main roads) to avoid obstruction to moving traffic. But it can also have wider restraint potential.

While parking controls may have some effect on vehicle ownership, the usual aim of restraint policy is to reduce car use by regulating parking space and by positive allocation of available parking space among different groups of users—usually seeking to deter car commuting for work. The effectiveness of parking as a restraint measure in developing countries is compromised by the ability of the rich to keep their vehicles on the street in the charge of their hired drivers, and by the fact that significant parts of the parking stock in many cities are not in the control of the traffic authority. While, in principle, publicly available but privately provided car parking can be required to charge "restraint-level" parking rates with the excess profit taxed away from them, in practice this enforcement measure is very difficult to implement in developing-country cities.

Even more difficult problems arise in respect of "private nonresidential" parking in the ownership of private sector companies or government agencies. Withdrawing the right to use these parking areas not only creates a political problem but also legal problems in some countries, where the private nonresidential parking may have been constructed in response to city parking standards for construction permits. There are still many developing-country cities where, even in city centers, minimum rather than maximum parking standards are set.

Despite these weaknesses a comprehensive parking policy is likely to be the starting point for demand management in most cities. Parking fees are the least contentious of user charges, and most cities have some form of parking policy. The number, location, and price of on-street parking spaces can be controlled. Publicly available off-street parking and private nonresidential parking capacity expansion can be limited, and charges regulated to prevent subsidized parking. Policies for these categories of parking consistent with general policy objectives should be included in all transport strategy plans. The integration of parking standards within development control strategies, such as in the Dutch ABC policy, is a good example of this.[4]

TRAFFIC RESTRAINT

Traffic demand can be restrained through the use of a range of physical measures such as:

- Limiting entry to environmentally sensitive city centers to "essential" traffic only, as in Tehran, Islamic Republic of Iran
- City-center pedestrianization, as in Buenos Aires and Budapest
- Cell systems that limit traffic within the city center by creating a system of cells between which there is no direct access for cars, as in Gothenburg (Sweden) and Bremen (Germany)
- Road-space reallocation to high-occupancy vehicles
- Traffic-calming measures (see chapter 5).

While the use of such measures may reduce traffic in the target areas (usually a city center), they are unlikely to reduce demand overall unless coupled with other measures, such as parking policy and encouragement to public transport.

Among the most popular restraint measures are schemes that limit use of vehicles on specific days according to their registration plate number. These have been introduced in many cities—including Athens (Greece), Bogotá, Lagos, Manila, Mexico City, Santiago, São Paulo, and Seoul—for both congestion and environmental reasons. There are obvious risks to the "odds and evens" policy and its variants. They may encourage shift to taxi use or an increase in the number of vehicles owned, and induce more trips by permitted vehicles than would otherwise have been made. Nevertheless, they have worked in the short term (Bogotá reports a 20 percent increase in average travel speeds). Above all, they have achieved acceptance by the public as a demonstration of commitment by government to reduce congestion and related air pollution, and have proved less difficult to enforce than one might have expected. Particularly if well designed to discourage peak use and if coupled with public transport improvements, as in Bogotá, they can at the very least give the government some breathing space to develop even more effective policies.

PRICING

Physical restraint measures have hitherto proved more acceptable than have direct charges for road use, both in industrialized and in developing countries. Even in industrialized countries, however, their effectiveness appears to have been exhausted; and some countries, such as the United Kingdom and the Netherlands, are now planning the introduction of direct charges. Singapore—now a rich country—is moving toward charges for vehicle use rather than charges and other controls on their ownership. In the few cases in countries of the Organisation for Economic Co-operation and Development (OECD) where direct cordon or area congestion prices are charged, part or all of the revenues have been earmarked for public transport improvements. For cities in developing countries, which lack resources to finance urban transport, the introduction of direct charges might thus be expected to have a double attractiveness as a source of finance as well as an instrument of restraint. The incorporation of direct charges within an integrated urban transport pricing policy is such a potentially important contributor to sustainable urban transport that it is discussed in detail in chapter 10.

One aspect of restraint is particularly important. Both theoretical research and practical experience indicates that combinations of car restraint and public transport improvement appear to work better than either in isolation, at least in their effect on travel to city centers. A coherent policy is therefore likely to include a combination of more than one measure.

INFRASTRUCTURE PROVISION

There is no magic number defining the appropriate level of transport infrastructure provision, which depends on the type of transport and land-use system that is being designed, as well as the topography and economy of the city. Predominantly auto-dependent cities in the United States may devote as much as 35 percent of their urban space to transport infrastructure.

European cities, which now have high car ownership levels, allocated 20 to 25 percent to roads before motorization. These cities now attempt to maintain system performance through traffic and demand management, and afford a degree of physical and fiscal priority to public transport systems. In contrast, Asian cities, many of which devote only 10 to 12 percent of their urban space to roads, do so by accident rather than by choice and do not have the appropriate policies in place to maintain efficient transport in the city with the road space available.

It is clear that cities with only 10 to 12 percent of their area devoted to movement cannot support unfettered motorization. Moreover, once the city fabric is established, it becomes increasingly expensive, and both socially and environmentally disturbing, to superimpose substantial additional road infrastructure. Furthermore, where congestion is already suppressing demand, increasing capacity may generate such a large amount of extra traffic that congestion is reduced much less than anticipated. Cities that have already grown to a size and density at which substantial traffic congestion exists may thus have lost forever the option of road-building their way out of congestion.

It is also the case, however, that as cities expand, so must their road systems. Cities need a basic amount of circulation space adequate for their size in order to operate efficiently (see discussion in chapter 2). Early planning of, and reservation of space for, transport infrastructure is thus a strategic requirement. Essential elements in the successful integration of land-use and transport facilities in well-planned cities (such as Curitiba and Singapore) have been the definition and protection of the basic transport infrastructure corridors. The requirement is not simply for roads for motor vehicles—pedestrians and NMT also need space for circulation. Some of the most attractive urban environments are those in which the circulation of motorized and NMT traffic has been separated and clear priorities in the allocation of space determined.

The strategy on road provision thus calls for a careful balance of judgment. On the one hand, the dynamics of city expansion must be recognized, because even the most environmentally aware cities only achieve their ends by adequate allocation and good planning of movement space. On the other hand, heavily congested cities cannot road-build their way out of congestion, and attempts to do so will almost certainly fail or carry very heavy social and environmental penalties. Only a strategy that recognizes these constraints and combines necessary road-capacity adjustment to support city expansion with clear and strict policies on the allocation and use of road space is likely to be able to reconcile city expansion with livability.

HIERARCHY AND SHAPE

Appropriate structuring of the road network is important (table 6.2). In many cases the city leaders want ring roads (China) and other primary roads and expressways (Moscow) when major problems arise from the absence of an appropriate structure and quantity of local distribution capacity (Bangkok, Manila, and Jakarta). It is true that limited-access arterial roads can handle several times more vehicles per hour in a given amount of space than can mixed-use roads. But it is also necessary to provide for pedestrian circulation and local distribution of traffic, as well as for longer distance trunk movements. These functions do not mix well, and a given amount of road space will always give better performance if it is classified and managed hierarchically to separate functions.[5] This type of road classification is often a basis for the allocation of financial responsibility for provision and an important aid to effective distribution of maintenance resources.

The shape of networks is also important. The classic "ring and radial" design of many Western cities evolved over time, with the ring roads being added as city centers became congested and the need to provide alternative routes for intracity crosstown movement became apparent. The innermost ring around the central area could be

TABLE 6.2 TYPICAL FUNCTIONAL CLASSIFICATION OF ROAD AND PATH NETWORKS

Classification	Principal functions	Separate NMT facilities	Segregated bus facilities	Percentage of street kilometers	Direct land access	Typical design speed	Motor vehicle parking	Comments
Pedestrian paths	Safe pedestrian circulation	Yes	No	n.a.	No restrictions	n.a.	Prohibited	Essential access to off-road property
Cycle paths	Safe cycle circulation	Yes	No	n.a.	No restrictions	n.a.	Prohibited	Preferably continuous system
Local streets	Land and property access	Sidewalks desirable	Not required	60–80	No restriction	30–40 km/h	Permitted	Through traffic should be discouraged
Collector streets	Links local and arterial streets	Sidewalks usually necessary	Not required	5–10	Generally unrestricted	40–50 km/h	Limited	Through traffic discouraged
Arterial streets	Intercommunity and intracity movement	Sidewalks mandatory; bicycle track if demand warrants	Desirable where both bus and general traffic levels high	15–30	Access only to major traffic generators	50–75 km/h	Limited or prohibited	Typically the backbone of urban street system
Freeways and expressways	Longer distance extra- and intrametropolitan traffic	None	Desirable if bus volumes high and route subject to congestion	n.a.	No land access permitted	75 km/h or more	Prohibited	Grade-separated intersections

n.a. Not applicable.
Note: km/h = kilometers per hour.
Source: Authors.

designed to discourage crosstown traffic from passing through the center and to allow more road space for local traffic, public transport, NMT vehicles, and pedestrians inside the ring. Some form of inner ring (coupled with appropriate freight access arrangements) is usually an integral part of major pedestrianization schemes. The critical element in such concepts is the management of traffic within the ring to prevent the capacity released from being filled by further newly generated through traffic. This was the basis on which the Bank was involved in financing of ring roads in Shanghai and Guangzhou. The main difficulty in this approach is to ensure that traffic or demand management measures are actually introduced, and then maintained over time.

Outer-ring roads, on the periphery of a city, may keep crosstown traffic out of the city where routes for crosstown traffic are inadequate, or they form part of the regional or national highway network. The critical element is not their form (ring) but their economic and environmental function (by-pass), and they should be judged on these grounds. Even where they are justified functionally, they may, as in Warsaw (Poland) and Budapest (Hungary), fuel auto dependency by attracting major shopping developments to the periphery, where access is much better by private than public transport. They should thus also be appraised in terms of the contribution that they make to the broader land-use and transport development strategy for the city.

Other structural considerations may arise. Grid networks, common in U.S. cities, spread crosstown traffic across parallel and alternative routes, but cannot avoid congestion in the downtown (central area) locations with the greatest concentrations of commercial activity. To avoid this it is likely to be less expensive and less disruptive to strengthen the hierarchy of the grid, rather than to superimpose new ring roads.

APPRAISING CAPACITY EXTENSIONS

It is observed above that an adequate basic infrastructure is essential to the efficient working of the city but that it may not be possible to eliminate congestion in established large cities by road-building. This observation still begs the question of where and when capacity should be added.

The classic test concerns the elimination of "bottlenecks," where the lack of capacity at one point in a system causes congestion and delay at the approaches to that point. Sometimes great benefits can be obtained inexpensively through enhancing the continuity of a network by removing a bottleneck or filling a missing link. Prima facie bottlenecks may appear to be a system design deficiency and an obvious case where capacity expansion is necessary. Of course, though, bottlenecks are not design faults in bottles. There they exist intentionally in order to restrict excessive flow at the point where it is most acceptable (in the bottle), and not at the point where the flow cannot be accommodated (in the glass). The same logic may be applied to road systems. Increasing flow into a city center that cannot accommodate further traffic may make things worse rather than better. Only if the total system performance is improved is the elimination of bottlenecks a sensible policy. "Opportunistic" measures to eliminate bottlenecks need to be very carefully appraised to ensure that the measures are not simply shifting traffic congestion to another point in the system.

The conventional way to address these issues is to attempt to compare costs and benefits in a rational, quantitative, framework. While this technique was originally developed for appraising interurban investments, the necessary technical adjustments for the appraisal of capacity expansion in congested cities have been part of the standard literature for 30 years. New traffic induced by a system improvement does imply some private benefit to those whose trips were previously suppressed, but it also reduces the extent to which existing traffic will benefit from extra capacity, and it generates an additional environmental impact. The net effect of allowing for generated traffic may thus be to reduce the estimated benefit of capacity expansion. A good demand analysis and evaluation model may be capable of considering this potential benefit, but where such sophisticated techniques are not available, the most obvious simplification—to assume a fixed matrix of trips—will probably significantly overvalue capacity expansion.

Another theoretically well-analyzed phenomenon is the impact of traffic and demand management on the economic value of capacity expansion. The possibilities of improving the efficiency of existing infrastructure by traffic management, and of restraining traffic by demand management, should theoretically be considered in specifying the base case against which to assess additional capacity. In practice, however, it is too easy to presume that better management of the transport system is impossible, and hence too easy to evaluate proposed capacity expansions on a basis that consistently overestimates the benefits of improvements.

Other considerations are of more recent concern, and are less well established. Effects on NMT users of the road infrastructure are typically ignored in conventional road investment project appraisals. At the technical level, the poverty focus also requires that benefits to the poor should be given a higher value in economic appraisals than is often the case.[6] It is desirable that, at the very least, the order of magnitude of such issues be assessed.

The cost-benefit methodology is still used at a technical level and therefore must be amended to avoid the most obvious biases. The valuation issues for environmental externalities, the absence of a solid understanding of the feedback effect of road building on land-use changes and urban form, and the distributional effects of investments mean that the calculated economic rate of return is inadequate as a sole technical criterion. Economic evaluation therefore needs to be embedded in a multicriteria framework, designed for a participatory and politically frank decisionmaking process.

One of the strongest but most diffused protections against overinvestment is the involvement of the concerned public in consultation or participatory design arrangements. While there is a danger of a nihilistic "not-in-my-backyard" syndrome developing, capable of blocking good as well as bad developments, procedures of consultation and of public inquiry into major schemes force planners and engineers to think much more carefully than might otherwise occur. It follows from this that the data collection and modeling should also evolve to suit the participatory process.

PRIVATE FINANCING

Private finance has been mobilized for urban toll road construction in major cities such as Bangkok, Buenos Aires, Kuala Lumpur, and Manila. Insofar as such roads are tolled at levels that service the full resource costs of the construction, they would appear to be consistent with the policies advocated hitherto. Insofar as they also succeed in reducing congestion on the untolled public road network, they might be viewed as unambiguously beneficial.

That conclusion may not hold, however, for a number of reasons. If urban toll roads generate extra traffic on an inadequate secondary road network (as in Bangkok and Kuala Lumpur), the new toll roads may actually increase congestion and, thus, reduce welfare. The environmental impacts, both of infrastructure and extra traffic, are typically uncharged except insofar as they are internalized in the design requirements for new routes. There may also be contingent costs on the public purse for improving the feeder network that are unaccounted for (as in Manila). The conclusion is thus not that private finance is undesirable but that, because of the system effects, private sector schemes should be subject to the same overall planning, economic, environmental, and social analysis as they would be if undertaken in the public sector.

POVERTY FOCUS

The poverty impact of urban roads, as that of all other elements of urban transport, can be divided into the indirect effects, arising through their effect on economic growth, and the direct effects, arising through their effect on the livelihoods of poor individuals.

THE GROWTH EFFECT

The economic viability of the industrial and trading base of cities is important to the poor who find their employment there. Whereas in industrialized countries, peak-period congestion is predominantly caused by private cars, the same is not true everywhere. Many major cities in developing countries are the terminal nodes of national and international transport networks. Some are historic port cities, the dominance of which has been enhanced during the period of colonial rule. In these cities freight traffic is often a significant cause of urban congestion. Concentration of traffic to and from major urban commodity markets, as in Dhaka, may have the same effect as the concentration of port flows, as in Manila. Having a strategy for the location of major freight traffic generators, and their associated movements, is therefore an important part of an urban transport strategy in developing-country cities. Urban road strategy must also be linked to, and reflect, changes in the national economy, as is the case in some of the transitional economies, where dramatic changes in industrial structure and trade links have shifted freight from rail to road and necessitated changes in urban transport structure.

DIRECT POVERTY IMPACTS

The poverty reduction potential of road investments can be enhanced by the selection of types of road project for inclusion in programs concentrating on the road infrastructure essential to the basic needs of the poor. These needs can be identified and focused on in several ways.

The first way of focusing policy on the poor is to look at where they live. In many countries the very poor live in informal housing developments or slums that have no paved or even prepared road access. Because they lack road access, they are not served by formal public transport, and are in fact often not served by any mechanized transport at all. They are forced to walk long distances, often in insecure surroundings. The World Bank has frequently financed paving of roads to improve access to poor areas, particularly in Latin America and Africa (box 6.2). In the context of increasing security, lighting may become an important aspect of basic safe-access provision.

A second way of focusing on the poor is to look at the modes of transport that they use. For the very poorest, this usually means walking or other NMT. Too often the allocation of street space for walking and NMT vehicles is inadequate to allow safe movement. Moreover, as motorization increases, even this limited street space tends to deteriorate. For example, while during the 1970s and 1980s the provision of segregated cycling capacity was a standard design feature in new urban arterial roads in Chinese cities, such attention to cyclists now appears to be declining. Segregated infrastructure for cycling and pedestrian access is being financed in cities as diverse as Lima, Accra, Manila, Bogotá, Shanghai, and Liaoning (China). For other groups of the poor, and in other countries, the poor are heavily dependent on road-based public transport. Making sure that road space is available for road-based public transport can be facilitated in two ways. First, where roads have deteriorated, priority for rehabilitation may be put on the parts of the primary road network used for public transport (such as in a recent project in the Kyrgyz Republic). Second, where road space is scarce, priority can be given to public transport vehicles, not only by bus lanes and busways but also in more sophisticated ways, such as the incorporation of priority for public transport vehicles in signal control systems.

The third focus might be on how the poor make their living. In very poor rural areas, it has been common practice to consider labor-intensive road construction and maintenance processes, which tend to be easier to manage and which produce a relatively higher quality product where the road standards required are low. The same emphasis

BOX 6.2 PAVING ROADS IN LOW-INCOME AREAS IN BRAZILIAN CITIES

Unpaved roads in low-income areas in Brazilian cities, many of which used to be impassable in wet weather, were serious impediments to the access of buses and emergency vehicles. In São Paulo alone there were 800 kilometers of unpaved bus route in the early 1980s. To remedy this an extensive program of paving in low-income areas was included in the First Brazil Urban Transport Project. Under this project there was a tendency for the design agencies to produce excessively elaborate designs for drainage and basic pavement structure. Cost and time overruns resulted.

Because of these overruns, the Empresa Metropolitana de Transportes Urbanos in São Paulo undertook a comprehensive study of low-cost paving; the result was a low-cost paving manual and an economic feasibility study. In parallel, the national body Empresa Brasileira dos Transportes Urbanos (EBTU) commissioned a study of regional experiences in low-cost paving, which concluded that the benefits from an extensive bus-route-paving program would be substantial, and established guidelines for the selection of roads in a paving program.

The Third Brazil Urban Transport Project included a $63 million component—the (Programa de Pavimentacao de Baixo Custo em Areas de Baixa Renda (PROPAV) program—to pave 500 kilometers of bus route in low-income areas between 1981 and 1984. EBTU would be responsible for selecting the roads and supervising the execution, and would embody its experience in a revision of the manual. Local labor and local materials were extensively used. The program was considered so successful that it was extended to over 1,000 kilometers, not all of which were Bank financed.

Similar problems existed in other Latin American and Caribbean countries, and programs were launched in Chile, Jamaica, Peru, and Mexico. In some cases, where impassability due to rain was not a problem, even simpler surfacing was used to permit extended coverage. The most recent developments include local community participation in the selection of segments for inclusion in a project in Lima.

Source: World Bank project files.

---

has not been normal in urban areas, although experience in South Africa does indicate that there may be equivalent possibilities in urban areas.

Finally, a focus may be on the incidental impacts of road development on the poor. There is a strong temptation to route new road infrastructure through areas where land is inexpensive, which is often land occupied by the poor. That is likely to be the case, in particular, where the poor are illegally occupying publicly owned land. The stringent requirements of the Bank for resettlement planning and compensation stem from a concern for this kind of adverse spin-off effect.

CONCLUSIONS: A STRATEGY FOR ROADS

Roads are a necessary component of urban infrastructure. Inadequacy of current road capacity to carry current traffic results in congestion, damage to the city economy, increased environmental impact, and, often, particularly harsh impact on the poor. In larger established cities, however, it may not be socially or economically acceptable to balance supply and demand solely by increasing road capacity. A strategy for roads must therefore encompass traffic management and demand management, as well as the provision and maintenance of road infrastructure. A strategy must thus include:

For road planning

- Initial planning and reservation of space for transport infrastructure (not restricted to roads)
- Appropriate hierarchical structuring of the road network and clear lines of responsibility for provision and maintenance of each category
- Rigorous appraisal of investments in additional road capacity to take into account (a) the effects of induced traffic on benefits, (b) the benefits and disbenefits of alternatives to NMT, and (c) environmental impacts
- Identifying the most important person or freight movements (not necessarily vehicle movements) both for the economic health of the city and the welfare of the poor and concentrating road improvements to help those movements.

For road maintenance

- Introduction of maintenance management systems
- Funding for adequate maintenance of the economically sustainable road capacity
- Improvement of private sector contracting capability to improve maintenance efficiency.

For traffic management

- Management of traffic to maintain safe, efficient, and environmentally acceptable movement of people (and not just of vehicles)
- Prioritization of infrastructure management and use to protect (a) the economic efficiency of the city and (b) movements of public and NMT, against unrestricted expansion of private motorized transport.

For demand management

- Management of demand for road space to balance movement with capacity through restraint measures
- Full-cost charging for road use (see chapter 10).
- Integration of financing to recognize the interaction between roads and other modes of urban transport (see chapter 10)
- Development of agencies capable of managing and maintaining the urban road system.

NOTES

1. Heggie and Vickers 1998.
2. Robinson, Danielsson, and Snaith 1998.
3. A fuller review of available instruments of traffic control for developing countries can be found in Cracknell 2000.
4. NEA Transport Research and Training 2000.
5. We must bear in mind the need to provide adequate grade-separated crossings to prevent arterial roads from damaging the social integrity of established settlements.
6. Distributionally weighted values of time have been considered in some Bank projects (for example, in road projects in Vietnam), but there remain serious problems in the development of any formal procedure for assigning distributional weights. Where the evaluation is based on traffic data modeled at a fairly fine zonal level, it is possible to approximately identify the distribution of benefits by income group (as piloted in the appraisal of some public transport investments in Brazil). That is not difficult technically and should become a normal output of economic evaluations.

7 PUBLIC ROAD PASSENGER TRANSPORT

Public road passenger transport is a key element of a strategy to contain congestion and environmental air pollution, as well as being essential to the poor. When it is appropriately regulated, competition best guarantees efficient supply, and through franchises and concessions can mobilize low-cost operations to provide the best quality of service and price for any budget capability. Without adequate regulation, however, competition can have some very damaging effects. The informal sector can also contribute effectively to satisfy demand in competitive markets.

As cities increase in size to the point at which walking can no longer satisfy the major trip requirements of the citizens, public transport—together with bicycling—becomes the major mode of transport for the poor. Buses are the main mechanized mode, carrying 6.5 trillion (6.5 x 10^{12}) passenger kilometers per year in 3 million vehicles, of which over 2 million vehicles operate in cities. In addition there are over 2 million paratransit vehicles operating in these cities.[1]

Public transport should not be viewed as only for the poor, however, as the importance of public transport to all income groups in many rich European cities demonstrates. Improving efficiency in public transport must be concerned not only with keeping costs down but also with providing a flexible framework within which the less poor, as well as the poor, can use public transport with confidence and comfort. If adequate public transport is not available, then the rich will use private automobiles while the relatively poor will shift first to bicycles, then to motorcycles (Vietnam and Indonesia), then to taxis (China and Indonesia), and ultimately to inexpensive cars as their incomes increase. The failure of conventional public transport may also generate a burgeoning small-vehicle paratransit sector that can contribute to maintaining accessibility, but that may have adverse consequences for congestion, air quality (pollution), and urban structure.

THE URBAN BUS SECTOR

In many developing countries of Africa, Asia, and Latin America, bus services were at one time provided by regulated monopolies. In colonial regimes these monopolies were often owned and managed by expatriates as subsidiaries of major suppliers in the colonizing country. In the postcolonial period, they were taken over into national ownership but continued to operate as protected monopolies. In the socialist economies, nationally owned public sector monopolies were also the rule. In both situations—former colony and former socialist economy—the traditional monopolies have now mostly collapsed.[2] In some Latin American countries, they have been replaced by smaller, privately owned companies operating under permissions granted by the municipal authorities.[3] In Africa they have largely been replaced by a fragmented small-vehicle paratransit sector, while in Eastern Europe and central Asia, a similar process of decline is at various stages of completion.[4] Only in China—where operations remain in public ownership but are adopting increasingly commercial approaches to business—and in a few major cities in India and Eastern Europe do traditional public operators still dominate.

Although the details of history vary from country to country, the processes of public transport decline have much in common. In many cases governments have attempted to use the public transport industry as an instrument of social policy by simultaneously constraining fare levels and structures, and by guaranteeing favorable wages and working conditions to employees. As deficits mount, and in the absence of a secure fiscal basis for subsidy, first maintenance, then service reliability, and finally operating capacity disappear.[5] In the process of decline, public subsidy tends to be progressively captured by favored, but not necessarily very poor, groups (for example, unionized labor or middle-class students).[6] Overregulation also tends to discourage market responsiveness.

The decline is not solely a result of cash starvation. Public sector operations generally lack proper incentives for, or are constrained politically against, acting efficiently. This can be demonstrated by comparisons between public and private operators in the same country, as exemplified for Delhi, India, in table 7.1.[7] The significance of staffing ratios in these comparisons is a delicate issue. Clearly, if the opportunity cost of labor is very low because of high unemployment or low productivity throughout the economy, it may be quite economic to operate with high staff-to-output ratios. Indeed that is the basis on which small vehicles that are operated informally are so competitive in many low-income economies. But the institutionalized protection of labor in a public sector bus industry imposes the costs of maintaining the income of what is often a relatively privileged group (unionized labor) on a relatively poor group (public transport passengers), as well as entrenching a long-term disincentive to productivity improvement. Maintaining an artificially high labor complement in public sector bus operations is thus likely to be a very poorly targeted form of poverty reduction strategy. It is for this reason that competition is preferred.

COMPETITION TO MAKE PUBLIC SECTOR OPERATIONS MORE EFFICIENT

Competitive pressures can be introduced in various forms, both within the traditional monopoly and between firms either "for the market" or "in the market." Given the inherent defects of the traditional uncontested monopoly and the demonstrated potential of competition to gen-

TABLE 7.1 EFFICIENCY OF BUS OPERATIONS IN DELHI, 1995		
Measure	**DTC**	**Private**
Peak-period fleet utilization	83%	93%
Kilometers per bus per day	216	246
Passengers per bus per day	751	1,584
Staff per bus	9.6	4.6

Note: DTC = Delhi Transport Corporation.
Source: Authors.

erate cost reductions and service quality improvements, the critical issue is how to establish the best ways of organizing competition in order to secure the city's strategic objectives for its transport system.

Many public sector transport operators are engaged in competitive procurement of equipment and a range of support services (cleaning, catering, professional services, construction, maintenance, engineering, and so on) to reduce costs, improve product quality, even out internal workloads, and eliminate the need for peak capacity. It is good management practice to conduct regular assessments in order to compare the cost of undertaking functions in-house with that of subcontracting to outsiders. The combination of some freedom to subcontract with performance agreements between the operating agency and its political master is one way of attempting to improve performance. Competition in performance can also take place between units performing similar functions within an organization or by benchmarking on bus operators in other cities or countries. However, such arrangements tend to offer only weak incentives to management, poor leverage over factor suppliers (particularly labor), and to be poorly enforced.[8]

COMPETITION FOR THE MARKET
Firms can compete for the market in several ways.

- **Gross cost service contracting** involves the procurement by a public authority from an operator of specified services at a price determined through competitive tendering. Contracts are usually for three to five years. The operator passes all on-bus revenues to the procuring authority and does not take any revenue risk. This system requires a secure means of ensuring that the procuring authority actually gets any fares that are paid on the vehicle, and careful monitoring to ensure that suppliers actually do provide the service for which they have been contracted.

- **Net cost service contracting** is similar to gross cost contracting, except that the operator keeps the revenue and hence incurs both the revenue and supply-cost risks. This increases the incentive to the supplier to provide the service contracted for (otherwise he loses his fare revenue)[9] and obviates the need for complex fare collection and security arrangements. However, it makes modal coordination more difficult and often involves higher net cost for the authorities, since the supplier is incurring an extra revenue risk, against which he is averse, and for which he will require remuneration.

- **Management contracting** involves operator responsibility for the management of a system's operation, possibly including service specification, within agreed-on parameters. The customer authority usually owns operational assets, although the operator may be responsible for their procurement and maintenance as well as negotiating labor wages and conditions. Intermodal coordination is relatively easy to achieve with this device. As long as the payment arrangements are well structured, there is also a high incentive to provide high-quality service to attract customers. The weakness is that the competitive pressure may be fairly weak, trade union power relatively strong, and costs relatively high.

- **Franchising** involves the grant of an exclusive right to provide a service that meets a number of general quantity, quality, and price standards established by the authority, usually because of a competition. The franchise may be for a self-contained area, such as a town or sector of a larger city, but it is also possible to have route franchises—especially with fixed track systems. They differ from service contracts in allowing the contractor a greater degree of freedom to develop the system. The franchisee may have to be paid by the authority to provide service and fare combinations that are not commercially viable.

- **Concessions** involve the granting of an exclusive right to provide a service without payment by the authority, although the authority may attach conditions, such as maximum fares or minimum service requirements. In all other respects the concessionaire is acting on his own behalf and not as an agent of the authority. Contracts are usually for rather longer periods, often 10 years or more, to allow the contractor to benefit from his development of the market.

The relationship between these various forms is shown in figure 7.1. There is a rapidly developing body of experience with these competitive forms resulting largely from the wave of regulatory reforms in Western Europe. Competitive tendering of service rights has also begun to extend into the developing and transitional economies.[10]

COMPETITION IN THE MARKET

The most direct form of competition is that of a totally *open market,* in which there are no restrictions on transport operators except those imposed by general law on business practices, vehicle construction and use, vehicle emissions, and highway and traffic matters. Even where there is no quantitative limitation on competition, the open market is usually associated with some form of *quality licensing,* which specifies minimum conditions for entry, including vehicle specifications, environmental performance, and maintenance standards. In some cases the qualitative conditions may also cover the type of service to be operated (including stopping places), fares, and trading practices.

A more restricted form of competition in the market may occur where, although there may be several operators providing services in competition with each other, the total number of vehicles allowed to operate is limited by the authority. This is a very common form of regulation for taxi markets. Particularly where fares are also controlled, this usually results in licenses acquiring value as a "business asset."

Competition in the market gives suppliers the greatest degree of freedom to respond to consumer demand and gives to the consumer the most direct instrument—his willingness to pay—to influence what is supplied. But market competition is not responsive to several important types of "market failure." First, if there is insufficient demand to meet the costs of supply, then there will be no service, irrespective of the importance which society attaches to the provision of some basic minimum service level. Second, the market is not responsive to various external effects, such as congestion and environmental impact, unless they are directly charged for. Third, because of information asymmetry and the difficulties associated with "shopping around," the process of competition may result in a combination of price and quality of service supplied, which is not what the majority of consumers would prefer. Fourth, it will not be in the interest of the individual bus operators to adapt their services and fares to promote modal integration.

These drawbacks are not merely theoretical. Deregulation of public transport in Santiago, Chile, in 1988 resulted in massive overprovision of capacity, increased urban congestion, and environmental degradation, as old and unsuitable vehicles were introduced into service, and large increases in fares occurred as operators responded to declining load factors. A number of aspects of anticompetitive or antisocial on-the-road behavior have also occurred in deregulated or inadequately supervised markets, including:

- "Hanging back," to maximize patronage either on the road or at terminals (Accra)
- "Blocking," to obstruct rival operators' services (Santiago during deregulation)
- "Racing," to beat rivals' vehicles in picking up passengers (Nairobi and Bogotá)
- "Turning back," when lightly loaded, to pick up passengers waiting to travel in the opposite direction (Pusan, Republic of Korea).[11]

CHOOSING AN APPROPRIATE SYSTEM FOR MANAGING COMPETITION

Where well-managed competitive regimes have replaced public sector monopolies in cities in

FIGURE 7.1 URBAN PUBLIC TRANSPORT COMPETITION: REGIMES AND TRANSITIONS

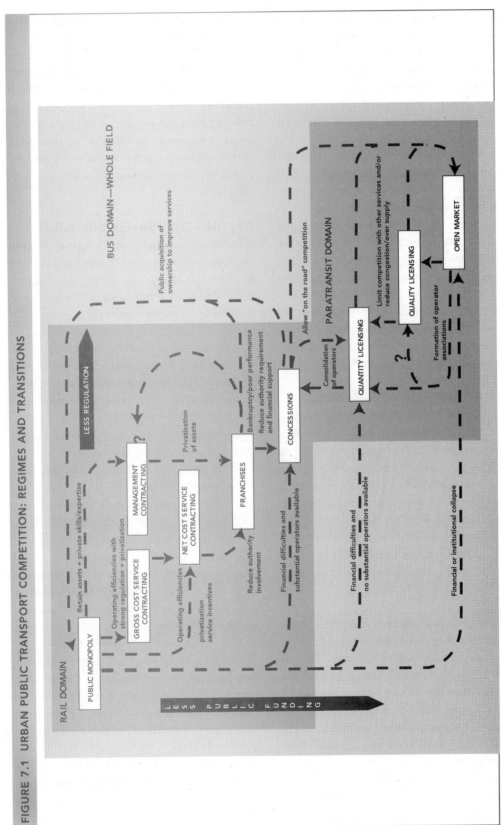

Source: Halcrow Fox 2000b.

industrialized countries—such as London (United Kingdom), Stockholm (Sweden), and Copenhagen (Denmark)—costs per unit of output have fallen between 20 and 40 percent,[12] and service levels have been maintained (figure 7.2).

The policy message is clear. Well-managed competition can be of great benefit to the poor, but badly regulated competition can have some very damaging consequences. Because of this, it is crucial to choose a competitive regime appropriate to the objectives of the procuring authority, the nature of the system being managed (particularly its size and number of modes), the potential strength of competition in the supply market, and the administrative capability of the procuring authority ("getting the right framework"). It is also crucial to make sure that the generic system is well adapted to the local circumstances and that it is well managed and regulated ("getting the framework right").

GETTING THE RIGHT FRAMEWORK

The objectives of the authority are the first concern. Both the achievement of multimodal coordination and the implementation of distributionally motivated subsidy structures are easier to achieve with a small number of suppliers (concessioning or area franchising rather than route contracting), and when the supplier is not dependent on direct fare revenue (gross rather than net cost contracts). On the other hand, costs are likely to be lowest where competitive pressures are strongest (with shorter contract-based route systems).

The larger the system and the greater the number of modes involved, the more complex will be the coordination problems. If the authority itself does not have the administrative skills to perform this function, then it may best obtain that service through a system concession with an experienced specialist company. Many French cities have either management contracts or system franchises for this reason.[13]

It is also clear that it is easier to operate a competitive system when there are already several suppliers to the local market of appropriate size and competence. This situation is, however, susceptible to change. If there is only one incumbent public sector monopolist, it can be split into several smaller competing units, as in London. If the operators are too numerous and too fragmented, they can be combined into a smaller number of groups, as with the "empresas" in Bogotá, Colombia, or the operators' associations more recently developed in the cities of Uzbekistan.

GETTING THE FRAMEWORK RIGHT

Whichever system is chosen, effective competition between private sector suppliers can only be achieved if the public sector itself is appropriately structured and capable. This imposes a number of critical institutional requirements:

- Political supervision of public transport that is separated from professional management
- Service planning that is separated from service provision, and adequately staffed and skilled
- Acquisition of new procurement skills, in the case of franchising or contracting
- Operations privatized, or at the very least commercialized
- Public company operation units restructured in a form conducive to competition, or subject to strong external competition.

This program of reforms may take time and require progressive refinement, especially where it involves concepts and procedures that are novel to the country (box 7.1).

Contracts must be of clearly defined duration. For route service contracts where the procuring authority is defining fare and service levels, the contracts can be of relatively short duration (three to five years). Particularly where there is a regular stream of contracts coming up for bid, it is not necessary for the contract length to reflect bus life, since vehicles can be switched between contracts either through secondhand markets or through leasing arrangements. Extension of con-

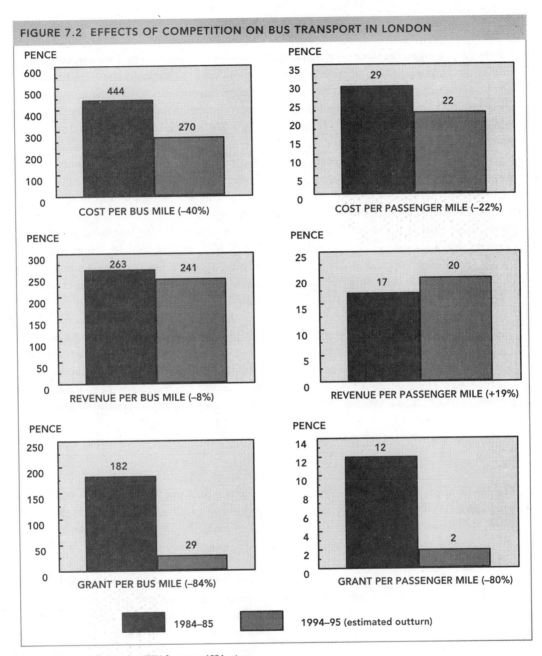

FIGURE 7.2 EFFECTS OF COMPETITION ON BUS TRANSPORT IN LONDON

COST PER BUS MILE (–40%)

COST PER PASSENGER MILE (–22%)

REVENUE PER BUS MILE (–8%)

REVENUE PER PASSENGER MILE (+19%)

GRANT PER BUS MILE (–84%)

GRANT PER PASSENGER MILE (–80%)

1984–85   1994–95 (estimated outturn)

Source: Transport for London (TFL) figures at 1994 prices.

tracts saves tendering costs but can blunt competition and, where it is allowed to become the norm, can be the basis on which an ostensibly competitive system becomes captured by a cartel of existing operators.[14]

Contracts must also define the rights and duties of the parties in as complete and consistent a way as possible. If fares are controlled, contracts should define the process for their adjustment to account for general cost inflation, as well as

BOX 7.1 INTRODUCING COMPETITIVELY TENDERED FRANCHISES IN UZBEKISTAN

Urban public transport services were traditionally supplied in Uzbekistan by state-owned enterprises that enjoyed areawide, sometimes citywide, monopolies. Beginning in late 1997, however, as part of the transformation of this former socialist economy into one that functions on market principles, the Uzbek government implemented radical changes in the organization and regulation of urban public bus transport services. Through a gradual and carefully planned process, which included experiments in a few cities, a study tour to London, and progressive scaling up to all secondary cities, responsibility has been given to the city administrations to organize all bus services on the basis of exclusive route franchises. These franchises are allocated through a competitive tendering process open freely to private companies and associations of small owner-operators as well as the state-owned enterprises. Tendering is under the responsibility of a special commission in each city, chaired by a deputy mayor, and operating under precise rules set by a transport regulatory agency in the central government. Bidders' discounts—if any—from the passenger fare ceiling, proposed service frequency, and bus fleet characteristics are the main selection criteria. Franchise duration, initially set at six months, renewable once for another six months, is progressively being extended (and is now at one year).

These reforms, completed in two years, have resulted in impressive changes. Numerous private operators have entered the public transport market, many new jobs have been created in the emerging bus service sector, and a healthy competition has developed (particularly for the rapidly growing minibus services). Private operators now supply more than 50 percent of all urban transport services. A bus route franchising system is also now being implemented in Tashkent.

Source: J-C. Crochet, from World Bank project files.

define the compensation for any discretionary fare adjustments introduced by the procuring authority. If this is not properly provided for, franchising systems are doomed to failure, as occurred in Jamaica.[15]

It is possible, in principle, for competition to operate between privately and publicly owned operators, but that type of operation can only work effectively if the public sector operators are strictly commercialized, subject to a bankruptcy constraint on their commercial behavior, free from specific public service requirements not imposed on private competitors, and not eligible to be "bailed out" directly or indirectly by central or local government. Such operation will probably require some legal change in the operators' status, and will probably only be secure if there is also an independent auditing arrangement to ensure that the operators do not bid below costs

to obtain business. These were the conditions under which public and private sectors competed in London for the interim period before the public sector operations were privatized.

A phased reform is possible as long as there is a sufficiently clear program and timetable to give private competitors the confidence that the reform will be consummated, and to give the public sector operators an incentive to adjust in preparation for competition and privatization, rather than to dig in politically to prevent it. In the case of the reform in London just mentioned, there was a timetable both for the extension of competitive tendering through the whole network and for the reorganization and privatization of the public sector operators. There will inevitably be a tendency to argue that subsidies should be phased out slowly in order to avoid any adverse impact on fares. In practice, most of the benefits are likely to arise in the initial round of tenders, so it is advisable that contracts be let from the outset on conditions that are likely to be financially sustainable in the long run.

PARATRANSIT

One of the most notable features of the public transport sector in the developing and transitional economies in recent years has been the explosive growth of publicly available passenger transport services outside the traditional public transport regulatory system, often referred to as paratransit.[16]

A number of characteristics are typical of paratransit services, although not necessarily applicable in all cases. These include:

- Services are usually unscheduled and often, though not always, on demand-responsive routes, filling gaps in formal transit provision.[17]
- The vehicles operated are typically small, including motorcycles,[18] partly because of the greater ease of financing and flexibility of operation of the small vehicles, and partly because controls over small vehicles are lax even in situations where entry to the large-vehicle market is strictly controlled. In some cities, such as Damascus, Syrian Arab Republic, small vehicles dominate the market.
- The vehicles used are often old, having been retired from other countries or other uses domestically, so that the capital investment necessary to enter the business may be small.
- The vehicles used are also often very simple, including, in many countries, NMT vehicles. Some of these vehicles, such as the motorized rickshaws of East and South Asia and the jeepneys of Manila, are very specialized, but in many cases they are simply adaptations for passenger carriage of whatever vehicle is inexpensively available (including converted trucks in Africa and motorcycle taxis in Bangkok).

Paratransit services are usually provided by informal operators with the following characteristics:

- They are "noncorporate," usually operating as single-person enterprises, although frequently with a vehicle owner who is not the operator. Often the driver pays a daily fee to the owner, incurs operating and maintenance costs, and keeps all revenue in excess of the fee. This gives a high incentive to work long hours and to obtain paying passengers by all available means, including touting, poaching, racing, and so on.
- They are often outside the tax system or benefit from favorable treatment of the noncorporate sector.[19] They may also have an advantage in competition with public sector operators, with costs inflated by minimum wage regulations, strict working hour requirements, neglect, and corruption.

Paratransit performs many roles. In Africa it is the dominant mode of public transport of the poor. In the former Soviet Union, it supplements a declining formal sector. In East and South Asia, and to some extent in Latin America, it complements the formal sector, providing differentiated services in identified market niches. In other parts of Latin America, it increasingly competes head-on with the traditional suppliers. Paratransit provides a range of services including:

- Feeder services linking inaccessible housing areas to the main transport routes (the four-wheel drives in the barrios of Caracas or the cycle rickshaws of Dhaka)
- Local distribution in inaccessible areas that are not served, or are underserved, by conventional public transport (Lima)
- Trunk services complementing, or competing by quality differentiation with, the formal sector on major routes (the minibuses of many central Asian countries or the "peruas" [passenger vans] of São Paulo and many other Brazilian cities)
- Direct longer-distance services on routes where the formal sector supply is slower or infrequent (the "truchos" of Buenos Aires)
- Duplication of franchised services.

There are many different combinations of informal transport structure, organization, service, and vehicle type. Table 7.2 classifies the examples mentioned above.[20]

THE PROBLEMS OF INFORMALITY

The informal sector is often viewed as a nuisance by national and municipal transport authorities, particularly when those authorities are responsible for the provision of conventional bus services. Despite this view, the sector has some important merits that have led the international institutions, including the World Bank, to view it more favorably, not least as a source of employment for the poor. In many countries it represents a very significant entry point to urban employment. For example, pedicab drivers in many Asian countries have some of the longest hours of work (typically 70 per week), lowest levels of education, and lowest incomes of all categories of workers, and include a disproportionately large share of recent rural-to-urban migrants. In many Asian

cities, it is estimated that over 15 percent of the population is dependent directly or indirectly on informal sector transport for their livelihood. In Dhaka, the proportion has been estimated at over 25 percent.[21]

The services that the informal transport sector provides are also valuable. Particularly in South Asia, informal transport performs a feeder function for relatively well-off people. In other cases, particularly in lower-income countries in Africa, it is often the mode of transport "of the poor" as well as "by the poor." In some cites it may do both—for example, in Manila 45 percent of trips are carried by the "down-market" jeepneys but another 12 percent by the "up-market" FX minivans. It is usually very market responsive, providing access to poor areas, direct routing, speed, and flexibility of service. If there is a demand for these characteristics that is not being met by the formal sector, the informal sector will invariably meet it if permitted (and often even if not per-

Vehicle type	Service features		Passenger capacity	Service niche	Market regime	Examples
	Routes	Schedules				
Large bus	Fixed	Fixed	25–60	Line-haul	Franchised	Buenos Aires; Rostov, Russian Federation
Minibus	Fixed	Fixed/semifixed	12–24	Line-haul	Franchised	São Paulo; Bangkok; Harare, Zimbabwe; Johannesburg, South Africa
Jeepney	Fixed	Semifixed	12–24	Line-haul	Franchised	Manila
Microbus and pick-up truck	Fixed	Semifixed	4–11	Feeder	Licensed	Caracas
Shared taxi	Variable	Variable	3–6	Short trips	Licensed	Casablanca, Morocco; Lima; Maracaibo, Rep. Bol. de Venezuela
Three-wheeler	Variable	Variable	2–4	Short trips, feeder	Unregulated	Phnom Penh, Cambodia; Delhi; Bangkok; Jakarta
Motorcycle	Variable	Variable	1–4	Feeder, some longer distances	Unregulated	Bangkok; Cotonou, Benin; Lomé, Togo; Douala, Cameroon
Pedicab and horse-drawn cart	Variable	Variable	1–6	Short trips, feeder	Unregulated	Dhaka; Vientiane, Lao People's Dem. Rep.; Mumbai

Notes: "Franchised" means holding official permission specifying task, area of operations, and so on. "Licensed" means holding unspecified permission to operate the vehicle.
Source: Based on Cervero 2001.

mitted!). This high degree of market responsiveness means that there may be little need for government support or economic regulation. It is inherently fragmented and hence highly competitive, although that has disadvantages as well as advantages, and typically results in the emergence of either formal regulation or informal self-regulation through operators' associations.

Despite these advantages, informal transport has a very poor image and reputation. It is often a very low earnings sector, with crews exploited by vehicle owners. It has an association with poverty, viewed as symbolically inappropriate by government, which tries to reduce its role as much as possible. There appear to be three main aspects of informal transport systems that contribute to this negative image:

- Dangerous on-the-road behavior and association with crime and violence
- Urban congestion and adverse environmental impacts resulting from use of small, old, and ill-adapted vehicles
- Undermining of basic network of existing services.

These defects are frequently exploited by vested interests. Police and other public officials may take advantage of the quasi-legal nature of the sector to supplement their incomes.[22] Traditional operators also exploit the limitations of the informal sector as reason for protecting the formal sector. The policy quandary is how to distinguish between real problems and the special pleading of vested interests.

Controlling operating practices

Paratransit is often criticized because the operator will only provide service where he considers it worthwhile to do so. But in many circumstances that will not matter. In particular, where the driver is leasing the vehicle on a daily basis, he may only be able to make a surplus over the rent by starting early or finishing late, or both, and plying his trade wherever there are passengers to be found. His standard of "remunerativeness," or prof-

itability, is thus very low, and his service coverage prolific. As experience has proved over many years in Buenos Aires, and more recently in the secondary cities of Uzbekistan, the organization of informal operators into route associations can ensure disciplined service.

Where there is a desire to provide even more services than the informal sector can provide commercially, it is argued that a monopolist public supplier is required. That is, of course, a fallacious argument. Directly subsidized services can be efficiently obtained through competitive tendering of franchises. Even cross-subsidy can be organized within a competitively tendered franchising system—as in London and several other large cities in Europe—either by packaging profitable and nonprofitable services together in tendered lots or by using fees from "positive" concessions to finance "negative" ones.

The most common concern about a fragmented informal sector is that the competitive pressure to earn a living will result in excess capacity, low load factors, and antisocial and often dangerous operating practices, such as lack of attention to passenger safety, racing, turning short, blocking intersections while touting for traffic, and so on. Certainly there is evidence of such behavior in a number of cities, including Kingston, Jamaica, and Harare.

Exponents of free markets have frequently argued that, in the long term, operators will see that it is not in their own interest to continue such undesirable practices. Typically this results in the formation of associations that limit entry and organize more disciplined service. Such associations are the norm in most of Sub-Saharan Africa and are common wherever the informal sector is unregulated.

There are several problems with such self-regulation. First, because it is outside public control, the association acts in the interests of its members and suppliers, and not in the interests of its customers. During the initial period of complete deregulation in Santiago, Chile, the action of the operators' cartels led to a rapid increase in fares.[23] Second, because self-regulation is not based on any legal rights of exclusion, it is often enforced by violent means, as occurred in the taxi (minibus) sector in South Africa. Third, the need to ensure fair allocation of revenues between members often results in suboptimal operating practices. In particular, ensuring that all vehicles are dispatched from the terminal with full loads equalizes incomes at the expense of passengers (forcing them to walk long distances to terminals to access the service) and utilization of vehicles (forcing delays as they queue for their turn to depart). Only the more secure and long-standing associations are able to adopt more efficient practices—and that extra security may involve more monopoly power.

Congestion and environmental impacts

The pressure of competition may also lead to an excess supply of vehicles (in the sense that more vehicles are in service than are necessary to provide uncrowded service at high frequency) and the use of small and often inexpensive older vehicles. Small vehicles are usually much simpler and lighter in construction than are conventional buses. Because of this, both capital and operating costs per vehicle seat vary relatively little with respect to vehicle size. If labor costs are also low, there is no incentive to use large vehicles, which the informal sector would find difficult to finance in any case. Because the effects of congestion and environmental impact are external to the individual operator, the main incentive is to operate inexpensive, and hence often older, vehicles. The result is that totally unregulated entry in low-income countries is likely to result in a higher level of congestion and environmental impact than is socially desirable.

Two economic distortions have contributed to the explosion of informal services in small vehicles. First, there is often an excess supply of labor in urban areas that coexists with minimum public sector wage rates and inefficient operation for the formal operators. Second, in the absence of any pricing system for the use of scarce road space or adequate proxy priority given to large

vehicles, the informal sector small vehicle is able to provide a faster, and sometimes less expensive, service than is the formal operator.

Undermining of basic network of services

A subtler problem has been emerging in recent years. In many cities in Latin America (such as Buenos Aires, São Paulo, and Fortaleza) and in some cities in East Asia (such as Bangkok), informal operators are beginning to operate services in direct competition with traditional large-vehicle services, whether operated by public or private enterprises. The basis for informal operators' ability to compete in this way has often been that, by operating smaller vehicles and a denser network of services, they are able to offer a quicker, more convenient door-to-door service than can the traditional operator. In some cases (as typical in Brazil), this service is provided at fares (and sometimes on routes) identical with those of the traditional operator.[24] In other cases the service may be operated at a premium fare. In either case, the effect may be to reduce the demand for the services of the traditional operator and thus either increase the breakeven fare or reduce the breakeven frequency. Both responses would be to the disadvantage of those passengers captive to the traditional services.

Probably the most serious impact is that on the development of integrated multimodal service and fare structures. In a number of Brazilian cities, where metros or suburban railways have been rehabilitated and bus networks restructured in the context of an integrated fare system, passengers are being lost to informal operators who provide direct service at competitive fares. The critical question is what, if anything, public authorities should do to respond to or control this market-oriented response.

THE FUTURE OF PARATRANSIT AND THE INFORMAL SECTOR

Given the importance of paratransit both as an income generator and, often, as a service provider to the poor, attempting to eliminate it by administrative action could generate significant unrest. Following action to control the sector in São Paulo in 1999, roads were blocked and 24 formal sector large vehicles were destroyed in a period of three months. Repression is thus not a likely solution to the perceived problems. Rather, governments should examine why the informal sector exists, and then try to identify a regulatory and administrative framework within which the potential of the sector can be mobilized and developed.

Many of the defects attributed to the sector can be attributed to its insecurity. Predatory behavior on the road is necessary to make a living in a context of very low opportunity costs and, hence, in the context of proliferation of capacity. Inadequate capitalization, and the consequent small size and poor quality of the vehicles used in many cases, may in turn be attributed to the absence of a sufficiently secure expectation of the future revenue to justify commitment of capital to large assets that lack versatility.

A number of different approaches have been adopted to overcome this lack of a secure field of operation. Several countries allow free access in certain specialized markets (local feeder buses in Seoul, air-conditioned services in Dhaka, commuter charter bus services in Delhi), but these tend to be limited niche markets, and often require a higher class of vehicle to attract patronage. In São Paulo, a provision for the formal sector operators to accommodate 15,000 "peruas" (passenger vans) to supplement their own services has failed to defuse an explosive situation that has involved the suppression of three times as many existing (albeit illegal) operations.

A rather different approach to the problem of the core supply of informal transport services is the creation of "curb rights," permitting registered informal sector operators to pick up and set down passengers in specific areas, but not otherwise constraining their activities. The aim is to give a supervising authority some leverage (withdrawal of registration) to discourage antisocial on-road behavior, while leaving freedom to the operators to respond flexibly to demand. It is very similar to the licensing arrangement found in rank-based taxi markets in many industrialized countries, but it is usually supplemented with some control on fares or capacity and also often overlaid with regulation or self-regulation to determine access priority. It has not been applied on any substantial scale to buses or minibuses, and would probably be very difficult to enforce in developing countries.

The more common solution in the bus sector has been found in the form of medium-term route franchise contracts. The immediate impediment to the inclusion of the informal sector in such a system is often the desire of the municipal authorities to guarantee regular, scheduled service on routes requiring a large number of vehicles. This impediment can be overcome by combining franchising (preferably competitively tendered) with freedom of establishment for (and indeed some encouragement to) operators' associations. That solution was the basis on which the urban bus sector in Buenos Aires operated very effectively until it began to be undermined by a new influx of illegal shared-taxi operations. It is also the basis on which competitively tendered franchising is being introduced in countries of the former Soviet Union, such as Uzbekistan and the Kyrgyz Republic. Some 2,700 informal sector vans have recently been legalized and regulated to give alternative services as cooperatives in Rio de Janeiro.

The main problem in pursuing that regulatory path is to determine how best to prevent collusion and the emergence of a grand cartel able to exploit monopoly power. In Argentina this was achieved, despite the absence of competitive tendering, by ensuring that route franchises granted to specific associations overlapped, so that there was a degree of competition on the road. In Uzbekistan it has been done by official encouragement for the creation of multiple associations.

Competitively tendered franchising arrangements also make it possible to address the issues of congestion (which can be addressed by limiting the amount of capacity franchised to operate in particularly congested streets) and environment (which can be addressed by putting qualitative standards or criteria in the selection process). Both problems have been very satisfactorily addressed in Santiago Chile, although road and rail passenger transport remain as competing alternatives, often serving different income groups, rather than as part of an integrated network in the absence of any institutionally systematic provision for improving modal coordination.

Some additional encouragement may also be needed. Restricted access to credit limits the ability of many operators to buy their own vehicles, forcing them into a dependence on an absentee owner. Even with the introduction of franchising, there will be a period, until the system is well established, in which it will be difficult for operators to secure funding for vehicles against a franchise contract. Assistance with vehicle finance may be a necessary component of reform. The ultimate objective should not be to maintain a highly fragmented bus industry for its own sake, but rather to encourage more informed and disciplined entrepreneurial structures on which competition can be based. In fact, most of the operators' associations in Buenos Aires developed naturally from pools of privately owned vehicles to shareholding companies. Some of the recently formed operators' associations in Uzbekistan are already beginning to undertake functions, such as joint purchasing, which are steps to corporate form.

In summary, there are two conflicting considerations concerning the role of the informal sector. On the one hand, the services provided by the informal sector may better respond to consumer demand than those of the formal sector, and employment in informal transport may be one of the few areas of gainful economic activity open to new rural-to-urban migrants. On the other hand, informal transport brings with it adverse effects on congestion, environment, and basic public transport network viability.

The balance of these considerations may be in favor of paratransit in smaller cities, where excessive supply is not a problem, but against it in larger, congested, and polluted cities. The critical question then becomes at what point does the growth of paratransit need to be controlled and redirected either to niche markets or more formal arrangements. In that progression, some policy measures should be specifically directed to attenuating congestion or environmental impacts directly where they occur. Limiting access to particular locations and enforcing environmental and safety regulations are the appropriate policy instruments—universal prohibitions of the informal sector are not. Even in larger cities, the appropriate policy response would seem to be one that permits informal operators to compete for franchises in sectors of the market where their flexibility is particularly advantageous but where their small vehicle size is acceptable. Authorities thus need to plan for the use, development, and migration of paratransit in a more positive way than has hitherto been common.

CONCLUSIONS: TOWARD A STRATEGY FOR PUBLIC TRANSPORT

Public transport is critical to the welfare of the urban poor and a crucial element in any poverty-oriented city development strategy. Yet it is failing to provide the necessary service and is actually in decline in many developing countries just at the time when many much richer, industrialized countries have begun to recognize its importance. That decline has some technical roots but is mostly a consequence of the inappropriateness, for the tasks expected of it, of the institutional and financial arrangements under which it typically operates.

The main elements of a strategy for urban public road passenger transport are suggested as follows:

On planning and integration
- Public transport provision should be treated as a key component of a city development strategy or structure plan.

- Public transport must be given a high priority in the design and use of scarce road space.

On competition
- Planning of public transport service should be separated from provision of public transport service.
- Competition should be recognized as the best way to secure good value for money in public transport.
- In complex cities the best form of competition for the market may be through tendered franchises or concessions.
- The competitive regime should be designed and regulated to maintain healthy competition and avoid excessive oligopolistic tendencies.
- City administrations should be restructured to facilitate competitive procurement of services (see chapter 11).

On paratransit and the informal sector
- The role of paratransit in satisfying dispersed trip patterns and in flexibly addressing the demands of the poor should be recognized.
- Anticompetitive or antisocial behavior within the sector should be controlled through the establishment and enforcement of quality standards.
- Cities should strive to find ways to mobilize the initiative potential of the informal sector through legalizing associations and through structuring franchising arrangements in order to give the small private sector the opportunity to participate in competitive processes.
- Cities must ensure that informal operators meet the same environmental, safety, and insurance requirements as formal operators, and that they meet their proper tax obligations.
- Cities should plan for a dynamic regime that will allow for a transition to a more formal role for the informal sector when appropriate.

On pricing
- General fare controls should be determined as part of a comprehensive city transport financing plan, and their effect on the expected quality and quantity of service carefully considered.
- Fare reductions or exemptions should be financed on the budget of the relevant line agency responsible for the categories of person affected (health, social sector, education, interior, and so on).

NOTES

1. Halcrow Fox 2000b.
2. Gwilliam 2001.
3. Aragão, Brasileiro, and Marar 1998.
4. For further detail, see Gwilliam 2000b.
5. Effective public sector operations still continue in some developed cities, such as Vienna (Austria), Stuttgart (Germany), and Zurich (Switzerland), even if relatively costly. The relevant ingredients for this outcome are efficient economies, high priority for public transport, and wealthy communities paying more attention to quality than to cost. Such conditions are rarely found in developing countries.
6. For an example of this, see Teurnier and Mandon-Adolehoume 1994.
7. Similarly, in São Paulo the now-defunct state operator had an average of 8.6 employees per bus compared to only 5.5 for private sector operators. Even after allowing for public sector employment associated with activities such as planning and coordination of the public transport system, labor productivity was still 28 percent below that of private sector operators.
8. World Bank 1995.
9. There may still be some service elements (the earliest bus, for example) that cost more to run than the revenue they earn, and for which there is an incentive not to supply, unless the supply is regulated.
10. See, for example, Gwilliam, Kumar, and Meakin 2000.
11. This is not in itself a bad practice as long as passengers are not seriously delayed or forced to pay twice. In the case of fragmented competition, these protections are rarely observed.
12. For a more detailed discussion of alternative forms of competition and some advice on their design, see Halcrow Fox 2000b.

13. Management contracting and system franchising are most common in France (Systra 2000).

14. See Aragão, Brasileiro, and Marar 1998 for a discussion of how this has happened in many Brazilian cities.

15. Gwilliam 1996.

16. This does not necessarily mean that they are operating illegally, as in many countries entry to the sector is effectively free, with operators subject only to the general rules of the road and law of the land. Nor does it necessarily mean that they are operating completely independently, since many informal sector operators are members of associations of operators.

17. Cervero 1998.

18. The motorcycle taxi is the most rapidly expanding segment of the market. It is estimated that there are 125,000 "moto-dubs" in Phnom Penh and 100,000 "rub-jangs" in Bangkok.

19. For example, in some of the Central Asian republics of the former Soviet Union, taxation on the informal sector amounts to less than 3 percent of revenue, compared with nearly 25 percent for the corporate sector.

20. For a fuller description and classification of types of informal transport, see Cervero 2001.

21. Gallagher 1992.

22. For example, the motorcycle taxi business in Bangkok involves buying off officialdom at several levels of the hierarchy (see Cervero 2001). Sometimes, as in Cairo, police become involved in ownership of the vehicles.

23. Dourthe and others 1998.

24. Associacão Nacional de Transportes Públicos 1999.

8 MASS RAPID TRANSIT

Mass rapid transit can contribute both to city efficiency and to the needs of the poor in the largest cities, but it can also impose a heavy fiscal burden. Alternative technologies should be evaluated both in operational and fiscal terms. More expensive rail-based systems should only be adopted within an integrated planning and financing structure ensuring system sustainability, effective coordination of modes, and affordable provision for the poor.

THE SCALE OF THE ISSUE

Mass rapid transit (MRT) comprises a spectrum of modes of urban public transport that use specific fixed-track or exclusive and separated use of a potentially common-user road track (such as metros, suburban railways, light rail transit, and busways). MRT usually has superior operating capacity and performance compared with unsegregated road-based public transport (such as buses, taxis, and paratransit). Rail-based metro systems in developing countries carry about 11 billion journeys a year, surface rail about 5 billion, and light rail about 2.5 billion. While the proportion of public transport trips by rail is more than 50 percent in Seoul and Moscow (and the proportion of passenger kilometers is even higher), rail systems dominate only in a very few cities.

MRT can, in principle, contribute to the achievement of all the main objectives of urban development policy. It can improve efficiency of the city economy by reducing travel costs and by maintaining a higher level of city-center activity and the associated economies of agglomeration than would otherwise be the case. The impact of poverty can be directly reduced where MRT is the major carrier of the poor, and indirectly reduced through the benefits the poor receive from economic prosperity. It can also improve the quality of life—immediately, through shifting movements to more environmentally benign modes of transport, and in the longer run, by supporting a more environmentally favorable land-use structure.

In practice, these benefits do not always accrue. Costs of rail investments are often underestimated and passenger flows overestimated.[1] Excessive indebtedness or unrealistic calls on municipal resources to finance expensive MRT modes can damage the local economy and preclude other socially desirable investments. Attempts to avoid that indebtedness through private financing or increased fares may disadvantage the poor by excluding them from use of the more expensive systems. The prohibition of parallel bus or minibus services may sometimes increase MRT financial viability by eliminating less-expensive, lower-quality modes on which the poor were most dependent. Potential congestion reduction and environmental benefit may be lost if the road space freed by a shift of passengers from conventional bus to MRT is allowed to be filled up by additional automobiles.

The central challenge with respect to urban MRT is to identify the strategic objectives being sought by the city, and then to identify means of implementation which best secure the benefits and evade the disbenefits listed above. Because there are a wide variety of city types, city objectives, MRT technologies, and pricing and financing mechanisms, there is a rich menu of strategic alternatives from which to choose. In many cases the problem is not simply that of exclusive choice *between* technologies, but more that of selecting the optimum mix of technologies and the optimum phasing of MRT capacity expansion. An appropriate strategic stance is thus not to be "for" or "against" MRT, or any particular variant of it, but to properly appreciate the critical factors affecting choice of technologies, operating, financing, and ownership arrangements, and to ensure that the choices made are consistent with city characteristics, objectives, and economic capability.[2]

Rather than advocating a "one-size-fits-all" MRT strategy, emphasis thus falls on the formulation of critical questions that must be addressed in designing an MRT strategy, and the presentation of evidence and experience relevant for addressing those questions. These critical questions include:

- What are the objectives and role of MRT within the city development strategy?
- How should MRT relate to urban structure and land-use policy?
- How does MRT impact on the urban environment?
- What factors should be considered in the choice of MRT technology?
- How should MRT be integrated within a broader transport sector policy?
- How should MRT be priced to gain maximum benefit?
- Who should own and finance MRT?
- What is the impact of MRT on the finances of national and local governments?

OBJECTIVES AND ROLE OF MASS RAPID TRANSIT WITHIN THE CITY DEVELOPMENT STRATEGY

The reduction of road congestion, with its consequent economic and environmental benefits, is usually the motivating factor for investments in MRT. Both because of its capability for carrying large volumes and for its superiority over buses in attracting traffic from, or limiting the trend of diversion to, the car, rail-based systems are usually preferred for the purpose of reducing road congestion. In fact, however, the studies of MRT outcomes in 1990,[3] and the recent update (Halcrow Fox 2000a), argue that congestion is rarely reduced. Rather, the effect is to permit the continued development of city-center activity while total movement volumes on the main radial links, along which metros are typically aligned, increase to levels that would have produced intolerable congestion in the absence of MRT.[4] It is hence the structuring effect to avoid sprawl of business activity and the consequential economies of agglomeration in production rather than reduction of transport costs over time that is the main source of economic benefit.

There are several corollaries of this argument. First, if the benefits of MRT are ultimately structural, then they should be planned and designed in the light of high-level objectives of a strategic structure plan. That is rarely the case, although it is notable that some of the more successful metro developments, such as that in Singapore, have been developed this way. Second, if MRT is designed to maintain the quality of access to the center, it needs to be supported by appropriate actions to feed the trunk links and hence needs to be developed in the context of a comprehensive transport plan. City-center development policies should be complementary to it. Third, if structural impacts are the objective, that should be reflected in the way MRT investments are appraised. Finally, for service to be maintained, the development needs to be properly financed. Cutting corners to reduce costs (such as the omission of elevators to high-level platforms on the new Bangkok Transit System [BTS] and Manila LRT3 systems) or charging high fares to maximize revenue for private concessions may actually reduce the economic benefit of the investment. A firm financial planning context is necessary to get the best out of efficiency-oriented MRT systems.

In cases where the main function of MRT is to provide basic accessibility in poor cities without alternative means of transport, the most important consideration might be the selection of a system that is affordable to users, or to the public budget, or to both. Where MRT is aimed primarily at reducing congestion and maintaining the central city, and predominantly carries middle-class passengers, it should be assessed in terms of its contribution to the economic viability of the city (from which the poor also benefit). The important poverty consideration in that context would be to ensure that the viability of the MRT system does not involve supporting policies that are damaging to the poor, and that its finance is supportable without damage to the maintenance of the desired level of other basic services to the poor.

RELATIONSHIP TO URBAN STRUCTURE AND LAND USE

The integration of MRT within the urban fabric makes some important demands on the planning system. Rights-of-way must be established and protected. Space must be released for depots and terminals. In addition, where high-density ancillary developments are intended, the land must be assembled into lots suitable for development and the appropriate densities of development sanctioned.

The most indisputable structuring effect of metros is that they allow central business districts in large, dynamic cities to continue growing, where service by road, either by car or bus, would be increasingly frustrated by congestion. Without the high-capacity links, activities would begin to be decentralized. This has implications both for city planning and for project evaluation. A conscious attempt to maintain the growth of the center will save on public infrastructure costs in other areas; avoiding these extra costs is an important part of the long-term benefit of MRT investments. Unfortunately the magnitude of those savings is little researched, particularly in developing countries, and the economic evaluation of MRT investments is usually based on the more conventional user cost-benefit appraisal. While that may still

be justifiable in the interest of avoiding the worst kind of "white elephants," a more wide-ranging multicriteria analysis may be the most suitable way of ensuring that those unmeasured effects are taken into consideration. An integrated land-use, urban transport, and air quality strategy, such as the PITU in São Paulo, is needed to ensure that the MRT system is adequately inserted in the urban structure.[5]

Obtaining desirable structuring effects outside the center is more difficult. Clustered multinuclear development associated with station locations sometimes occurs spontaneously, but normally requires either some preplanning by government (as in the cases of Singapore and Hong Kong, China) or close links between private ownership of the MRT system and contiguous developments (as is common in Japan). In both cases this requires land to be assembled for development in relatively large lots. This has been achieved by comprehensive public ownership of land in Hong Kong, China, by compulsory public purchase in Singapore, and through market mechanisms in some Japanese private railway developments.[6]

MASS RAPID TRANSIT AND THE URBAN ENVIRONMENT

One of the most common arguments for MRT systems is that by reducing more polluting private road traffic, they benefit the environment. Within the MRT family, rail systems are preferred to bus systems[7] because their use of electric traction is believed to mean that they are cleaner.[8] Whether this is true, of course, depends both on the source of electricity for the MRT and on the kind of road-based system with which the MRT is compared. Underground systems are often preferred to at-grade or elevated systems, because they are considered less intrusive in the urban fabric.[9] Underground metros are thus regarded as the most environmentally beneficial, even where the main diversion is from another public transport mode—the bus—rather than from the private car. Environmental benefits were accordingly among those taken into account by the World Bank in its initial appraisal of the Line 4 metro investment in São Paulo.

The main caveat to be entered against the environmental benefits of MRT concerns longer-term, less-direct effects. Insofar as metro investments allow a higher level of activity to be sustained in the historic city business centers than would otherwise be the case, the absolute level of inner-city road traffic may be little affected in comparison with the "without metro" case.[10] The critical question is then to what extent does it obviate growth of environmentally damaging traffic. Most assessments fall short of a thorough analysis of this counterfactual, though implying the net effect is beneficial.

CHOICE OF MASS RAPID TRANSIT TECHNOLOGY

The selection of technology has long been the most controversial element in discussions of MRT. Both costs and performance vary from location to location according to stop spacing, vehicle and system design, and so on. Table 8.1 gives data from systems recently completed or still in construction. In broad orders of magnitude, at-grade busway systems formed by conversion of existing roadway (including vehicles) cost between $1 million and $8 million per route kilometer, with the costs increasing to as much as $15 million where either the vehicles (as in Quito) or the infrastructures (as in Bogotá) become more sophisticated. Light rapid transit (LRT) costs are typically between $10 million and $30 million, though where the most sophisticated technology is used in a fully segregated system, as in the PUTRA system in Kuala Lumpur, the costs can approach those of a heavy rail system. Full heavy rail metros cost between $30 million and $100 million, the most expensive being fully automatic, fully underground systems. The capacity of the systems varies from busways, which can carry up to 20,000 passengers per hour in the peak direction (pphpd) at an average speed

of 17 to 20 kilometers per hour (km/h), to metros, which can carry up to 80,000 pphpd at an average speed of 40 to 50 km/h (where there are long stop spacings). Conversions of existing suburban railways, as in Recife or Linha Sul, Brazil, may offer high-potential capacity at reasonable cost, although many are not appropriately located to exploit this potential.

Busways are the least-expensive form of MRT, extensively developed (and now being extended) in Brazil, Colombia, and Ecuador.[11] They provide substantial capacity as trunk carriers in major corridors, as in São Paulo. They can be operated as a high-quality network, as in Curitiba; with electric traction if required, as in the San Mateus-Jabaquara system in São Paulo;[12] even retrofitted into existing road systems, as in Quito.[13] Yet, outside Latin America, they are rare in the developing world. This is partly due to their association with what is regarded as a relatively primitive technology, with a "bottom-of-the-market" image, not to be adopted when a metro can be afforded or reasonably aspired to. Their capacity is seen as limited, due to the small size of vehicles and interactions with other traffic at intersections.[14] In the technologically upgraded form of bus guidance systems, they are now being advocated as possible means of efficiently using space at bottlenecks, while being relatively inexpensive to retrofit.[15]

Many of these perceived problems can be overcome. Well-designed large buses (23-meter, double-articulated buses with five doors are used in Curitiba), off-vehicle ticketing, passing lanes at bus stops, and even platoon operation can bring effective capacity up to 20,000 pphpd. The original four-lane busway on Avenida Caracas in Bogotá managed 36,000 pphpd, albeit with reduced speed performance.

Good system design and specification of state-of-the-art clean and efficient vehicles, as in Curitiba, can change both the environmental image and the reality. Electric trolley vehicles, as used in Quito, can further reduce both air and

Example	Caracas (line 4)	Bangkok (BTS)	Mexico City (line B)	Kuala Lumpur (PUTRA)	Tunis (SMLT)	Recife (Linha sul)	Quito Busway	Bogotá (TransMilenio, phase 1)	Porto Alegre Busways
Category	Rail metro	Rail metro	Rail metro	Light rail	Light rail	Suburban rail conversion	Busway	Busway	Busway
Technology	Electric, steel rail	Electric, steel rail	Electric, rubber tire	Electric, driverless	Electric, steel rail	Electric, steel rail	AC electric duo-trolleybus	Articulated diesel buses	Diesel buses
Length (kilometers)	12.3	23.1	23.7	29	29.7 km	14.3	11.2 (+ext 5.0)	41	25
Vertical segregation	100% tunnel	100% elevated	20% elevated 55% at grade 25% tunnel	100% elevated	At grade	95% at grade 5% elevated	At grade, partial signal priority	At grade, mainly segregated	At grade, no signal priority
Stop spacing (kilometers)	1.5	1.0	1.1	1.3	0.9	1.2	0.4	0.7	0.4
Capital cost (millions of dollars)	1,110	1,700	970	1,450	435	166	110.3	213 (inf only)	25
of which:									
Infrastructure/TA/equipment (millions of dollars)	833	670	560	—	268	149	20.0	322	25
Vehicles (millions of dollars)	277	1,030	410	—	167	18	80 (113 vehs)	Not included (private operation)	Not included (private operation)
Capital cost/route kilometers (millions of dollars)	90.25	73.59	40.92	50.0	13.3	11.6	10.3	5.2	1.0
Initial (ultimate) vehicles or trains/hour/direction	20 (30)	20 (30)	13 (26)	30	—	8	40 (convoy operation planned)	160	—
Initial maximum passenger capacity	21,600	25,000	19,500	10,000	12000	9,600	9,000		20,000
Maximum passenger capacity	32,400	50,000	39,300	30,000	12000	36,000	15,000	35,000	20,000
Average operating speed (km/h)	50	45	45	50	13/20	39	20	20+ (stopping) 30+ (express)	20
Rev/operating cost ratio (percent)	—	100	20	>100	115% in 1998	—	100	100	100
Ownership	Public	Private (BOT)	Public	Private (BOT)	Public	Public	Public (BOT) under consideration	Public infrastructure, private vehicles	Public infrastructure, private vehicles
Year completed	2004	1999	2000	1998	1998	2002	1995 (ext 2000)	2000 (1998 prices)	Mostly 1990s

— Not available.

Note: BOT = Buy-own-transfer.

Sources: Pattison 1999; and BB&J Consult 2000.

noise pollution, at the expense of a near doubling of total system costs. In cities where roads are wide (as in much of the former Soviet Union) and the bus industry fairly concentrated, electric trolley vehicles can provide an affordable and flexible MRT alternative that is acceptable both to passengers and to the traditional carriers. However, they do require strong political commitment and effective public sector planning in overcoming impediments to finance, in ensuring priority treatment in traffic management and infrastructure design, and in service procurement and supervision. Systems in Curitiba and Bogotá have shown that this can be done, but it requires effective forward planning, strong local political leadership, and a degree of stability and nonpartisanship in policy that is not found everywhere.[16]

Light rapid transit (LRT) ranges from the conventional on-street tramways of Eastern Europe and the Arab Republic of Egypt to the sophisticated elevated and completely segregated systems of Singapore. LRT is expanding rapidly in industrialized countries in cities with low corridor volumes, as a secure and high-quality alternative to the private car, and sometimes serving as a feeder to heavy rail systems. In developing countries, where the need is for adequate capacity and speed for captive low-income public transport passengers, its role is less obvious. Where it operates at grade, without priority or protection from obstruction by other traffic, it has little or no performance advantage over busways.[17] Although low-cost rehabilitation of on-street tramways may sometimes be worthwhile (an example is the Bank-assisted rehabilitation in Budapest), they are usually an expensive proposition for the volume and speed achieved. Their main advantages are that they have less local air pollution impact, signal a more permanent commitment to public transport, and have an image that triggers support for complementary measures, which buses have great difficulty achieving.

With the exception of the conventional tram systems of Eastern Europe and the former Soviet Union, LRTs exist, or have been planned, only in relatively wealthy cities—such as Hong Kong, China; Singapore; Tunis; and Kuala Lumpur—or for high-income developments—such as the Tren de la Costa of Buenos Aires. Some newer road-based light transit systems, such as the Fura Fila guided trolleybus in São Paulo, have lower infrastructure costs than have a similarly segregated LRT. At the moment, LRTs are usually low-capacity prestige systems of doubtful value in poorer cities in the earlier stages of development. However, if viewed as mixed systems, partly at grade and partly elevated or underground, and as interim steps to the creation of a full metro in larger and more dynamic cities, they may have some role to play, not least as a means of preserving the necessary right-of-way for a subsequent metro development.

Suburban railways are often well located for radial journeys. Although even in relatively well-served cities (Mumbai, Rio de Janeiro, Moscow, Buenos Aires, and Johannesburg), they carry fewer than 10 percent of trips, they can be very important in providing for longer commuting trips. Existing, but less-well-used lines can be converted to effective local passenger service either in the form of a conventional rail service sharing facilities with other rail traffic or by replacement on the same right-of-way by a light rail system.[18] Suburban railways can have significant disadvantages, however. Sometimes, because they were developed before the growth of motorization, they have at-grade crossings that reduce their speed and capacity, and present serious safety hazards. Where the center of activity in the city has shifted, the central stations may not be well located; and in some cases underused rights-of-way become encumbered by poor people living illegally on publicly owned land (squatters), which makes redevelopment difficult. In some cases the sharing of track with freight or long-distance passenger services, as well as frequent grade crossings, also reduces their capacity.[19] Despite these problems, several systems could be converted into surface metros at a fraction of the cost of underground or elevated systems, even if there is a need to add an underground or elevated link to the central business district or any other populated area.[20] Several Asian cities (Mumbai, Delhi, Manila, Bangkok) and African cities (Abidjan, Côte d'Ivoire; Maputo, Mozambique; Cape Town, South Africa) are possible candidates for conversion of suburban railways into modern systems operated with diesel multiple units or electric multiple units.

The most serious impediments to suburban railways are frequently institutional. When operated by national rail organizations, suburban railways tend to be given low priority and are poorly coordinated with other urban public transport services (as in Colombo, Sri Lanka; Moscow; and Mumbai). In some cases the weakness of publicly owned national rail undertakings leaves their capacity severely underdeveloped (as in Manila). Recent experience has shown what can be achieved by addressing these problems. A program of concessioning to the private sector in Buenos Aires has revitalized the system, doubling patronage over a five-year period while reducing the budget burden of the system by nearly $1 billion per year. In Brazil the transfer of responsibility for suburban railways from the highly centralized Companhia Brasileira de Trens Urbanos (CBTU) to local (state) control, together with a government-funded rehabilitation program, has improved service in most of the major cities,[21] and, assisted by a program of concessioning,[22] is greatly reducing the fiscal burden (box 8.1). The costs of developing existing rights-of-way can be very reasonable; there is considerable scope for such developments. Serious attention should be given to eliminating the institutional impediments to the development of suburban railways as part of metropolitan MRT networks.

Metros are usually the most expensive form of MRT per route kilometer, but have the greatest capacity and best performance. With 10-car train sets and two-minute headways, the first Hong Kong, China, line has carried as many as 80,000 pphpd. The Moscow metro has regularly achieved headways below 90 seconds. São Paulo's East line has consistently carried more than 60,000 pphpd. However, many metros are designed for capacities around 30,000 to 40,000 pphpd, and few actually carry more than that.

Costs can vary greatly. Total capital costs can be as low as $8 million per kilometer where an at-grade right-of-way is available for conversion, and can rise to over $150 million per kilometer for an underground railway in difficult terrain.

A study of recently built metros showed total costs per kilometer for the underground systems in Latin America to be from two to three times higher than those for Madrid (table 8.2).[23] To a large degree, this was attributed to differences in project management arrangements. In Madrid, there was a high political commitment to complete the project, full financing was ensured from the beginning, and contractors were paid without delay. In most Latin American cases, there were delays and interruptions caused by lack of available finance and changing political priorities. Moreover, the small but highly experienced project management team of the Madrid metro company was given full power to make on-the-spot technical and financial decisions, thereby avoiding work delays and ensuring quick progress payments to the contractors. The government was seen to be a credible client by the contractors, whose prices thus included a lower risk element than is sometimes the case elsewhere. Additional reasons for the lower costs in Madrid have been ascribed to the technology adopted. Civil works costs were kept low by using the earth pressure balance method for tunneling, by strong geotechnical supervision monitoring, and by a standardized station design. Equipment cost differences were attributed to the choice of conventional steel-wheel technology with overhead current collection, and carefully phased acquisition of signal and communications equipment, the technology of which was specified to be slightly lower than that in some of the Latin American cases. Madrid also benefited from the option of extending a previous supply contract, which permitted the acquisition of new rolling stock at a relatively low cost.

BOX 8.1 LEVERAGING URBAN TRANSPORT COORDINATION IN BRAZIL

Responsibility for urban public transport in the Brazilian conurbations has historically been very fragmented. The federal government owned and operated suburban railways, the states were responsible for intermunicipal buses within the conurbation, and municipalities were responsible for intramunicipality bus services. Metros were under either state or municipal control. Policy was not coordinated, especially when the various levels of government were under different political control. In the early 1990s, as part of a policy of decentralization, the federal government decided to rehabilitate the various urban rail systems and transfer them to the states.

The World Bank financed part of the rehabilitation in several cities (Recife, Belo Horizonte, Rio de Janeiro, São Paulo, Salvador, and Fortaleza). As part of the process, the opportunity was taken to address the broader issues of urban transport coordination. In addition to funding infrastructure or rolling stock rehabilitation, each project contained the following elements:

- Establishment of a regional transport coordination body
- Completion of an integrated urban transport, land-use, and air-quality strategy and a regional public transport plan
- Introduction of financing mechanisms to establish the basis for financially sustainable public transport
- Increased involvement of the private sector in operations and investment in the sector.

The reforms have limitations. The coordinating bodies usually lack executive power, because mayors and governors are unwilling to delegate their regulatory powers. Even good transport plans do not ensure consistent implementation. The financial provisions may simply be the inclusion of a budget line rather than a secure, long-term source of finance—and private participation does not exclude all need for public funding.

Nevertheless, the achievements have already been considerable. In Rio both the metro and the suburban railways have been successfully concessioned to the private sector. In São Paulo metro and suburban rail systems are being linked, and their development coordinated. In Fortaleza, state and municipality work together to restructure networks and introduce integrated ticketing systems.

Source: J. Rebelo, based on World Bank internal documents.

The financial performance of some of these systems is shown in table 8.3. For a fully privately financed metro, operating costs only account for about 40 percent of total cost, with capital charges accounting for the remainder. On that basis, only Hong Kong, China, appears to come close to covering total costs; many do not cover operating costs. The table also indicates that, while costs do differ substantially between systems, the two main factors affecting financial viability are the corridor volumes and the revenue per passenger. Although the existence of large external effects (about one-half of the benefits typically accrue to remaining road users) means that economic rates of return may be positive and acceptable even where the financial return is negative, the same factors that affect financial viability also affect the conventional measures of economic viability.

TABLE 8.2 VARIATION OF COST IN RECENT METRO CONTRACTS

Costs per kilometer[a] (millions of dollars)	Madrid extensions	Caracas line 4	Percent of Madrid	Santiago line 5 extension	Percent of Madrid
Total costs per kilometer	31.18	93.56	300	70.1	225
Civil works	19.69	31.41	160	33.68	171
Equipment costs	5.13	22.48	438	11.56	225
Track	1.27	2.67	210	3.57	281
Power supply	0.85	8.45	994	2.36	278
Signaling and so on	0.96	6.51	678	4.36	454
Station equipment	0.61	2.13	349	0.35	57
Escalators and lifts	0.99	2.00	202	0.72	73
Ticketing equipment	0.12	0.68	567	0.20	167
Rolling stock	5.54	25.77	465	17.84	322
Rolling stock (adjusted)[b]	4.87	10.74	221	8.35	171
Design and management	0.69	4.64	672	8.54	1,237

a. All costs are in U.S. dollars at September 2000 exchange rates.
b. Adjusted to capacity of 10,000 passengers per hour, at four standing passengers per square meter.
Source: Authors.

Capital costs, which may account for as much as two-thirds of total costs, are very largely determined by international prices for the metro technology. In contrast it is typical for about three-quarters of conventionally measured economic benefits to be in the form of time savings for metro passengers and bus passengers; these savings are a function of local incomes. Hence it is not only the financial but also the economic benefit of metros that depend critically on income levels.

OWNERSHIP AND FINANCING

Most metros require subsidy. As table 8.3 shows, some are able to cover operating costs, excluding depreciation of assets; full-cost coverage would require an operating cost cover ratio of about two. While relatively low operating costs offset low revenues per passenger in the cases of Santiago and Singapore, the differences in the level of cost coverage are more strongly influenced by variations in revenue per passenger than in costs. As a result, new metros are likely

to impose a heavy fiscal burden unless the systems are very heavily utilized *and* fares are relatively high. Even a relatively rich city—such as Pusan, the Republic of Korea—found its metro to be such a burden that it had to be transferred back to the national government account. It was estimated that the 70 percent central government contribution to the proposed Bogotá metro (shelved in 2000) would have required 30 percent of the uncommitted national investment budget for the next 10 years. Such a burden might well preempt other social expenditures that would be of great benefit to the poor.

In recent years the mobilization of private finance has been seen as a way of escaping the adverse fiscal burden, with two systems in Kuala Lumpur and one each in Bangkok and Manila being privately financed. In all cases the projects appear to have been constructed to time and budget, but all have fallen short of estimated passenger demand. The revenue risk in the Manila project fell to government under the build, lease, and transfer (BLT) structure adopted. The two Kuala Lumpur projects have

TABLE 8.3 FINANCIAL PERFORMANCE OF SOME METRO SYSTEMS

City	System length (kilometers)	Population (millons)	Passengers per kilometer (millions)	Revenue per passenger (dollars)	Cost per passenger (dollars)	Operating cost per kilometer (millions of dollars)	Revenue to operating cost
Santiago	37.6	4.9	4.92	0.35	0.19	37.8	1.84
Singapore	83.0	4.0	4.67	0.57	0.34	71.9	1.67
Hong Kong, China	82.0	7.1	9.36	0.96	0.61	65.2	1.56
Buenos Aires	47.4	12.6	5.46	0.59	0.43	78.8	1.39
São Paulo	49.2	17.8	9.32	0.62	0.61	65.4	1.02
Seoul	286.9	12.5	6.56	0.38	0.44	64.6	0.87
Pusan	54.2	4.0	4.43	0.39	0.46	103.2	0.83
Mexico City	191.2	18.1	6.66	0.15	0.28	41.9	0.53
Kolkata	16.45	12.9	4.86	0.11	0.23	47.6	0.42

Note: Conversion to U.S. dollars at official exchange rates.
Source: Data from annual reports of companies for year 2000.

had to be restructured with government effectively bailing them out. The viability of the Bangkok Transit System (BTS), the first to be purely privately financed, has not yet been proven. Furthermore, reliance on private finance has discouraged integration with other modes or other MRT lines, so that the contribution to the total urban system has been less productive than it might have been.[24]

In the case of busways, it has proved difficult to structure private concessions for the provision of infrastructure and services, with failed attempts in São Paulo (1995) and Bogotá (1996).[25] Despite their proven operational and financial performance, it appears that without active government participation in the implementation process, the risk may be too great to attract private finance.[26] Bogotá's recent TransMilenio project thus concessioned only the provision and operation of its 470 buses, but the physical busway was financed and implemented by the municipal government (box 8.2).

A different approach to private involvement has been employed in the concessioning of existing metro and suburban rail systems in Buenos Aires, Rio de Janeiro, and other Brazilian cities, and is now being considered in Mexico City. In Buenos Aires the contracts have involved government financing of major rehabilitation as well as operating subsidies based on winning bids. In the Brazilian cities the rehabilitation took place largely before concessioning, under the terms of the transfer of responsibility for suburban railways from the federal to state governments. In Mexico City the concession of 200 kilometers of suburban railways is being designed in three gross-cost-type contracts to enable the authorities to control fares within a coordinated system.

Private management has greatly improved service supply and cost recovery and reduced the fiscal burden. In Buenos Aires between 1993 and 1999, metro and suburban rail line coach kilometers increased by 75 percent, proportion of trains on time by 20 percent, and train kilometers cancelled fell by 80 percent. Although fares rose by 30 percent in real terms over the period, patronage increased by 125 percent. The result was that the subsidy cost per passenger fell by 90 percent, from $1 to $0.10. Experience thus

BOX 8.2 TRANSMILENIO: BOGOTÁ'S BUS RAPID TRANSIT SYSTEM

As part of a comprehensive urban mobility strategy including promotion of nonmotorized transport (NMT) and restriction of automobile use, the municipality of Bogotá, Colombia, has developed a bus rapid transit system called TransMilenio.

The infrastructure of the system includes exclusive busways on central lanes of major arterial roads, roads for feeder buses, stations, and complementary facilities. Trunk line stations are closed facilities with one to three berths, varying from 40 to 180 meters in length, located in the median every 500 meters, on average. Trunk lines are served by articulated diesel buses with 160-passenger capacity, while integrated feeder lines are served by diesel buses with capacity of 80 passengers each. To maximize capacity, trunk lines accommodate express services stopping at selected stations only, as well as local services stopping at all stations. This combination allows the system to carry up to 45,000 passengers per hour per direction.

Services are operated by private consortia of traditional local transport companies, associated with national and international investors procured under competitively tendered concession contracts on a gross cost basis. A separate marketing contract covering production and distribution of smart cards, acquisition and installation of turnstiles and validating systems, and passenger information and money handling was also competitively tendered. All revenues are deposited in a trust fund, from which operators are paid according to their contracts.

Overall system management is performed by a new public company (TransMilenio S.A.) funded by 3 percent of the ticket sales. TransMilenio S.A. operates a control center, supervising service and passenger access. Each articulated bus is equipped to use global positioning system to report its location every six seconds. Turnstiles also report passenger movements to the control center, allowing supply to be efficiently adjusted to demand.

The system was developed in less than three years starting January 1998; service commenced in December 2000. By May 2001 it carried 360,000 trips per weekday, at a ticket cost of $0.36 and without operating subsidies, on 20 kilometers of exclusive lanes, 32 stations, 162 articulated buses, and 60 feeder buses. Productivity was high, with 6.21 passengers per kilometer, 1,945 passengers per day per bus, and 325 kilometers per day per bus. Fatalities from traffic accidents involving buses had been eliminated, some air pollutants reduced by 40 percent, and users' travel time reduced by 32 percent.

When the first phase of TransMilenio is fully operating, in 2002, more than 800,000 passengers per day are expected on 41 kilometers of exclusive lanes, with 62 stations, 470 articulated buses, and 300 feeder buses. It is intended to expand over a 15-year period to include 22 corridors with 388 kilometers of exclusive lanes.

Source: Hidalgo Guerrero 2001.

suggests that private construction and management can yield substantial benefits, but that the benefit of private participation is likely to be greatest within a well-considered and carefully planned overall strategy, and where the public sector accepts the financial implications of such public policy objectives and builds in well-constructed concession arrangements.

MRT often raises the value of land near stations, suggesting the possibility of mobilizing finance from "development gain." In practice, concentrated development often fails to occur because of the fragmentation of landownership. Even where landownership is concentrated, as in Hong Kong, China, the direct contribution to the public funding of metros has been limited to between 10 and 15 percent of the capital costs. Subtle interactions and incentives may arise where there is common ownership of the MRT and contiguous developments or land, as in some urban railways in Japan. Even then, development may be slow to occur (as in Kuala Lumpur's PUTRA system). Perhaps the clearest lesson of the Hopewell saga in Bangkok is that linking transport infrastructure development to profits of property development is a very insecure basis for ordered progress (box 8.3).

Where ownership of land contiguous to MRT systems is fragmented, development gain can usually only be recouped through taxation. This has two main drawbacks. First, it is only recouped ex post and therefore cannot contribute to the initial capital finance. Second, because the definition of both area and magnitude of impact is difficult, specific betterment taxation tends to be politically contentious. It is therefore much more common for taxes related to MRT-financing to be system related (such as the French "versement transport" and the Buenos Aires subway tax) than project related.

The project preparation process must be thorough. Premature commitment to unsolicited proposals has usually involved some contingent obligations, which have come back to haunt government, and a lack of coordination, which has been very damaging to the transport system as a whole. For projected corridor flows exceeding 10,000 pphpd, alternative MRT solutions should be carefully evaluated within an integrated urban transport, land-use, and air-quality strategy. When choosing the technology, the need to maintain a competitive supply environment as the system expands should also be borne in mind: unusual proprietary technologies can create serious problems in this respect. A very sober economic evaluation of the system using cost-benefit analysis (including resettlement analysis, environmental analysis, and an analysis on the impact on accidents), as well as a multicriteria analysis weighing the objectives to be achieved, should be undertaken. A qualitative analysis of the effects on urban structure should be also prepared. An

---

BOX 8.3 THE HOPEWELL PROJECT IN BANGKOK

A concession to the Hopewell Company for a 60-kilometer multimodal transport system was approved by the Thai government in 1991. It included an elevated toll road, an MRT system, grade separation of the Thailand State Railway (SRT) track, local road improvements, and a port rail line from Makkasan. The financial attractiveness of the project stemmed substantially from the grant of property development rights on SRT-owned land.

At the time of the collapse of the Bangkok property boom, in 1997, work progress came to a standstill, and the project remained only 14 percent completed for over nine months. The government unilaterally announced the termination of the concession in spring 1998, an action renounced by an official panel in March 1999. Negotiations for continuation of the project have been based on the elimination of the toll road, given the completion in the interim of other road schemes that reduce its attractiveness.

Source: World Bank 1999.

analysis of the financial impacts and breakeven fares will always be required, and should include analysis of the impact of the breakeven fares on the poor along with their willingness to pay. Finally, the impact of the project on state finances must be evaluated.

PUBLIC TRANSPORT INTEGRATION

The planning and evaluation of many mass transit projects presume that there will be effective modal integration, including the creation of appropriate interchange facilities (which the Bank funded in the case of Pusan metro and is proposing to fund for Manila MRT3) and bus service restructuring. If the objective of an MRT investment is primarily to improve road transport conditions, the restructuring of public road passenger transport may be critical to the achievement of the desired objective.

There are two main problems in this respect. First, it may take many years for the posited restructuring to take place. There are a number of reasons for this.

- Fragmentation of operational responsibility between modes (and in the case of bus systems, within the mode) means that there is no initial institutional responsibility for providing appropriate interchange.
- Jurisdictional fragmentation often accentuates this, with responsibility for rail-based modes resting with state or central governments but responsibility for buses resting with the municipality.
- Bus services are often regulated by agencies that operate largely independently of the other transport institutions.
- Bus operators, who are often a powerful political lobby, may resist the reduction in their overall market share.
- Restructuring of the formal bus services, if not clearly seen as beneficial by the vast majority of passengers, may be undermined by the emergence of informal paratransit

services retaining direct point-to-point connections on a "many-to-many" (from many origins to many destinations) basis.

A second main problem is that, even if the institutional arrangements are conducive to an organized physical restructuring, it may not be seen as politically or socially feasible because of its effects on some disadvantaged groups. Restructuring of bus services to feed rail stations increases the number of interchanges, imposing both interchange time penalties and fare penalties where there is no integrated fare system. In order to overcome this impediment, attempts to develop physically integrated systems in major Brazilian cities have been accompanied by integration of fares and careful attention to fare structures to avoid adverse distributional consequences (see section on pricing below). The key to effective modal integration is the existence of a strong regional coordination authority backed by the different levels of government.

PRICING

Public transport serves very disparate markets. In many large cities, it serves the basic movement needs of those without private transport. In more congested cities, it may also aim to attract commuting trips of higher-income car owners or potential car owners. The problem is that the two markets are likely to require quite different price and quality combinations. For buses this can be reconciled by the provision of higher-quality services (air conditioned, seat only, limited stop) on the same infrastructure as that for more basic services at lower costs. Despite the possibility of having two classes of service on the same train, it is more difficult to price-discriminate effectively for rail-commuting journeys.

There are various ways of attempting to address this disparity, including flat fares to allow the peripherally located poor to have reasonable access to centrally located employment; person-related subsidies, such as the "vale-transporte" (subsidy provided through employers to employees) in Brazil; and integrated fare systems to eliminate the disadvantage of modal interchange. These devices are discussed in chapter 10. The important point to bear in mind with respect to MRT strategy is the high level of fixed costs of the rail systems, and the substantial external effects and interactions between modes. It is therefore not advisable to take a purist view that all modes should be independently self-financing. Cross-modal financial transfers may certainly be justifiable in such circumstances. It is often true that motorized road users do not meet the full costs of the infrastructure that they use. Insistence on "pure" private financing of public transport infrastructure, as in the BTS system in Bangkok, may result in the adoption of price levels and structures that maximize revenues at low traffic volumes, hence lose substantial external benefits and exclude the poor from use of the system. It is equally important, however, to avoid arrangements that effectively tax bus users to subsidize a minority of rail users.

The fact that some subsidies may be efficient and acceptable does not mean that any subsidy is efficient and acceptable. The minimum criteria for subsidy should include the following:

- The subsidy should not be open-ended but should be embodied in a contract.
- The right to provide subsidized service should be subject to competitive tender.
- The level of acceptable subsidy for a service or agency should be subject to explicit cost-benefit appraisal.
- The cost of the subsidy must be fiscally sustainable.

CONCLUSIONS: TOWARD A STRATEGY FOR MASS RAPID TRANSIT

MRT plays an important part in maintaining the viability and environmental quality of very large cities, but it can also be expensive and can impose a severe burden on municipal finances. It

is therefore important that a wide range of different technologies be considered in the MRT family, and that cities adopt technologies appropriate to both their physical and their financial situations. The main elements of a strategy for MRT would therefore seem to be as follows:

On planning

- Several MRT technologies should always be considered and the selection among them based on a thorough and systematic comparison of their costs and benefits, and their financial sustainability.
- The interaction of MRT with land use, and its sheer financial magnitude, requires its careful integration into the planning of metropolitan structure, transport, and finance within a comprehensive long-term structure plan for the city.
- The public sector must set strategy, identify infrastructure projects in some detail (including horizontal and vertical alignment, and station locations) and confirm the acceptability of environmental consequences, tariffs, and any contingent changes to the existing transport system.
- The public sector must acquire the necessary land and rights-of-way, ensure development permissions, commit funding, and provide some necessary guarantees. If development at terminals is desired, it may need to facilitate consolidation of landholdings.

On finance

- There must be a comprehensive financial plan within which the costs of infrastructure and publicly funded operations are foreseen and securely provided for.
- MRT systems should normally be incorporated in citywide price-level and structure plans.
- Especially when private finance is involved, MRT investments should be consistent with an approved city structure plan; opportunistic development on an ad hoc basis has usually proved to be damaging to welfare, and ultimately costly to the budget.

- Financing for project implementation must be fully ensured to avoid the delays and cost overruns that have plagued past schemes.
- The full cost of new mass transit investments on municipal budgets, on fares, and on the poor should be estimated in advance; development should only proceed on the basis of a sound financial plan and a reasonable commitment from funding agencies for any planned financial support.
- No commitment to major expenditure on new systems should be made in the absence of secure funding to complete the investment.

On management and pricing
- Modes of public transport require physical coordination (to achieve convenient modal interchange) and fares coordination (to keep public transport attractive and to protect the poor). Stakeholders need to agree on a comprehensive transport strategy plan, within which the relationship between MRT and other modes (both physical and financial) are understood.
- There must be strong political support and competent implementation management, with arrangements put in place to facilitate coordination between multiple public agencies.
- Modally integrated fare schemes should be assessed for their impacts on the poor.

NOTES

1. This is particularly likely to occur when those making the forecasts have a positive incentive to be optimistic—for example, where free counterpart funding is available from central government for "promising" projects, or where private developers want to present a positive view to prospective lenders.

2. That approach is discussed in a recent World Bank discussion paper (Mitric 1997).

3. Fouracre, Allport, and Thompson 1990; Gardner, Cornwell, and Cracknell 1991; and Gardner 1993.

4. Halcrow Fox 2000a.

5. Rebelo 1996.

6. PADECO 2000.

7. For example, the "9th of July Busway" in São Paulo, despite being a cost-efficient mass people-mover, had negative environmental and community impacts, including accidents to pedestrians entering or leaving the system. While these effects can be minimized by changes in fuel, more pedestrian overpasses, and maybe grade separation, these all increase costs.

8. Note, however, that there are increasing efforts to reduce air pollution through innovative bus propulsion systems, including natural gas, clean diesel, hybrid diesel and electric, and fuel cells (see chapter 4). Moreover, two recently developed busways, in Quito and São Paulo are operated by electric trolleybuses.

9. The elevated BERTS (Bangkok Elevated Road and Train System) in Bangkok has given rise to sufficient concern about the "tunnel effect" it has had on trapping the road-generated congestion below it that the government of Thailand has resolved that all future rail systems in the central area of the city be underground.

10. Fouracre, Allport, and Thompson 1990.

11. Total costs for a 32-kilometer system of busways in Bogotá, including 470 articulated trunk buses and 1,000 feeder buses to operate off the busway, were recently estimated as approximately $8 million per route kilometer (Ardila and Menckhoff forthcoming).

12. Rebelo and Machado 2000.

13. The critical feature when a phased development of technology is planned is that the initial land reservation and the subbase construction must be sufficiently strong to support subsequent expansion.

14. Congestion was experienced at stops on Avenida Caracas in Bogotá despite there being two lanes in each direction with 400 small-medium buses per hour; the newly developed TransMilenio system will improve performance by the exclusion of small vehicles.

15. Quinn 1998.

16. For more details, see Halcrow Fox 2000a.

17. The highest capacity for a true street-running system is the 12,000 pphpd achieved on

the Alexandria-Madina line with 275 passenger vehicles operating every 80 seconds, albeit at a very low speed of 6 km/h. The highly segregated Tunis system has a capacity of 13,000, and the 95 percent segregated Alexandria-Rami line has a capacity of 18,000. All currently have patronage much below these theoretical capacities. The largely segregated Tuen Mun system in Hong Kong, China, is reported to have a capacity of over 25,000.

18. Caetano Roca Giner 2000.

19. An important component of a World Bank–funded urban transport project in Buenos Aires was a program of grade separation of railroad crossings in the city.

20. Such a conversion is being done, at relatively low cost, in Fortaleza, Brazil.

21. Rebelo 1999b.

22. Rebelo 1999a.

23. BB&J Consult 2000.

24. For example, physical transfer between different rail lines is very difficult in Kuala Lumpur and Manila, and between rail and bus in Bangkok, Kuala Lumpur, and Manila. Moreover, there is no fare coordination in any of these cases.

25. The city of São Paulo awarded concessions for a 241-kilometer bus network, but none of the winning bidders could obtain financing to implement the schemes. In 1995 the city did successfully concession the São Mateus-Jabaquara trolley busway, which benefited from the fact that most of the infrastructure was already in place. In Bogotá in 1996, the Metrobus consortium failed to close the financing necessary to implement.

26. Menckhoff and Zegras 1999.

9 THE ROLE OF NONMOTORIZED TRANSPORT

Despite its economic importance to the poor—both as a mode of transport and a source of income—and its environmental advantages, the potential of nonmotorized transport is often unmobilized or even actively suppressed. A combination of infrastructure investment, traffic management, and financial measures can make nonmotorized transport safer and more attractive, to the benefit not only of the very poor, who are economically captive to nonmotorized transport, but also of the less poor.

THE IMPORTANCE OF NONMOTORIZED TRANSPORT

Nonmotorized transport (NMT) has an unambiguously benign environmental impact. In many cities it is the main mode of transport for the poor, and in some a significant source of income for them. It therefore has a very significant poverty impact. Where NMT is the main transport mode for the work journeys of the poor, it is also critical for the economic functioning of the city. Despite these obvious merits, NMT has tended to be ignored by policymakers in the formulation of infrastructure policy and positively discouraged as a service provider. The purpose of this chapter is to understand why that has happened, and in light of the evidence on its characteristics, role, costs, and benefits, to suggest a framework within which NMT's potential may be better exploited.

Some governments appear to have an ideological preference for motorized over NMT because they regard it as technologically more advanced. The World Bank concern for NMT is certainly not based on any ideological preference for low technology in urban transport. Indeed, the environmental impacts of motorized transport are often accentuated by outdated engine and fuel technology, while modern nonmotorized vehicles may benefit from advanced materials technology. Rather an explicit strategy for NMT is necessary to redress a historic vicious policy circle that has biased urban transport policy unduly in favor of sacrificing the interests of pedestrians and cyclists to those of motor vehicle users. Because of this policy, NMT becomes less safe, less convenient, and less attractive, making the forecast decline of NMT a self-fulfilling prophecy. That process is unacceptable, because it stems from a failure to recognize some of the external effects of motorized transport that distort individual choice against NMT, and hence militates particularly against the poor who do not have the means to use even motorized public transport.

The two major modes of NMT are walking and various forms of cycling, which can be personal or public transport. The NMT public transport sector, which is particularly important in South Asia, comprises many load-carrying variants. Particularly in higher-income countries, many people also walk or bicycle for exercise and pleasure. We exclude such activities from our consideration here to concentrate on NMT only as a mode of necessary transport. NMT accounts for between 40 and 60 percent of all trips in several major cities in Asia. In the poorer cities in Africa, that proportion is even higher.

WALKING IS TRANSPORT

For very short trips, walking is the main mode of transport in most societies, rich or poor. Indeed, most trips in all countries involve some walking as access and egress to the main mode. The modal share of walking can be very high. Recent studies show that between 25 and 50 percent of trips in the major Indian cities,[1] and around 50 percent of all trips in major African cities, are entirely on foot, and that trips undertaken primarily by public transport also involve significant walking distances. In medium and smaller cities, the share of all-walking trips increases to 60 to 70 percent. Clearly, walking dominates for shorter trips, but even in terms of distances traveled, walking accounts for over 50 percent of all trips in Morogoro, Tanzania.[2]

The political attitude toward pedestrians is often neglectful or curiously hostile. Pedestrian space is continually being eroded. Fewer than one-half of the major roads in most Indian cities have sidewalks, and those that exist are frequently occupied by street vendors, encroached upon by shop premises, or blocked by parked cars, motorcycles, and bicycles.[3] As city authorities have found it difficult to manage and control street market and footway activities, the trend has been toward getting rid of them altogether, rather than taking a functional approach to road hierarchy, whereby the functions of some roads could be for pedestrians and market activities and not for fast-flowing motor vehicle traffic. Whereas in many industrialized countries the advantage of pedestrianization of shopping streets has been recognized by shoppers and traders alike, it remains difficult to give priority to pedestrians in developing countries.

In some very rapidly growing countries, such as China, there has been an attempt to plan for pedestrians—though planning for pedestrians has lagged behind planning for vehicles. Attempting to cater to fast and free-flowing motor vehicle traffic has resulted in the gradual physical segregation of pedestrians by over-passes, subways, and barriers, many of which are poorly designed. Locations are often chosen for convenience of construction rather than to best satisfy pedestrian desire lines. While physical segregation can provide safe facilities for pedestrians to cross roads, it also results in severance and inconvenience for them.

WALKING ON WHEELS

Bicycles are a desirable mode of transport in many cities, but it is important to analyze who is using them, what the prevailing social and political attitudes are to the use of the mode, and whether there are particular obstacles to their use by women.

WHO BICYCLES?

The bicycle represents a trade-up from walking. In many of the poorer developing countries, only middle-income households can afford bicycles. For example, in 1996, 54 percent of bicycle users in Delhi had a monthly family income of over 2,000 rupees (about US$41), and only 19 percent of the users earned less than 1,500 rupees (about US$31). A similar survey in León, Nicaragua, showed 89 percent of users to be relatively well-off.

Data from Guangzhou, Delhi, León, and Accra show that the NMT share of each age cohort correlates closely with its share in total mobility, the age cohort 25 to 35 dominating both NMT use and overall mobility. In Vietnam, however, nearly all secondary-level schoolchildren go to school by bicycle, while motorcycles are rapidly taking the place of the bicycle as a means of transport for the age group 25 to 35. Men dominate the use of bicycles in most countries, with the exception of China and Vietnam.[4]

In some large countries, the proportion of bicycle trips has declined, and is continuing to decline, as incomes increase and as the perceived safety and security of cycling diminishes. Even in traditional cycling cities, such as Guangzhou and Delhi, those using NMT are apparently doing so because there is no affordable alternative—that is, they may be viewed as (at least temporarily) captive passengers. But there are exceptions. In some European countries, already at high income levels, the use of bicycles as a mode of transport is steady or increasing, both as a main mode and as a subsidiary or feeder mode.

ATTITUDES TOWARD THE BICYCLE

Some insight into attitudes toward cycling can be obtained from a survey carried out in five different cities across the world (Accra, Delhi, Gangzhou, León, and Lima) in 1996.[5] Most bicycle users in these cities preferred bicycle to bus primarily because it was less expensive, but the majority also found it more flexible in routing, faster, and more reliable. The survey did suggest, however, that many would change to motorcycles except for the cost. In Ouagadougou, a city almost exclusively dependent on two-wheeled transport, and having made better provision for it than most, bicycles were still clearly viewed as an inferior mode to be abandoned as soon as the household could afford a motorcycle.

In two of the cities, public transport users were also asked about the relative merits of bicycle and public transport. Interestingly, most of the perceived benefits of cycling were the same as those perceived by the cyclists, namely, cost, speed, and flexibility. The main disadvantages that this group perceived (which by definition were clinching in their decision to use public transport) were the danger of cycling, the risk of thefts and assaults, the lack of bicycle paths, and the motorists' lack of respect for traffic laws (also by implication safety concerns). Only a minority quoted excessive trip distance or topography as clinching factors. One implication is that if these factors could be overcome, the use of NMT might be even greater. Another, less-comfortable implication is that if private motorized transport could be afforded and were to have the same flexibility as NMT, it would be preferred. Certainly that would seem to be consistent with the recent rapid increases in motorcycling in the richer developing countries.

The attitudes of public authorities toward the modes are often inconsistent with individuals' responses. While efforts have been made to segregate motorized and NMT in China, relatively little is being done elsewhere on a national basis, and improvement in the conditions for NMT depend heavily on the enthusiasm of specific municipal governments. Only a few (as for example, Bogotá under Mayor Penalosa) have attempted major initiatives. As far as public NMT is concerned, a number of governments—most notably that of Indonesia—have taken positive actions to eliminate it.

The reasons for these official attitudes appear to be rather complex, as Chinese experience shows (box 9.1). There is almost certainly a lack of interest by engineers (a lack of interest shared, until comparatively recently, in industrialized countries), who favor dealing with more technically rewarding road and bridge design. Police often focus on the difficulties of enforcing NMT routes and the lack of respect of cyclists for traffic regulations. Similarly, the richer and more politically influential classes are likely to be car users and to have a vested interest in reducing the nuisance offered by slow-moving and congesting NMT. Lack of transport-planning skills and design solutions appropriate for the large NMT volumes found in developing countries also contributes. Where local government is dependent on central government for road infrastructure funding (not the case in China), this may also limit local initiatives in providing for NMT.

WOMEN AND BICYCLING

In many countries women are largely excluded from the use of bicycles. This is partly a consequence of general economic and social norms, which can be addressed by community awareness programs to overcome cultural constraints to women's use of NMT. There are often more direct transport policy constraints—associated with access to credit mechanisms, design of vehicles, and personal safety and security during travel—that may impinge more on women than on men and that should be addressed in a policy package.

In *Shanghai,* the development of NMT routes has been slow; the pace of development has super-seded many proposals. But such problems did not affect the rapid development of motorized vehicle routes. In retrospect, it would appear that the Shanghai agencies saw the creation of NMT routes as a way of increasing the capacity and facilitating the operation of motorized vehicle routes, rather than providing safer and easier passage for NMT on a network of routes. The NMT routes suffered from problems of motorized vehicle access and parking.

In *Guangzhou,* the piecemeal development of elevated city-center routes has severed NMT and pedestrian routes, and again, the development of segregated NMT routes was seen by the Guangzhou agencies as a way of improving capacity for motorized vehicles.

In *Urumqi,* NMT volumes have decreased dramatically since 1992 with the introduction of minibuses, particularly in the central area. Weather and geography also result in NMT volumes lower than in other Chinese cities. Consequently, existing and previously physically segregated NMT lanes in the city have been converted into service roads and footways. Cycle lanes on central area roads are being converted to bus lanes.

In *Beijing,* NMTs are increasingly being squeezed by motorized vehicle parking in physically seg-regated NMT lanes and by the reallocation of space in wide NMT lanes to through motorized vehicle traffic. On the Second Ring Road, the outside half of the NMT lane has been reassigned to motorized vehicles, and the inside half is used by buses and taxis. NMT parking at work units is increasingly being moved to distant, inconvenient locations to provide more convenient space for motorized vehicle parking. A recent high-profile closure to NMTs of a commercial street at Xidan in Beijing epitomizes current practice.

Source: Frame 1999.

THE POLICY PACKAGE

In most countries NMT has developed sponta-neously and remains largely outside the normal processes of transport planning. Provision for NMT, if made at all, tends to be "retrofitted" to existing infrastructure, and to concentrate on minimizing the disturbance that it causes to the flow of motor-ized traffic. The consequence is that the provisions are not only expensive but often inconvenient for NMT (for example, open pedestrian footbridges for crossing busy roads). Even where it is neces-sary to retrofit, the chances of designing an attrac-tive NMT package are much greater when there is a willingness to modify elements of the system not originally designed for NMT. For example, meas-ures of traffic calming to reduce speed differen-tials between motorized and nonmotorized traf-fic may be an essential requirement if pedestrians are to be kept safe and bicycle traffic is to be attracted to unsegregated roads.

The more successful schemes, whether provid-ing for NMT as a feeder mode or a main mode, have been incorporated in initial urban system design. For example, the plan for Tama New Town in Tokyo provides for pedestrian and bicy-cle access to town centers and railway stations completely segregated from vehicular road traf-fic. The basis for such comprehensive attention to NMT is a combination of national strategy and local implementation planning.

Unless bicycle infrastructure networks are sufficiently dense, continuous, and direct, and both links and intersections perceived as safe, the impediments to cycling will continue to be strong. That will involve understanding desire line flows and identifying missing links, safety black spots, and other major impediments to bicycle use. Many attempts to mobilize the potential of NMT have failed because the attempts did not contain the minimum package of elements to ensure that NMT became an attractive proposition to a significant number of people. Given the need for a safe, secure, and direct transit, this minimum package would need to include the provision of safe, adequately segregated infrastructure; direct routings without major intersection conflicts with motorized traffic; secure bicycle parking to preclude theft; and financially affordable means of vehicle procurement. Hence, it is desirable that there be a local cycling master plan that should be the basis both for planning infrastructure specifically for bicycles and for incorporating cycling into general traffic infrastructure and management planning. Such plans have been drawn up and implemented in Dutch cities such as Delft.[6] An ambitious bicycle master plan for Bogotá, Colombia, has recently been published (box 9.2).

Local planning alone may not be enough. At the national level, it is necessary to identify objectives for the sector and to ensure that the crucial elements of the facilitating framework that can only be handled at the national level (such as the creation of a legal basis for traffic management, promotional campaigns, financing instruments, and so on) are put in place. The Dutch Bicycle Master Plan specifies a general objective and identifies a number of "spearheads" for action; the plan is an element of the long-term transport strategy for the Netherlands. A similar central government initiative has recently been taken by the government of South Africa in establishing a national bicycle transport partnership (box 9.3).

INFRASTRUCTURE POLICIES

Network planning must be supplemented by detailed road section planning (what to do with the layout: separation or mixing) and junction and intersection planning. This will involve a combination of measures to determine the function, physical characteristics, and use of each element in the network.

The starting point is function. There are several different functions (such as access, distribution, or transit) for each kind of mode. Since the inter-

---

BOX 9.2 THE BOGOTÁ BICYCLE MASTER PLAN

In year 2000 the municipality of Bogotá, Colombia, published a master plan for bicycles in the city. The plan includes the construction of 320 kilometers of cycleways over a nine-year period at an estimated cost of $120 million. It also provides for the necessary ancillary infrastructure, including bicycle parking, urban street furniture, landscaping, and traffic signals. The plan has been subject to detailed economic and environmental appraisals. For a shift in modal split to the bicycle of 2.5 percent, an economic rate of return of 15 percent was estimated. Higher shifts give correspondingly higher returns.

The launch of the first phase of the plan, for the construction of 200 kilometers of cycle track at a cost of $50 million, was accompanied by an ambitious marketing effort. This showed the program to be well integrated with parallel development of the TransMilenio urban public transport scheme and other transport facilities, as well as offered links to neighboring municipalities.

Source: Mauricio Cuellar, from local Bogotá press reports .

In his 2000/01-year budget speech, the minister of transport of South Africa announced a plan to promote greater self-reliance through a national bicycle transport partnership. The minister himself is the champion of this partnership and has the overall authority to define its course. The national department of transport is responsible for overall project management and implementation.

At the core of the partnership is a project called the National Bicycle Transport Demonstration Program. The aim of this program is to demonstrate the transport benefits of bicycle promotion targeted at low-income users in relatively low-traffic rural and medium-size city areas. It consists of a road show to raise awareness and to leverage support, including targeting women, girls, and youths; procuring and providing low-cost new and used bicycles; training in riding and maintenance skills; developing a container microbusiness outlet to support users; reviewing infrastructure safety; and providing detailed training, planning, and evaluation exercises.

This program is funded by the national department of transportation (NDoT), with the aim of leveraging additional support from other parties. The objective of Phase 1 (2000/01) is to implement at least 10,000 bicycle transport packages at one or more sites in each province across South Africa. The objective of Phase 2 (2001/02) is to implement a further 15,000 bicycle packages at the nine existing and eight new sites. Phase 3 (2002/03) aims to implement 50,000 bicycle packages at the 17 existing and 18 new sites.

In addition to the national demonstration program, the partnership has also developed rural and urban pilot projects. The urban project is a partnership between the NDoT and the Midrand Local Council. As part of their Ecocity initiative, Midrand has committed 300,000 rands (about US$30,675) to promoting 1,000 subsidized bicycle transport packages in the township of Ivory Park, east of Johannesburg, together with a container microbusiness. Midrand, together with its partners, has also designed six kilometers of bicycle infrastructure in Ivory Park in order to ensure safety and maximize the promotion of township cycling.

Source: De Langen and Tembele 2000.

ests of various modes may differ (and conflicts are endemic), the planner must develop a functional classification of roads and road hierarchy and identify the appropriate measure to reconcile conflicts. If the functions for different modes are incompatible—such as the use of "rat-runs" through residential areas as segments of main trunk movement routes—it will be necessary to judge on priorities and modify both physical characteristics and regulation of use accordingly. Some cases (for example, major arterials designated for faster, longer-distance move-ments or urban busways) might justify the exclusion of nonmotorized vehicles on both efficiency and safety grounds. Nevertheless, even in those circumstances, it is important that steps are taken to avoid serious severance of short-distance movements. Moreover, any decisions to restructure roads (for example, to introduce new restraints on categories of use or to take away protected bicycle lanes) should be appraised in terms of the net benefit to all types of user and not merely in terms of the speed of motorized traffic.

Intersection design and design of motor vehicle access to buildings on NMT routes are both extremely important, particularly, as in China, where bicycle volumes may be very high.

It may often be possible to reconcile functions of a road section by changing its physical layout. Motorized and nonmotorized traffic can coexist in three ways.

a. Full integration gives no exclusive right or special protection for bicyclists or pedestrians using a mixed road and relies on driving behavior to protect the more vulnerable categories.

b. Partial segregation reserves a strip on the carriageway for bicyclists or pedestrians, but does not protect it physically.

c. Full segregation gives exclusive rights to pedestrians or cyclists and makes it physically difficult for motorized traffic to trespass on that right. Even in this case, however, it is likely that there will be at best only partial segregation at major intersections.

These alternatives are in ascending order of capital cost but descending order of enforcement cost. The choice between them will depend on the traffic mix, primary road function, relative free flow speeds, and traffic volumes. Experience in Africa (Ghana) and Latin America (Peru) have shown that if the volume of bicyclists is too low, it will invite infringement, at least by pedestrians, particularly if there is no pedestrian alternative.

Where NMT volumes are high, it will not only be safest but also most efficient in terms of travel speed for all categories of traffic to provide for full segregation. It may then also be efficient, as increasingly practiced in larger cities in China, to provide for grade separation of traffic at intersections, though there may be a danger that, for cost reasons, cyclists are assigned a cumbersome route that reduces the relative comfort of that mode. At the very least, it will be justified to pro-vide for separate NMT phases in signal-controlled intersections.

Where motorized traffic volumes are low and the location sensitive (for example, in residential areas), it may be more appropriate to use traffic-calming devices to slow all movements to speeds at which they are safely compatible (as in the Dutch "woonerf"—sharing space between vehicles and pedestrians). The adoption at the national level of advisory standards for traffic separation is one basis on which a more NMT-sensitive attitude to road design can be effectively disseminated.[7]

TRAFFIC MANAGEMENT

Survey evidence makes it clear that safety is the most critical feature for the preservation and development of NMT. Physical separation of space for NMT can be made largely self-enforcing. Where there are no physical barriers to infringement, separation will only work if there is a sufficiently powerful combination of monitoring, enforcement, and legal penalties, particularly on vehicle infringements to run or park in NMT space. Most difficult of all is the protection of NMT in shared space; evidence in many countries suggests that this will have to be done through strong, physically enforced, traffic calming. Experience in the Netherlands and elsewhere shows that traffic-calming measures in neighborhoods and shopping or market areas are among the most effective supports to NMT programs.

Theft is a strong deterrent to bicycle ownership. A household survey in Guangzhou in 1995 revealed that each household had on average one bicycle a year stolen from it, and that 62 percent of these thefts occurred in residential areas. Protection against theft has proved elusive. Nearly all the stolen bicycles in Guangzhou were locked. They were also registered with the police, who were, however, unwilling even to record the thefts and who recovered fewer than 10 percent of the stolen bicycles. (In Jiangmen City, where a new bicycle number plate practice is in place, results are different.) Guarded parking facilities, common in Japan and the Netherlands, offer better protection.[8] Unfortunately, most cities do not have suitably located or sufficiently inexpensive parking facilities at major destinations (stations, markets, offices, and so on).

SAFETY EDUCATION AND TRAINING

An important requirement of a strategy to promote NMT is to establish and make known to the general public the rights and responsibilities of pedestrians and cyclists, as well as the traffic rules that deal with safety. In many Organisation for Economic Co-operation and Development (OECD) countries, these rights and rules are clear. In contrast, in many developing countries cyclists and pedestrians are often mentioned in legislation only for definition purposes and have no specified legal rights in the use of road space. Traffic law should clearly define the rights and responsibilities of nonmotorized users of roads, as well as those of motorized users.

Establishing rules is only one part of the solution to the problem. The second part is to get them known and applied. Training and educating children to understand more about traffic rules can be addressed both by incorporation of such training in the school curriculum and by campaigns outside school. In the longer term, knowledge of the rights of pedestrians and cyclists should be incorporated in driver license testing. In the shorter term, the problems are twofold: many existing drivers are unlicensed, and few police have been educated to think of the safety of pedestrians and cyclists as a responsibility of drivers of motorized vehicles. Treatment of NMT should thus be a central part of comprehensive road-safety programs (see chapter 5).

MUNICIPAL INSTITUTIONS AND ORGANIZATION

Provision for NMT in urban areas is almost exclusively a municipal responsibility. As such it suffers from the typical paucity of municipal funding in developing countries. The virtual impossibility of charging users directly for the infrastructure provided accentuates this disadvantage. Even secure bicycle parking, which is provided commercially in some industrialized countries, is difficult to finance in developing countries.

In some of the higher-income developing countries, it may be possible to learn from more industrialized countries, where adequate provision for NMT—especially walking—is a planning requirement for commercial shopping mall development. But that requires both a degree of effectiveness of development controls and a political commitment to adequate provision for NMT. The critical question is how such commitment and capability can be developed.

One approach, being pursued in some African cities, is to set up a special-purpose multidisciplinary and interdepartmental team within the municipal authority to take initiatives, to plan, and to implement interventions. Such a team might support intensive user participation in the planning and design process and focus on widely supported interventions with a high benefit-to-cost ratio (value for money). A template for such an approach has been provided for African cities.[9]

That approach is most likely to be effective where the modal share of NMT is large and its importance is already recognized. In less propitious circumstances, it may be more important to create alliances rather than to risk further fragmentation of responsibility for urban infrastructure. It may then be more effective to build capacity by embedding NMT expertise in existing forums, such as municipal engineering departments, national road-safety councils, road fund administrations, and so on. In either case, the starting point needs to be recognition of the potential for NMT and a commitment to providing for it.

STAKEHOLDER PARTICIPATION

It might be expected that user and stakeholder participation would improve the quality of the decisions by exploiting local knowledge and desires, and spotting and solving potential problems, as well as by smoothing the execution of public sector interventions. In practice, experience with user participation in NMT schemes has been very variable. In the NMT project in Lima, staff and authorities showed little commitment to participation, and ad hoc meetings were organized only in response to local protests. Similarly, the Kenyan authorities lacked commitment in implementing the Sub-Saharan Africa Transport Program (SSATP), and success was limited. However, in Tanzania the SSATP results were positive, partly because of the urgency of the problems and the expectation that the outcome of the entire process would be positive for the user group involved (box 9.4).

FINANCING

Many of the impediments to cycling and walking arise from the inadequacy of infrastructure that is not addressed through the traditional funding mechanisms. For example, none of the recently developed second-generation road funds appears to pay any attention to NMT or to have NMT interests represented in the roads authority boards managing the funds. Given that the commercial rationale of user involvement in fund management is that those who benefit should pay, and vice versa, this is perhaps not surprising. Nevertheless, it highlights a weakness of the device in addressing the interests of noncommercial stakeholders.

While the operating costs of cycling are very low and the benefits very great where no other alternative is affordable, the cost of bicycles is a serious impediment to cycling in many countries (especially where the probability of loss by theft is high). Previous efforts to overcome this impediment have had mixed success but offer some useful lessons for design of future schemes.[10] For example:

- A World Bank–funded credit program directed to the poorer sections of the urban population of Lima met its credit targets, but was hampered by the mutual distrust between staff of the Caja Municipal and the poor in the administration of the scheme.
- An African pilot scheme giving incentives for employers to establish credit and savings schemes failed in situations where the credits were to be prefinanced by employers.
- Bicycle sale-on-credit programs have had limited success in pilot projects in Africa, due

---

BOX 9.4 STAKEHOLDER PARTICIPATION IN NONMOTORIZED TRANSPORT DEVELOPMENT IN TANZANIA

In experiments undertaken in East Africa as part of the SSATP, different forms and roles of user participation were employed at different stages of the projects. For example, in Dar es Salaam 64 user groups of about 10 people each discussed general problems with mobility and NMT and provided information on problems, road-use behavior, potential solutions, and priorities to the planners. Subsequently a general user platform of about 20 nonpolitical, nongovernmental citizens was asked to review, articulate, and prioritize the problems mentioned by user groups; this user platform acted as an intermediary between the authorities and the community. Local user platforms were used to create and review plans, and propose changes; to provide control during construction; to mobilize resources; to organize repairs; and so on. Finally, formal user associations with legal status and able to mobilize finances through contributions of members or users may also have a part to play. In the case of Dar es Salaam, a garden park was planned that is to be handed over to a user association for maintenance and protection.

Source: De Langen and Tembele 2000.

to the perceived high risk of lending to poor clients.

- In Morogoro, Tanzania, entrepreneurs who rent or lease bicycles welcomed the concept of bicycle lease contracts, though they were unable to prefinance enough bicycles.
- In contrast, a scheme for promotional bicycle sales to women and children entering secondary school in Morogoro, showed a high price elasticity of demand for bicycles, and suggested possibilities of extending bicycle use by identifying promising target groups.

CONCLUSIONS: A STRATEGY FOR NONMOTORIZED TRANSPORT

The major elements of a strategy for NMT should include the following:

- Clear provision for the rights, as well as responsibilities, of pedestrians and bicyclists in traffic law
- Formulation of a national strategy for NMT as a facilitating framework for local plans
- Explicit formulation of local plans for NMT as part of the planning procedures of municipal authorities
- Provision of separate infrastructure where appropriate (for safe movement and for secure parking of vehicles)

- Incorporation of standards of provision for bicyclists and pedestrians in new road infrastructure design
- Focusing traffic management on improving the movement of people rather than of motorized vehicles
- Training of police to enforce the rights of NMT in traffic priorities, as well as in accident recording and prevention
- Incorporation of responsibilities for provision for NMT in road fund statutes and procedures
- Development of small-scale credit mechanisms for finance of bicycles in poor countries.

NOTES

1. Sachdeva 1998.
2. De Langen and Tembele 2000.
3. Sachdeva 1998.
4. Men's share in New Delhi, Accra, Lima, and León is 100 percent, 99 percent, 84.6, and 90 percent, respectively.
5. Interface for Cycling Expertise 1997.
6. Interface for Cycling Expertise 2000.
7. Interface for Cycling Expertise 2000.
8. At one of the very few places in Lima where you can park your bike—the Catholic University—students have to show their identification before entering the university compound. So far, not a single bike has been reported stolen.
9. De Langen and Tembele 2000.
10. Interface for Cycling Expertise 1997.

10 URBAN TRANSPORT PRICING AND FINANCE

Prices allocate resources and raise revenue. Urban transport pricing is complicated by the multiplicity of objectives pursued and by the institutional separation of road infrastructure from operations, of infrastructure pricing from charging, and of roads from other modes of transport. In the interests of both urban transport integration and sustainability, developing countries should move toward prices reflecting full social costs for all modes; to a targeted approach to subsidization reflecting strategic objectives; and to an integration of urban transport funding.

THE ROLE OF PRICES IN URBAN TRANSPORT

In most markets, prices have two main functions: to ration and allocate the use of resources between the production of different products, and to finance production. In transport in general, but in urban transport in particular, the performance of these functions is subject to three major complications:

a. The separation of responsibility for infrastructure from that of service provision

b. The pursuit of multiple objectives, particularly in public transport policy

c. The separation of infrastructure financing from charging.

In this chapter we address each of these complications and suggest ways in which municipal governments may improve their effectiveness in the provision of transport services by developing better pricing and funding arrangements.

CHARGING FOR THE USE OF INFRASTRUCTURE

Roads are "congested" when traffic volume reaches a level at which the flow of traffic is significantly impaired. In such circumstances the extra cost to society of the marginal trip is not only the cost that the extra vehicle itself incurs but also the sum of the marginal delays that it imposes on all existing road users. Unless the cost charged to, and perceived by, each user reflects that extra cost imposed on society, there will be an incentive to make road trips for which the benefit to the trip maker is lower than the extra total cost to society.[1]

In practice, in most countries—industrialized and developing—urban roads are provided to their users without any direct charge. The only payments from the private user to the public supplier that vary with the amount of road use come indirectly in the form of taxes (primarily on fuel). Underpricing is endemic. Even in developing countries with relatively higher taxes on fuel, taxes do not reflect the costs of urban congestion.

The fact that these taxes do not cover costs has several adverse effects. First, it distorts the choice of mode in favor of road transport, particularly private cars. Second, it encourages excessive use of the infrastructure (which may cause "excess" congestion). Third, because there is no direct revenue, it is not logically possible to use conventional commercial investment criteria in deciding how much capacity should be provided. Fourth, because the revenues do not accrue to the responsible local authority, there may be inadequate money for proper maintenance of the existing infrastructure. For all these reasons, it is desirable to ensure that the price charged to users at the margin covers the full social cost of their trips.

CONGESTION PRICING

The concept of congestion pricing is that road users should pay a price that reflects the short-run marginal social cost of road use, and that hence varies according to the prevailing level of congestion.[2] Congestion pricing has long been advocated by economists on the grounds that, unlike the various administrative controls which are often used to manage traffic, it gives correct incentives over the whole range of dimensions involved in travel decisions, including choice of destination, time of travel, mode of transport, route, and so on. Moreover, if congestion pricing were applied in the context of a flexible land and property market, the city would evolve toward a more compact form, with more mixed land use, fewer resources devoted to the spread of the road network into surrounding areas, and more funds available for upgrading infrastructure in the already urbanized area.[3] Above all, unlike administrative restraint alternatives, congestion pricing yields revenue rather than being a cost to the public purse (box 10.1).

For these reasons the World Bank strongly advocated congestion pricing in the 1975 urban transport policy paper (World Bank 1975), and has subsequently examined its applicability in industrialized countries.[4] Nevertheless, attempts to introduce it in Kuala Lumpur and Bangkok in asso-

ciation with Bank projects foundered, as did the initiative in Hong Kong, China, in the early 1980s. To date, the most sophisticated application remains that in Singapore, where an area licensing scheme (ALS) first introduced in 1973 has now been developed into a much more sophisticated electronic pricing system. Instead, various surrogate measures, such as the use of parking restraints and pricing policies, have been adopted in many countries. Even in industrialized countries, there is growing concern that these surrogates have not worked well. Direct charges for urban roads have been introduced to generate revenue in some Norwegian cities, and congestion pricing is now under serious consideration in the Netherlands and the United Kingdom.

Many of the objections raised against congestion pricing have already been overcome. Initial concerns about the cost and reliability of the technology have been superseded by developments in electronics. Fears about intrusion on privacy—which contributed to undermining the Hong Kong experiment—can be overcome through the choice of a technology not relying on any centralized record of vehicle movements. Fears about the effects of congestion charging on lower income groups, which have been a significant obstacle to its political acceptability in highly motorized societies,[5] are much less justified in developing-country cities, where most people remain dependent on public transport or nonmotorized modes.[6] Even some of the rapidly motorizing major cities of Eastern Europe still offer much more extensive and frequent public transport services as an alternative to the private car than are available in many of the Western countries. Specific inequities that do arise in the shift to a more direct and efficient system of charging for road use can also be compensated by provision of case-specific subsidies, such as free or reduced-price smart cards or stickers during a transition period. Congestion pricing is increasingly being viewed as a concept whose time has come.

Congestion prices can be charged with different degrees of precision through a variety of tech-

Traffic congestion in Seoul increased dramatically during the 1980s and early 1990s despite extensive construction of new urban freeway and subway lines. In 1996 the Seoul metropolitan government commenced charging 2,000 won (US$2.20) for the Namsan #1 and #3 tunnels, two corridors with high private vehicle use linking downtown Seoul to the southern part of the city. Charges were set for one- and two-occupant private vehicles (including driver) and collected in both directions per entry or exit from 7:00 a.m. to 9:00 p.m. during weekdays and from 7:00 a.m. to 3:00 p.m. on Saturdays. Private cars with three or more passengers, taxis, and all kinds of buses, vans, and trucks were exempted from charges, as was all traffic on Sundays and national holidays.

In the two years following commencement of the congestion pricing scheme for the Namsan #1 and #3 tunnels, there was a 34 percent reduction in peak-period passenger vehicle volumes, the average travel speed increased by 50 percent, from 20 to 30 km/h, and the number of toll-free vehicles increased substantially in both corridors. On the alternative routes, traffic volumes increased by up to 15 percent, but average speeds also increased as a result of improved flows at signalized intersections linked to the Namsan corridors and increased enforcement of illegal on-street parking on the alternative routes.

The whole of the annual revenue from the two tunnels (equivalent to about US$15 million) goes into a special account used exclusively for transport projects, including transport systems management and transport demand management measures throughout the city.

Source: Hwang, Son, and Eom 1999.

niques of different degrees of technological sophistication and cost. While, theoretically, different prices can be set for each link in the network for each time period, in practice a rather rougher approximation may be used both for reasons of practicability of application and for predictability of response from drivers. Three principal forms of congestion pricing have been developed to date:

Cordon pricing, or area licenses, can be implemented with simple technology, to charge for the right to access or circulate within limited geographical areas, with some degree of time differentiation. The principal application has been the area licensing scheme for downtown Singapore in operation between 1975 and 1998. The scheme being prepared for central London is of this type.

Time-dependent tolling of individual roads or road lanes can charge for congestion on major highways and improve traffic flows on the affected facility (though not necessarily beyond it). In developing countries it has been used on a number of tunnels in Hong Kong, the Namsan tunnels in Seoul, as well as on the expressways in Singapore.

Electronic road pricing (ERP) enables more precise differentiation of charges by road, time of use, and type of vehicle for whatever area is covered. Recent developments in intelligent transport system technologies make this much more attractive, and several large test applications have been undertaken. In 1998 Singapore replaced its ALS by an ERP system that applies to the city center and some major access roads, and is gradually being extended as needed (box 10.2).[7]

In principle, once roads are charged at a price equal to the marginal social cost, the decision by the road authority as to whether and when to invest in expansion of the road should depend on the relationship between congestion-pricing revenues and the costs of the expansion.[8] In practice, where the pricing system is only roughly applied, it may still be necessary to undertake a cost-benefit analysis of proposed investments. Nevertheless, the application of the pricing scheme will create the proper base on which to undertake the appraisal and will have generated a revenue pool that can be used to finance extra capacity.[9]

The fact that efficient congestion prices, or parking charges used as a proxy for them (see discussion below), yield revenues in excess of the total direct costs of congestion is sometimes used as an argument against them. This should not be seen as a problem but as an opportunity. High user prices are quite apposite to the shortage of street space relative to built area in many developing-country cities. The distributional implications are very progressive because those who do have cars are predominantly high-income earners likely to attach the highest value to reduced travel time and journey predictability. They may also be democratically viable, since only a minority of the wealthier citizens would be called upon to pay the increased charges due to low car ownership. For all of these reasons, congestion pricing, accompanied by use of the revenues to improve public transport and other city amenities to the benefit of the poor, can be recommended for the typical cash-strapped municipality in a developing or transition economy.

BOX 10.2 ELECTRONICS IMPROVES ROAD-PRICING EFFICIENCY IN SINGAPORE

In September 1998 the government of Singapore replaced the manually enforced ALS by ERP. It generally covers the same area as that for the ALS, but has been extended to work on principles similar to ALS, but with extension to approach and bypass roads. All vehicles are required to have an electronic in-vehicle unit (IU) that accepts credit in the form of a smartcard. Tolls are automatically paid when the vehicle passes under a gantry and a liquid crystal display indicates the current credit balance. Tolls do not fluctuate in relation to actual traffic volumes but are adjusted quarterly to ensure optimum traffic speeds. The system cost $200 million in Singapore dollars (US$125 million) to implement, one-half of which was for the free fitting of IUs.

The ERP system was not implemented to increase government revenue. ERP charges are generally less than the corresponding ALS fees, although the ERP system's per-pass charging principle means that those motorists who use the priced roads must now pay more. Overall, revenue is about 40 percent less than that previously collected from the ALS, but electronic charging gives greater flexibility to set charges that are just sufficient to keep the roads free of congestion.

Once new traffic patterns stabilized, weekday traffic volume entering the restricted zone dropped by 20 to 24 percent, from 271,000 vehicles per day to between 206,000 and 216,000. With those lower traffic volumes, average traffic speeds in the zone increased from 30–35 km/h to 40–45 km/h. Improvements are less clear on the three expressways in the ERP scheme, and the Land Transport Authority is reviewing ERP charges to further optimize traffic flow.

Source: PADECO 2000.

FUEL TAX AS A SURROGATE USER PRICE

For the moment, however, the tax element of the pump price of fuel is the main charge directly associated with road use. Fuel price is thus very important in urban transport. For the private motorist, it is usually the only incurred cost that is perceived in making a marginal trip. It may thus directly affect the amount of travel undertaken, choice of transport mode, and choice of vehicle technology, and may less directly affect the trade-off between location and transport expenditure.

In an ideal world, the price of fuel should cover its resource cost (the border price); maintenance of roads and congestion costs should be charged for directly through highly differentiated tolls; environmental costs should be charged for through emissions charges; and any redistribution objectives should be pursued through nondistorting lump sum taxes.

In reality, that prescription is not achieved currently in either industrialized or developing countries. Most roads are open access (particularly in urban areas), and cannot be subject to highly differentiated direct charges. The technology for location- and pollutant-specific emissions charging does not exist. Lump sum transfers or naïve direct distributional taxes are not possible. In the absence of direct charging mechanisms, fuel taxation is often looked to as a proxy for a number of other, theoretically preferable, taxes or charges relating to road maintenance, congestion, and environmental and distributional objectives. It is thus important to examine the potential of fuel taxation to perform these various functions.

As a charge for *road maintenance,* fuel tax does not differentiate well by vehicle type, and needs to be supplemented by axle-weight charging. Similarly, as a *congestion charge,* fuel tax does not reflect the structure of congestion well because fuel consumption is not sufficiently sensitive to vehicle speed variation. As an *environmental charge,* it is likely to be a very good proxy for carbon emissions taxation, but many other emissions are not proportional to fuel consumption and vary by fuel type, vehicle type, and extent of emissions technology employed. As a *distributional* instrument, it has the right combination of low price elasticity and high income elasticity, and is therefore a very promising redistributor in developing countries.

Fuel tax does have one great advantage compared with taxation on vehicles (vehicle excise duties, registration taxes, insurance charges, and so on), which does not vary with vehicle use. That concerns the relationship with public transport fares, which vary directly with use (period passes are relatively unpopular in developing countries because of the element of advance payment involved). If taxation on private cars is not related to use, the consequence is that the cost of car use for the marginal trip may appear very inexpensive in comparison with that of public transport. One of the great advantages of increasingly including payment of what are presently fixed charges within fuel taxation, or other distance-based charges,[10] is that it puts private and public transport pricing structures on a more-comparable, and hence less-distorting, basis.

Reliance on fuel taxation as a surrogate for direct charging faces some severe administrative difficulties. There are multiple transport fuels, used in multiple sectors, to achieve multiple objectives. Diesel, which may merit heavy taxation for local air pollution reasons, is also the primary fuel for road freight transport, for which reason, as an intermediate input rather than a final consumption good, it would justify a relatively low tax burden. Kerosene typically carries low taxation, or is even subsidized, because of its use for domestic heating in many countries. Unfortunately, if these fuels carry low tax, there is a high likelihood of substitution of diesel for gasoline vehicles, or the adulteration of gasoline with kerosene or diesel, either of which could be environmentally very damaging. Particularly where there is spatial differentiation of fuel taxation for congestion charging reasons, fuel carrying could also be a problem in everything except the very largest cities.

Above all, however, fuel taxation is usually a national prerogative, with revenues accruing to the national treasury rather than to the municipality. For this reason it is likely to be difficult to fit it into, or coordinate it with, a city-level strategy, except on the basis of a countrywide agreement on allocation of all transport-related tax revenues and expenditure responsibilities.

OTHER LESS-DIRECT TAXES AND CHARGES FOR ROAD USE

Other vehicle taxes may also perform a function of allocating road costs equitably and efficiently among vehicle categories. In particular, annual charges based on standard axles are widely used to correct for the fact that road wear is much more a function of axle weights than of fuel consumption. Even though these taxes may be fixed centrally, the revenues yielded sometimes accrue directly to a local jurisdiction.

Some taxes have a very clear allocation function. In Denmark and Hong Kong, acquisition taxes that approximately triple the cost of cars have been major factors limiting motorization (presently some 330 and 60 cars per 1,000 inhabitants, respectively).[11] The most extreme form of this is in Singapore, which in 1990 introduced a system in which a rationed number of entitlements to own a motor vehicle (the so-called Certificates of Entitlement) are auctioned each month. In combination with preexisting taxes, this has resulted in new cars retailing at some four or five times their world market price. Other relevant experiences are those of Tokyo, where prospective car purchasers are required to provide proof of having an off-street parking space; and of various Chinese cities, where entitlements to register a motorcycle have been sold and local circulation of motorcycles registered elsewhere banned.

Parking charges are often used in place of direct road-use charges. While they cannot deter people from driving through an area or reflect the different distances or routes drivers take, they can be varied by time and place in such a way as to capture a significant part of the congestion externality and encourage better spatial or temporal distribution of demand for movement on the roads.[12] They are already manipulated in quite sophisticated ways in many European cities, and both the United Kingdom and France are debating taxation of downtown parking spaces provided by employers for their employees.[13] Transferable permits for a given number of available parking spaces would be a way of auctioning the right for commuters to drive to work.

In summary, an ideal charging regime for the use of infrastructure should allocate all of the associated costs (congestion, environmental, wear and tear on the infrastructure, and so on) to the users incurring them, as far as possible directly in proportion to the costs imposed. That is not completely achievable even in principle because there are some costs (such as lighting, street cleaning, and so on) that have the characteristic of public goods and hence must be allocated more arbitrarily. Because the imposition of the different types of cost varies between vehicle types according to a range of characteristics of vehicles and their use, only the simultaneous application of a number of different charging devices could meet this ideal.

The design of a charging system thus needs to be constructed from a carefully designed combination of different charging components. For simplicity's sake, it may be desirable to limit the number of these components, but a number of general elements can be recommended.

- Fuel should never cost less than border price in any circumstances.
- Where direct congestion charges are possible, these should be varied by time of day and structured according to the congestion-creating equivalents of different vehicle types.
- Wear-and-tear costs should preferably be recouped on a basis variable both by wearing effect and distance traveled (standard axle kilometers). Where this is not possible, the

wear-and-tear cost may be incorporated partly in a fuel tax surcharge and partly in vehicle category–related charges (preferably also based on actual annual use of each vehicle).

- Marginal environmental impact costs and marginal public costs of accidents might be recouped through local fuel tax and insurance surcharges.
- Any sumptuary, or "luxury" taxation, levied on road users for general taxation (nontransport) reasons should be levied on passenger transport rather than freight transport in order to minimize economic distortion.
- Where diesel fuel is taxed at a low rate, some compensating tax should be imposed on the procurement and use of diesel-powered light passenger vehicles to minimize adverse environmental consequences.

PUBLIC TRANSPORT PRICING AND FINANCE

Setting public transport prices and raising the necessary finance, raises problems because of the multiple objectives faced by decisionmakers. The primary objective of public transport pricing is to generate revenue that can ensure an efficient and adequate supply of public transport service. Public transport pricing may also be expected to contribute to the reduction of congestion and environmental impact of road traffic, efficient coordination between public transport modes, and the reduction of poverty. It is commonly argued that if urban public transport is to satisfy these latter objectives, it cannot be expected to cover its full costs. Urban public transport is consequently subsidized in many major cities in industrialized countries.

Similar policies have traditionally been applied in the transition economies and some postcolonial developing countries, but many of these countries are no longer in a position to fund such policies, and their public transport sectors are facing decline because of cash starvation. This section considers how to establish a basis for setting policies on pricing and cost recovery in urban public transport that best reconciles the multiple objectives.

EFFICIENT SUPPLY

There are two important aspects of supply efficiency. First, it is necessary to provide the most beneficial range of services with the resources available—"doing the right thing." Second, it is necessary to supply the required services at the least-possible cost—"doing the thing right." Neither is simple and neither is well achieved in most developing countries.

The difficulty in doing the right thing is that there may be legitimate reasons, both on equity and efficiency grounds, why a pure market outcome would not be optimal. For these reasons, municipal governments may intervene to define both the services to be provided and the fares to be charged. In the absence of the capability to make any more sophisticated calculation, this typically takes the form of setting flat fares for a defined network of basic services. Public sector monopolies are often protected because of the difficulty of enforcing a flat-fare policy with multiple operators.

Such monolithic simplicity is rarely optimal. Transport users have different preferences (partly as a result of differences in income). It may therefore be possible to increase consumer welfare while increasing profitability by supplying different products to different segments of the market. In urban bus transport, this means the provision of "premium" services—such as express services or air-conditioned services—at premium prices. Price discrimination, in this sense, may benefit all users. Operators should therefore be encouraged to examine such revenue-enhancing strategies as an alternative to reliance on subsidy. This strategy has already been widely adopted as a means of maintaining urban bus service in Seoul, Buenos Aires, Bangkok, and many other developing-country cities.

Doing the thing right is what commercial competition usually ensures, since the threat of bankruptcy is a powerful stimulant to internal efficiency. The possibility of subsidy weakens that incentive. Particularly in parastatals, subsidies strengthen the likelihood that organized labor will appropriate part of it to support better wages and working conditions than a competitive market would be able to support. In the United Kingdom it was estimated that over one-half of subsidies aimed at lowering fares or improving service quality actually "leaked" into benefits for management or workers or were lost through reduced efficiency of operation.[14] Exploring measures to reduce subsidy requirements through improved efficiency and reduced costs is thus the first step to take in formulating a public transport subsidy strategy.

Much of the argument for transport deregulation and privatization (see chapter 7) derives from a need to reduce subsidies. Attempts to increase efficiency of operation through the introduction of competitive pressures within the sector may enable lower prices to be charged without recourse to subsidy. The implication is that, for any level of cost recovery lower than 100 percent, subsidies should be specifically targeted at the objectives sought and should be embodied in competitively tendered service contracts.

The macroeconomic effects of urban transport subsidies also need to be considered. In the short run, they may reduce the general price index if transport has a disproportionately heavy weight in the index. Particularly where urban transport is a significant item in the consumption pattern of strongly unionized labor groups, there may be some associated relief from wage pressure. In the longer run, however, it is inevitable that the inflationary pressure will spill over to other items that will have to be taxed to finance the subsidy, or through increased direct income taxation—inducing compensatory wage claims. Deficit budgeting has similar inflationary consequences. The general World Bank position is that subsidy is the wrong tool to deal with inflation; there is nothing special about the transport sector to vitiate this view.

THE IMPACTS ON ROAD CONGESTION

In industrialized countries it is commonly argued that public transport should be subsidized in order to entice trip makers out of private cars and hence reduce road congestion. Where road congestion is concentrated in particular locations or at particular times of the day, this implies a highly differentiated structure of subsidy. Where road congestion is systemwide and pervasive throughout the day, general public transport subsidy may be called for on this argument.

Despite the superficial attractiveness of this line of reasoning, there are several considerations that counsel caution in the use of public transport subsidy as a countercongestion instrument. First, there is the supply efficiency impact discussed earlier. Only if the benefits resulting from a more efficient modal split were greater than the disbenefit of any reduction of supply efficiency associated with subsidy would there be a net benefit overall.[15]

Second, there is a problem of targeting. Where congestion is limited in time or spatial extent, it becomes increasingly difficult to target public transport subsidies as a response to the problem. Highly peaked road congestion calls for peak-hour public transport subsidies, which may have the perverse side effect of shifting public transport demand from off-peak to peak periods. For spatially variable congestion, differential subsidy policy by route may be extremely difficult to structure even if competitively tendered service franchising allows each route to be treated differently.

Third, there is a problem of fiscal cost. Where the basic purpose of the subsidy is to divert traffic from the private auto to public transport, the ideal situation would require very high cross-elasticity of demand for auto use with respect to public transport pricing. Empirical evidence (albeit mostly from industrialized countries) suggests that in fact this cross-elasticity is very low (perhaps 0.1) in the short run. While it may be somewhat higher in the long run due to effects on car ownership, it would still appear to be an instrument of relatively weak leverage.

Finally, there is a problem of perverse land-use effects. Public transport subsidy to countervail systematic undercharging for private transport will mean that all transport is subsidized. This will tend to generate excessive travel and inappropriately sprawling land use. Measures to redress inadequacies in the system of charges for private transport should always be a condition attached to the financing of "second-best" subsidies.

PUBLIC TRANSPORT COORDINATION

Allocation of traffic between competing modes within an urban transport system would be efficient if prices were everywhere equal to short-run marginal social costs. The general prescription for covering fixed costs where these will not be recouped by short-run marginal cost pricing is to minimize distortion by loading the fixed costs most heavily on those parts of the market for which the demand is least likely to be affected by a price increase. This is known as the "Ramsey pricing rule" (box 10.3). In multimodal urban transport systems, which are, as a whole, in financial equilibrium, this may imply cross-subsidy between modes, particularly when the modes have different cost structures. The application of this approach to urban public transport pricing requires consideration, not only of the implications of the relative congestion externalities of alternative modes but also of their different cost structures.

Where two modes are operated within a single organization, and entry is regulated, it is possible to reconcile different levels of cost recovery for the two with any overall cost-recovery requirement (including breakeven overall). It is quite common for this to occur in metropolitan public transport undertakings (though it should be remarked, in

---

BOX 10.3 RECOVERING FIXED COSTS: THE RAMSEY PRICING RULES

The Ramsey inverse elasticity mark-up rule concerns the allocation of fixed costs between alternative products within a production agency. If a multimodal transport system is viewed as a single supply agency, the Ramsey pricing rule can be interpreted as a rule about the allocation of system-fixed costs between modes. For example, in typical bus operations, over 90 percent of costs vary with respect to either the number of vehicles employed or the number of bus kilometers run. Short-run marginal cost pricing would nearly cover full cost. The same is not the case for rail systems, where typically only 50 or 60 percent of costs are directly related to the service provided. In such conditions, the most efficient outcome may involve different levels of total cost coverage by the modes and transfers between them.

If cross-elasticities between alternative transport forms are zero, the objective of efficiently covering total costs will be achieved by adding mark-ups to the marginal social cost in proportion to the reciprocal of the price elasticity of demand. The rule then becomes rather more complex. Consider, for example, the ratio of peak and off-peak prices. If the peak demand were completely inelastic and the off-peak demand infinitely elastic, the whole of the burden would fall on the peak price. More realistically, some users may shift from peak to off-peak as relative prices change. With nonzero cross-elasticities, the ratio of the mark-ups of different service should take into account the cross-elasticity as well as the own-price elasticities.

Source: Authors.

passing, that where it does occur, it is often regarded as a form of illegitimate cross-subsidy).

However, when the modes are operating in competition with each other, attempting to apply the inverse elasticity rule creates a conflict between the interests of pricing for allocative efficiency and those of pricing for commercial viability. Competitive operation of such mixed-mode systems on a purely commercial basis will result in a suboptimal level of patronage for those modes with the greatest proportion of fixed cost (empty trains and overfull buses). It will also affect the structure of services provided. For example, commercial operation of buses and metros within an urban area may lead to a smaller amount of restructuring of bus services to take advantage of the complementarity of the modes and a larger amount of trunk service by buses than would be optimal. Recent experience in Rio de Janeiro suggests that concessions of urban rail operations to the private sector may make the achievement of fare integration more difficult.

Not all modal coordination considerations militate in favor of public transport subsidy. Because congestion must, by definition, be greater at peak than at off-peak hours, the marginal social cost of the peak period private car user must always exceed the average cost. The marginal social cost of peak-hour public transport may also exceed its average cost, because peak service requires extra vehicle capacity costs and may impose high marginal labor costs (resulting from labor agreements requiring payment for a minimum number of hours per day exceeding the number of peak hours, and premiums for any splitting of working shifts). The marginal social cost of peak public transport provision thus depends not only on the level of congestion but also on the disparity between peak and off-peak demand levels and the industrial relations context in which the service is being supplied. For cities with relatively low levels of road congestion but high public transport peak-to-off-peak demand ratios, optimal peak public transport subsidies may be small (or even, conceivably, negative).

EQUITY

In many cities public transport fares are controlled in an attempt to maintain an affordable service to the poor who have no alternative form of travel. While in principle lump sum transfers would be a preferable way to redistribute income, in practice they are rarely feasible politically. Increases in public transport fares are therefore politically sensitive. (Five people died in riots following a fare increase in Guatemala in April 2000.) The question is thus not whether the objective of maintaining affordable public transport service is important and desirable, but whether it can be practically and cost-effectively achieved with the policies typically adopted for the purpose. The main characteristics to review in this context are the general fare level, fare structures, fare concessions, and fare discrimination.

Fare levels. In most low- and middle-income developing countries, the average income of public transport users is below that of motorized private transport users, and below the overall average income. If fares are set below cost in such circumstances and operating deficits covered either from a progressive income tax or a tax on private motoring, the distributional (poverty alleviation) impact will be positive. If, however, the control on fares is not directly funded, the long-term effect will be to reduce first the quality and eventually the quantity of public transport available. Whether the poor actually benefit from price controls then depends on the tradeoff between less expensive fares and poorer service. There is considerable evidence, even in relatively poor countries, such as the Kyrgyz Republic, that the poor are willing to pay more for a better service than that provided at existing controlled fares. In the extreme, the poor get no benefit at all from setting very low fares if that causes supply to disappear altogether. Decisions on the control of fares should thus be taken in the context of an assessment of the effects of the control on the quality of service and in the context that the continuation of an appropriate level of service can continue to be financed.

Fare structure. Flat fares are frequently adopted throughout a municipal or conurbation area in the belief that this is equitable. Where longer work journeys have been forced on the poor, either through racial discrimination in housing (as in South Africa) or through market-unaware housing planning (as in many former command economies), flat fares may indeed compensate for other forms of discrimination against the poor. The danger, however, is that in larger cities, a flat fare may need to be set at such a high level that it encourages shorter-distance travelers to seek alternative modes, and hence to undermine any "within-mode" cross-subsidy. It is therefore recommended that such spatial distribution issues be handled through specifically designed services and fares, rather than through a general flat-fare system.

Designing a service and fare structure that is both equitable and efficient is particularly difficult in multimodal systems. There may be an efficiency case for structuring bus services to feed high-capacity trunk rail systems and for allowing the buses to cross-subsidize the rail system. In many cases, however, the average bus user is poorer than the average rail user, so what may look efficient from a coordination viewpoint involves the poor subsidizing the rich. The lack of multimodal ticketing accentuates this problem The moral is that wherever explicit attempts are made to secure modal coordination within urban public transport systems, it should be in the context of an integrated fares and charges strategy taking particular cognizance of the effects on the poor.

Fare reductions or exemptions. The distribution of poverty-oriented subsidies should ideally be explicitly related to the income levels of service users. There may be some vulnerable categories of passenger (schoolchildren and senior citizens not in receipt of a full income) that can be easily distinguished and for which charging a lower price is possible. The advantage of discrimination on this basis is that it can be applied to all services and can even be nuanced (for example, to exclude retired people with incomes above some mini-

mum level). In many countries, and particularly in the transitional economies, there is a pervasive tradition of providing free or reduced-fare transport for a wide range of public servants. This raises two major problems. First, the categories in receipt of free fares are often not the most needy, so that the redistribution effects of supporting the concessions by internal cross-subsidy are perverse. Second, where there are a large proportion of non-fare-paying passengers, it becomes more difficult to enforce payment by those who are supposed to pay. Explicit consideration of the extent and justification of fare exemptions and the extent and means of combating fare evasion should therefore be a sine qua non of any fare-determination process. Moreover, where reduced fares are mandated for the support of other sector policies (health, social security, policing, and so on), the costs of the subsidies should be charged directly to the other sector budgets.

Fare discrimination. Where residential locations are highly segregated by income group, specific routes may also be identified for subsidy on income-distribution grounds. For example, at one stage a fare differential existed between Lines 1 and 2 of the metro in Santiago, Chile, with the line serving the lower-income population charging lower fares per kilometer. Less well targeted approaches may have perverse effects. For example, the provision of minimum levels of network density and frequency throughout an urban area at the standard fare level will tend to provide higher levels of service or lower price to areas with low residential density than would be commercially sustainable. In middle-income countries, these areas are areas of high incomes and high car ownership. If such a policy were pursued within a system covering its costs in total, the effect would be a perverse cross-subsidy from the poor to the rich. Maintaining specified network density or frequency by external subsidy has other disadvantages. In particular, there will be a systematic tendency to overprovision, because both those who receive the subsidized service and those who supply it develop a vested interest in high levels of provision.

THE DYNAMICS OF POLICY REFORM: MAKING SUSTAINABILITY PARAMOUNT

There is a close relationship between charges for infrastructure and charges for public transport service. If road use were efficiently priced, there would be no economic second-best case for public transport subsidy. Logically, this suggests the need not only for action to secure optimal pricing for both infrastructure and services but also for careful attention to the dynamics of change. Eliminating public transport subsidy in the absence of efficient infrastructure charges might simply further distort the choice of transport mode. The counsel of perfection would thus be to link any move to improved cost recovery for public transport to the progress made in introducing efficient road pricing.

Within the context of political reality, however, that may be a difficult prescription to observe, particularly where, because of fiscal collapse, the short-term alternative to fare increases is not continued subsidy but loss of service. Generating an adequate cash flow is the most serious problem for many public transport operators in developing countries. Attempts to control fares at uncommercial levels in the absence of a secure fiscal foundation threatens sustainability of service, not only for parastatals (as in many cities in West Africa) but also for franchised private operators (as in Jamaica). Without a secure financial basis, it is impossible to achieve the other objectives discussed. For that reason it is suggested that, while increased cost recovery through the farebox should not be the primary concern of public transport policy per se, the maintenance of a sound financial basis should be at the heart of the pricing policy process.

This is not always well understood. In transitional economies, where parastatal operators are not accustomed to commercial accounting principles, it may be particularly difficult to ensure that proper provision is made for the financing of depreciation. Even where some of the capital investment is sunk in long-lived assets that are fixed or cannot be profitably resold or devoted to any other use, system sustainability still requires enough revenue to cover costs of operation, maintenance, and replacement of rolling stock.

URBAN TRANSPORT FINANCING

The financing of municipal transport is complex and difficult both because of the separation of road infrastructure from operations and because of the multiple objectives that public authorities are pursuing in urban transport policy. In this section we first consider the problems of financing public sector infrastructure, then examine the possibilities of private sector participation in infrastructure finance, and finally consider the institutional possibilities of mobilizing the pricing devices that have been discussed above to solve the financing problem.

PUBLIC FINANCING OF INFRASTRUCTURE

The sources of funding for public sector investments may include transfers from central government, local borrowing, local taxation, and service charging. Public expenditures on urban transport in capital cities may be fully financed by the central government. More generally, and almost exclusively in noncapital cities, the main responsibility for finance will rest with the regional or municipal government with some degree of counterpart funding from the central government. That sharing of financial responsibility can induce overinvestment in infrastructure if it takes the form of automatic counterpart funding of locally generated schemes. Projects should therefore be subject to some formal economic appraisal of investments as a condition for cost sharing.

Local borrowing may be secured against general municipal revenues or occasionally against toll revenue. Some municipalities are at least as creditworthy as their national governments and may be able to issue bonds of their own. That is not usually the case for smaller cities, however, and borrowing may have to be by government on their behalf. In this context it is essential that all claims for capital resources be based on, and assessed according to, a common investment appraisal criterion and that the municipality should meet the servicing costs of its borrowing.

Local taxing capability is also very limited in many countries, often being restricted to property taxation and various minor licensing revenues. In many developing countries, sales tax and income tax are central government prerogatives. Other local taxes, or taxlike impositions, are sometimes used to supplement user charges for transport services. The French "versement transport" is an earmarked payroll tax. The "vale-transporte" in Brazil is an obligation imposed on employers to finance part of the commuting costs of their employees.

On the principle that "he who benefits should pay," it may seem desirable to capture in tax revenues part of the benefit due to infrastructure investment accruing to local residents or businesses, and to use these funds to finance investments. A "betterment" tax, which appropriates part of the gain in the value of properties resulting from infrastructure investments, does this in principle but is difficult to assess and apply in practice. It is also collected after the investment rather than in advance. Development charges and infrastructure contributions, when assessed systematically, can provide for the extension of infrastructure as cities expand, but can rely on the existence of very strong development controls, which are often lacking in developing countries. The national government of Japan has issued administrative guidance on integrated rail and new town development mandating contributions of the land developer to the rail enterprises with several provisions to be included in their agreement.[16]

Direct charges for service from users of a particular piece of locally funded infrastructure is normally treated as a trading revenue that accrues automatically to the supplying authority—but these direct charges for service are very rare. Indirect charges, such as fuel taxation, usually accrue to the central government. A critical question is whether congestion charges are to be treated as a charge for service or a tax. One of the reasons that road pricing has made so little progress in industrialized countries is that it is often legally classified as a tax, accruing to the central treasury. The British Parliament has recently passed a law to allow municipal authorities to keep road-charging revenues, and hence gives municipalities an incentive to introduce congestion charges.

MOBILIZING PRIVATE FINANCE

Where public transport service is franchised to the private sector, the financing of vehicles and their supporting infrastructure normally becomes the responsibility of the franchisee. The main difficulty in this context is that unless the contracts are well defined, and of reasonable duration, it may be difficult for a private operator to finance the necessary vehicles. For example, one of the major difficulties confronting the introduction of competitive tendering of franchises in Uzbekistan is that in the absence of any history of contracting, neither borrowing for nor leasing of vehicles is possible.

Recent experience in some Latin American and East Asian countries has shown that private finance can also be mobilized for urban transport infrastructure through concession arrangements. Urban expressways have been totally privately financed in Argentina, Malaysia, and Thailand, and the first urban metro in Bangkok was privately financed. In other cases, such as the concessioning of the existing suburban railways in Argentina, where prices were fairly tightly constrained, public contribution was necessary to make private financing of new investment viable.

The need for public sector contribution is not a reason for forgoing private participation, but it does emphasize the need to establish both the principles and procedures through which public contributions should be appraised. Essentially, if the private concessionaire is able to exploit consumer surplus of users of the new infrastructure, the public sector should require that the value of external and nonuser benefits be sufficient to justify the required contribution on its normal evaluation conventions. The danger is that the government will become committed without any clear understanding of the costs and benefits.

One of the major impediments to private sector initiative in urban transport infrastructure is the problem of acquiring many fragmented parcels of land and assembling them into a linear right-of-way. For "greenfield" developments, transport infrastructure may so improve the value of adjoining land that it should be in the interests of landowners to facilitate infrastructure construction. This potential gain has been effectively exploited in a number of urban rail systems in Japan through a process of land assembly and reparceling (box 2.4 in chapter 2).[17] The codification of a basis for such private sector initiatives is worth exploring as a means of facilitating private sector investment in large-city transport infrastructure. In areas of existing development, however, that goal is more difficult to achieve. For this reason the public sector usually uses its powers of eminent domain to assemble and provide the right-of-way, as in the cases of the private investments in new metro systems in both Bangkok and Manila.

URBAN TRANSPORT FUNDING

It is widely agreed that urban transport planning and operation should be an integral part of urban strategy. It is even more obvious that the activities of the different modes and functions within the transport sector should be well integrated. By implication that requires consistency of financial arrangements within an overall strategic framework. In most countries, however, no more than lip service is paid to that prescription. We therefore need to explore how financing arrangements might be structured to secure more effective integration both within the sector and between sectors.

The usual institutional context for this has two complicating characteristics. First, responsibility for public transport is increasingly being decentralized to the cities in the absence of an adequate local fiscal base. This means either that the sector has to be financially self-supporting or that it must be dependent on intergovernmental transfers. Second, the supply of transport facilities and services is typically very fragmented, both between private and public sectors and functionally within the public sector itself. This means that the provision of service usually depends on separate and independent financing arrangements for the modes.

Intergovernmental transfers

With respect to intergovernmental transfers, a mechanism is needed that channels finance in a way that neither distorts the allocation of resources between alternative modes or instruments nor weakens the incentives to efficient operation of the individual modes. Unfortunately, the two most commonly used transfer mechanisms—counterpart funding of infrastructure investments and direct subsidy of bus operations—fail these tests.

Counterpart funding by national governments of urban transport infrastructure investment, particularly in capital cities, is common, while current account support to the municipalities for transport purposes is rare. The effect of this is to bias the cities in the allocation of resources at their disposal in whatever way attracts the most generous counterpart funding. The partiality of cities for road investment in many countries, and even for heavy rail investments in some countries, often derives from the high degree of counterpart funding that such investments attract. It may also undermine collaboration, because authorities see more benefit in competing for the "cheap" counterpart funds than in collaborating to develop effective programs.

Three devices can contribute to limit or eliminate this rent-seeking behavior. First, allocation of funds from central to local government should be based on the quality of the project. Second, all such investments in conurbations may be required to be in conformity with an agreed-on conurbation development plan. Third, support can be channeled through block grant arrangements that leave the cities free and responsible to decide how central government contributions are best used.

Subsidization of public transport operations by the central government is typically channeled through deficit funding of publicly owned transport companies. This discourages the search by municipalities for more efficient supply mechanisms, and has ultimately failed to provide a sustainable basis for public transport operations in most of the developing and transitional economies where it has been applied. To avoid this it is necessary to replace the funding of publicly owned supply agencies by the provision of untied funds with which the municipalities can procure services, in whatever way they find it most effective. In some cases where municipal government has been captured by the supply agencies or their employees, it may be necessary to link the provision of such funds with requirements for the introduction of a competitive procurement process.

Intrasectoral coordination

The pricing principles set out earlier clearly do not result in balanced budgets for each and every urban transport mode. In the case of congested urban roads, short-run marginal cost pricing would yield a surplus over road maintenance and operation costs. While in many sectors this would justify increasing capacity so that short-run costs fell, that may not be possible in the case of urban roads because of the high land and environmental costs of increasing the capacity. In contrast, setting public transport fares below cost in order to redistribute income, to act as a countervailing distortion to the underpricing of road space, or to affect modal split for environmental reasons would all leave a deficit in public transport financing. This might be implemented in a competitive regime through negative price franchising of transport services. Even *within* the public transport sector, an optimum pricing structure might require different cost-recovery rates for road- and rail-based systems because of differences in cost structures between modes and indivisibilities in supply. In all these cases, a systemwide approach to urban transport finance makes more sense than a strict financial balance for individual modes or suppliers.

Political attitudes to cross-subsidy are somewhat paradoxical. Within the bus sector, cross-subsidy of unprofitable routes or schedules by profitable ones is often viewed as a good thing and the loss of that capability to be the major disadvantage of competitive regimes. Yet, at the same time, there is great resistance to the transfer of surpluses from one mode to another. Road pricing is frequently opposed because the benefits of the surplus are not likely to be returned to those who pay the charges. The future of congestion charging will depend largely on the political acceptability of the proposed uses for the large revenues that will be generated.

Public opinion on this appears to be changing in the industrialized countries. The emerging professional consensus that "net revenues from congestion charging (after some reduction of other road-user taxes in cases where they are already high) should be devoted largely to transport improvements" certainly reflects the results of public opinion surveys. European discussions usually give particular emphasis to use of a significant portion of the revenues for support to public transport, partly on grounds that drivers in congested areas benefit directly through reduced private travel time and cost from the decisions of others to use public rather than private transport. Various formulas have been proposed to combine transport service objectives with social and fiscal desiderata so that the benefits of the scheme would be distributed as fairly as possible and would be perceived as being fair.[18] The emergence of such a view could be very significant in influencing policies in developing countries.

Integrated urban transport finances

These considerations suggest the need for a mechanism to integrate urban transport finances, whether secured from users, from local taxes, or from intergovernmental transfers, and to ensure their efficient allocation among uses. For smaller, unitary cities, an existing all-purpose administration might be quite adequate without the creation of any special new institution. Many Chinese cities appear to operate very satisfactorily this way. In these circumstances there may already be sufficient fungibility of funds both within the transport sector and between sectors to serve the area well. But the larger the city size and the more complex its jurisdictional and functional organization, the more likely it is that a "ring fenced" fund and authority will be beneficial.

One straightforward solution for larger conurbations is the creation of an urban transport fund into which all local transport trading profits, transport-related intergovernmental transfers, or local tax allocations should be paid, and from which all local public sector transport expenditures should be financed. The creation of such a fund does not depend on any specific tax source being earmarked for transport, although it would be an essential part of such a scheme that local congestion charges be treated as municipal trading revenues and not as general tax revenues.[19] The essential features to be sought in an arrangement would thus be the pooling of all available transport revenues and their allocation between uses on the basis of the contribution made to the overall municipal development objective.

Neither does the creation of such a fund require any unique local political structure. While the funds would need to be administered by a professional urban transport executive, there are many possible structures for the strategic control of the executive. Where there is a strong local democratic process with competent administration, it might be directed by the local political authority (as is being considered in Buenos Aires); in multiple-jurisdiction authorities, it might be responsible to a joint committee of contiguous authorities (as is being developed in many large, multijurisdictional Brazilian conurbations). It might

be administered by a "special purpose district," as is common in the United States. The controlling authority might even include direct user representation, as is commonly advocated for national road funds. These alternatives are considered in more detail in chapter 11.

CONCLUSIONS: A STRATEGY FOR URBAN TRANSPORT PRICING AND FINANCING

The essence of the urban transport pricing and financing issue is that in a system where the modes are highly interactive and policy objectives are complex, the separation of responsibilities for road infrastructure from operations, for infrastructure provision from infrastructure charging, and for roads from that of other modes creates significant policy distortions. The irony is that with such a heavy demand for road space, and such palpable undercharging for its use, cities are short of financial resources to support the investments and the modes of transport that can best contribute to the relief of urban transport problems. In the interests of urban transport integration and sustainability, developing countries should move toward prices reflecting full social costs for all modes, to a targeted approach to subsidization reflecting strategic objectives, and to an integration of urban transport funding. At the same time, however, it is desirable to retain institutions and objectives for the individual modes or components that give high incentive to operational efficiency and cost-effectiveness. A monolithic public sector monopoly is thus not the solution.

The components of a strategy to achieve this logical integration include:

On charging for road infrastructure
- Vehicular users of congested urban road space should be charged a price at least equal to the short-run marginal cost of use.
- Cordon pricing and tolling of specific roads may make an interim contribution, but the

long-term solution must lie in a more thorough application of congestion charges.

- Fuel tax, although a poor surrogate for congestion or road maintenance impact pricing, should in the absence of direct charging be structured along with vehicle license duties to give the best available proxy.
- Taxes on different fuels should be structured to reflect their relative contributions to urban air pollution, again in conjunction with the structuring of vehicle license duties.
- Parking charges, although a poor proxy for congestion charges, should always cover the full opportunity cost of land used for parking.
- Where parking policy is the only available proxy for efficient pricing, controls need to cover all forms of parking space (including that provided privately by employers for employees), and should be designed to secure a level of restraint equivalent to that of efficient prices.
- All road congestion charges, or fuel tax surcharges operating as a proxy for them, should accrue to the municipal or metropolitan authority, and not to the central government treasury.

On public transport pricing and finance

- Pricing principles for public transport modes should be determined within an integrated urban strategy and should reflect the extent to which road infrastructure is adequately charged.
- Given the high level of interaction between modes, and the prevalent undercharging of road use, no absolute value should be ascribed to covering all costs from fares, either for public transport as a whole or for individual modes.
- Transfers between roads and public transport services, and between modes of public transport, are potentially consistent with optimal pricing strategies.
- In the interests of efficient service supply, transport operators should operate com-

petitively with purely commercial objectives, with financial transfers achieved through contracts between municipal authorities and operators for the supply of services.

- Any noncommercial objectives imposed on operators should be compensated directly and transparently, where appropriate by nontransport line agencies in whose interests they are imposed.
- In the absence of appropriate contracting or other support mechanisms, the sustainability of public transport service should be paramount and generally have precedence over traditional price regulation arrangements.

On urban transport financing

- Given the degree of interaction between modes, urban transport financial resources should be pooled within an urban transport fund administered by the strategic transport authority at the municipal or metropolitan level.
- Intergovernmental transfers should normally be made to the fund and should be structured in such a way as to avoid distorting the efficient allocation of resources within the transport sector at the local level.
- Private sector financing for transport infrastructure should be raised through competitive tendering of concessions that may be supported by public contributions as long as these have been subject to proper cost-benefit analysis.
- When allocating funds to urban transport, the relationship between transport policy and other sector policies, in particular housing, should be borne in mind.

NOTES

1. That does not mean that the optimum would be a situation without any congestion at all. In urban areas, where the cost of extra road capacity is usually very high, some people may be willing to pay a surcharge over their own direct costs for the benefits that they receive from making a

trip, but the benefits of eliminating congestion are not sufficient to justify the high costs of the extra capacity.

2. Mohring 1999.

3. Wheaton 1996.

4. Hau 1992b.

5. See, for example, Richardson and Bae 1998.

6. Equity concerns have not been a major concern in Singapore's repeated raising of taxes and charges on motor vehicle ownership and use, and family budget surveys make it clear that the vast majority of these taxes and charges are paid by the 30 percent of the households with the highest incomes.

7. See Willoughby 2000b.

8. Hau 1992a.

9. Roth 1996.

10. For a discussion of distance-based charges, see Litman 1999.

11. Other countries, too, have sometimes justified new taxes on car acquisition as measures to ration access to road space, but the relatively low rates of the tax make it harder to identify specific impact. For the case of the United Kingdom, see Newbery 1990.

12. Verhoef, Nijkamp, and Rietveld 1995.

13. Conseil National des Transports 1999; and Department of Environment, Transport, and the Regions 1998.

14. TRL 1985.

15. Given widespread evidence that demand for public transport is more elastic with respect to level of service—particularly network density and frequency—than to price, policies aimed at securing high levels of service quality may well be more effective than those directed at prices.

16. PADECO 2000.

17. PADECO 2000.

18. Small 1992.

19. Without such a provision, municipalities are inevitably resistant to the introduction of direct charges on local road users. The recent resurgence of interest in congestion charging in the United Kingdom has resulted partly from the passing of legislation to allow local authorities to keep any road congestion charge revenues.

11 STRENGTHENING URBAN TRANSPORT INSTITUTIONS

Institutional weaknesses are the sources of many observed failures in urban transport in developing countries. At the municipal level, institutional structures for transport are weak and inadequately staffed. The need to integrate policies both within the transport sector and between transport and other aspects of urban development calls for the development of institutions that minimize jurisdictional and functional impediments to policy integration and allow for extension of the role of the private sector within an integrated strategy.

THE IMPORTANCE OF INSTITUTIONS

This review shows the heterogeneity and technical complexity of urban transport issues, as well as their political sensitivity. At the same time, it emphasizes the need for strategy integration both within the urban transport sector and between the sector and the rest of the urban development process to which it contributes. This is an enormous institutional as well as intellectual task.

Urban transport strategy operates at three levels:

Strategy for the city is the concern of national and regional governments, which have the responsibility for formulating regional development policy, for allocating intergovernmental funding transfers, and for establishing the legal framework within which lower-level authorities and agencies operate.

Strategy of the city is the concern of municipal authorities, which have the responsibility for determining their own internal priorities, supplementing the resources available from local sources, and allocating the resources at their disposal to achieve city objectives. It is also the concern of citizens who may not be well heard or represented through the local political process.

Strategy in the city is the concern of implementing agencies, both private and public sector, who have the responsibility for performing the tasks, or supplying the services, attributed to them, but who have some degree of technical autonomy in undertaking these duties.

Table 11.1 lists the functions commonly associated with each level of strategy making and the wide range of agencies that are involved. For urban transport strategy to be effective, each of these three levels must have a technical competence to perform their tasks, and the levels of strategy must be consistently aligned and efficiently coordinated. Many of the failures to achieve desired objectives (such as safety, environmental protection, and public transport integration) or to implement policy instruments effectively (for example, traffic management) that have been observed earlier can be attributed, at least in part, to institutional weaknesses. In many cases collaboration is necessary between institutions or actors operating under different incentives and having no inducement to act in concert with each other. Cities that have failed to find acceptable institutional mechanisms have also frequently failed to address the problems of increasing road congestion, environmental deterioration, and the decline of public transport.

TABLE 11.1 ALLOCATION OF STRATEGIC FUNCTIONS

Strategy level	Function	Agency	Comments
"For the city"	National roads Public enterprises Tax levels Intergovernmental transfers Regulation and competition policy Vehicle registration and safety	Ministry of construction Ministry of economy Treasury Treasury Ministry of economy Ministry of transport	Private sector construction Sometimes municipal May be function of a quasi-independent commission
"Of the city"	Urban structure planning Strategic transport planning Local road management Public transport planning and procurement Traffic management Law enforcement Road safety	Planning department Transport department Roads department Public transport agency Traffic department Police department Interdepartmental unit	 Direct responsibility to mayor Sometimes national
"In the city"	Public transport operations Road construction and maintenance Local facility consultation	Private companies Private companies NGOs and individuals	Franchised or contracted Some force account maintenance typical Sometimes under formal public inquiry laws

Note: NGO = nongovernmental organization.
Source: Authors.

MAJOR INSTITUTIONAL WEAKNESSES

There are a number of sources of potential weakness including a lack of technical capability, poor spatial and jurisdictional coordination, poor functional coordination, and poor operational coordination.

The weakness of urban transport institutions is frequently noted in this review. Few cities have any comprehensive strategic land-use and transportation-planning agency. There is often no traffic management institution or unit worthy of the name, and often not even an adequately trained transport or traffic engineer within the municipal institution. Traffic police are often involved with traffic management planning simply because there is no professional civilian alternative. They are often underequipped, not well trained in traffic management enforcement, and do not appreciate the role and function of traffic management.

The public transport planning and regulatory function is too often tied to operations. If the institutions exist, they tend to be understaffed and their staff poorly trained. The net result is that politicians and senior executives without transportation training are making important transport decisions without informed professional input and with predictable adverse consequences.

If the professionalism of the relevant institutions cannot be improved, it is unlikely that the substantive problems will be solved. Action is therefore required on two levels. First, authorities must recognize what kind of technical organization is necessary to address urban transport issues. Second, the organizations must have adequate human and physical resources to perform their functions.

SPATIAL AND JURISDICTIONAL COORDINATION

Suburbanization of population growth, particularly where associated with continuing centralization of employment and economic activity, leads to a situation where the major traffic flows are *between* traditional local government jurisdictions rather than *within* them. The city region, rather than the municipality, becomes the effective unit of major transport interaction.

Overlapping levels of authority within a hierarchical system are often the source of jurisdictional conflicts. In many transitional economies, responsibility for financing urban public transport has been transferred to the municipalities, while the central government retains some powers (often embodied in law) to determine fare levels. In countries with a federal structure, it is common to find very complex allocations of responsibility for urban transport between the central government, state government, and municipality. In Brazil, for example, suburban railways were, until very recently, the responsibility of the federal government, intermunicipal buses the responsibility of the state government, and intramunicipal buses the responsibility of the municipalities. In many cases the major metropolitan areas are made up of several autonomous municipalities. Particularly where political control is in the hands of different political parties, agreement may be very difficult to reach.

Contiguous authorities, at the same hierarchical level, make up many metropolitan areas in developing, as well as in industrialized, countries. Where transport interaction occurs significantly across the boundaries between them, it is desirable that they should act in concert. Sometimes there is a dominant central authority whose leadership is acceptable to all others. That is particularly likely to be the case where, as in Bangkok, the capital city has a special legal status or is more favorably treated by the central government than are other local authorities. More commonly, however—as in Manila, Caracas, and Lima—multiple jurisdictions of equivalent size and status may be unwilling to yield any significant amount of power or financial control to another authority at the same hierarchical level.

Local district and municipal interests may not be well aligned on detailed matters of transport policy even in unitary cities. Local impacts of new infrastructure and of public transport service and fare-level changes may be much better understood at the neighborhood level than at the city level. For this reason, even countries with an active local democratic process, commonly subject major transport infrastructure to a parallel process of detailed local consultation and review.

FUNCTIONAL COORDINATION

The inability to avoid congestion by simply increasing road capacity leads to interaction between modes of transport (particularly between private cars and public transport) and between functions (particularly between land-use management, infrastructure provision, road-traffic management, and public transport planning and operation). The transport system, rather than the individual mode or function, becomes the effective unit of transport supply.

Coordination between land-use and transport development is fundamental to efficient city development. Singapore and Curitiba, the two developing cities widely considered to have best managed their motorization, benefited immensely from the early establishment of a long-term structure plan. In both cases the structure plans have permitted rational procurement of land for future rights-of-way for main transport arteries and were the basis for the location of high trip generators (such as shopping centers) in locations conveniently accessible by public transport. It has been possible to provide a high level of accessibility to major activities by public transport and, as a consequence, to reduce the dependence on the private car. In both cities the institutional basis for this successful structure planning experience has been the early establishment of a strong technical planning capability.

Coordination between transport modes is required to secure effective physical interchange between modes, particularly when the modes are independently and privately operated. It is also necessary to ensure efficient economic exploitation of the potential of all modes within a system while at the same time maintaining affordable basic service for the poorest. As far as public transport is concerned, cities that have institutionalized a central functional responsibility for planning and procurement appear to be most capable of achieving both technical and economic coordination of the modes.

Coordination in traffic management and enforcement depends critically on the relationship between transport policy and policing functions. In most countries police have extensive, and often exclusive, powers to direct road traffic, supported by powers of arrest. This gives them a critical role in policy implementation in traffic management, road safety, public transport priority, nonmotorized transport (NMT), the informal transport sector, and so on.

OPERATIONAL COORDINATION

Private and public sectors interact increasingly as central and municipal governments find themselves incapable of financing their strategies alone. Unfortunately, their objectives do not naturally coincide. What is external to the private enterprise is internal and central to the enlightened municipal government. Incompatible and uncoordinated development of infrastructure (as in Bangkok's expressways and mass rapid transit systems) creates long-lasting burdens on the traveler. Unregulated operational competition creates environmental and safety hazards. This does not mean that the private sector cannot contribute importantly to the resolution of urban transport problems. But it does mean that there must be appropriate public institutions for the planning, procurement, and regulation of private sector services in order to reconcile the different interests and efficiently mobilize private participation.

ORGANIZATIONAL OPTIONS

These coordination issues are difficult to handle because transport is but one of a number of services with differing degrees of spatial interaction and hence different "natural spatial boundaries."

Even within transport, some functions, such as parking enforcement, may be appropriately administered at a very local level, while others, such as infrastructure planning, need to be addressed on a much wider scale. Moreover, countries have very widely differing political systems and administrative competencies. There is thus no unique, universally applicable, structural solution. Arrangements may even change over time within a country as priorities, problems, and the political attitude toward planning change. For example, the United Kingdom has fluctuated between joint transport committees of smaller autonomous authorities and allocation of primary powers to city-region jurisdictions. Nevertheless, some general guidelines may be derived from experience in countries that have addressed the problems reasonably successfully.

ESTABLISHING THE NECESSARY FUNCTIONAL BASIS

The basic organizational requirements for good urban transport are that each major function is recognized, that responsibility for each function is clearly assigned to an identified management unit, that the units are properly resourced for their tasks, and that their relationship with other organizations is clearly designated. The majority of local planning and day-to-day operational functions will fall to the municipal or metropolitan level. A typical organization for the performance of these functions, together with the responsibilities and resource requirements of the departments or agencies, is shown in table 11.2.

Managing public transport is particularly difficult when there are many modes, operating over boundaries of autonomous municipalities, some in the private and some in the public sector. In these circumstances, it is important that responsibility to ensure the coordination of physical infrastructure, service systems, fares, and finances is clearly allocated.[1] There are several different patterns for this, including:

- A regional *coordinating committee* composed of political representatives of all the jurisdictions, but without its own executive powers. This sort of institution has been set up in several Brazilian metropolitan areas.

- A regional *coordinating authority* governed by a board of political representatives of the constituent authorities, having a professional executive agency to implement its policies, with operators either directly controlled by the executive or operating under contract to it. This was the pattern of the Passenger Transport Authority/Executive arrangement in the United Kingdom until the mid 1980s. Some of the German "Verkehrsverbund" (for example, Hamburg and Karslruhe) also follow this pattern.

- A regional *mixed coordinating authority* governed by a board containing both political representatives of the constituent authorities, and operators. This is the form of "Verkehrsverbund" in Stuttgart.

- A *two-tier arrangement,* in which there is a political body and an operators' body linked by a formal agreement. This is the arrangement in Berlin.

- A *legally established independent authority* governed by a broadly based representative board of directors, including directors nominated by the political jurisdictions but not under direct political control. An example of this structure is the Madrid Transport Consortium.

The distinguishing feature of good examples of each of these structures is the ability to manage the system as one, and to introduce and maintain integrated service planning and pricing. For example, the recovery of public transport patronage in Madrid is closely linked to the establishment of the Madrid Transport Consortium and its introduction of a multimode transit "commuter card" (figure 11.1).

An appropriate starting point for a city wishing to improve its urban transport capability might usefully be to fill out and expand a basic functions table and, by benchmarking on the organization and capabilities of peer cities, to identify where its institutional and human resource weaknesses lie (table 11.2).

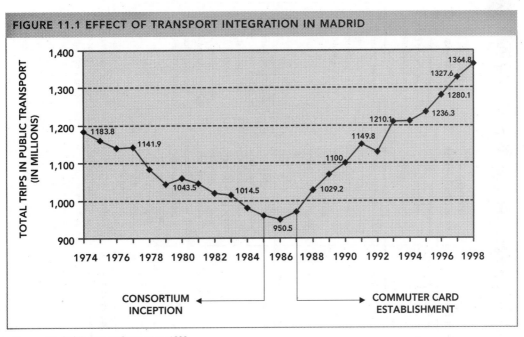

FIGURE 11.1 EFFECT OF TRANSPORT INTEGRATION IN MADRID

Source: Madrid Transport Consortium 1999.

TABLE 11.2 PROFESSIONAL ORGANIZATION FOR MUNICIPAL TRANSPORT FUNCTIONS

Function	Principal responsibilities	Policy functions	Professional skills	Relationship to other organizations	Comments	References in review
Urban structure planning	Prepare and maintain metropolitan structure plan.	Shape development structure, create basis for development controls.	Land-use planners, environmental specialists, sociologists	Responsible to mayor or city council		Chapter 2
Strategic transport planning	Conduct strategic transportation studies Prepare comprehensive transportation plans for the city or metropolitan area.	Prepare broad strategies that other organizations should follow.	Transport planners, economists, civil engineers	Responsible to strategic transport authority. Receives input from other municipal transport units in preparing strategies and plans	Must be consistent with the strategic land-use planning and function.	Chapters 2, 3, 9, 10
Traffic management	Prepare traffic management plans; review development proposals with traffic impacts; operate Traffic Control and ITS (Intelligent Transport Systems); manage vehicle inspection and maintenance scheme; monitor environmental impacts.	Determine traffic priorities consistent with general strategy. Create parking and traffic management framework for lower-level districts.	Traffic engineers, economists, parking specialists, electrical engineers	Responsible to strategic transport authority. Must work in coordination and consultation with local police authority.	Some activities (such as inspection and maintenance) can be contracted out to private sector.	Chapters 2, 3, 4, 6, 9
Public passenger transport	Plan and regulate public transport systems including buses, trams and light rail, taxis, and metros. Procure services.	Prepare passenger transport policies consistent with strategy and with financial capability. Set parameters for procurement agency.	Public transport and regulatory specialists	Responsible to strategic transport authority. Should be separate from any passenger transport operations	Procurement preferably by an arms length agency.	Chapters 3, 7

		Police officers		Chapter 6
Traffic enforcement	Enforce traffic regulations; manage traffic events and incidents; collect accident data.	Collaborate in traffic management system design. Enforce traffic management policy.	Traffic police provide traffic accident and traffic incidence information to safety and traffic management organization.	Traffic police typically part of a city police department with wider enforcement functions.
Road design, construction, and maintenance	Responsible for designing, constructing, and maintaining streets.	Maintenance prioritization	Civil engineers	Work closely with Traffic Management Organization to implement detailed traffic engineering works	Could be part of a city public works department.	Chapters 3, 6, 9
Traffic safety	Road traffic safety strategy. Coordinate all departmental inputs, including those from health, education, and so on.	Analyze safety data; orchestrate inter-departmental collaboration to implement strategy.	Statisticians; traffic engineers	Directly responsible to mayor or city council. Relationship with health authorities necessary	Must be a primary responsibility of a lead department, such as traffic engineering. Police commitment essential.	Chapters 5, 9

Source: Authors.

REDUCING THE SCOPE FOR HIERARCHICAL CONFLICT

Interactions between different layers of government may be very complex. Very clear and explicit separation of function between levels in the hierarchy may avoid many problems. For example, in the process of decentralization in Brazil, the federal government transferred responsibility for suburban rail operations to the states. That has certainly contributed to improving modal coordination in major Brazilian cities. Even with strategic issues retained at the metropolitan or regional level, however, the interests of individual lower-level jurisdictions need to be taken into account.

It does not always work, however. In the Brazilian case, transfer was usually smooth because the federal government accompanied the transfer with appropriate financial arrangements, generally consisting of a thorough rehabilitation of the capital stock before transfer. In contrast, in many of the newly independent countries of the former Soviet Union, the transfer of responsibility was not accompanied by a transfer of funding. In some cases the responsibility of funding public transport was even transferred to municipalities or regions, while the central government retained powers to determine fares or to grant discounts or exemptions. The result has usually been a disastrous decline in service.

COORDINATING OVERLAPPING AUTHORITIES

There are a number of different ways in which coordination between authorities may be sought. At one extreme is the creation of a single-tier conurbation authority with plenary powers, not only for transport but also for associated functions, such as land-use planning and control. A less monolithic arrangement is to have a two-tier local government structure, with powers for transportation planning and conurbation transport policy formulation assigned to the conurbation-wide level and other, less strategic, responsibilities, such as local parking control, left for exercise at the second level. In these arrangements the

high-level authority has its own independent budget with either its own direct revenue sources or predetermined allocations from either lower or higher levels of government. A third, less radical, arrangement would be the creation of a joint committee of the independent authorities. The participants on the committee would remain financially autonomous and agree on the allocation of costs among them.

The difficulty with associations based on voluntary collaboration is that there will be significant likelihood of rent-seeking behavior in the dealings between authorities. Three institutional devices reduce that possibility.

First, there should be a national legal framework within which collaboration between authorities must take place. This is clearly established by law for public transport in France.[2]

Second, the authorities should have some freedom to determine the boundaries of the collaboration. In France this is done by authorities having the freedom to set up their own planning boundary by agreement.

Third, there may need to be some externally injected financial inducement to collaborate. In France, this is achieved by requiring the establishment of an organizing authority as a condition for being able to levy a local transport tax (the "versement transport") or to receive certain central government contributions. In Brazil, development of regional transport coordinating committees was a condition of financing urban rail developments in the major cities. This arrangement may be strengthened by making all expenditure involving government aid subject to certification by the regional authority that it is in accordance with policies for the region.

The metropolitan authority would typically be charged with:

*   Integrating strategic urban land-use and infrastructure planning with transport system

and network planning, including the development and publication of a strategic planning framework for transport and land use in the metropolitan region

- Integrating road network planning with public transport planning
- Integrating the planning, policy, regulation, and pricing of the various public transport modes.

COORDINATING FUNCTIONS— PLANNING AND OPERATIONS

Recognition of the interaction between modes and functions requires the development of mutually compatible policies through a process of strategic transport planning. Often this is embodied in a transport and land-use plan, or structure plan, which offers the strategic framework within which separate but consistent functional and modal policies are developed. Shorter-term plans often take the form of a rolling five-year program and an annual plan and program. Modern management tools, such as planning, programming, and budgeting systems, and the adoption of a range of standards and guidelines for service provision can assist in converting good planning into well-managed implementation. A typical logical structure for the planning process is shown in figure 11.2.

A wide range of *strategic functions* is usually devolved to the metropolitan region level agency, including:

- Land-use development strategy
- Environmental strategy

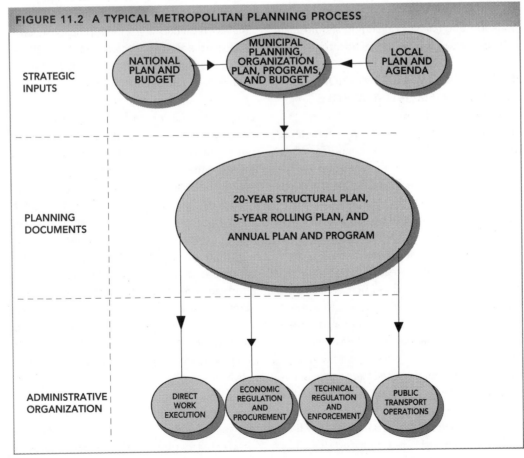

FIGURE 11.2 A TYPICAL METROPOLITAN PLANNING PROCESS

STRATEGIC INPUTS

NATIONAL PLAN AND BUDGET → MUNICIPAL PLANNING, ORGANIZATION PLAN, PROGRAMS, AND BUDGET ← LOCAL PLAN AND AGENDA

PLANNING DOCUMENTS

20-YEAR STRUCTURAL PLAN, 5-YEAR ROLLING PLAN, AND ANNUAL PLAN AND PROGRAM

ADMINISTRATIVE ORGANIZATION

DIRECT WORK EXECUTION | ECONOMIC REGULATION AND PROCUREMENT | TECHNICAL REGULATION AND ENFORCEMENT | PUBLIC TRANSPORT OPERATIONS

Source: Authors.

- Road planning, including supervision of private concession development
- Traffic management strategy
- Parking and road pricing strategy
- Public transport planning and service procurement.

Assigning this range of functions to the metropolitan region authority requires it to develop integrated strategies, knowing that, subject to the limits of a normal democratic process, it has the ultimate power to implement them. The implementing agencies should operate within this overall strategic framework, whether they are subsidiaries to the metropolitan region authority, quasi-independent agencies, or units within existing ministries. Where enforcement is an integral part of a function, the resource requirements for enforcement should be recognized and allocated as part of the decision process. The critical issue is that the agreed-on strategy for transport and land-use planning should take precedence over ad hoc, independent initiatives.

INTEGRATING IMPLEMENTATION AND ENFORCEMENT—THE ROLE OF THE POLICE

Traffic management faces one very intractable institutional element in most countries. While traffic management measures should be designed to be as self-enforcing as possible (physical dividers on bus lanes, guardrails to prevent illegal parking, and so on), some police enforcement is always likely to be necessary. While in some cities traffic police have proved to be the only agency ready to take action to resolve serious traffic issues (such as the installation of median strips in Colombo to prevent traffic accidents at crossings), they tend to operate to their own agenda. Their main objective is usually to "keep traffic moving," particularly on main routes. For example, the failure of area traffic control in Bangkok is largely attributed to the police propensity to override the system. Similarly, successful enforcement of with-flow bus lanes, standard in industrialized cities, has proved difficult in many developing cities. The

inability to develop a strong traffic safety campaign in Buenos Aires was similarly attributed to difficulties in coordination between police and transport agencies.

That independence of action has institutional roots. Traffic police are often organized at a national level, responsible to a central ministry of the interior, and are often suspected of being both corrupt and politically partisan. In some countries, such as Mexico and Venezuela, city traffic police forces also exist and work in parallel with the national force. In some countries, traffic police are separated from the general police force. Even where they are, as in the Russian Federation, the law allows the traffic police to be used for the maintenance of public order. A poor police image inevitably damages the credibility of, and respect for, any traffic measures—such as bus lanes and speed control—that rely on strict and impartial enforcement. It also creates a reputational risk for multinational donor or lending agencies, such as the World Bank, with a responsibility under charter to avoid involvement in local political matters.

Despite these problems it is difficult to make progress in urban transport management without the involvement of the police. The World Bank has therefore financed transport projects with traffic police components in all regions of the world.[3] Police components usually comprise equipment to assist traffic regulation enforcement, technical assistance for traffic accident reporting and analysis systems, and technical assistance for traffic regulation enforcement. Efforts to mitigate the risk of misuse of investments include such measures as ensuring that equipment financed was not of a kind that could be used for nontraffic purposes, monitoring of equipment use, and covenants on traffic police activities.

The recommended institutional basis for this involvement is that the traffic authority should be responsible for planning, design, and operation of traffic schemes, including computer-controlled traffic signal systems.[4] Traffic police responsibilities should be confined to traffic regulation enforcement, but they should be involved through consultation in scheme design and on a continuous basis in an advice and assistance role. Securing such coordination and cooperation is likely to be more easily achieved where police and transport authorities are responsible to the same jurisdiction.

COORDINATING PUBLIC AND PRIVATE SECTORS

There is no need for a strategic planning authority to have any direct operating responsibility or to own any transport service supply capacity. Success in mobilizing private sector participation in urban transport has already occurred in a number of areas, including:

- Investment in new road and public transport infrastructure
- Concession of existing public transport operations, with responsibility for future capital finance
- Concession or privatization—whole or in part—of ports and airports.

In all of these areas, institutional arrangements have been necessary to ensure that there is a basis for commercial operation that is consistent with an integrated urban transport policy.

The first step in a successful involvement of the private sector in urban transport is the separation of planning from operations to ensure that the benefits of competition can be obtained without the strategic planning agency's feeling the need to protect its "own" operating agency. Restructuring of existing line supply agencies is usually necessary to achieve this, because national or municipal transport undertakings typically perform both planning and operational functions. That is not an insuperable problem. In several industrialized countries, the planning and procurement skills of the monopoly agency have been transferred to a quasi-independent procurement agency. However, as the nature of the procurement task is changed from the procurement of goods to the procurement of transport services, some additional skills may need to be developed.

The residual operating function is also likely to need restructuring. The fact that the public sector currently has a monopoly of the necessary skills is often used as an argument that competition is impossible. In many countries the central government has washed its hands of formal financial responsibility for its traditional supply agencies by converting them into state joint stock companies, the majority of shares of which may still be held by a state property agency. Experience suggests that unless a much more thorough separation is made, and a real opportunity for independent management and initiative created, the change will have little effect. In reality nothing is immutable. The operating company can be restructured as a number of independent profit centers to compete with each other and eventually to be privatized. This kind of transformation may need some time (it took nearly 10 years to complete in London), but can be done if the political will is there.

Capacity building in the private sector is often a key issue and should be taken into account in designing policies and programs. Where some competitive potential already exists in a fragmented, small-scale private sector, it needs some institutional fostering. This may take two forms. First, it may be necessary to create a legal basis for the establishment of operators' associations with the appropriate standing to engage in competitive tendering competitions. Such associations were long the basis of public transport operations in Buenos Aires, and have more recently been provided for in law in some of the Central Asian countries, such as Uzbekistan, where tendering is being introduced. Second, a more difficult point is that attention may need to be given to the institutional arrangements for vehicle finance, and particularly the legal arrangements for vehicle leasing. The weakness of these institutions in some of the transitional economies has been a serious impediment to the transformation of the private sector from a low-quality, peripheral, service provider to a mainstream part of the public transport system.

Restructuring of government budget arrangements may also be necessary. In many countries, and particularly in the transitional economies of Eastern Europe, public transport operators are legally obliged to offer free or reduced-fare transport for many categories of passengers. The adverse impacts of these obligations on the sustainability of service and on the welfare of those who most need support have been discussed in chapter 3. To avoid such impacts, and to ensure that resources devoted to the social services are used to their best effect, it is desirable that all transport subsidies supporting other sector objectives (health, education, police, and so on) should be directly funded through those sector budgets. Where the finances are not available to fund the exemptions, operators should be under no obligation to honor them.

Some regulatory requirements will remain. As far as technical conditions of vehicle construction and use are concerned, it is likely that these will remain the function of a national regulatory agency, both for rail- and road-service providers. General business behavior will need to be controlled by whatever general regulator is responsible for control of monopolization or of restrictive and predatory practice (although this is often weak in developing countries). Where there has already been a broad extension of private provision of traditional public utility services, a regulatory agency responsible for adjudicating price increases under concession contracts may already exist. Where concession contracts themselves attempt to cover the conditions of operation of the concessions completely, it may be necessary to ensure that the relevant courts have the skills for the kind of contract adjudication that might arise.

ENGAGING CIVIL SOCIETY

Even in industrialized countries with well-developed, formal, local democratic processes, it is common practice for civil society to be engaged in validating major infrastructure investments or policy changes. This may occur through advance exposure of plans to a free press and other media, as well as through more formal processes of public consultation or public inquiry. This participation can operate at several levels. For small-scale localized projects, it may be possible to incorporate local preferences in the design process itself. For example, local residents' associations in Lima have been involved in identifying desired improvements in access roads to informal housing areas. Similarly, public transport users may be involved in service franchising arrangements through provision for direct complaints to the regulating authority (as in Buenos Aires), for consumer consultation on new routes, and through the involvement of the media in assessing performance of franchised operators (as in Bogotá).

At a more strategic level, and for larger, more complex, projects, consultation often functions more as a means of giving voice to local concerns in the process of trying to reconcile inherently competing or conflicting interests. It is inherently more difficult to mobilize citizen involvement at the strategic level in the development of consensus-based city development strategies.

Developing such strategic involvement requires action at two levels. First, particularly where formal local political processes are weak, the existence of effective local community groups is extremely important. In developing countries such groups are often well developed in rural areas, but much less so in cities. The Bank can strengthen this development by very positively seeking the involvement of urban community groups in project implementation. There are some promising examples. In Mumbai, slumdwellers' organizations have been involved from the outset in planning and implementing resettlement associated with improvement in the urban railways (box 11.1). Efforts are also being made to encourage a more inclusive decisionmaking process in Indonesia. To aid this process, the World Bank has developed a participation toolkit, bringing together advice on good practice in the organization of participation.

Second, the public processes must be organized to facilitate timely but well-informed consultation. An interesting example of this is the presentation of long-term transport strategies to ban cars in the center of Bogotá during peak hours after the year 2015 in a referendum in Bogotá in October 2000. While such long-term commitments are susceptible to being overturned in the future, the significance is to raise the level of interest, understanding, and debate on critical strategic issues.

CAPACITY BUILDING

Skills development is required in a number of different areas, including planning and engineering, and traffic management and enforcement.

Other important issues that need to be addressed include how to distribute and retain key staff, and when to train them.

PLANNING AND ENGINEERING

Institutions responsible for urban transport in developing countries, whether at a local or national level, are generally short of adequate professional skills. While there may be enough highway or construction engineers, other professional staff (such as traffic engineers, transport planners, economists, and public transport regulators) tend to be in short supply. In Bangkok and Jakarta, it is conservatively estimated that there are about one-tenth the number of traffic engineers that would be found in cities of a similar size in industrialized countries.

Technical and administrative staff to support the professional staff may be adequate in number, but also frequently lack necessary skills. Even those staff who do have technical skills in urban

---

BOX 11.1 ENGAGING CIVIL SOCIETY IN PLANNING RESETTLEMENT OF THE POOR IN MUMBAI

The Mumbai Urban Transport Project envisages improvements in urban transport in Mumbai, primarily to encourage public transport. The project will require resettlement of over 75,000 people, most of whom are squatters. Because of the size of resettlement, project preparation has emphasized a strong participatory approach and involvement of Mumbai's civil society in the project. This is being achieved through the reliance on local nongovernmental organizations (NGOs) as partners. The NGOs are responsible for community organization and data gathering, and construction of temporary and some permanent housing. This process is being carried out in a participatory manner with groups of project-affected people. The project resettlement policy was also prepared in a participatory manner using a task force headed by a retired chief secretary with members from government agencies, local NGOs, and the private sector. The project will also establish an independent monitoring panel of eminent citizens of Mumbai who will ensure that the Bank's safeguard policies are followed, and provide a last-resort grievance redressal mechanism for the affected people. A main problem with the participatory process has been reconciling the use of NGOs as partners with the Bank's procurement guidelines. There has been close collaboration among all parties to find solutions that would meet both the Bank's procurement guidelines and the objectives of partnership with local NGOs.

Source: Harald Hansen, from World Bank project files.

transport may not be in positions to make the most effective use of them, having achieved management status outside their technical field or being in units where administrative, jurisdictional, or functional limitations restrict the extent to which they can apply their specialized knowledge. Many trained staff lack the necessary experience to guide them through the social and political issues they face in applying their technical expertise. Technical support tools such as local design standards and guidelines, good practice manuals, and more sophisticated knowledge management systems also tend to be underdeveloped.

TRAFFIC MANAGEMENT AND ENFORCEMENT

Traffic management skills are particularly scarce. Although traffic management schemes are of relatively low cost, they require a high staff input and the resolution of many detailed and interrelated planning, design, and procurement issues. Success depends on staff capabilities and thus on staff training. Countries such as Brazil and Chile have a well-established traffic management capability and staff training, but in many countries traffic management is not recognized as a distinct discipline, and staff capabilities and training procedures are deficient. Capacity building can be assisted in a number of ways. Traffic management can be introduced as an established part of curriculums in institutes of higher education. Some universities in industrialized countries already have "twinning" arrangements with universities in developing countries, often with the assistance of bilateral funds. There have also been successful examples of twinning of transport and traffic agencies as between Gothenburg (Sweden) and both Hanoi (Vietnam) and Ibadan (Nigeria).

Traffic police training is mostly carried out at police-run training centers, and normally emphasizes routine policing (such as license checking, stolen vehicles, city-checkpoint security controls, and so on) rather than traffic management matters (traffic scheme enforcement, particularly

selective enforcement techniques, gaining familiarity with traffic laws and regulations, dealing with traffic emergencies, accident reporting and analysis, and so on). As with training for professional transport planners and engineers, a systematic approach to traffic police training is needed. Training for traffic police is a specialist task: few traffic engineers have an adequate background to identify and plan such programs. Programs can only be devised by traffic police specialists. Furthermore, operational methods of traffic police forces vary widely from country to country, and training must conform to local cultures (although it will sometimes be advantageous to improve operational practices) and have a high local input in its preparation.

DISTRIBUTION AND RETENTION OF SKILLS

What professionals there are tend to be concentrated in central government departments or in metropolitan areas, which are not necessarily where they are most needed. Making the best use of scarce professional skills may call for some institutional flexibility. Where problems are greatest in a capital city, it may be sensible to establish a specialist unit in the capital city, which is designed to develop people and techniques that can be used elsewhere in the country. For example, the London Traffic Management Unit, though it had a London remit, boosted traffic management capability throughout the United Kingdom. In developing countries a similar approach is being attempted; an example is the Office of the Commission for Management of Land Transport in Bangkok. Such units need to be linked to national research and development agencies, as well as to leading academic institutions. Support for such breeding grounds for technical skills may be an essential instrument for the multilateral development agencies.

Not all the skills need to be in the public sector. Particularly where government salary levels make it difficult to retain staff, it may be more efficient and cost-effective for scarce specialist skills to be maintained in centralized specialist technical units and brought in when required by municipalities. Another option is to focus on developing the local consulting industry and for government agencies to contract out services to consultants on a project-by-project basis or comprehensively on a term basis (as is being done in the United Kingdom). Whichever option is chosen, the best results are likely to be achieved by spreading resources geographically while developing a number of units as "centers of excellence," particularly in more advanced fields such as transport modeling and Intelligent Transport Systems.

TRAINING INSTITUTIONS

Developing the necessary human resources for urban transport is not a simple or short-term task. For basic training, particularly for technicians or categories of staff where there is a high turnover, either in-house or external training may be adequate. Increasing the numbers of professional specialists requires an expansion of tertiary education coupled with subsequent practical professional training. The main options available are for public sector transport organizations to expand their own facilities, to expand the local tertiary education sector, or to use already existing facilities in industrialized countries. In practice a combination of all three options is likely to be necessary in the short term. Over time the objective should be to develop local technical and tertiary education, with the public service sectors gradually devolving training to these facilities. In parallel, a professional accreditation and licensing system should be put in place. This can be managed by the government and fostered by a learned society (as in the United States) or be both fostered and managed by the learned society (as in the United Kingdom). Twinning with organizations having similar technical responsibilities in developing and industrialized countries enables staff to gain valuable practical technical and city management experience. Regional special initiatives (such as the Latin America Clean Air Initiative and the Asia Clean Air Initiative) permit knowledge sharing on emerging topics of common interest.

CONCLUSIONS: A STRATEGY FOR INSTITUTIONAL REFORM IN URBAN TRANSPORT

No single institutional blueprint for urban transport is appropriate for all countries. Nevertheless, there is enough experience of the difficulties arising from the failure to align policies between jurisdictions and agencies, or to secure collaboration between them, to establish some general principles for the reduction of institutional impediments to effective policy integration.

A strategy for institutional reform should address the main areas of human resource development and coordination, and be based on the following principles:

For functional capability and human resource development

- Municipal or metropolitan transport agencies should establish an administrative structure within which responsibility for all necessary technical functions in urban transport are clearly identified and allocated.
- Central governments should develop a training strategy for professional and technical skills in urban transport.
- Scarce professional skills should initially be concentrated, and retained by adequate remuneration, in either public sector "centers of excellence" or in private sector consultant organizations.
- Collaboration between authorities should be encouraged both nationally, to share available skills, and internationally, to further develop skills and experience.

For jurisdictional coordination

- Allocation of responsibility among levels of government should be clearly established by law.
- Intergovernmental transfers should be carefully planned to be consistent with the allocation of responsibility.
- Formal institutional arrangements should be made for collaboration where multiple

municipalities exist within a continuous conurbation.

- Central government should use intergovernmental transfer arrangements to encourage coordination at the metropolitan level.
- Obligations statutorily imposed on local authorities should be linked to specific channels of finance (such as direct-line agency funding of reduced-fare or free public transport).

For functional coordination

- There should be a strategic land-use and transport plan at the municipal or metropolitan level with which detailed planning, both of transport and land use, should be aligned.
- Functions should be clearly allocated between agencies, with more strategic functions being retained at the higher level in metropolitan areas.
- Traffic police should be trained in traffic management and safety administration and should be involved collaboratively in transport and safety policy planning.
- Responsibility for traffic safety should be explicitly allocated with an institutional responsibility at the highest level of the local administration (mayor's office or its equivalent).

For effective involvement of the private sector

- Planning and operating responsibility for public transport should be institutionally separated.
- Technical regulation should be separated from procurement and economic regulation.
- Operating agencies should be fully commercialized or privatized.
- The development of new competitive private suppliers of service should be encouraged through legal recognition of associations, and so on.
- A clear legal framework should be established for competition in public transport supply, either in the market or for the market.
- The public sector should develop professional service procurement and contract enforcement skills.

NOTES

1. The alternative forms are discussed in detail in Prointec Inocsa Stereocarto 2000.
2. See Louis Berger S.A. 2000.
3. The countries include Albania, Armenia, Bangladesh, Brazil, China, Costa Rica, Egypt, Hungary, India, Lithuania, Pakistan, Poland, Romania, Turkey, and the República Bolivariana de Venezuela.
4. Barrett 1986.

12 MEETING THE DEVELOPMENT CHALLENGES: HOW CAN THE BANK CONTRIBUTE?

The urban transport scene is changing rapidly, with a sharper focus on poverty reduction, decentralization of responsibilities, increase of private participation, and deterioration of environmental, safety, and security conditions. These developments pose new challenges, but at the same time create new opportunities to redress the defective pricing and financing practices and institutional fragmentation to which poor urban transport performance has been attributed in the past. This final chapter suggests how the World Bank can best support the development of sustainable urban transport institutions and policies in these new conditions.

DEVELOPMENT CHALLENGES

The general objectives of this review have been (a) to develop a better understanding of the nature and magnitude of urban transport problems in developing and transitional economies, particularly with respect to the elimination of poverty; and (b) to articulate a strategy to assist national and local governments to address urban transport within which the role of the Bank and other agencies can be identified. This chapter completes the review by identifying how the Bank can take forward the substantive agenda.

The context for the review has been continuing urbanization in developing countries and some, but not all, transitional economies, and increasing motorization of the urban areas. In that context, the focus has been on the "fundamental paradox of urban transport," namely, the coexistence of excess demand for road space with an inability to adequately finance public transport services. The review started by examining the urban transport–poverty nexus, arguing that urban transport impacts on poverty indirectly, through its effect on economic growth (chapter 2), and directly, through its impact on the lives of the poor themselves. The direct impacts are not only economic (chapter 3) but also relate to the environmental quality of life (chapter 4) and its safety and security (chapter 5). These impacts were subsequently explored with respect to the main modes of private road transport (chapter 6), public transport (chapters 7 and 8), and non-motorized transport (chapter 9). What emerged was an explanation of the paradox in terms of a combination of inappropriate pricing and financing mechanisms (chapter 10) and fragmented institutions (chapter 11). In particular, the problem is seen to result from the separation of road charging from road provision and finance, the separation of the provision of urban transport infrastructure from operations, and the inadequate integration of modes within the urban transport sector and of urban transport with the rest of development strategy.

This diagnosis is neither new nor specific to the developing world, but there are some emerging trends, which pose new challenges, but also create new opportunities for progressive reform. The most notable of these trends are:

- Intensified focus on poverty reduction

- Decentralization
- Increasing private participation in urban transport supply
- Deteriorating safety and security
- Increased concern about the local and global environment.

In this chapter we present, for each of these challenges, (a) a synthesis of the policies advocated, (b) a review of progress so far in assisting the implementation of these policies, and (c) an agenda for World Bank action to take the policies further.

STRENGTHENING THE FOCUS ON POVERTY

The very poor often cannot afford public transport and are dependent exclusively on NMT, mainly walking. It is clear that few governments recognize the importance of such modes to the poor and devote inadequate attention and resources to them. In many middle-income countries, the efficiency of public transport operations is critical to the welfare of the poorer groups who are primarily dependent on it. Governments frequently impose general fare controls to ensure public transport affordability, fare controls that are often not well targeted to the poor, that "leak" to suppliers or privileged user classes who are not poor, and, where no external means are provided to finance them, reduce the quality or quantity of service. The vulnerable poor are offered insufficient protection. The main policy prescriptions to address these deficiencies are:

- Emphasize road and public transport access to low-income housing areas.
- Give priority in road planning and management to the needs of public transport.
- Develop competitive regimes to reduce costs of public transport.
- Focus any fare subsidies narrowly, and fund them securely.
- Protect against adverse spin-off effects, such as resettlement and redundancy.

PROGRESS SO FAR

The development of the Comprehensive Development Framework and Poverty Reduction Strategy Papers (PRSPs) has brought infrastructure activity under increasingly critical scrutiny. While both governments and civil society continue to stress the importance of infrastructure in meeting the fundamental problems of exclusion,[1] the emphasis in urban transport has clearly changed. The emphases in Bank urban transport in the past decade include the following:

- *Concentrating on the transport modes of the poor.* In the current urban transport portfolio, more is being invested in public transport than in roads. Urban road maintenance projects, as in the Kyrgyz Republic, often concentrate on the main public transport routes. The Bank has encouraged the provision of infrastructure facilities for NMT in Accra, Lima, and Manila; it has also—in Lima—addressed the problems of finance of bicycles for the poor.
- *Improving public transport efficiency.* The Bank has long advocated competition as the best way of ensuring public transport efficiency. However, experience now suggests that, particularly in the larger cities, competition for tendered bus franchises within a well-monitored and enforced regulatory framework may yield lower fares and both environmentally cleaner and safer services than total deregulation. It has supported such reforms in Uzbekistan and Senegal. In urban rail transport, Bank-supported concessioning to the private sector has also yielded significant efficiency improvements in Argentina and Brazil.
- *Encouraging sustainable public transport fares strategy.* In projects in the Russian Federation and some of the Central Asian republics, the Bank has emphasized the importance of sustainable financing through cost reduction, direct funding of reduced fares by line agencies (health, education, and so on) and, where necessary to sustain service, fare increases. Multimodally inte-

grated fare schemes to protect the poor have been developed in Bank projects in several Brazilian cities.

- *Protecting the vulnerable.* During the past decade, the formal safeguard policies of the Bank have been strengthened substantially to ensure that anyone whose residence or location of livelihood is directly affected because of a Bank project is resettled or compensated so that the change imposes no detriment to them. The Bank has also financed redundancy and retraining compensation in rail reforms in Argentina, Brazil, and Poland both through project loan funds and through adjustment lending.

THE AGENDA

Despite these efforts the poverty focus is still not sharp enough. Better understanding is required of the impact of urban transport infrastructure and service policies on poverty. There is a danger that, in the absence of effective demand management, road investments to eliminate bottlenecks will tend to benefit the rich at the expense of the poor. NMT and walking remain underfinanced, and the special needs of women and the mobility impaired are neglected. Competition is still seen too simply as total absence of regulation, and hence is associated with undisciplined chaos. Formal requirements for line agencies to finance subsidies to their client groups are not honored. Resettlement and redundancy compensation is often viewed as a bureaucratic enclave requirement of Bank projects, to be avoided by judicious choice of projects for Bank financing. The Bank can further assist in strengthening the poverty focus of its urban transport activities in the following ways:

- *Emphasize the importance of facilities for NMT, particularly adequate sidewalks for pedestrians and creation of a friendlier regulatory environment and better traffic management for all nonmotorized modes.*
- *Seek to develop new forms of finance for bicycles for the poor.*
- *Require, as far as practical, the inclusion of the full economic, social, and environmen-*

tal impacts, including those on affected NMT users, in the formal cost-benefit appraisal of projects.

- *Increasingly support the development of competitive franchising systems, through technical assistance in the reform process, and where appropriate, through financing of refurbishment of public transport systems in the process of reform. The technical assistance will also assist countries in designing systems that, while permitting the informal sector to play a continuing role, ensure that unfair competitive advantage is not taken at the expense of safety or environmental quality.*
- *Encourage infrastructure and service design to better accommodate the mobility impaired.*
- *Emphasize the importance of institutionally sustainable finance of public transport operations. Where direct income transfers to the poor are not possible, do not oppose, in principle, well-targeted subsidies of services essential to the poor.*
- *Support general fare control only where the finance necessary to maintain the system is ensured or the implications of fare controls on supply have been carefully considered and the quality of service implied by such controls explicitly chosen.*
- *Continue to emphasize adequate compensation for locational or occupational disturbance arising from projects.*
- *Encourage the further participation of nongovernmental organizations in the design and implementation of adjustment arrangements and require evidence of early and adequate consultation among affected parties.*

FACILITATING DECENTRALIZATION

In many countries (particularly in the former Soviet Union and in Latin America) responsibility for urban transport is being decentralized. Sometimes this is merely a by-product of the failure of traditional central fiscal sources. Frequently, where specialized skills are scarce, decentralization reduces the availability of expertise at the local level. Rarely does it provide an adequate fiscal basis for the transferred responsibilities. This creates new challenges in municipal management. It requires local authorities to acquire technical competencies to fulfill new responsibilities. It gives municipalities the incentive to incorporate urban transport in their city development strategies and to consider the tradeoffs and synergies among sector policies. It may also encourage autonomous municipalities within a city region to collaborate in the development of metropolitan strategies and may provide a new foundation for more-integrated financing arrangements. The main policy prescriptions to exploit these opportunities include the following:

- Metropolitan regions should develop metropolitan-scale transport planning and financing arrangements.
- Cities should prepare human resource development plans for their new responsibilities.
- Cities should develop integrated, fungible, urban transport funding arrangements.
- Cities should develop integrated road use and public transport charging strategies to make the urban transport sector financially sustainable.

PROGRESS SO FAR

The Bank has already begun to respond to these challenges.

- *Institutional development.* Functional coordination and human resource development have been successfully pursued in many urban transport projects. For example, regional transport coordination institutions have been reestablished in several of the major Brazilian conurbations in association with Bank-funded mass transit investments; similar efforts are being undertaken to reestablish an effective metropolitan planning function in Metro Manila and in Dakar.
- *Human resource development.* The Bank has attempted to provide technical assistance and training for new responsibilities.

For example, study tours to acquaint municipalities with franchising experience abroad have become a common feature of public transport projects in Eastern Europe and Central Asia.

- *Financing arrangements.* Modally integrated ticketing systems are being supported in Brazil. Where there are multiple municipalities in a metropolitan region, the creation of a single-purpose authority or the pooling of metropolitan transport funding may make resources more fungible between modes, as well as give a new incentive to the development of new road taxation or charging systems to meet the metropolitan-level needs. In some of the transition economies of the former Soviet Union, efforts are being made to ensure that adequate allocations are made to urban roads from national road funds.

THE AGENDA

Integrated planning of urban transport infrastructure and services is important in any setting. As responsibility for the management of urban services is decentralized to the cities, such integration becomes more feasible. For integration to be successful, there must be a conscious effort to develop a strategic structure plan to control land use and to coordinate the development of urban services within the long-term development strategy. The Bank can contribute to improving the effectiveness of decentralization in the following ways:

- *Support the formulation of city development strategies and the technical instruments, such as land use and development controls, that implement the plans.*
- *Assist institutional reform as far as possible by technical assistance components in traditional Project and Sector Adjustment loan instruments, as well as by use of newer instruments (such as the Learning and Innovation Loan [LIL] and programmatic lending instruments) to give a broader and more continuous support to reform programs.*

- *Continue to encourage the development of sustainable metropolitan and municipal transport financing, both by encouraging institutional reform within urban transport projects and, more generally, by programmatic lending to municipalities.*
- *Where governance is not good, or where jurisdictional or functional fragmentation is particularly damaging, support metropolitan-level single-purpose government organizations with appropriate integrated urban transport funding arrangements.*

MOBILIZING PRIVATE PARTICIPATION

Inability to support the increasing fiscal burden of public sector operations, associated with a desire to secure investment off-budget, has led many countries, including those in traditional public sector–dominated areas such as the former Soviet Union, to turn to the private sector for financing and operation of transport infrastructure and services. But they have often done so without realizing, or adequately addressing, the very important role that they still must play. Fares and tolls have often been set without regard to the sustainability of the service to be provided. Where there is an effective competitive alternative, the greatest degree of freedom in fare setting is desirable. However, the grant of concessions or franchises usually confers a degree of monopoly power, which might in some cases result in profits being maximized at relatively high prices and low utilization. The exclusion of poorer users may reduce overall welfare even though it increases profitability. Ad hoc opportunism in the sanctioning and support of private sector–financed infrastructure in developing-country cities has often led to poor physical and commercial coordination of developments (as in Bangkok and Kuala Lumpur) and significant, unplanned, contingent costs falling on the public authorities (as in Manila). The main policy prescriptions to address these deficiencies are the following:

- Government should prepare framework laws and model contracts for infrastructure concessions and competitively tendered service franchising.
- Cities should prepare strategic infrastructure plans with which private sector developments should be consistent.
- Cities should establish public transport planning and procurement units, independent of operating agencies.
- Cities should develop criteria for appraising the public financial contribution to public-private participatory schemes, such as concessions.

PROGRESS SO FAR

The Bank has done much to encourage private participation in the sector, attempting to assist in the development of efficient and equitable forms for private participation. The main areas of development have been as follows.

- *Infrastructure concessioning.* The Bank has been instrumental in assisting the concessioning of some urban railways to the private sector, particularly in Latin America. That experience has shown that urban mass transit systems can benefit from private management and that front-end-loaded contributions to a private-public participatory arrangement can improve service quality and reduce the budget burden. Urban motorway concessions have also increased capacity, but have created problems where they are not established within a broad city infrastructure development plan.
- *Urban road–passenger transport franchising.* The Bank has for many years advocated reliance on competitive private sector supply, often in the form of an increasing role for the informal sector and small vehicles. However, different experiences in countries such as Chile, Peru, and Sri Lanka have shown that, particularly in large conurbations where environmental and congestion externalities are most significant, well-regulated competition "for the market" may better meet the aspi-

rations of the city than free competition "in the market." The Bank has extensively used project preparation funds to acquaint decisionmakers in the transitional economies with a range of competitive market forms, and with the administrative experience of countries that have successfully employed market forms.

- *Bus finance.* Past lending to public sector bus companies has assisted in meeting immediate supply problems (as in Russia), but has often failed to ensure the sustainability of that improvement. Consequently, recent projects in Kazakhstan and Uzbekistan have concentrated on finding an institutional basis on which affordable public transport supply can be maintained, particularly through the introduction of competitive private sector supply. Direct financing of public sector vehicles tends to undermine that competitive initiative, as well as to confront serious problems of vehicle specification for procurement. For that reason the Bank has tried to encourage the development of supplier finance or commercial leasing arrangements, which can be accessed by all forms of supply agency, but which require them to be able to meet the full costs of vehicle finance and maintenance.
- *Affordable fares.* The Bank has supported various devices to ensure that private participation does not make public transport unaffordable, including financing initial government contributions to concession agreements and public specification of fare tables in contract documents in Argentina, using fare level as a selection criterion in tenders in Uzbekistan, or subjecting tariff or profit levels to an independent regulator, as in several rail concessions.
- *Strengthening the planning context.* The Bank has addressed this, ex ante, through the development of coordination arrangements in the context of urban rail developments in Brazil and, ex post, through the financing of modal interchange between buses and light rapid transit in Manila.

- *Public-private participation.* Privately financed urban transport infrastructure can yield benefits not only to its users—who should normally be willing to pay for the benefits accruing to them—but also to nonusers, whose travel conditions are relieved by the transfer of some traffic to the new facilities. This highlights the importance of treating these developments as genuine public-private partnerships to which public sector–funding contributions are entirely appropriate. This contribution might be new capital, existing complementary infrastructure, or even operating support. It also points to the possibility of combining Bank investment in the public sector element with an International Finance Corporation (IFC) participation in the private finance. This requires attention to both the institutional arrangements for and the evaluation of private sector participation in infrastructure finance. The Bank has funded public sector contributions to concessioning arrangements in Argentina and Brazil.

THE AGENDA

While World Bank Institute (WBI) training and dissemination efforts in infrastructure finance have raised the awareness of many problems, much remains to be done to consolidate the developments of private participation in urban transport. Concession contract design deficiencies have created some severe problems (for example, the Bangkok Second Expressway). The need to renegotiate obsolete contracts has been a source of much friction in Argentina. Regulatory provisions have often been inadequate for both infrastructure concessions and service franchises. It is also important that private sector developments should be consistent with a city strategy for physical development, and justified in system cost-benefit, as well as private financial, terms. The Bank can contribute to more-effective private sector participation in urban transport in the following ways:

- *Disseminate good practice in franchising and concessioning through WBI activities, including newly developed distance-learning packages.*

- *Further develop and tailor guarantee arrangements to the special needs arising in transport concessions.*
- *Only be involved in finance of vehicles where it contributes to a desirable reform, either in the introduction of cleaner or safer technologies or in sustainable competitive supply arrangements.*
- *Support the development of commercial financing arrangements for vehicles and seek means to provide microcredit to small operators and for a wide range of vehicle type.*
- *Continue to encourage the development of forms of concession and franchise contracts that ensure the benefits of competition are passed on to poor users and that environmental standards are maintained.*
- *Finance the development of skills in procurement and regulation, through both project and reform program loan financing.*
- *Continue the effort to improve the forms of competition in service provision, with particular emphasis on the LIL instrument as a vehicle to support experimentation and preparation, but also through the incorporation of institutional audits and analysis as a routine part of the preparation of all lending activities.*
- *Support the physical and commercial coordination of private and public transport facilities both through specific investments to deal with defects in existing systems and through technical assistance to establish and to staff planning and coordinating agencies.*
- *Support the effective extension of private sector participation in urban transport infrastructure finance by requiring that such developments be consistent with an established city development plan, and that public sector contributions, in whatever form, be subject to an economic appraisal similar to that undertaken for purely public projects.*

INCREASING TRANSPORT SAFETY AND SECURITY

Road accidents already represent a global pandemic, and deteriorating security is a growing problem, particularly in Latin America. Absence of sidewalks, inadequate lighting, and poor segregation of motorized and nonmotorized traffic make pedestrians and bicyclists vulnerable both to traffic accidents and to criminal attack. Dangerous public transport operating behavior has been a significant contributor to road traffic accidents in some countries in the absence of effective policing of traffic behavior. The poor suffer disproportionately from these deficiencies. Transport safety and security in developing countries suffer because, although they require wide collaboration among agencies (transport, health, police, and so on), they are often "nobody's baby." To overcome this it is necessary both to develop appropriate interagency coordination mechanisms and to develop the necessary skills. The main policy prescriptions to address these deficiencies are the following:

- Cities should identify and empower a unit of its administration, or quasi-independent agency, with police involvement, to be responsible for safety and security in urban transport.
- All urban transport infrastructure and traffic management plans should be subject to a mandatory safety audit before approval.
- Traffic police should be involved in design of traffic management schemes, but should be subject to instructions from the traffic management authority on the objectives of traffic management policy and enforcement.
- All urban transport franchises or operating permissions should carry strict requirements for safe operating practice and be should be rescindable for nonobservance of that practice.

PROGRESS SO FAR
Attempts to address the problems so far include the following:

- *Infrastructure design.* Recent Bank-financed projects have provided segregated facilities for cyclists in Lima, Accra, and Manila, as well as tried to maintain good cycling facilities in Chinese cities. That concern must now be mainstreamed into all urban projects. In some cases (for example, in many residential areas), the best solution may not be complete separation of motorized and nonmotorized traffic but the adoption of measures to "calm" motorized traffic to speeds at which it is not a threat to pedestrians or cyclists. Protection of pedestrians has also been pursued through the financing of sidewalks in many cities (for example, Accra, Nairobi, and Dakar).

- *Institutions.* Despite the reputational risk issues of World Bank association with investments in policing in many countries, the Bank has recognized that it is unlikely that traffic-safety problems can be adequately addressed without substantial police involvement. Most recently, in conjunction with an urban transport project in Moscow, the Bank has found it necessary to further refine the criteria for acceptability of such involvement, and to ensure that the police are adequately involved in traffic system design and trained to perform traffic management functions in an efficient manner consistent with the city traffic safety and traffic management strategies.

- *Regulation, market structure, and safety.* In some cases, such as in Lima, deterioration in both safety and security has been associated with market liberalization. In others, such as the concessioning of the Buenos Aires suburban railways, the passenger-security situation has been improved by private involvement. More understanding is required of the relationship between safety, security, and market structure in urban passenger transport, but there already appears to be a close association between the quality of economic regulation and the safety and security situation.

THE AGENDA

Personal security is only partly a transport sector phenomenon per se, but it has particularly serious impacts on the sector. In both areas, the challenge to the Bank is to help clients develop ways of confronting these pressures in the context of an increasingly fragmented public transport supply situation. The Bank can contribute to the development of a concerted effort to improve transport safety and security in the following ways:

- *Require adequate safe provision for pedestrians, including mobility-impaired pedestrians, and NMT (especially bicycles) in all new road investment, rehabilitation, and traffic management interventions. Moreover, safety should not be used as a justification for greatly inconveniencing these categories of road user to facilitate easier flow of motorized vehicles.*

- *Support broader institutional involvement in transport-related security and traffic-safety issues, including improved coordination between traffic management and police agencies.*

- *Further refine the criteria under which specific items of investment in policing are appraised, paying special attention to the need to invest only in facilities and equipment that cannot easily be converted to purposes of civil repression.*

- *Attempt to ensure that the safety of operation of vehicles and the security of passengers, including the mobility impaired, are properly addressed in public transport reform measures, particularly where existing monopolies are replaced by multiple operators.*

- *Avoid, or adopt appropriate mitigating measures against, any serious potential risks to the environment and public health and safety associated with projects or programs.*

PROTECTING THE ENVIRONMENT

Although environmental impacts of transport are reaching the top of the agenda in many megacities, municipalities still tend to ignore the environmental implications of their strategies until too late in the process of growth, to ignore global warming issues at any level, and to fail to recognize the distributional implications of environmental impacts. One of the lessons of experience is that while traffic management can improve network performance, it cannot be a *substitute* for adequate capacity provision and network planning in rapidly growing cities. The weakest link in the development of the strategic position has concerned the efforts to advocate demand management, particularly through road pricing or other surrogate devices to ensure that users pay the full social costs of road use. The general strategy that is recommended for protecting the environment is a combination of better management of urban transport operations in the short term, with technological improvement and urban structural change in the longer term. The main policy prescriptions to achieve this are the following:

- National programs should be established, where necessary, to eliminate leaded gasoline and to improve or replace the technology of gross emitters of particulate matter where that is cost-effective.
- Cities should establish a traffic management department or agency with responsibility for measures to reduce environmental impact of traffic, as well as measures to improve its efficiency.
- Municipal action should improve public transport as a high priority.
- Traffic system management and traffic demand management programs should be developed.

PROGRESS SO FAR

The ways in which these prescriptions have been pursued in Bank operations include the following:

- *Supporting technological development.* Because much of the necessary technological development occurs in the private sector, it may fall outside the ambit of traditional Bank lending. A number of new instruments may help to overcome this limitation. The IFC may invest or lend for innovations of commercial potential. In addition, new instruments are

becoming available in some areas. For example, technological development of means of improving fuel efficiency in transport may receive funding, both through Operational Program 11 of the Global Environment Facility (GEF) and through investments undertaken by the Prototype Carbon Fund.

- *Traffic management.* The Bank has put much emphasis on traffic management in its past urban transport strategies. It has achieved considerable success in improving traffic flow in countries such as Brazil, Chile, and Korea, and has included similar measures in current projects in Beirut (Lebanon) and Moscow, including substantial investments in traffic control equipment. Among the most recent developments has been an increasing emphasis on providing for NMT and pedestrians, as in Lima and Manila. The Bank is also administering GEF grants in process or in preparation, aiming at improved air quality through traffic management measures in Lima, Manila, and Santiago.
- *Road infrastructure.* Road-related expenditures account for about one-third of the Bank's urban transport portfolio. About one-half of that has been on capacity rehabilitation rather than expansion, with even that effort concentrated on the roads that carry the main public transport flows, as in the Kyrgyz Republic urban transport project. For larger established cities, it is recognized that it is neither possible nor desirable for countries to attempt to invest their way out of road congestion. That said, it is clear that the Bank has not withdrawn entirely from the support of urban road infrastructure investment, nor does it intend to do so. Nevertheless, it is critical that any Bank lending for urban road investment be conditional on the implementation of effective policies of traffic management and restraint.
- *Demand management, prices, and taxes.* Despite disappointing past experience, the devolution of responsibilities to the cities in the context of severe fiscal pressure, together with a developing interest and

experience with road pricing in some industrialized countries, makes it now opportune to make the development of road-pricing mechanisms a priority.

- *Bus mass transit.* The concept of physically separating buses from worsening traffic congestion was supported by the Bank in projects in Brazil, Chile, and elsewhere. The recent revival of bus segregation as a more extensive mass transit system, first introduced in Curitiba, is now being supported in Bogotá and is being considered in Lima.
- *Rail mass transit.* Previous policy statements and actions taken have given the impression that the Bank was resolutely opposed to any fixed-rail investment in urban areas for fear that investment in such large, expensive projects would preempt municipal funds, which might yield higher social returns elsewhere. The portfolio review shows how substantially that position has been amended. The position that is now adopted is that where urban rail systems already exist, it is usually desirable to sustain them (for example, the projects in Argentina and Brazil) and that new urban rail investments must be seen in the wider context of a long-term urban development strategy. What remains of the traditional position is a determination that rail investments must be fiscally sustainable. What has been added is a determination that such developments must be integrated into a comprehensive urban transport strategy and that arrangements should include physical and fare integration between modes to ensure that the poor are not excluded from or disadvantaged by the investments. At the technical level, this is associated with recommendations both about the way in which the distributional consequences of urban rail investments should be estimated and about the way in which the economic benefits should be evaluated.

THE AGENDA

The Bank retains its strong commitment to environmental improvement. It is recognized that this cannot be approached as a technically and institutionally separate activity but must be integrated in an urban transport policy with other objectives with which it has to be reconciled. The Bank can assist countries and city governments to make their urban transport sectors more environmentally sustainable in the following ways:

- *Emphasize the importance of road planning for the movement of people and not just of vehicles. Increase the emphasis on the needs of public transport passengers, pedestrians, and users of nonmotorized modes of transport in urban road operations.*
- *Advocate a balanced strategy in urban areas, combining the provision of a necessary basic amount of road capacity with a program of traffic management, demand restraint, and public transport development; link any urban road investments to the introduction of supporting traffic management and pricing measures to ensure that planned environmental and efficiency benefits are widely distributed.*
- *Attempt to ensure that the methodologies for financial and economic appraisal of investments are consistent and comparable between modes.*
- *Renew efforts to secure the introduction of effective measures of demand restraint, through both price and nonprice instruments. Where compliance with environmental standards requires other management measures to be associated with investments, require evidence that the management measures are being implemented before the investment funding is committed.*
- *Support the introduction or extension of bus rapid transit systems, linking it to a reform of public transport supply where appropriate, especially where this can be shown to enhance the environment.*
- *Support the exploitation of the potential of urban rail, particularly where the basic infrastructure already exists, but continue to be cautious in ensuring that the appraisal of any such investments is realistic and that*

the long-term fiscal burden of any investment in urban rail is properly assessed and
seen not to deflect from other, more beneficial investments.

- *Search for and support technological developments to increase efficiency of fuel utilization in transport, but recognize that
technological development in transport is
primarily a private sector prerogative and
responsibility, and act as agents of the GEF
and the Prototype Carbon Fund.*
- *Ensure that reasonable allowance is made
for the effects of induced traffic in assessing the economic and environmental
impacts of road infrastructure investments.*

CONCLUSIONS

We turn finally to the question of *how* the strategy will be implemented, with particular emphasis on the instruments, processes, and procedures to be adopted.

INSTRUMENTS

The context for this review is a general shift in
World Bank policy on its approach to infrastructure sectors. Three shifts in Bank corporate policy
deserve mention:

First, there is the shift from infrastructure project finance toward **knowledge building, advisory services, and capacity building.** The LIL is
a small, quick-disbursing instrument devised to
enable reforms to be introduced on an experi-
mental basis, and to decouple support of such
experiments from investment lending. It is
administratively expensive, however, and has
generated only limited enthusiasm on the part of
both staff and clients. In any event, institutional
reform is usually a slow, learning process, and
may need a more protracted and systematic
presence than the LIL allows. Associated with
the emphasis on knowledge building is a new
emphasis on output-based aid, where support
is linked not to investment in public sector supply,
but to the development of efficient procedures

of procurement of privately provided services to
the poor.

Second, there is a shift from stand-alone project
finance toward **more-programmatic lending.** This
may take several different forms, including the
following:

- Funding a time slice of a single-sector program based on agreement about the associated policy objectives and reforms, such
as traditional sectoral investment and adjustment lending
- Multisector lending aiming at the integration of sector inputs within a comprehensive
strategy, such as the transport component
of the Rio de Janeiro State Private Sector
Development Project
- A tranched approach linked to and triggered
by the sequential achievement of reform targets, as in Adjustable Program Lending, such
as the Urban Mobility Project for Senegal.

Several critical issues in this review—such as
municipal institutional reform, regulation of concession contracts, local air pollution, and so on—
are transport applications of more-generic
problems. An increasing proportion of the Bank
assistance to reforming urban transport institutions may thus appear in wider projects dealing
with municipal reform or air quality over a range
of sectors. In that context it is important to ensure
that sectoral matters continue to be dealt with
in a technically competent manner that does not
weaken the strong professional links that have
always been so important in transferring knowledge and securing developing-country commitment at the appropriate technical and political
levels. The rigorous World Bank loan procurement rules, the objective of which is to ensure
fair competition and to avoid possibilities of corruption, will remain in place.

Third, there is a desire to shift from conventional
to **high-impact lending.** This includes novel activities, particularly in public-private participation,
which are intended to have a high demonstra-

tion effect. For example, the Bank partial risk guarantee can protect franchisees against default by government in performance of their contractual obligations, although in practice there have been no such guarantees to date. In some other important aspects of urban transport policy—particularly the development of NMT and the informal public transport sector—the critical need is the provision of relatively small amounts of finance to multiple, usually private, borrowers. The Bank's experience with lines of credit—particularly with those tied specifically to selected sectors—has not been good. It is therefore important that the best experience of the Bank in addressing the financing needs of small and medium-size enterprises be incorporated in urban transport sector developments. It is also now being explicitly recognized that in some areas, the Bank has global advocacy goals that may be in advance of current client perception and preferences. In the urban transport sector, the Bank has already entered such a campaign for improved transport safety and security.

LENDING TO CITIES

As responsibility for urban transport is decentralized, cities are increasingly forced to make their own decisions about financing, including borrowing. City credit risks can be particularly serious because the Bank's loans are typically denominated in foreign currencies and cities' revenues are in local currency. Unlike some of the other multinationals,[2] the International Bank for Reconstruction and Development (IBRD) is constrained by its charter from lending directly to cities, unless there is a sovereign guarantee. In contrast, the IFC can lend only to the private sector, and must do so without sovereign guarantee. Cities therefore fall between the IBRD and IFC conditions as imposed on government and private borrowers.

The effects of this situation are complex. On the one hand, cities may face the moral hazard of an incentive to unduly risky borrowing if guaranteed by the central government. This perverse incentive can be countered by appropriate pricing for

the guarantee (for example, both the Polish and Colombian governments have charged a 2 percent fee up front for the guarantee). On the other hand, as an incentive to reform, governments may offer guarantees on a competitive basis to cities undertaking reforms that will increase their fiscal sustainability.[3] Properly priced or conditioned sovereign guarantees may thus contribute to the achievement of the sustainability objective. The most serious concern, given the Bank's emphasis on supporting effective decentralization, is that a central government may use its guarantee power as leverage over city governments of a different political persuasion from the central government, or may shy away from the unpleasant task of discriminating between creditworthy and noncreditworthy cities.

In some cases channels of finance other than direct or guaranteed lending to municipalities may be found to meet the needs of urban transport. The IBRD has lent to public banks in Colombia, which have then on-lent to cities. In Uzbekistan a loan to a public sector leasing agency, operating within a "sunset clause," has been used to enable vehicles to be made available to public and state joint stock companies in the secondary cities. The IFC can lend to private, or mixed public-private, banks, which can on-lend on commercial terms to transport service suppliers. The experience of developing microcredit for urban transport vehicles is not very promising, however, and supplier credit for leased vehicles has been difficult to stimulate in some of the transitional economies where it is most required; the need for a wider range of lending instruments remains.

The crucial issue from the Bank's point of view is whether the instruments available are able to forward the objectives of strengthening the capacity of the cities to become fiscally self-reliant and to access private capital markets. Some traditional lending—for example, to state-owned enterprises for bus replacement—may have actually discouraged the development of that sustainability. The emphasis is therefore shifting to the development of supplier credits, microcredit, and other more commercially based financing arrangements, and away from the financing of public enterprises. The IFC may have a role to play in assisting the establishment of commercial agencies able to lend to municipalities, such as Infrastructure Finance Corporation Limited in South Africa; the IFC is unlikely, however, to be involved in financing direct lines of credit for municipalities.

PROCEDURES: OWNERSHIP, PARTICIPATION, AND COLLABORATION

The Bank's lending programs emerge from a "top-down" process, at the apex of which is the Country Assistance Strategy or, for heavily indebted poor countries, the Poverty Reduction Strategy Papers. These strategic documents are increasingly a joint product of the national government and the Bank, often supported by wider stakeholder consultation. The inclusion of urban transport components in country programs thus depends on urban transport's having been identified as a priority problem area in national development strategy. Although urban transport pervades the whole urban economy, its influence tends to be diffused. It is therefore important that the urban transport–poverty nexus is better understood, and that urban transport developments are increasingly linked both to general urban development activities and to other specific social sector developments, including the acknowledgment of women and the mobility impaired as important stakeholders.

Local ownership is always essential to project success. In the rural context, civil society is increasingly being engaged in the process of community-driven development. That is more difficult in urban areas, where populations are often more transitory and local institutions correspondingly weaker. But there are some very important policy questions on which transport-user participation is being increasingly fostered in the interests of more-sensitive project or program design. These include the following:

- *Design and implementation of resettlement provisions.* In the Mumbai Urban Transport

Project, local slumdwellers' associations are engaged in defining strategy and selecting locations and phasing of resettlement provisions.

- *Design and implementation of paving programs in poor areas.* Citizens of the municipality of Villa el Salvador, on the outskirts of Lima, have developed their own local road-paving strategy and scheme. In the preparation of an urban transport project for Lima, inhabitants of poor areas ("pueblos jovenes") participate in the selection of road links for paving to give vehicular access to poor areas.

- *Service quality and fare tradeoff.* Social surveys of public transport passengers are an essential element of public transport project design. Such surveys in Cali, Colombia, showed that the proposed expenditure on a metro system was not perceived as helping the poor, despite the politicians' claims. Conversely, in Uzbekistan and the Kyrgyz Republic, user surveys showed a much greater concern with the availability of service than politicians had asserted.

- *Safety and security policy formulation.* Far too little is usually done to establish how and where transport users are most vulnerable, both to road accidents and, more significant, to personal violence on transport. In the project under preparation in Lima, a detailed survey of women has demonstrated the significant impact of on-vehicle violence and harassment on the activity patterns of women and hence their ultimate well-being.

In undertaking the present review, the Bank has attempted to involve nongovernmental organizations and individual members of civil society, as well as governmental and professional bodies, to respond to the proposals being made.

The Comprehensive Development Framework also raises the question of the comparative advantage of the Bank in each specific area of activity. The Bank is already frequently involved in collaboration with other international lend-ing and donor organizations, and some of those institutions have financed background studies for this review. The European Union has recently expressed a parallel wish to improve collabora-tion on transport development matters. Typically, collaboration involves joint or parallel financing of projects. In some cases, however, such as the urban Sub-Saharan Africa Transport Program, the collaboration extends to the program level. One of the main purposes of publishing a strat-egy review such as this is to solicit comment from peer institutions with the aim of increas-ingly aligning the positions of the institutions on major development strategy issues. The eco-nomic, environmental, and social problems of urban transport are large, and in many countries these problems continue to grow. The issues need, and deserve, the concentrated and coher-ent attention of the whole development com-munity.

NOTES

1. The concerns expressed in the *Voices of the Poor* studies were approximately equally divided between health, education, and infrastructure issues (Narayan 2000b).

2. For example, the European Bank for Reconstruction and Development is able to lend to cities without sovereign guarantee if the con-ditions merit it, while the European Investment Bank, although requiring a guarantee, can accept a guarantee purchased by the borrower from a commercial bank.

3. For example, the government of the Russian Federation offered a guarantee for funds used from the First Urban Transport loan to secondary cities, conditional on the cities promising to achieve a preset level of cost recovery deemed necessary to make their operations sustainable. In the event, though, the city finances were not in good condi-tion and yet were able to meet the terms.

APPENDIX: URBAN TRANSPORT PORTFOLIO IN THE WORLD BANK

A.1 URBAN TRANSPORT PROJECTS UNDER PREPARATION AND IMPLEMENTATION AS OF FEBRUARY 26, 2002

Country	Name of Project	Fiscal Year Approved	Status	Project Cost (US$M)		WB Loan (US$M)		Principal Urban Transport Thrust	Number of Cities in Project	Project Team Leader
				Total	Urban Transport	Total	Urban Transport			
Africa Region										
Benin	First Decentralized City Management (phase 1)	2000[a]	Ongoing	28.3	21.8	25.5	19.2	Urban road rehabilitation & drainage	3	Larbi
Burkina Faso	Urban Environment Project	1995	Ongoing	49.7	9.1	38.0	6.8	Urban road improvement & rehabilitation	2	Ouayoro
Cameroon	Douala Infrastructure Project	2002	Under preparation	86.0	86.0	38.0	38.0	Urban road rehabilitation & management	1	Inal
Chad	Transport Sector Strategy (PAProNaT)	2001	Ongoing	91.1	2.2	67.0	1.6	Road safety improvement	1	Schliessler
Ghana	Urban 5 (phase 1)	2000[a]	Ongoing	22.0	5.0	11.0	2.0	Urban road improvement	23	Bahal
Kenya	Urban Transport	1996	Ongoing	155.0	155.0	115.0	115.0	Transport infrastructure and management	26	Morrell
Malawi	Road Maintenance & Rehabilitation (ROMARP)	1999	Ongoing	39.0	4.0	30.0	4.0	Urban road rehabilitation & maintenance	2	Brushett
Mali	Urban Development & Decentralization	1997	Ongoing	93.5	30.0	80.0	25.4	Urban road rehabilitation & maintenance	10	Inal
Mauritania	Urban Development Program	2001[a]	Ongoing	100.0	17.0	70.0	14.0	Transport infrastructure improvement & road construction	13	Inal
Mauritius	Transport Sector	2002	Under preparation	100.0	70.0	20.0	3.0	Environmental infrastructure improvement	4	Ghzala
Nigeria	Lagos Urban Transport	2002	Under preparation	140.0	140.0	100.0	100.0	Institutional reform, road rehabilitation & bus operation improvement	1	Schelling
Senegal	Urban Mobility Improvement	2000[a]	Ongoing	132.0	132.0	98.0	98.0	Infrastructure improvement and private sector support	1	Bultynck
Tanzania	Urban Sector Rehabilitation	1996	Ongoing	141.0	32.0	105.0	30.0	Road rehabilitation & construction	8	Carroll
Togo	Urban Development	1994	Ongoing	29.0	26.2	13.0	11.0	Urban road & drainage	1	Cave
Zambia	National Road	1998	Ongoing	454.0	40.0	70.0	11.0	Urban road rehabilitation & support of urban road management	3	Brushett
			Totals	1,660.6	770.3	880.5	479.0			
East Asia and Pacific Region										
China	Guangzhou City Center Transport	1998	Ongoing	586.0	586.0	200.0	200.0	Road investment & maint., traffic mgmt./safety, environment, public transport	1	Scurfield
China	Liaoning Urban Transport	1999	Ongoing	384.0	384.0	150.0	150.0	Road investment & maint., traffic mgmt./safety, environment, public transport	3	Scurfield
China	Urumchi Urban Transport	2001	Ongoing	250.0	250.0	100.0	100.0	Road investment & maint., traffic mgmt./safety, environment, public transport	1	Dotson

Country	Name of Project	Fiscal Year Approved	Status	Project Cost (US$M)		WB Loan (US$M)		Principal Urban Transport Thrust	Number of Cities in Project	Project Team Leader
				Total	Urban Transport	Total	Urban Transport			
China	Shijiazhuang Urban Transport	2001	Under preparation	286.0	286.0	100.0	100.0	Road investment & maint., traffic mgmt./safety, environment, public transport	1	Scurfield
China	Wuhan Urban Transport	2003	Concept	500.0	500.0	200.0	200.0	Road investment & maint., traffic mgmt./safety, environment, public transport	1	Dotson
Indonesia	Strategic Urban Roads Infrastructure	1996	Ongoing	168.0	168.0	87.0	87.0	Reducing traffic bottleneck, decentralization of responsibility of urban transport	8	Scouller
Indonesia	Strategic Urban Road Infrastructure II (Java)	2003	Under preparation	150.0	150.0	150.0	150.0	Reducing traffic bottleneck, decentralization of responsibility of urban transport	TBA	Dotson
Republic of Korea	Pusan Urban Transport Management	1994	Ongoing	332.0	332.0	100.0	100.0	Effectiveness of an urban rail transit & policy reforms	1	Burningham
Philippines	Metro Manila Urban Transport Integration	2001	Under preparation	87.0	87.0	56.0	56.0	Improving integrated access to public Iransport & NMT	12 cities and 5 mun. in metro Manila	Burningham
Thailand	Bangkok Air Quality Management	2002	Under preparation	80.0	80.0	80.0	80.0	Reduce local emissions	1	Capannelli
Vietnam	Urban Transport Improvement	1998	Ongoing	47.0	47.0	43.0	43.0	Operational efficiency & safety improvement	1	Burningham
			Totals	2,870.0	2,870.0	1,266.0	1,266.0			
Europe and Central Asia Region										
Armenia	Armenia Transport Project	2000	Ongoing	47.0	0.5	40.0	0.5	Urban transport study	1	Talvitie
Kyrgyz Rep.	Urban Transport	2001	Ongoing	24.2	24.2	22.0	22.0	Urban road rehabilitation & finance	3	Podolske
Latvia	Municipal Services	1995	Ongoing	45.4	15.0	27.3	15.0	Bus service improvement in Riga	1	Balkind
Russian Federation	Urban Transport	1995	Ongoing	391.0	391.0	330.0	330.0	Expand fleet & reform public transport operations	14	Podolske
Russian Federation	Bridge Rehabilitation	1997	Ongoing	466.0	93.0	350.0	69.8	Bridge rehabilitation in Moscow	1	Podolske
Russian Federation	Moscow Urban Transport	2001	Under preparation	100.0	100.0	60.0	60.0	Traffic management + associated institutional development	1	Podolske
Uzbekistan	Urban Transport	2000	Ongoing	31.4	31.4	29.0	29.0	Public transport reform & leasing of buses	5	Crochet
			Totals	1,105.0	655.1	858.3	526.3			
Latin America and the Caribbean Region										
Argentina	Second Municipal Development	1995		600.0	186.0	210.0	65.0	Road paving	Many	Miguel Mercado-Diaz

Country	Name of Project	Fiscal Year Approved	Status	Project Cost (US$M)		WB Loan (US$M)		Principal Urban Transport Thrust	Number of Cities in Project	Project Team Leader
				Total	Urban Transport	Total	Urban Transport			
Argentina	Buenos Aires Urban Transport	1997	Ongoing	364.0	364.0	200.0	200.0	Support rail concessions & institutional reform	1	Menckhoff
Argentina	Pollution Management	1998	Ongoing	36.0	15.0	18.0	7.5	Air pollution	1	Tlaiye
Bolivia	Decentralization	2001	Ongoing	67.0	3.0	54.0	2.4	Road rehabilitation & paving	20+	Rojas
Brazil	Belo Horizonte Metropolitan Transport	1995	Ongoing	197.0	197.0	99.0	99.0	Rehabilitate & transfer commuter rail from federal to local government	1	Rebelo
Brazil	Recife Transport Decentralization	1995	Ongoing	204.0	204.0	102.0	102.0	Rehabilitate & transfer commuter rail from federal to local government	1	Rebelo
Brazil	São Paulo Integrated Urban Transport (BF)	1998	Ongoing	95.1	95.1	45.0	45.0	Build link to integrate commuter rail systems	1	Rebelo
Brazil	Rio de Janeiro Mass Transit	1998	Ongoing	316.0	316.0	186.0	186.0	Rehabilitate & concession trains; improve integration	1	Rebelo
Brazil	Salvador Urban Transport	1999	Ongoing	308.0	308.0	150.0	150.0	Build new metro line (BOT)	1	Rebelo
Brazil	Fortaleza Urban Transport	2001	Ongoing	176.0	176.0	85.0	85.0	Rehabilitate & transfer commuter rail from federal to local government	1	Rebelo
Brazil	São Paulo Line 4	2002	Ongoing	1,800.0	1,800.0	209.0	209.0	Build new metro line (BOT)	1	Rebelo
Brazil	Recife Urban Upgrading	2002	Under preparation	100.0	22.0	56.0	12.3	Road & walkway widening & paving	1	V. Serra
Colombia	Regulatory Reform TA	1997	Ongoing	33.0	2.0	13.0	0.8	TA for busways, metro, & suburban rail	3	Challa
Colombia	Bogotá Urban Services	2003	Under preparation	332.0	136.8	150.0	68.0	Feeder routes, traffic mgmt., street maint. & institutional reform	1	Persaud
Mexico	Medium-Size Cities Urban Transport	1993	Ongoing	471.0	471.0	200.0	200.0	Urban transport systems in medium-size cities	12	James
Mexico	Second Air Quality and Transport Project	2004	Under preparation	100.0	TBA	70.0	TBA	Air quality mgmt. & urban transport mgmt.	TBA	Vegera
Peru	Lima Urban Transport	2003	Under preparation	94.0	94.0	35.0	35.0	Busway & air pollution; improved accessibility to low income areas & safety	1	Guitink
Venezuela, Rep. Bol. de	Urban Transport	1993	Ongoing	220.0	220.0	100.0	100.0	Street and traffic improvement, institutional strengthening	10	Rebelo
Venezuela, Rep. Bol. de	Caracas Slum Upgrading	1998	Ongoing	153.0	30.0	60.0	11.6	Road & walkway widening & paving	1	Cira
			Totals	5,066.1	4,639.9	1,832.0	1,513.6			
Middle East and North Africa Region										
Algeria	Transport Technical Assistance	2002	Ongoing	11.3	3.9	8.7	2.8	Institutional reforms, assistance to metro concessioning	1	Loir
Lebanon	Urban Transport Development	2002	Under preparation	115.0	115.0	65.0	65.0	Roads, traffic and parking management, transport planning	1	Feghoul
Lebanon	First Municipal Infrastructure	2000	Ongoing/ Supervision	100.0	100.0	79.0	79.0	Municipal roads, retaining walls, sidewalks, municipal capacity		Benouahi

A.1 URBAN TRANSPORT PROJECTS UNDER PREPARATION AND IMPLEMENTATION AS OF FEBRUARY 26, 2002 (CONTINUED)

Country	Name of Project	Fiscal Year Approved	Status	Project Cost (US$M)		WB Loan (US$M)		Principal Urban Transport Thrust	Number of Cities in Project	Project Team Leader
				Total	Urban Transport	Total	Urban Transport			
Tunisia	Transport Sector Investment (APL Phase I)	1998[a]	Ongoing	117.2	117.2	82.0	82.0	Transport services reforms		Loir
Tunisia	Transport Sector Investment (APL phase II)	2001[a]	Ongoing	57.0	39.3	37.6	26.6	Transport Services reforms	1	Loir
			Totals	400.4	375.4	272.3	255.4		1	
South Asia Region										
Bangladesh	Dhaka Urban Transport	1999	Ongoing	234.2	234.2	177.0	177.0	Urban transport services improvement	1	Qureshi
Bangladesh	Municipal Services	1999	Ongoing	154.0	10.0	139.0	9.0	Urban road rehabilitation program	4	Kamkwa-lala
India	Mumbai Urban Transport	2002	Under pre-paration	838.0	838.0	485.0	485.0	Sustainable public transport (rail/bus)	1	Swamina-tha
India	Tamil Nadu Urban Development - II	1999	Ongoing	205.0	55.0	105.0	28.2	Urban infrastructure services improved	…	Suzuki
			Totals	1,431.2	1,137.2	906.0	699.2			

Note: The data are based on the project appraisal document at the time of the approval. Whenever the detailed information did not exist in the project appraisal document, the values were estimated.

a. Adaptable Program Lending, where "lending" refers to an International Bank for Reconstruction and Development loan or International Development Association credit.

Source: World Bank project files.

A.2 SPECIAL PROJECT FEATURES

Country	Project	Fiscal year approved	Poverty	HIV	Concessions and franchises	Air pollution control	Transport safety	Transport planning	Traffic management institutions	Public transport regulation	Transport system integration	Improved transport finance
Africa Region												
Benin	First Decentralized City Management	2000ᵃ		X							X	
Burkina Faso	Urban Environement Project	1995	X									
Cameroon	Douala Infrastructure Project	2002										
Chad	Transport Sector Strategy (PAProNaT)	2001	X	X			X					
Ghana	Urban 5 (phase 1)	2000ᵃ										
Kenya	Urban Transport	1996					X					
Malawi	Road Maintenance & Rehabilitation (ROMARP)	1999										X
Mali	Urban Development & Decentralization	1997	X									
Mauritania	Urban Development Program	2002ᵃ	X	X								
Mauritius	Transport Sector	2002				X	X	X			X	X
Nigeria	Lagos Urban Transport	2002	X		X		X		X	X		X
Senegal	Urban Mobility Improvement	2001ᵃ		X	X	X	X	X			X	X
Tanzania	Urban Sector Rehabilitation	1996	X				X					
Togo	Urban Development	1994	X									
Zambia	National Road	1998					X			X		X
East Asia and Pacific Region												
China	Guangzhou City Center Transport	1998				X	X	X	X	X	X	
China	Liaoning Urban Transport	1999				X	X	X			X	
China	Urumchi Urban Transport	2001				X	X	X	X	X	X	
China	Shijiazhuang Urban Transport	2001				X	X	X	X	X	X	
China	Wuhan Urban Transport	2003				X	X	X	X	X	X	
Indonesia	Strategic Urban Roads Infrastructure	1996						X				
Indonesia	Strategic Urban Road Infrastructure II (Java)	2003				X		X				
Korea, Rep. of	Pusan Urban Transport Management	1994						X			X	X
Philippines	Metro Manila Urban Transport	2001				X	X			X		X
Thailand	Bangkok Air Quality Management	2002										
Vietnam	Urban Transport Improvement	1998					X					

Country	Project	Fiscal year approved	Poverty	HIV	Concessions and franchises	Air pollution control	Transport safety	Transport planning	Traffic management institutions	Public transport regulation	Transport system integration	Improved transport finance
Europe and Central Asia Region												
Armenia	Transport Project	2000				.	X	X	X			X
Kyrgyz Republic	Urban Transport	2001	X		X							X
Latvia	Municipal Services	1995					X					X
Russian Federation	Urban Transport	1995			X	.						X
Russian Federation	Russia Bridge Rehabilitation	1997					X					
Russian Federation	Moscow Urban Transport	2001					X	X				X
Uzbekistan	Urban Transport	2000			X							X
Latin America and the Caribbean Region												
Argentina	Second Municipal Development	1995										X
Argentina	Buenos Aires Urban Transport	1997			X	X	X	X			X	X
Argentina	Pollution Management	1998				X						
Bolivia	Decentralization	2001										
Brazil	Belo Horizonte Metropolitan Transport	1995	X		X	X		X	X	X	X	X
Brazil	Recife Transport Decentralization	1995	X		X			X		X	X	X
Brazil	São Paulo Integrated Urban Transport (BF)	1998	X		X	X		X		X	X	X
Brazil	Rio de Janeiro Mass Transit	1998	X		X		X	X		X	X	X
Brazil	Salvador Urban Transport	1999	X		X			X	X	X	X	X
Brazil	Fortaleza Urban Transport	2002	X		X			X		X	X	X
Brazil	São Paulo Line 4	2001	X		X	X		X			X	X
Brazil	Recife Urban Upgrading	2002	X									
Colombia	Regulatory Reform TA	1997			X							
Colombia	Bogotá Urban Services	2003	X			X	X		X		X	
Mexico	Medium-Size Cities Urban Transport	1993		X	X	X		X			X	X
Mexico	Second Air Quality and Transport Project	2004				X	X					
Peru	Lima Urban Transport	2003	X		X	X	X			X	X	
Venezuela, Rep. Bol. de	Urban Transport	1993	X				X	X	X		X	
Venezuela, Rep. Bol. de	Caracas Slum Upgrading	1999	X									

A.2 SPECIAL PROJECT FEATURES (CONTINUED)

Country	Project	Fiscal year approved	Poverty	HIV	Concessions and franchises	Air pollution control	Transport safety	Transport planning	Traffic management institutions	Public transport regulation	Transport system integration	Improved transport finance
Middle East and North Africa Region												
Algeria	Transport Technical Assistance	2001			X	X		X	X	X		
Lebanon	Urban Transport Development	TBD				X		X	X	X		
Lebanon	First Municipal Infrastructure	2001	X				X					
Tunisia	Transport Sector Investment (APL Phase I)	2000a			X	X						X
Tunisia	Transport Sector Investment (APL Phase II)	1998a						X	X	X	X	
South Asia Region												
Bangladesh	Dhaka Urban Transport	1999	X			X	X	X	X			
Bangladesh	Municipal Services	1999		X								
India	Mumbai Urban Transport	2001			X	X	X	X			X	X
India	Tamil Nadu Urban Development II	1999	X					X				

Note: HIV = human immunodeficiency virus. For technical assistance, feature categories may overlap.

a. Adaptable Program Lending, where "lending" refers to an International Bank for Reconstruction and Development loan or International Development Association credit.

Source: World Bank project files.

A.3 URBAN PORTFOLIO: PROJECT COST AND WORLD BANK GROUP LOAN AND GRANT AMOUNT ALLOCATION (MILLIONS OF U.S. DOLLARS)

Urban transport component

Legend: □ Project cost ▨ World Bank Group loan or grant amount

In each cell the values are shown as **project cost / World Bank Group loan or grant amount**.

Country	Project	Fiscal year approved	Road and bridge construction	Road and bridge rehabilitation and maintenance	Traffic management	Bus lanes and HOV facilities	Pedestrian and bicycle facilities	Bus, trolleybus, tramway	Metro	Commuter rail	Vehicle emission control	Other investments	Technical assistance engineering and construction supervision	Other technical assistance	Total
Africa Region															
Benin	First Decentralized City Management	2000[a]		18.6 / 16.1									3.2 / 3.2		21.8 / 19.3
Burkina Faso	Urban Environment Project	1995		9.1 / 6.8											9.1 / 6.8
Cameroon	Douala Infrastructure Project	2002		75.1 / 29.1									5.3 / 4.6	5.7 / 4.7	86.0 / 38.4
Chad	Transport Sector Strategy (PAProNaT)	2001	1.0 / 0.7	0.3 / 0.2	0.8 / 0.6									0.1 / 0.1	2.2 / 1.6
Ghana	Urban 5 (phase 1)	2000[a]		4.8 / 2.4											4.8 / 2.4
Kenya	Urban Transport	1996	25.7 / 19.1	78.7 / 58.4	6.3 / 4.7		4.7 / 3.5							39.6 / 29.4	155.0 / 115.0
Malawi	Road Maintenance & Rehabilitation (ROMARP)	1999		3.5 / 3.5									0.5 / 0.5		4.0 / 4.0
Mali	Urban Development & Decentralization	1997		26.7 / 22.4									3.6 / 3.0		30.3 / 25.4
Mauritania	Urban Development Program	2002[a]	14.3 / 10.8										3.5 / 3.2		17.8 / 14.0
Mauritius	Transport Sector	2002						70.0 / 3.0							70.0 / 3.0
Nigeria	Lagos Urban Transport	2002		67.0 / 41.1	9.2 / 7.3			15.6 / 13.3				4.6 / 3.6	22.2 / 18.9	21.7 / 15.9	140.3 / 100.0
Senegal	Urban Mobility Improvement	2000[a]		32.3 / 24.0	19.5 / 14.5		1.0 / 0.7	29.8 / 22.1		27.3 / 20.3	12.9 / 9.6	0.7 / 0.5	9.6 / 7.1		132.1 / 98.1
Tanzania	Urban Sector Rehabilitation	1996	31.0 / 29.1												32.0 / 29.8
Togo	Urban Development	1994	9.8 / 8.5										2.9 / 2.9		12.7 / 11.4
Zambia	National Road	1998		33.0 / 8.5	1.6 / 0.5								4.5 / 1.1	0.9 / 0.9	40.0 / 11.0
East Asia and Pacific Region															
China	Guangzhou City Center Transport	1998	505.0 / 172.4	7.0 / 2.4	25.7 / 8.8	9.2 / 3.1	6.8 / 2.3	13.4 / 4.6			9.0 / 3.1		10.0 / 3.4		586.1 / 200.0
China	Liaoning Urban Transport	1999	292.0 / 114.1	26.0 / 10.2	26.8 / 10.5	17.4 / 6.8	6.8 / 2.7	7.2 / 2.8				1.5 / 0.6	6.5 / 2.5		384.2 / 150.1
China	Urumchi Urban Transport	2001	219.5 / 87.8	3.5 / 1.4	10.0 / 4.0	3.8 / 1.5	2.0 / 0.8	3.1 / 1.2			4.6 / 1.8		3.5 / 1.4		250.0 / 100.0
China	Shijiazhuang Urban Transport	2001	219.0 / 76.6	16.5 / 5.8	9.6 / 3.4	6.4 / 2.2	15.9 / 5.6	13.0 / 4.5			2.6 / 0.9			3.4 / 1.2	286.4 / 100.1
China	Wuhan Urban Transport	2003													500.0 / 200.0
Indonesia	Strategic Urban Roads Infrastructure	1996	147.0 / 76.1										16.8 / 8.7	3.8 / 2.0	167.6 / 86.8
Indonesia	Strategic Urban Road Infrastructure II (Java)	2003			48.2 / 12.2										150.0 / 150.0
Korea, Rep. of	Pusan Urban Transport Management	1994							281.2 / 86.2						331.5 / 100.0
Philippines	Metro Manila Urban Transport	2001	18.9 / 12.6	20.5 / 10.5	26.0 / 18.0	10.0 / 7.0	10.0 / 7.2							2.1 / 1.6	86.4 / 56.3
Thailand	Bangkok Air Quality Management	2002												1.0 / 1.0	80.0 / 80.0
Vietnam	Urban Transport Improvement	1998			34.1 / 3.3								8.6 / 1.2		42.7 / 4.5
Europe and Central Asia Region															
Armenia	Armenia Transport Project	2000											0.5 / 0.5		0.5 / 0.5
Kyrgyz Republic	Urban Transport	2001		21.7 / 19.6									2.5 / 2.5		24.2 / 22.1
Latvia	Municipal Services	1995						15.1 / 14.5					0.5 / 0.5		15.6 / 15.0
Russian Federation	Urban Transport	1995						378.0 / 318.0					13.0 / 11.0		391.0 / 329.0
Russian Federation	Bridge Rehabilitation	1997		83.7 / 62.8									9.3 / 9.3		93.0 / 72.1

Note: The following reproduces the legible portions of a large landscape table ("Urban Transport Portfolio in the World Bank"). The two columns of the table that carry the grand totals (each summing to 100 percent) are the total amount column and the Bank lending column.

Region / Country	Project	Fiscal year	Total	Lending
Russian Federation — Moscow Urban Transport		2001	97.6	56.9
Uzbekistan — Urban Transport		2000	31.4	29.0
Latin America and the Caribbean Region				
Argentina	Second Municipal Development	1995	186.0	65.0
Argentina	Buenos Aires Urban Transport	1997	367.0	200.0
Argentina	Pollution Management	1998	14.5	7.2
Bolivia	Decentralization	2001	3.0	2.4
Brazil	Belo Horizonte Metropolitan Transport	1995	196.0	98.5
Brazil	Recife Transport Decentralization	1995	204.0	102.0
Brazil	São Paulo Integrated Urban Transport (BF)	1998	93.1	45.0
Brazil	Rio de Janeiro Mass Transit	1998	316.0	186.0
Brazil	Salvador Urban Transport	1999	308.0	150.0
Brazil	Fortaleza Urban Transport	2001	176.0	85.0
Brazil	São Paulo Line 4	2002	1,800.0	209.0
Brazil	Recife Urban Upgrading	2002	22.0	12.0
Colombia	Regulatory Reform Technical Assistance	1997	2.0	1.0
Colombia	Bogota Urban Services	2003	136.9	68.0
Mexico	Medium-Size Cities Urban Transport	1993	467.0	200.0
Mexico	Second Air Quality and Transport Project	2004	100.0	70.0
Peru	Lima Urban Transport	2003	94.0	35.0
Venezuela, Rep. Bol. de	Urban Transport	1993	220.0	100.0
Venezuela, Rep. Bol. de	Caracas Slum Upgrading	1999	30.0	12.0
Middle East and North Africa Region				
Algeria	Transport Technical Assistance	2002	3.9	2.8
Lebanon	Urban Transport Development	2002	115.0	65.0
Lebanon	First Municipal Infrastructure	2000	78.6	78.6
Tunisia	Transport Sector Investment (APL Phase I)	1998[b]		15.1
Tunisia	Transport Sector Investment (APL Phase II)	2001[a]	39.3	26.6
South Asia Region				
Bangladesh	Dhaka Urban Transport	1999	226.2	177.0
Bangladesh	Municipal Services	1999	10.0	9.0
India	Mumbai Urban Transport	2002	838.0	485.0
India	Tamil Nadu Urban Development - II	1999	54.9	28.2
Totals (all regions)			10,356.6	4,861.0
Percentage			100.0	100.0

Note: HOV = high occupancy vehicles. Figures in the shaded area represent loan amounts allocated for a component.

a. Adaptable Program Lending, where "lending" refers to an International Bank for Reconstruction and Development loan or International Development Association credit.

Source: World Bank project files.

BIBLIOGRAPHY

Note: Background reports for the review (indicated with symbol §) were commissioned with the assistance of national trust funds (France, Japan, the Netherlands, and Spain) or direct government finance (Germany and the United Kingdom). They are all posted on the Urban Transport Strategy Review Web page, and can be downloaded directly from that page, which may be accessed from the World Bank Transport Web site at http://www.worldbank.org/transport.

The word *processed* describes informally reproduced works that may not be commonly available through libraries.

Aeron-Thomas, A., A. J. Downing, G. D. Jacobs, J. P. Fletcher, T. Selby, and D. T. Silcock. 2002. "Review of Road Safety Management Practice: Final Report." TRL Ltd., with Ross Silcock, Babtie Groups, Ltd.

Affonso S. A., F. Rezende, and F. P. Vitor. 1998. "Peace within Traffic: A Revolution of Attitudes in Brazilia." In Freeman, P., and C. Jamet, eds., *Urban Transport Policy: A Sustainable Development Tool.* Proceedings of the International Conference CODATU VIII, Cape Town, South Africa. Rotterdam: Balkema.

Amundsen, F. H. 1996. "Review of World Bank Experience in Traffic Safety Concerning Motorized and Non-Motorized Traffic (1989–94)." TWU. World Bank, Washington, D.C. Processed.

APOYO Group. 1999. "Profile of Socioeconomic levels in Metropolitan Lima." Apoyo, Opinion y Mercadeo.

Aragão, J. J., A. Brasileiro, and R. Marar. 1998. "The Brazilian Bus Industry and the New Legislation on Public Procurement Procedures." In Freeman, P., and C. Jamet, eds., *Urban Transport Policy: A Sustainable Development Tool.* Proceedings of the International Conference CODATU VIII, Cape Town. Rotterdam: Balkema.

§ Arcadis Bouw/Infra. 2000. *The Development of Logistic Services* (The Netherlands). http://www.worldbank.org/transport

Ardila, A., and G. Menckhoff. Forthcoming. "Busways: Lessons from Latin American Cities." World Bank, Washington, D.C.

Armstrong-Wright, A. 1986. "Urban Transport Systems: Guidelines for Examining Options." World Bank Technical Paper, Urban Series No. 52. Washington, D.C.

———. 1993. *Public Transport in Third World Cities.* TRL State of the Art Review. London: HMSO.

Associacão Nacional de Transportes Públicos. 1999. *O Transporte Clandestino no Brazil.* Documentos Setoriais. São Paulo.

Barrett, R. 1986. "Institution Building for Traffic Management." Technical Paper 78. World Bank, Washington, D.C.

Barter, P. 1999. "Transport and Urban Poverty in Asia: A Brief Introduction to the Key Issues." *Regional Development Dialogue* 20 (1).

§ BB&J Consult. 2000. "Implementation of Rapid Transit (Spain)." http://www.worldbank.org/transport

§ BCEOM. 2000. "Review of French Experience in Institutional Framework for Planning and Programming in Urban Transport (France)." http://www.worldbank.org/transport

Bertaud, A. 1999. "Bangalore Land-Use Issues." World Bank, Washington, D.C.

Bertaud, A., and B. Renaud. 1997. "Socialist Cities Without Land Markets." *Journal of Urban Economics* 41.

Bloy, E. 2001. "Rentabilité et financement des micro-entreprises de transport collectif en Afrique subsaharienne." Sub-Saharan African Transport Policy Program Report 54F. World Bank, Washington, D.C.

Burchell, R. W. 1998. *The Costs of Sprawl—Revisited.* Transit Co-operative Research Program Report 39. Transportation Research Board. Washington, D.C.: National Academy Press.

Button, K. J., and E. T. Verhoef, eds. 1998. *Road Pricing, Traffic Congestion and the Environment.* Cheltenham: Edward Elgar.

§ Caetano Roca Giner (PriceWaterhouseCoopers). 2000. "Conversion of Railway Lines for Suburban Passenger Services (Spain)." http://www.worldbank.org/transport

Canning D., and E. Bennathan. 2000. "The Social Rate of Return on Infrastructure Investments." Policy Research Working Paper 2390. World Bank, Washington, D.C.

§ CATRAM. 2000. "Land Use and Transport Development: The Case Study of Cairo, Egypt (France)." http://www.worldbank.org/transport

Centro de Estudios del Transporte del Area Metropolitana. 1999. "Estudio de Transporte y Circulacion Urbana." Universidad de Buenos Aires.

Cervero, R. 1998. "Paratransit: The Gap Fillers." *Habitat Debate* 4 (2).

———. 2001. "Informal Transport: Mobility Options for the Developing World." Paper Prepared for UNCHS (Habitat), Nairobi.

Conseil National des Transports. 1999. "Les transports et l'environnement: vers un nouvel equilibre." La Documentation Française, Paris.

§ Cracknell, J. 2000. "Experience in Urban Traffic Management and Demand Management in Developing Countries (United Kingdom)." http://www.worldbank.org/transport

Cusset, J. M. 1998. "Accessibility to Urban Services and Mobility Needs of Peripheral Population: The Case of Ougadougou." In Freeman, P., and C. Jamet, eds., *Urban Transport Policy: A Sustainable Development Tool.* Proceedings of the International Conference CODATU VIII, Cape Town. Rotterdam: Balkema.

De Langen, M., and R. Tembele, eds. 2000. "Productive and Liveable Cities: Guidelines for Pedestrian and Bicycle Traffic in African Cities." Interface for Cycling Expertise, Utrecht, the Netherlands.

De St. Laurent, B. 1998. "Overview of Urban Transport in South Africa." In Freeman, P., and C. Jamet, eds., *Urban Transport Policy: A Sustainable Development Tool.* Proceedings of the International Conference CODATU VIII, Cape Town. Rotterdam: Balkema.

Department of Environment, Transport, and the Regions. 1998. "A New Deal for Transport: Better for Everyone." Cmd 3950. London: HMSO.

Diaz Olvera, L., D. Plat, and P. Pochet. 1998. "Les multiple visages de la mobilité feminine dans les villes d'Afrique." In Freeman, P., and C. Jamet, eds., *Urban Transport Policy: A Sustainable Development Tool.* Proceedings of the International Conference CODATU VIII, Cape Town. Rotterdam: Balkema.

Dimitriou, H. 1998. "Developing a Strategy to Address Problems of Increasing Motorization." Report prepared for the United Nations Development Programme.

Dollar, D., and A. Kraay. 2001. "Growth is Good for the Poor." Policy Research Working Paper. World Bank, Washington, D.C. http://www.econ.worldbank.org

Dourthe, A., M. Wityk, H. Malbran, and O. Figueroa. 1998. "Dereglementation et re-reglementation du transport public urbain: le Cas de Santiago" In Freeman, P., and C. Jamet, eds., *Urban Transport Policy: A Sustainable Development Tool.* Proceedings of the International Conference CODATU VIII, Cape Town. Rotterdam: Balkema.

Dowall, D. 1995. "The Land Market Assessment: A New Tool for Urban Management." Urban Management Program Discussion Paper, World Bank, Washington, D.C.

Dutt, A. K., Y. Xie, F. J. Costa, and Z. Yang. 1994. "City Forms of China and India in Global Perspective." In Dutt, A. K., F. J. Costa, A. G. Noble, and S. Aggarwal, eds., *The Asian City: Processes of Development, Characteristics and Planning*. Boston: Kluwer Academic Publishers.

ECLAC (Economic Commission for Latin America and the Caribbean). 1991. "The Impacts of Subsidies, Regulation and Different Forms of Ownership on the Quality and Operational Efficiency of Urban Bus Services in Latin America." Santiago, Chile.

Eskeland, G. S., and S. Devarajan. 1996. "Taxing Bads by Taxing Goods: Pollution Control with Presumption Charges." Directions in Development Series. World Bank, Washington, D.C.

Eskeland, G. S., and J. Xie. 1998. "Integrating Local and Global Environmental Benefits: Mechanisms and Case Studies in the Transport Sector." World Bank, Washington D.C.

European Commission. 2000. "Developing Urban Management and Safety." Report of an international research team (The DUMAS Report). European Union, Brussels, Belgium.

European Conference of Ministers of Transport. 1995. "Urban Travel and Sustainable Development." OECD/ECMT, Paris.

———. 1999a. "Improving the Environmental Performance of Vehicles: Fleet Renewal and Scrappage Schemes." Report of the ECMT Committee of Deputies. Paris.

———. 1999b. "Improving Transport for People with Mobility Handicaps: A Guide to Good Practice." Paris.

———. 1999c. "Traffic Congestion in Europe." Report of 110th Round Table on Transport Economics. Paris.

Fouchier, V. 1997. "Les densites urbaines et le developpement durable: I[er] cas de l'Ile de France et des villes nouvelles." Secretariat General du Groupe Centrale des Villes Nouvelles, Paris.

Fouracre, P. R., R. J. Allport, and J. M. Thomson. 1990. "The Performance and Impact of Rail MRT in Developing Countries." TRL Research Report RR278. Transport Research Laboratory, Crowthorne, United Kingdom.

Fouracre, P. R., A. Astrop, and D. Maunder. 1999. "Accessibility for the Urban Poor." TRL Project Report 153/99. Transport Research Laboratory, Crowthorne, United Kingdom.

Frame, G. 1999. "Traffic Management and Road Safety in World Bank Projects in Chinese Cities: A Review." World Bank, Washington, D.C.

Gallagher, R. 1992. *The Rickshaws of Bangladesh*. Dhaka, Bangladesh: University Press.

Gannon, C., and Zhi Liu. 1997. "Poverty and Transport." Discussion Paper TWU-30. Transport, Water, and Urban Development, World Bank, Washington, D.C.

Gardner, G. 1993. "The Performance of Light Rapid Transit in Developing Countries." TRL Project Report. Transport Research Laboratory, Crowthorne, United Kingdom.

Gardner, G., P. R. Cornwell, and J. A. Cracknell. 1991. "The Performance of Busway Transit in Developing Countries." TRL Research Report RR329. Transport Research Laboratory, Crowthorne, United Kingdom.

Garreau, J. 1991. *Edge City: Life on the New Frontier*. New York: Doubleday.

Ghee, C., D. Silcock, A. Astrop, and G. D. Jacobs. 1997. "Socio-economic Aspects of Road Accidents in Developing Countries." TRL Report 247. Transport Research Laboratory, Crowthorne, United Kingdom.

§ Godard, X., and L. Diaz Olvera. 2000. "Poverty and Urban Transport: French Experience and Developing Cities (France)." http://www.worldbank.org/transport

Gold, P. 1999. *Using Engineering to Reduce Accidents.* Inter-American Development Bank, Washington, D.C.

Gomez, L. M. 2000. "Gender Analysis of Two Components of the World Bank Transport Projects in Lima, Peru: Bikepaths and Busways." World Bank Internal Report, World Bank, Washington, D.C.

§ GTZ (Deutsche Gesellschaft für Technische Zusammenarbeit). 2002. "Urban Transport Strategy Review: Experiences from Germany and Zurich (Germany)." http://www.worldbank.org/transport

Gwilliam, K. M. 1996. "Getting the Prices Wrong: A Tale of Two Islands." Infrastructure Note UT-6. Transport, Water, and Urban Development, World Bank, Washington, D.C.

———. 2000a. "Natural Gas as a Transport Fuel." Infrastructure Note UT-8. Transport, Water, and Urban Development, World Bank, Washington, D.C.

———. 2000b. "Private Participation in Public Transport in the Former Soviet Union." Discussion Paper TWU-40. Transport, Water, and Urban Development, World Bank, Washington, D.C.

———. 2001. "Competition in Passenger Transport in the Developing World." *Journal of Transport Economics and Policy* 35 (1/January).

Gwilliam, K. M., and R. G. Scurfield. 1996. "Constructing a Competitive Environment in Public Road Passenger Transport." Discussion Paper TWU-24. Transport, Water, and Urban Development, World Bank, Washington, D.C.

Gwilliam, K. M., A. J. Kumar, and R. T. Meakin. 2000. "Designing Competition in Urban Bus Transport: Lessons from Uzbekistan." Discussion Paper TWU-41. Transport, Water and Urban Development, World Bank, Washington, D.C.

§ Halcrow Fox, in association with Traffic and Transport Consultants. 2000a. "Mass Rapid Transit in Developing Countries (United Kingdom)." http://www.worldbank.org/transport

§ Halcrow Fox. 2000b. "Review of Urban Public Transport Competition (United Kingdom)." http://www.worldbank.org/transport

Hau, T. 1992a. "Economic Fundamentals of Road Pricing: A Diagrammatic Analysis." Policy Research Working Paper 1070. Transport, Water, and Urban Development, World Bank, Washington, D.C.

———. 1992b. "Congestion Charging Mechanisms for Roads: An Evaluation of Current Practice." Policy Research Working Paper 1071. Transport, Water, and Urban Development, World Bank, Washington, D.C.

Heggie, I. G., and P. Vickers. 1998. "Commercial Management and Financing of Roads." World Bank Technical Paper 409, World Bank, Washington, D.C.

Henry, E. 2000. "Mobility, Motorization and Income: Does Urban Growth Mean More Transport?" The French Research Institute for Development (IRD—Institut de recherché pour le développement). henry@bondy.ird.fr.

Hidalgo Guerrero, D. 2001. "TransMilenio: The Mass Transport System of Bogotá." A paper prepared for the Latin American Urban Public Transport Congress (KLATPU), Havana.

Holgate, S. T., J. M. Samet, H. S. Koren, and R. L. Maynard, eds. 1999. *Air Pollution and Health.* London: Academic Press.

§ Howe J., and D. Bryceson. 2000. "Poverty and Urban Transport in East Africa (Netherlands)." http://www.worldbank.org/transport

Hughes, G., and M. Lovei. 1999. "Economic Reform and Environmental Performance in Transition Economies." Technical Paper 446. World Bank, Washington, D.C.

Hwang, K. Y., B. Son, and J. K. Eom. 1999. "Effect of Congestion Pricing at the Namsan Tunnels in Seoul." *Journal of the Eastern Asia Society for Transportation Studies* 3 (4).

Ingram, G., and Zhi Liu. 1999. "Determinants of Motorization and Road Provision." Policy Research Working Paper 2042. World Bank, Washington, D.C.

Interface for Cycling Expertise. 1997. *Cycling Promotion and Bicycle Theft.* Local background studies in León, Nicaragua; Lima, Peru; New Delhi, India; Guangzhou, China; and Accra, Ghana. Utrecht, Netherlands.

§ ———. 2000. "Nonmotorized Traffic in Developing Countries (Netherlands)." http://www.world-bank.org/transport

IPCC (Intergovernmental Panel on Climate Change). 1996. *Climate Change 1995: The Economic and Social Dimensions of Climate Change.* Cambridge (U.K.): Cambridge University Press.

Jacobs, G., and A. Aeron-Thomas. 2000. "A Review of Global Road Accident Fatalities." Paper commissioned by the Department for International Development (United Kingdom) for the Global Road Safety Partnership.

JICA-Chodai. 1996. "Master Transportation Plan of Bogotá." Bogotá.

Jones, P. 1998. "Urban Road Pricing: Public Acceptability and Barriers to Implementation." In *Road Pricing, Traffic Congestion and the Environment Issues of Efficiency and Social Feasibility.* Cheltenham: Edward Elgar.

Joos, E. 2000. "Kunming: A Model City for a Sustainable Development and Transport Policy in China." *Public Transport International* May 24–27.

Karan, P. P. 1994. "The Distribution of City Sizes in Asia." In Dutt, A. K., F. J. Costa, S. Aggarwal, and A. G. Noble, eds., *The Asian City; Processes of Development, Characteristics and Planning.* Boston: Kluwer Academic Publishers.

Kojima, M., C. Brandon, and J. Shah. 2000. "Improving Urban Air Quality in South Asia by Reducing Emissions from Two-Stroke Engine Vehicles." South Asia Environment Unit, World Bank, Washington, D.C.

Kojima, M., and M. Lovei. 2001. "Urban Air Quality Management: Coordinating Transport, Environment, and Energy Policies in Developing Countries." World Bank Technical Paper 508, World Bank, Washington, D.C.

Koster, J. H., and M. de Langen. 1998. "Preventive Transport Strategies for Secondary Cities." In Freeman, P., and C. Jamet, eds., *Urban Transport Policy: A Sustainable Development Tool.* Proceedings of the International Conference CODATU VIII, Cape Town. Rotterdam: Balkema.

———, eds. 2001. *Low-Cost Mobility in African Cities.* Proceedings of the Expert Group Meeting, Delft, Netherlands. Delft: IHE.

Kranton, R. 1991. "Transport and the Mobility Needs of the Urban Poor: An Exploratory Study." Discussion Paper INU 8. Infrastructure and Urban Development Department, World Bank, Washington, D.C.

Krugman, P. R. 1991. *Geography and Trade.* Belgium: Leuven University Press.

Kumarage, A. S. 1998. Formulation of a Policy Framework for Poverty Alleviation: Transport. University of Moratuwa, Sri Lanka.

Kwakye, E., P. Fouracre, and D. Osufa-Dorte. "Developing Strategies to Meet the Transport Needs of the Poor in Ghana." *World Transport Policy and Practice 3.*

Lee, D. B. 1999. "The Efficient City: Impacts of Transport Pricing on Urban Form." Paper presented at the Annual Conference of the Associated Schools of Collegiate Planning, Cambridge, Mass.

Lee, K. S. 1989. *The Location of Jobs in a Developing Metropolis.* A World Bank Research Publication. New York: Oxford University Press.

Litman, T. 1999. "Distance-Based Charges: A Practical Strategy for More Optimum Vehicle Pricing." Transportation Research Board's 78th Annual Meeting, Washington, D.C.

§ Louis Berger, s. a. 2000. "Review of French Experience With Respect to Public Sector Financing of Urban Transport (France)." http://www.worldbank.org/transport

Lovei, M. 1996. "Phasing Out Lead from Gasoline: Worldwide Experience and Policy Implications." Environment Department Paper 40. World Bank, Washington, D.C.

Lvovsky, K., G. Hughes, D. Maddison, B. Ostro, and D. Pearce. 2000. "Environmental Costs of Fossil Fuels: A Rapid Assessment Method with Application to Six Cities." Environment Department Paper 78. World Bank, Washington, D.C.

Madras Metropolitan Development Authority. 1990. "Survey of Pavement Dwellers, Madras City 1989–90." Madras.

Madrid Transport Consortium. 1999. *Annual Report*. Madrid.

Menckhoff, G., and C. Zegras. 1999. "Experiences and Issues in Urban Transport Infrastructure." IRF Symposium on Innovative Financing in Transportation Projects, Hanoi.

Merilainen, A., and R. Helaakoski. 2001. "Transport, Poverty and Disability in Developing Countries." World Bank, Washington, D.C. Draft.

Midgley, P. 1994. "Urban Transport in Asia: An Operational Agenda for the 1990's." Technical Paper 224. World Bank, Washington, D.C.

Mitric, S. 1997. "Approaching Metros as Development Projects." TWU Discussion Paper 27. Transport, Water, and Urban Development, World Bank, Washington, D.C.

Mohring, H. 1999. "Congestion." In *Essays in Transportation Economics and Policy: A Handbook in Honor of John R. Meyer*. Washington, D.C: Brookings Institution Press.

Moser, C. A. 1996. "Confronting Crisis: A Summary of Household Responses to Poverty and Vulnerability in Four Poor Urban Communities." Environmentally and Socially Sustainable Development Studies and Monographs Series No. 7. World Bank, Washington, D.C.

Moser, C. A., and L. Peake. 1987. *Women, Human Settlements, and Housing*. London: Tavistock.

Narayan, D. 2000a. *Voices of the Poor: Can Anyone Hear Us?* New York: Oxford University Press.

———. 2000b. *Voices of the Poor: Crying Out for Change*. New York: Oxford University Press.

§ NEA Transport Research and Training. 2000. "Relationship between Urban Land Use Planning, Land Markets, Transport Provisions and the Welfare of the Poor (Netherlands)." http://www.worldbank.org/transport

Newbery, D. 1990. "Pricing and Congestion: Economic Principles Relevant to Pricing Roads." *Oxford Review of Economic Policy* 6 (2).

Newman, P. and J. Kenworthy. 1989. *Cities and Automobile Dependence: A Sourcebook*. Aldershot: Gower Technical.

———. 1999. *Sustainability and Cities: Overcoming Automobile Dependence*. Washington, D.C: Island Press.

§ PADECO Co. Ltd.. 2000. "Study on Urban Transport Development: Japanese Experience (Japan)." http://www.worldbank.org/transport

Pattison, T., ed. 1999. *Jane's Urban Transport Systems 1999–2000*. 18th edition. Coulsdon, United Kingdom, and Alexandria, Va.: Jane's Information Group.

Pendall, R. 1999. "Do Land-Use Controls Cause Sprawl?" *Environment and Planning B: Planning and Design 26*.

§ Prointec Inocsa Stereocarto. 2000. "Urban Public Transport: Integration and Financing (Spain)." http://www.worldbank.org/transport

Quinn, D.J. 1998. "The Leeds Guided Busway: A Low Cost Solution for Developing Countries?" In Freeman, P., and C. Jamet, eds., *Urban Transport Policy: A Sustainable Development Tool*. Proceedings of the International Conference CODATU VIII, Cape Town. Rotterdam: Balkema.

Rebelo, J. 1996. "Essentials for Sustainable Urban Transport in Brazil's Large Metropolitan Areas." WPS 1633. World Bank, Washington, D.C.

————. 1999a. "Rail and Subway Concessions in Rio de Janeiro: Designing Contracts and Bidding Processes." Viewpoint #183. World Bank, Washington, D.C.

————. 1999b. "Reforming the Urban Transport Sector in the Rio de Janeiro Metropolitan Region: A Case Study in Concessions." WPS 2096. World Bank, Washington, D.C.

Rebelo, J., and P. Machado. 2000. "The São Mateus–Jabaquara Trolleybusway Concession in Brazil." Policy Research Working Paper 2353. World Bank, Washington, D.C.

Richardson, H., and C. Bae. 1998. "The Equity Impacts of Road Congestion Pricing." In *Road Pricing, Traffic Congestion and the Environment Issues of Efficiency and Social Feasibility.* Cheltenham: Edward Elgar.

Rickert, T. 1998. *Mobility for All: Accessible Transportation Around the World.* San Francisco: Access Exchange International.

Robinson, R., U. Danielsson, and M. S. Snaith. 1998. *Road Management: Concepts and Systems.* London: Macmillan.

Ross, A. 1993. "Review of World Bank Experience in Road Safety." Discussion Paper INU 93. Infrastructure and Urban Development Department, World Bank, Washington, D.C.

Roth, G. 1996. *Roads in a Market Economy.* Aldershot: Avebury.

Sachdeva, Y. P. 1998. "Walk and Bicycle Travel Characteristics in Indian Cities." In Freeman, P., and C. Jamet, eds., *Urban Transport Policy: A Sustainable Development Tool.* Proceedings of the International Conference CODATU VIII, Cape Town. Rotterdam: Balkema.

SACTRA (Standing Advisory Committee on Trunk Road Assessment). 1994. "Trunk Roads and the Generation of Traffic." United Kingdom.

Schipper, L., and C. Marie-Lilliu. 1999. "Transportation and CO_2 Emissions: Flexing the Link—A Path for the World Bank." Environment Papers No 69. Environmentally and Socially Sustainable Development, World Bank, Washington, D.C.

Schwela, D., and O. Zali. 1999. *Urban Traffic Pollution.* London: E & FN Spon.

Small, K. 1992. *Urban Transportation Economics.* Chur: Harwood Academic Publishers.

§ Sodeteg. 2000. "Review of French Experience in Respect of Characteristics and Potentialities of Urban Fixed Track Systems in Developing Countries (France)." http://www.worldbank.org/transport

§ Systra. 2000. "Review of French Experience in Private Financing of Public Urban Transport (France)." http://www.worldbank.org/transport

Teurnier, P., and B. Mandon-Adolehoume. 1994. "L'Integration du Transport Artisanal dans un Service Public de Transport Urbain: Le Cas de Dakar. " Paris: TTD.

Thompson, I. 1993. "Improving Urban Transport for the Poor." *CEPAL Review* (49).

TRB (Transportation Research Board). 1998a. "Guidebook for Evaluating, Selecting and Implementing Fuel Choices for Transit Bus Operations." Transportation Co-operative Research Program Report 38. TRB, Washington, D.C.

————. 1998b. "The Costs of Sprawl Revisited." Transportation Co-operative Research Program Report 39. TRB, Washington, D.C.

TRL (Transport Research Laboratory). 1985. "The Demand for Bus Transport." TRL, Crowthorne, United Kingdom.

————. 1995. "Costing Road Accidents in Developing Countries." Overseas Road Note ORN 10. TRL, Crowthorne, United Kingdom.

§ TRL (Transport Research Laboratory) and R. Silcock. 2000. "Review of Road Safety in Urban Areas (United Kingdom)." http://www.worldbank.org/transport

United Nations. 1996. *World Urbanization Prospects.* New York.

UNCHS (United Nations Centre for Human Settlement). 1998. "Global Urban Indicators Database." Urban Indicators Programme, Nairobi.

Verhoef, H., P. Nijkamp, and P. Rietveld. 1995. "The Economics of Regulatory Parking Policies: The (Im)possibilities of Parking Policies in Traffic Regulation." In *Transportation Research, Part A, Policy and Practice* 29 (A): 2.

Weaver, C. S., and L. M. Chan. 1996. "Bangkok Particulate Study." Report to the Thai Government and the World Bank. World Bank, Washington, D.C.

Wheaton, W. 1996. *Land Use and Density in Cities with Congestion.* Cambridge, Mass.: MIT Center for Real Estate.

White, P.R. 1999. "Impacts of the Cairo Metro." Paper presented at the Sixth International Conference on Competition and Ownership in Land Passenger Transport, Cape Town.

Willoughby, C. 2000a. "Managing Motorization." TWU Discussion Paper 42. Transport, Water, and Urban Development, World Bank, Washington, D.C.

————. 2000b. "Singapore's Experience in Managing Motorization and its Relevance to Other Countries." TWU Discussion Paper 43. Transport, Water, and Urban Development, World Bank, Washington, D.C., and the Web site of the Singapore Land Transport Authority http://www.lta.gov.sg.

World Bank. 1975. "Urban Transport." A World Bank Policy Paper. Washington, D.C.

————. 1986. "Urban Transport: Sector Policy Paper." A World Bank Policy Paper. Washington, D.C.

————. 1995. *Bureaucrats in Business: The Economics and Politics of Government Ownership.* Oxford: Oxford University Press.

————. 1996. "Sustainable Transport: Priorities for Policy Reform." A World Bank Policy Paper. Washington, D.C.

————. 1998. "Fuel for Thought: a New Environmental Strategy for the Energy Sector." A World Bank Policy Paper. Washington, D.C.

————. 1999. "Bangkok Urban Transport Sector Review." Washington, D.C.

————. 2000a. "Cities in Transition: World Bank Urban and Local Government Strategy." World Bank Policy Paper. Washington, D.C.

————. 2000b. "Reforming Public Institutions and Strengthening Governance." Poverty Reduction and Economic Management Network, Washington, D.C.

————. 2000c. *World Development Report.* Washington, D.C.

————. 2001. "Mexico Energy Environment Review." ESMAP (Energy Sector Management Assistance Programme). Report 241/01. Washington D.C.

WHO (World Health Organization). 1992. *Urban Air Pollution in Megacities of the World.* Oxford U.K. and Cambridge, Mass.: Blackwell Reference.

————. 1999. *World Health Report.* Geneva.

Wright, C.L., ed. 2001. *Facilitando o Transporte para Todos.* Banco Interamericano de Desenvolvimento, Washington D.C.

Zegras, C. 1998. "The Costs of Transportation in Santiago de Chile: Analysis and Policy Implications." *Transport Policy Journal* 5.

INDEX

Accessibility poor, 27

Accidents, incidence, 65, 68; location, 68; prevention programs, 68–69; Sri Lanka, 66; statistics, 68

Adjudication, land invasions and informal acquisitions, 19

Advisory services, 179

Affordability, 34–36

Agglomeration economies, 5, 8, 10, 16

Air pollution, 42–59; economics, 8; mortality and morbidity and, 39; pollutants, 42–45; *see also* Environment

Ancillary infrastructure, costs, 19

Area licenses, 137

Argentina, safety and security, 66–67, 74

Authority: contiguous, 155; overlapping, 155, 160–61; strategy, 167–68

Bangkok Transit System (BTS), 15

Basic knowledge, 60

Blocking, 96

Borrowing, 146

Bottlenecks, 87

Brazil, 14, 72, 90, 116

Buenos Aires Urban Transport Project, 66–67

Built environment, 39

Buses, 58, 80–81; accidents, 68; design, 112; financing, 174

Bus sector, 93–106; competition, 95–96; contracts, 98–100, 105; efficiency, 94–95; financing, 94; franchises, 100, 105; institutional requirements, 98; mass transit, 178; monopolies, 93; ownership, 93–94; policy, 98–101; private sector role, 15; rapid transit system, 119; ridership, 93; Uzbekistan, 100

Busways, 112; financing, 118

Capability, institutions, 167

Capacity building, 179; institutions, 163–64, 165

Capacity extensions, economics, 87–88

Capital cities, 16, 22

Car ownership, income and, 8

Carbon dioxide (CO_2), 40

Carbon monoxide (CO), 43, 45

Catalyst technologies, 51

Catalytic converters, 50, 51

Charges: system, 140–41; vehicle use, 84

China, 93, 128, 131

City characteristics, 6–7

City development strategies (CDS), 5, 11–12, 22–23

Civil society, engaging, 164–65

Collaboration, 181–82; voluntary, 160

Collusion, prevention, 105

Colombia, 74, 119, 129

Community severance, 42

Commuters, 25

Competition, 34, 37, 171; bus sector, 95–96; effective, 98; informal sector, 103, 104; managing, 96, 98; strategy, 107

Comprehensive Development Framework, 170, 181–82

Compressed natural gas (CNG), 47–48

Concessioning, 95–96, 173

Conflict reduction, institutions, 160

Congestion: city development, 7, 10, 22; environment, 58; impacts, 142–43; poverty reduction and, 29, 32–33; reduction, 110

Congestion pricing, 135, 136–38

Contracts, 15, 98–100; gross cost service contracting, 95; net cost service contracting, 95

Control system, 19

Coordinating authority, 157

Coordination, 22, 116, 143–44; committee, 156–57; functional, 168; institutions, 154–56, 160–62, 163–64, 167–68; jurisdictional, 167–68

Cordon pricing, 137

Cost-benefit, capacity extensions, 88

Costs, 37; accidents, 65; ancillary infrastructure, 19; congestion, 142–43; cycling, 133–34; demand management, 83; I/M programs and, 54–55; infrastructure, 19, 20; MRT, 112; metros, 115–17; recovering, 143; unit transport, 19; undercharging, 19; sprawl, 19; *see also* Economics; Finance

Counterpart funding, 148

Country Assistance Strategy, 181

Credit, bus sector, 106

Crime, 73, 75

Cultural factors, 28

Curb rights, 105

Cycling, 30–31, 125, 126–28; attitudes, 127; women, 127

Cyclists, 126–27, 131

Decentralization, 14, 15, 22; facilitating, 171–73; policy, 172; political and financial responsibility, 1–2; progress, 172; WB agenda, 172–73

Demand for transport, 12

Demand management, 60, 83–84, 91, 171, 177–78

Densification, 17

Development: challenges, 169–70; control skills, 23; planning, 14

Disabilities, 27

Distance, 7, 26–27

District interests, 155

"Doing the right thing," 141–42

Drunken driving, preventing, 71

Easements, 13, 111

Economics: capacity extensions, 87–88; cities in developing countries, 5; deconcentration, 16; dynamics, 8, 9–11, 22; efficiency, 28; paratransit, 104; poverty impact of urban roads, 89; subsidies, 142; see also Agglomeration economies; Costs; Finance

Edge cities, 11

Education sector, 21

Efficiency: development strategies for, 12–15; economists and, 16; equity vs., 31–32

Electric vehicles, 48–49

Electronic road pricing (ERP), 137–38

Emergency medical services, 71

Emissions, 40, 45, 50–51; high emitters, 53

Energy-poverty, 27

Engineering, institutions, 165–66

Engines, 51–52; two-stroke, 51–52

Environment, 39–63; densification and, 17; dumping, 56–57; MRT and, 111–12; policy, 177; progress, 177–78; protecting, 176–79; standards application, 53–58; strategies, 60–61; WB agenda, 178–79; see also air pollution

Equity, 144–46

Ethanol, 48

Ethiopia, road safety, 67, 72

Exclusion, 28

Facilities location, 21

Fares: affordable, 34–36, 37, 174; discrimination, 145; exemptions, 36, 145; informal sector, 104; levels, 144; reduced, 21, 145; service quality and, 181; structure, 145

Fatalities, causes, 70, 71

Finance, 37, 146–50, 172; buses, 94, 174; channels, 180; cross-modal transfers, 122; infrastructure, 146–47, 150–51; integrated, 149–50; metros, 117; MRT, 117–20, 122–23; NMT, 133–34; planning, 22; private, 15, 88, 117, 147–48; public transport, 141–46; road maintenance, 77–79; strategy, 151; see also Costs; Economics

Firms, location, 10–11

Focus on poverty: policy, 170; progress, 170-71; strengthening, 170–71; WB agenda, 171

Framework, urban planning and market forces, 16

Franchises, 173–74; bus sector, 95, 100, 105–6

Freight transport policies, 13–14

Fuel, 40–41; adulteration, 46; biofuels, 48; consumption, 49–50; diesel, 41, 55–56; economy, 50; fossil, 41, 43, 44; improving quality, 45–47; gasoline octane, 50, 52; leaded vs. unleaded gasoline, 51; policy, 45–50; regulation, 46; staged strategy, 51; standards, 50; substitutes, 47–49; tax, 139–40

Fuel-cell technology, 50

Full integration, 131

Full segregation, 131

Funding, 148–50

Gasoline. See Fuels

Gender-related disadvantages, 27–28, 127

Global Environment Fund (GEF), 41

Global overlay, 41

Global Road Safety Partnership, 67

Global warming, 40–42

Government: budget restructuring, 164; freight movement, 14

Greenhouse gases (GHG), 40–42; technological measures, 41
Grid networks, 87
Gross domestic product (GDP), 8
Growth, urban roads and the poor, 89
Guidelines, road safety, 69

Hanging back, 96
Health services, 21
Hierarchy, conflict reduction, 160
Hopewell Project, 120
Household: budget, 26; characteristics, 28
Housing, 19
Hoy no circula {do not drive today] scheme, 59
Human resource development, 167, 172; *see also* Staff
Hybrid diesel-electric vehicles, 49
Hydrogen fuel cell, 49, 50

Implementation and enforcement, institutions, 162–63
Incentive systems, 60
Income, 6, 7, 10; car ownership and, 8; car-users, 32; personal vs. national, 28–29; proportion spent on transport, 26; urban roads and, 89–90
Income poor, 27, 28
Independent authority, 157
India, 6, 72, 165
Industrial development, 14
Industrialized countries, urban sprawl, 11
Informal sector services, 35
Informal transport sector, 37; congestion, 104; controlling operating practices, 103–4; environmental impact, 104; formal services and, 104; future, 104–6; negative image, 103; paratransit, 101–4; problems, 102–3
Infrastructure, 22, 28, 37, 84–88; charges, 135–36, 146–47; concessioning, 173; costs, 20; design, 69, 175–76; finance, 150–51; NMT policies, 129–31; policy focus, 29–32; public financing, 146–47; roads, 177
Inspection and maintenance (I/M) programs, 53–55; introduction, 54
Institutions: capability, 167; capacity building, 165; civil society, engaging, 164–65; con-flict reduction, 160; coordination, 154–56, 160–62, 163–64, 167–68; development, 172; environment, 60–61; functional basis, 156–59; human resource development, 167; implementation and enforcement, 162–63; jurisdiction, 167–68; NMT, 132–34; organization, 156–65; planning and engineering, 165–66; planning and operations, 22, 161–62; police role, 162–63; public and private sectors, coordinating, 163–64; safety, 71–72, 176; skills, 166–67; strategy, 167–68; strengthening, 153–68; traffic management and enforcement, 166; training, 167; weaknesses, 154
Instruments, 179–80
Intelligent Transport Systems (ITS), 71
Intergovernmental transfers, 148–49
Intersections, 131
Intrasectoral coordination, 149

Japan, 20
Jurisdiction, institutions, 155, 167–68

Knowledge building, 179
Kyrgyz Republic, 78

Land: characteristics, 17–18; development costs, 19; readjustment, 20; values, 21
Land use: administrative control, 17–18; change, 19; congestion, 143; control, 14; coordination, 155; implementation, 18–19; markets and distribution, 19–21; MRT and, 111; planning, 15–16, 18; planning and management, 16–19; roads, 13; technical skills, 18
Lead, 42–43, 44, 45
Leapfrogging, 11
Legal framework, 160; *see also* Regulations
Lending: to cities, 180–81; high-impact, 179–80; programmatic, 179
Licensing fees, 79
Light rapid transit (LRT), 114
Limited use, 84
Liquefied petroleum gas (LPG), 48
Logistic networks, 14

Malaysia, 68
Management contracting, bus sector, 95

Market, 22; activity and, 16; bus sector, 95–96; failure, 96; land-use distribution, 19–21; public transport, 121; structure, 176

Mass rapid transit (MRT), 31, 109–24, 178; benefits, structural, 110; environment and, 111–12; financing, 110–11, 117–21, 122–23; management, 123; metros, 31, 115–17; objectives and role, 110–11; ownership, 117–21; planning, 122; pricing, 121–22, 123; project preparation, 120–21; public transport integration, 121; ridership, 109; strategic objectives, 109–110; strategy, 122–23; technology, choice of, 112–17; timeframe, 121; urban structure and land use and, 111

Mechanized transport, private, 27

Medical policies, 71

Megacities, 5, 6, 16

Merit good, 33

Methane, 40, 41

Methanol, 48

Metros, 31, 115; costs, 115–17; see also Mass rapid transit

Mexico, 54, 66, 67

Microcredit, 180–81

Migration, discouraging, 16

Modes of movement, 5–6

Monopolies, 93, 105

Motor vehicles, ownership and use, 7

Motorcycles, 51–52; information base, 52, 53; injuries, 67–68; standards, 52; taxes and fees, 53; two-stroke engines, 52, 53

Motorized transport, 39; two-wheelers, 6

Multimodal integration, 37

Multimodal systems, 32

Municipal interests, 155

Nepal, 49

Netherlands, 17

Network: completeness and integrity, 33; planning, 129

Nitrous oxides (NO$_x$), 40, 41, 43

Noise, 42

Nonmotorized transport (NMT), 30–31, 37, 59, 89, 125–34; financing, 133–34; institutions and organization, 132–34; policy, 128–32; safety education and training, 132; stake-holders, 132–33; strategy, 134; traffic management, 131–32; volume, 131

Odds and evens policy, 84

Opportunity cost, 41

Organization, institutions, 156–65

Ownership: MRT, 120–21; procedures, 181

Ozone, 43

Pakistan, 74

Paratransit, 101–4; future, 104–6; growth, 106; services provided, 101; strategy, 107

Parking: charges, 140; demand management, 83; private nonresidential, 83

Partial segregation, 131

Participation, 181

Passenger transport, 93–108

Paving programs, 181

Pedestrians, 42, 125, 126; safety and security, 67, 74

Peripheral infrastructure, 14

Performance, deteriorating, 6, 8

Personal characteristics, deprivation and, 27

PHARE program, 67

Physical disabilities, aids, 27

Planning, 174; institutions, 154, 161–62; MRT, 121, 122; strategy, 106–7, 161–62

Police: female, 74; officers, 74; role, 162–63; training, 166

Policy: accident prevention, 68–69; bus sector, 98–101; coordination, 21–22, 23; decentralization, 172; environmental protection, 177; focus on poverty, 170; fuel, 45–50; fuel taxation, 55–56; infrastructure, 29–32; medical, 71; NMT, 128–32; private participation, 173; public expenditures, 57–58; reform, 146; safety and security, 175; social sector, 21–22; system management, 58–59; vehicle, 50–53

Politics, 149; history, 6; processes, 164–65; violence, 74

The Poor, residence, 89

Population: concentration, 8; growth, 5; rates, 7

Poverty, concept, 25

Poverty Reduction Strategy, 2–3; Papers (PRSPs), 170, 181; urban transport and, 25–38

Price distortions, 23

Prices and pricing, 84, 135–46; congestion, 136–138; efficient, 19; fuel tax, 139–40;

infrastructure charges, 135–36; MRT, 121–22, 123; public transport, 141–46; role, 135; strategy, 107, 150–51, 177–78

Primacy, 16

Priorities, private sector, 15

Private sector: financing, 15, 147–48; institutions, 163–64; MRT, 117–18; participation, mobilizing, 173–75; policy, 173; progress, 173-74; public sector and, 156, 163–64; role, 14–15; traffic management, 81–; vehicle inspection and maintenance, 54; WB agenda, 174–75

Privatization, 34

Property rights, 19

Propoor economic growth, 28–29

Prototype Carbon Fund, 41

Publicly owned lands, recycling, 19

Public opinion, 149

Public-private participation, 174

Public processes, 165

Public sector: administrative activities, 21–22; bus sector, 93–94, 100; expenditure policies, 57–58; infrastructure financing, 146–47; pricing, 20; private sector vs., 100

Public transport, 7; accidents, 68; buses, 93; competition, 107; economic liberalization, 58; efficiency, 170; implementation, 81–82; markets, 121; MRT integration, 121; poverty reduction, 25, 28, 32–34, 37; planning and integration, 106–7; pricing, 107, 141–46; priorities, 58; strategy, 106–7; subsidies, 57; traffic management, 80–82; *see also* Paratransit

Racing, 96

Rail systems, 20; investments, 31–32; mass transit, 178; private sector role, 15; suburban, 114–15, 117

Ramsey pricing rules, 143

Redevelopment, 19

Redistribution, perverse, 21

Refineries, 46–47

Reform, phased, 100–101

Regulations: development strategies, 19–20; environment, 176; fuel quality, 46; institutions, 164; legal framework, 160; municipal, 8; traffic law enforcement, 72

Rent-seeking behavior, 148–49

Research octane number (RON), 50, 52

Resettlement: civil society, 165; design and implementation, 181; rail systems and, 32

Residence: choices, 10, 11; location, 26–27, 28, 89

Ridership: buses, 93; MRT, 109

Rights-of-way, 13, 111

Ring and radial design, 85, 87

Roads: design, 69; infrastructure, 8, 12–13, 150–51, 177; investments, 23, 29–30; locating, 90; low-income areas, 90; maintenance, 77–79, 91; network, 85; planning, 91

Road systems, 77–91; capacity extensions, 87–88; hierarchy and shape, 85, 87; poverty focus, 88–90; private financing, 88; strategy, 90–91

Safety, 8, 66–72, 75–76, 79; cost-effectiveness, 69; education and training, NMT, 132; evidence, 67; funding, 71–72; infrastructure design, 69; institutions, 71–72; NMT, 132; policy formation, 68–69; strategies, 75; traffic management, 70–71

Safety and security: increasing, 175–76; policy, 175, 181; progress, 175-76; WB agenda, 176

Safety-net approach, 33–34

Safety poor, 27

Scrappage programs, 55

Second generation road funds, 78, 79

Security, 65–66, 72–76; paratransit, 105; strategies, 75–76; threats to, 73

Severance, 42

Sexual harassment, 74

Signals, 80

Singapore, electronic road pricing, 138

Size and size distribution, 6

Social exclusion, urban poverty and, 25

Social sector, 21–22

Social security, 21

Social violence, 74

South Africa, 74, 130

South Korea, 137

SO_x. *See* Sulfur oxides

Speed, 7

Speed limits, 70

Sri Lanka, 66

Staff, 165–66, 166–67

Stakeholders, NMT, 132–33

Statistics, road accidents, 68

Strategies, 3, 6; city development, 22–23; coordinating sector policies, 21–22; environment, 60–61; institutions, 167–68; motorcycles, 52–53; MRT, 122–23; NMT, 134; operational levels, 153–54; poverty focus, 37; pricing and finance, 151; public transport, 106–7; roads, 77, 90–91, 150–51; safety and security, 75–76; structural change, 15–21; transport efficiency, 12–15

Structural change: planning capabilities, 22; strategies, 15–21

Subsidies, 57–58, 122, 142, 149

Suburban railways, 114–15, 117; see also Rail systems

Sulfur, 51

Sulfur oxides (SO$_x$), 43, 45–46

Supply efficiency, 141–43; congestion, 142

Sustainability, 146, 170–71

Synergy, local and global effects, 41

System management, policies, 58–59

Tama Garden City Development Project, 20

Tanzania, 133

Targeting: congestion, 142; financing, 36–37; subsidies, 34

Taxation, 20; environment, 41–42, 177–78; financing, 147; fuels, 55–56, 139–40; infrastructure, 136–37; relative levels, 56; vehicle, 140

Technology: priorities, 60; supporting development, 177

Thailand, 15, 46, 120

Theft: by stealth, 73; by force, 73

Three-wheel motor vehicles, road accidents, 67–68

Ticketing systems, 32

Time-dependent tolling, 137

Time poor, 27

Title, 19

Tokyu Railway Company, 20

Tolls: roads, 88; shadow systems, 15

Trade liberalization, 56–57

Traffic, 43; authority, 162–63; calming measures, 70; control, 79–80; law enforcement, 72, 156, 166; restraint, 58–59, 84

Traffic management, 23, 58, 79–82, 91; agency, 70; coordination, 156; cycling and, 131–32; environment, 177; implementation, 81–82; institutions, 166; process, 81; safety and security, 70–71

Training, 166, 167

Transport: investments, land values and, 21; modes, 155–56, 170; patterns, urban poor, 25–28; planning, 15–16

Transport sector, growth and change, 45

Travel time, 7–8, 26

Trickle down, 29

Trip rates, 25–26, 27

Trucks, road accidents, 68

Turning back, 96

Two-tier authority, 157

Urban development, 5–23; lower-order, 16; MRT and, 111; planners, 16; strategy, 2–3

Urbanization, 5

Urban sprawl, industrialized countries, 11

Uzbekistan, 100

Vale-transporte, 147

Vandalism, 73–74

Vehicles: age limit, 57; charges for use, 84; electric, 48–49; existing stock, 53; hybrid diesel-electric, 49; policy, 50–53; quality, 46; replacement, 41–42, 52, 53, 55; taxes, 140; technology, 50–51

Venezuela, 74

Versement transport, 147, 160

Vietnam, 72

Violence, 73

Vulnerable populations, protecting, 171

Walking. See Nonmotorized transport; Pedestrians

Women, 27–28; cycling, 127

World Bank: contribution, 169–82; policy shifts, 179–80; review content, 2–3; review objective, 2; vision vs. reality, 2; WB policy paper, 2; WB portfolio, 1

World Bank Institute (WBI), 174

Zimbabwe, 67

Zoning, 19